S0-DTQ-870

Preparing
America's
Foreign
Policy
for the 21st CENTURY

Preparing America's Foreign Policy

JZ
1480
.P74
1999
West

**David L. Boren and
Edward J. Perkins**

University of Oklahoma Press : Norman

Library of Congress Cataloging-in-Publication Data

Preparing America's foreign policy for the twenty-first century /
    David L. Boren and Edward J. Perkins [editors].
        p. cm.
    Based on papers presented at a conference held at the
University of Oklahoma, Sept. 12–16, 1997.
    Includes index.
    ISBN 0-8061-3123-3 (cloth : alk. paper)
    1. United States—Foreign relations—Congresses. I. Boren,
David Lyle, 1941– . II. Perkins, Edward J. (Edward Joseph),
1928– .
    JZ1480.P74   1999
    327.73'009'049—dc21   98-43713
                                                                  CIP

The paper in this book meets the guidelines for permanence and
durability of the Committee on Production Guidelines for Book
Longevity of the Council on Library Resources, Inc.

Copyright © 1999 by the University of Oklahoma Press, Norman,
Publishing Division of the University, except for Chapter 8,
"Protecting and Defining Our National Security in a Changed
World," by Sam Nunn, © 1997 by Sam Nunn; Chapter 11, "A Strategic
Look at Intelligence in the Future," by George J. Tenet (in the public
domain); Chapter 16, "Trade Liberalization," by John S. Wolf (in the
public domain); Chapter 23, "A Geostrategy for Eurasia," by Zbigniew
Brzezinski, reprinted by permission from *Foreign Affairs* 76, no. 5
(1997), © 1997 by the Council on Foreign Relations, Inc.; Chapter 24,
"United States Relations with Nations Emerging as World Leaders,"
by Jeane J. Kirkpatrick, © 1997 by Jeane J. Kirkpatrick; Chapter 25,
adapted from "U.S. Global Policy: Toward an Agile Strategy," by
David M. Abshire, *The Washington Quarterly* 19, no. 2 (Spring 1996):
41–61, © 1996 by the Center for Strategic and International Studies
(CSIS) and the Massachusetts Institute of Technology. All rights
reserved. Manufactured in the U.S.A.

1 2 3 4 5 6 7 8 9 10

Table of Contents

Foreword

William J. Crowe Jr.

David L. Boren and Edward J. Perkins have put together a must-read book for all who are interested in the role and responsibilities of the United States, the world's only superpower, as we begin the twenty-first century. These two editors' combined public careers in state and national government (both legislative and executive); in national security, diplomacy, and the corporate world; and in education uniquely qualified them for their task. Moreover, their careers gave them the personal relationships to assemble into one volume the informed, sound, and creative thinking of a remarkably experienced, knowledgeable, and brilliant group of practitioners and scholars. Where else between the covers of a single volume could one hear and learn from such varied and articulate voices as Secretary of State Henry A. Kissinger and Vice President Walter Mondale, Chinese Ambassador Li Daoyu and novelist Colleen McCullough, environmentalist Richard Sandor and media pundit David Gergen, Wall Street money manager Michael F. Price and Yale historian Gaddis Smith? The book, as seen in the biographical notes on the contributors, is a *Who's Who* of noted authorities from several fields to address the international challenge of our day. Their wisdom, logic, and advice (individually and collectively) are a significant contribution and a step forward in the debate in which our country is now engaged about America's need for a new paradigm for the conduct of foreign policy.

When the Chinese say, "May you live in interesting times," I think they had in mind a period such as we are experiencing right now. I wrote in my book, *The Line of Fire*, that I sometimes regretted that my military professional life was shaped by a single global factor: the challenge of the Soviet Union, which was constantly in the forefront of our minds as our one formidable military adversary. Those times certainly were not uninteresting, but the current global situation is even more intellectually diverse and challenging. My postmilitary life has deepened and widened the already broad world perspective I had acquired as chairman of the Joint Chiefs of Staff, as a unified area commander, and in other military assignments. I am the current George Washington University Shapiro Professor in the Elliott School of International Affairs; at the Center for Strategic and International Studies; on various corporate boards and national commissions; and have been a professor at the University of Oklahoma, briefly in campaign politics, and for three years, United States ambassador to the Court of Saint James, London.

Our world is truly in flux. It is moving so rapidly that perspectives, goals, and strategies that seemed appropriate a few years after the end of the cold war are continuously being rethought and reshaped. Certainly the global picture has altered dramatically in an extremely short period of time and continues to change rapidly. In essence we are witnessing firsthand one of the great watersheds of history. We are actually experiencing it and reading about it in our newspapers and seeing it on our televisions. We saw the edifice of communism shatter, the Soviet empire crumble, and now, throughout much of the world, people are throwing off their shackles and moving—in a very halting and uncertain way—toward pluralism and free markets.

As Americans we, of course, applaud these developments, while we are aware that all our problems are not solved and our future is not necessarily secure and assured. I submit that we are in for a protracted period of uncertainty and struggle. The current transitions are bringing new pockets of poverty and new pockets of wealth, with a widening divergence between the two. New governments have in several cases fashioned important improvements through economic liberalization and greater individual freedom, but the world and its nations will still suffer a great deal of confusion, trauma, frustration, and disillusionment before they can seize their destiny. And although each nation and each people must be responsible for their own problems and actions, the United States—as the world leader for individual freedom and economic development and as the world's only current superpower—will undoubtedly be deeply involved in this global, revolutionary process.

For the first time in fifty years we live in an international community with no superpower adversary. Third World threats, although real, are more ephemeral, individually less dangerous in the short term (although not so cumulatively), and not especially predictable. Without the consuming confrontation between two armed camps, not every crisis or every challenge requires American reaction or intervention. Washington's primary international problem now is to determine when our interests are genuinely at risk and what their relative priorities are—in other words, to be selective as to our involvement. Unfortunately, this is a perplexing task, and our republican system of government has difficulty in coping with ambiguous, low-stakes, political-military conflicts.

Such challenges abound. In many parts of the world traditional enmities grounded in ethnic feuds and national rivalries are thriving, and local rivalries have the capacity to blossom into wider challenges. The doomsday anxieties that so deeply marked the collective psyche of the cold-war generation are not totally a thing of the past. The possibility of several countries employing nuclear, chemical, or biological weapons of mass destruction on their neighbors is made more likely by proliferation. Witness the 1998 decision of both India and Pakistan to set off nuclear devices. In a very real sense, the United States is being expected to act as an international policeman and conciliator for regional wars, to control rogue states, and to settle low-intensity conflicts within recognized countries. That is the burden of our role as the world's only superpower. Winston Churchill once commented: "With great power comes great responsibility."

To exercise successful global leadership and assume global responsibilities, domestically we must be economically strong, and—within broad parameters of democratic debate and diversity—we must be united in purpose and resolve. Immediately after the cold war there was much concern about the economic resilience and competitiveness of the United States vis-à-vis Europe and Japan. A half century of spending heavily and disproportionately on the free world's security seemed to have left us with a deteriorating infrastructure. Worries also have been expressed that growing diversity within the United States, which we previously had regarded as a strength, is becoming so pervasive that we are on the verge of fracturing permanently the consensus on national ideals and purpose that made us a superpower during the last half of the twentieth century. Preoccupation with our economic competitiveness has receded since 1992, but comparative economic capacity and relative political influence among the great powers are somewhat cyclical. The debates over diversity and political correctness continue unabated. America's preeminence is not assured without continuing effective leadership, dialogue, and self-examination among our culturally rich and diverse groups, and continuous renewal of a consensus on America's fundamental goals and missions.

The domestic challenges are profound in a period of incredible and rapid technological change that has thrust America headlong into the information age and given it a temporary advantage over other major powers, while at the same time crafting many new ways of living and doing things. Each of the developments requires painful adjustments. By the government's beginning to put its fiscal house in order and the corporate world's boosting productivity through downsizing, outsourcing, and the revamping of regulatory régimes, the United States has made great strides in reinvigorating its economy. There is still much to be done, however, to rebuild and add to a domestic infrastructure that was neglected during the long cold war.

A reappreciation of government is also in order. Relations between the federal government and business, and with state and local governments, are still to be satisfactorily tuned. We confront immense challenges to protect the environment, to manage and resolve social ills such as drug consumption, and to incorporate the less advantaged members of society into the mainstream economy and into our nation's social and political life. The right level of spending on national security and the conduct of diplomacy must be reached—not so great as to overextend us into decline, but ample enough to fulfill our duties. And finally, we have to create a more constructive information media, and to provide our youth—kindergarten through doctorate—the best education in the world.

In 1989, at the conclusion of a military career that spanned four decades and before President Clinton appointed me ambassador to the United Kingdom, I came to the University of Oklahoma as a new professor of geopolitics.

When I entered my first class and looked out on the faces of those bright and expectant students, I was as nervous as I had been in briefing my superiors in the government hierarchy. At least I knew something of what they expected of me. It did not take me long to learn that I did have something to offer them, but just as importantly, they also had much to offer me. I found that as I pressed these students to think seriously about the world around them, they challenged me to rethink my own suppositions. My time at the University of Oklahoma taught me that the same spirit of interest, commitment, and dedication to the country that is so common among the young men and women of our armed forces is shared by the new generation of Americans living in our nation's heartland.

I am confident that we Americans will hearken to the call of history and assume the leadership role the world has thrust upon us. As a nation we should be rethinking our basic assumptions about the changed world in which we reside. We must find new ways to contemplate and approach our problems. We must continue to set our own house in order and to create a vision of and a sense of direction for navigating in the new world order. This book attempts to provide this. The editors and contributors discuss the obstacles to and propose the components of a paradigm for the United States to follow in the conduct of foreign policy at the beginning of the twenty-first century.

Preface

Edward J. Perkins

This book is only one example of the myriad results of the University of Oklahoma's (OU's) recent transformation and growing excellence. The book is the by-product of a foreign-policy conference held at the University in late 1997 and papers solicited from foreign-policy authorities subsequent to the conference. The conference, on preparing America's foreign policy for the twenty-first century, was held September 12–16, 1997. America's foremost authorities, in terms of their experience as practitioners and their knowledge as scholars, shared views and wisdom not only with students, faculty members, and the people of Oklahoma but also with all of America. The conference was covered by the national media and sessions were broadcast on C-Span.

University of Oklahoma President David L. Boren noted at that conference that a new architecture was created at the end of World War II for American foreign policy, and that as the twentieth century draws to a close, America again faces a changed world landscape which requires a new foreign-policy framework. International-relations specialists surveyed the state of the world, with special attention on Asia. They also delved deeply into defense, the intelligence function, international environmental policy, the impact of the media, and trade policy and economics, as well as the elements of a coherent and effective United States foreign policy for the twenty-first century.

To complement the superb presentations at the conference, an equally distinguished group of statesmen, practitioners, and academics was invited to provide papers for the book. They examined more profoundly United States–Asian relations, criteria for the employment of military force, the priority of economics, and again, a new architecture for a changed world.

I am pleased to join President Boren in his efforts to make this public university a pacesetter for the nation in the "internationalization" of public higher education.

J. W. Fulbright said, "we must try to expand the boundaries of human wisdom, empathy and perception, and there is no way of doing that except through education."[1] The university, through the entire educational process—teaching, research, and service—has a responsibility to develop informed citizens who are literate about the increasingly global community in which they live. Today's students must be cognizant of and function effectively in the different cultures of the world and meet the broad global challenges that confront our nation. The United States' role in the international arena and its prosperity and security depend on its citizens' ability to cope with the challenges and take advantage of the opportunities of the increasingly interdependent society of the twenty-first century.

President Boren has emphasized repeatedly that the University must further internationalize its curriculum, including that of the professional schools such as law, engineering, and business, to prepare students for the world in which they will live and work. First-rate universities must make studies of world affairs an important and permanent dimension of under-graduate programs. Graduate and professional schools must be competent to teach and conduct research on international aspects of their disciplines and professions. The University of Oklahoma is setting an example by pro-viding specialized programs in international studies in its professional schools that are built on strong international, area, and language studies in the College of Arts and Sciences.

The goal of the International Programs Center, which began operations in August 1997, is to foster interdisciplinary education that will prepare OU graduates for success in the global environment, and to enhance the Univer-sity's role as a regional actor in our nation's international relations. The cen-ter encourages and facilitates an ever-increasing number of international activities and programs as a means of enriching students' education and preparation for professional careers.

As a state-supported institution, the University has a major commit-ment to increase its outreach qualitatively and quantitatively. The intent is to educate and involve the public in civic dialogue about international affairs and to provide citizens of this region a greater role and voice in our nation's international relations and the formulation of foreign policy. This goal is in accord with the rapidly increasing globalization of the world's economy. There is a feeling by citizens in much of the interior of the United States that they often have had a limited and primarily reactive voice in the making of our nation's foreign policy. President Boren is determined to change this.

This book is one effort in that direction. The theme, *Preparing America's Foreign Policy for the Twenty-first Century*, is timely as Americans discuss and evaluate the inescapable issues affecting the United States' role in interna-tional affairs. The University of Oklahoma and its International Programs Center are enabling the interior of the United States to play a more promi-nent role in formulating our country's foreign policy. We are pleased that you join us in this important endeavor by your reading, reflecting and, it is hoped, acting on what you learn from the thoughts and suggestions of the varied group of foreign-policy experts who are contributors to this volume.

NOTES

1. J. William Fulbright, *The Future of the United Nations: A Roundtable held on November 16, 1976* (Washington: American Enterprise Institute for Public Policy Research, 1977).

Acknowledgments

We the editors, David L. Boren and Edward J. Perkins, gratefully acknowledge that this book reflects the wisdom, lifework, thought, research, writing, and long hours of toil and effort of many distinguished persons. There are many individuals, some publicly well known and others not so, to whom we are obliged. First, we wish to thank the foreign-policy practitioners and scholars who contributed their thinking and precious time from extremely busy and complicated schedules to participate in the University of Oklahoma foreign-policy conference and to write their portions of this book.

Second, we wish to express appreciation to benefactors of the University whose generosity helped make possible the foreign-policy conference on which this volume is based. These include lead corporate sponsors Conoco Inc., Mobil Oil Corporation, Phillips Petroleum Company, Southwestern Bell Telephone; sponsors American Airlines, Bank of Oklahoma, Central and South West Corporation, Globe Life and Accident Insurance Company of Oklahoma City, Kerr-McGee Corporation, the Samuel Roberts Noble Foundation, Inc., the Nordam Group, OG&E, Texas Instruments Inc., Tulsair Beechcraft Inc., Wagner & Brown; patrons Aurora Natural Gas, B-P Investments, Ltd., Helmerich & Payne Inc., Integris Health Inc., The Kerr Foundation, Manhattan Construction Company, Marc Nuttle/Sam Hammons, Attorneys, Public Service Company of Oklahoma, Ramco Operating Companies; and supporters American Fidelity, Security National Bank, Vintage Petroleum.

Third, we thank those hardworking and diligent professionals at the University of Oklahoma who organized and staged the conference. Among those who deserve special recognition are Ambassador Edwin G. Corr, Catherine Bishop, Tom Godkins, Amy Monsour, Lee Ann Bratten, Kelly O'Brien, David Maloney, Paul Massad, Sandy Waterkotte, Josh Galper, Kimberlee Hefty, Nanette Shadid, David Smeal, Bob Taylor, Linda Baker, Donna Epperson, Millie Audas, Gary Cohen, Julie Horn, and Kathy Shahan.

Finally, we wish to extend our gratitude to those who had a special role in the compiling and editing of this book, including John Drayton, editor, Kimberly Wiar, senior editor, and Sarah Iselin, associate editor, of the University of Oklahoma Press. We thank Hazel Rowena Mills, copy editor. We also wish to thank Edwin G. Corr for his extensive work in organizing the compilation of the book, and OU graduate students James Hochtritt and John Van Doorn, who reviewed some of the transcripts from the conference.

Finally, we are indebted to Kathy Shahan and Claudia J. Braun, whose help in editing and whose untiring, repeated, and patient typing of the manuscript resulted in this volume.

PART I

The State of the World as We Enter the Twenty-first Century

Chapter 1

Introduction:
The Context and the Challenge
David L. Boren

We have gone through a period of enormous change in our own country and in the world around us during the last decade of this millennium—more change than in any other comparable length of time in our history. When we look back on the industrial revolution, for example, the pace of change was slow compared with what we are now experiencing. Change unsettles and worries us even when it presents us with new opportunities. Then Secretary of State James Baker, interviewed at the time of the fall of the Berlin Wall, took little time to celebrate before worrying out loud that the movement toward democracy had not taken place on our projected timetable and that we did not know what to expect next.

At the end of World War II the United States also confronted an immediately changed and very different world. Some countries which had been allied with us in World War II, such as the Soviet Union, became enemies, and some adversaries became allies in the long cold war that was to follow. We had to adjust very rapidly and find new ways of thinking, a new architecture for a new world. And we did that very successfully. The results are history. The National Defense Act of 1947 reorganized our defense and international-affairs agencies. The Marshall Plan and Point Four Program were enunciated to rebuild and build the free world. NATO and other regional alliances embodied the concept of collective security. The policy of containment was devised to stop the spread of Communism. Containment made the Soviets pay a price when they tried to extend their empire and influence. That price ultimately contributed to the economic collapse of the Soviet Union.

We had a policy. We had a construct. We had an architecture. We had a set of concepts such as collective security and containment that allowed us to weigh and make judgments about what our nation should do, what our national interests were, and how we should conduct ourselves. There was increasing predictability throughout the period of the cold war and nuclear menace about what each side would do. These policies provided a framework that enabled the United States to provide leadership and protect the free world.

Dean Acheson, in writing his autobiography and thinking about the policies that were developed at the end of World War II, titled his book *Present at the Creation*.[1] He was indeed not only present as a witness but as a key participant in the creation of a new architecture for United States foreign policy which protected and advanced our national security and asserted American leadership and ideals. Viewing what has gone on in our country since the end of the cold war, few people would declare that they have yet witnessed the creation of a new concept, architecture, or rationale that now enables us to judge our own interests or to understand our future role in the world.

This book has been written in the hope that it will contribute to the formation of a critically needed new paradigm for the United States to help us understand and act responsibly in the rapidly changing world we now confront.

As indicated by my coeditor, Ambassador Edward J. Perkins, this volume is based on a conference held at the University of Oklahoma in late 1997, from which the thoughts of eminent guest speakers were collected to share with the national foreign-policy community and the general public. Other authorities' papers were added to these. The book reflects our national struggle to develop concepts and an analytical framework for making important strategic decisions—often life-or-death decisions—about how and when to commit American soldiers, American influence, and American resources in the world. It asks how we can best use this window of opportunity, when the world is not yet polarized into competing groups of superpowers, to create a world that will be safer and more orderly for our children and grandchildren.

When the atomic bomb was first exploded, Albert Einstein commented that everything in the world had changed except our thinking. By that, he was reflecting on how difficult it is for man's understanding, analysis, and concepts to keep pace when everything is in rapid flux in the world around us. That certainly is the case as we approach and enter the twenty-first century.

Dr. Henry Kissinger, whose groundbreaking work, *Nuclear Weapons and Foreign Policy,*[2] I read while I was a student in political science and international relations, first made me aware of the change in our world which came with the production of nuclear bombs. These awesome weapons of mass destruction with their hair triggers in a delicate balance of world power had a terrifying and profound impact on all of us, even if an unconscious one. About ten years ago there was an experiment in elementary schools across the country in which, during a free-drawing period, third-grade students were asked to draw anything that came to mind. More than half of them drew pictures of mushroom clouds, missiles, elements of war, and agents of mass destruction. When it was repeated a decade later, virtually none drew a mushroom cloud or scenes of mass destruction.

We again find ourselves in a brand-new world. We are not at this moment locked into the kind of arms race we had prior to World War I, nor are we living in a world that is divided and polarized into competing superpower camps. We are not trapped in a nuclear arms race. We are not engaged in a cold war in which each side has nuclear hair triggers. We no longer live in a cold-war situation in which international organizations are unable to function because the UN Security Council vetoed nearly every major action. With the end of the cold war, we are facing a totally new world. We live in a unique moment of opportunity. Unlike earlier generations when the world was polarized, we have a moment in which to bring the leading nations of the world together to create a new framework for stability. We have a chance to establish what President George Bush called a new world order.

This window of opportunity will not remain open indefinitely. There is no time to waste. A wise observer once said that those who mill around at the crossroads of history do so at their own peril.

There are many questions which need to be answered. Many of them we have not yet faced.

How can we keep the United States from entering a new period of isolationism and attempted withdrawal from the world? After each perceived victory in the past, Americans weary of the struggle have had a tendency to withdraw, thereby creating a dangerous vacuum of power in the world. Even today we are disengaging from the world, closing or downgrading diplomatic posts, especially in Africa and Central and South America. Foreign policy is neglected in presidential elections. Fewer members of Congress hold passports or travel to other nations to learn about them firsthand than has been true for many decades. Although we have fewer troops stationed around the world and have an even greater need of early warning of threats to our interests, the intelligence budget remains under pressure. All this is happening at a time when more American jobs depend on the stability and prosperity of the rest of the world than ever before.

How can we avoid the terrible choice between standing on the sidelines as regional crises develop in other parts of the world and moving in to play the world's policeman or humanitarian savior all by ourselves? Can we find ways under Article 43 of the United Nations Charter to set up a multinational force to train together and to deploy together in a crisis without compromising our own national sovereignty or losing our will to act alone when it is absolutely necessary?

How can we seize the opportunity to create an alliance of the world's leading nations to build an effective inspection effort to stop the spread of weapons of mass destruction? How far are we willing to go in allowing inspections on our own soil of our own weapons systems to give us the moral authority to get others to abide by the same rules?

How do we build a relationship for future friendship with China, emerging as the other most powerful nation in the world in the next century? How do we build on our common interests in a predictable way as China begins a potential political transition as great as its economic changes of the last two decades? How do we prevent the warnings of some people of a new cold war with China from becoming a self-fulfilling prophecy?

How do we prevent a new polarization of the world along economic lines if a united Europe with a new currency competitive with the dollar becomes protectionist and hostile to free and fair trade for American products? Some have suggested that the polarization of the world in the next century could be along economic instead of political lines, pitting Europe against North and South America and parts of Asia.

How can we prepare the next generation of Americans to live and compete in an increasingly international environment when our educational system remains provincial, with a lower percentage of our students studying other languages or studying abroad than is true of virtually every other country in the world?

We have yet to ask ourselves many of the most important questions and are far from adequately answering the few which we have asked.

One of the problems pointed out by the contributors to this work is that in dealing with our role in the world there has been a tendency for domestic political issues to intervene excessively in foreign-policy decisions. This is exactly what happened after World War I, and I am concerned about the present. It can be said that the temptation for American political leaders to make short-term decisions for temporary domestic political gain often leads the United States to take actions harmful to our long-term interests. It is not possible in a democracy for the president to exercise international leadership without exercising domestic leadership. The two areas have in fact become so intertwined that political scientists have coined the term *intermestic* to describe the phenomenon.

How do we find offsetting ways to keep politicians from being so tempted to focus only on the short term? The political response to media coverage of the Somalian intervention is illustrative of the danger of making decisions on the basis of instant emotional reactions without reference to history and the long term. We saw on CNN television the vivid images of a mob in Mogadishu dragging an American soldier through the streets. Immediately, there was a proposal in Congress to prevent American forces from ever serving under the command of anyone other than an American. The motion almost passed! I recall helping to lead the filibuster against it. Senator Sam Nunn, who is a contributor to this book, also spoke against it. In the debate, those of us who opposed the proposal pointed out that at the Battle of Yorktown, none other than George Washington put units of American soldiers under the command of French military leadership, and that with the help of French military leaders our Revolution succeeded. We also pointed out that in the North African campaign during World War II, American soldiers fought under General Montgomery with much success. Other examples were given.

Americans were simply reacting to TV images on Somalia. They had little knowledge of Somalia's history and what caused the events they were seeing on television. They could not have named the heads of the various factions involved. They could not have told you why our policy went wrong—how "mission creep" got us engaged in a civil war when the original objective was only to help feed hungry people. Americans merely learned that American forces there were in danger, and they wanted their young women and men home within twenty-four hours. The drew the wrong conclusions from what they saw on television. It was not the idea of a joint international effort that was to blame, it was taking sides in a civil war when we had solely a humanitarian mission. They did not want American young men and women to be put in harm's way overseas ever again.

What do we do about that? Is there anything that we can do to give people a broader and deeper perspective, including our political leaders? Can we, especially members of Congress and the media, pause to take a deep breath, learn about, consider, and present a little of the historical context of conflictive and dangerous situations, no matter the level of human suffering and despair, before clamoring for precipitate actions by our government?

Our great American historian Daniel Boorstin has warned us that we must not confuse mere information with knowledge. The fact that we have had an exponential increase in information does not make us wiser. In fact, it could make us less wise, because the volume of information often overwhelms our ability to analyze it or put it into its proper context. I watched during my term as chairman of the Senate Intelligence Committee while the CIA greatly increased its information, its raw data, but became overwhelmed and unable to separate the important from the unimportant.

Again on the matter of leadership, three or four years ago Senator Clayborne Pell and I had an interesting series of conversations on our visits to Pakistan, India, China, and Russia. We talked with officials in each country about their willingness to have intrusive and very detailed international inspections of nuclear weapons and other potential weapons of mass destruction. The Pakistanis said, of course, "We are not willing to allow this unless the Indians are." The Indians said to us very pointedly, "We are a great nation and are not about to agree to such inspections unless the Chinese do." The Chinese leadership, Jiang Zemin and others, said, "We are not willing to do it unless the Russians are." And the Russians said very directly to us, "We are not willing to have any more intrusive inspections than you in the United States are." So it again comes down to leadership, both internationally and domestically. If we are going to lead the world's nations to have international inspections with teeth in them for weapons of mass destruction, the willingness to allow really intrusive inspections must begin with us to some degree. Do you think we have thought enough about what kind of an inspection régime we ourselves are willing to accommodate to lead the world in stopping the spread of dangerous weapons? Are we examining this matter sufficiently, explaining it adequately to the American people, and building political support for desired measures among the American public? With greater leadership we might have gotten an inspection régime that could have forestalled India's and Pakistan's nuclear-bomb testing in 1998.

A short-term focus on domestic politics is causing people to forgo learning about what is going on in the rest of the world. Just during the last two or three months, three former colleagues of mine in Congress have called me to say, "We have been planning to go to China, but we are about to back out. Do you think we should go? We are afraid we will be criticized if we go to see China for ourselves." I replied to all three, "You cannot afford not to go. That relationship is so critical to the future of our country and our people. Whether it is a positive relationship or the source of a new cold war as we go into the next century, it is vital; and you are going to be voting on crucial issues affecting that relationship. How can you afford not to go, if you are a responsible legislator? You would not think about voting on health care and never visiting a hospital or an outpatient clinic or a research facility or looking at what is happening to insurance rates. You must comprehend what is going on in China." Yet many are afraid to go. It is alarming. They have become concerned almost exclusively with domestic politics.

A look at what is happening at the state and local level is also essential to understanding how dramatically the conduct and nature of international relations are changing. This is demonstrated by something that we have been studying in the class I teach on introduction to American politics. We have read and discussed an article written by a journalist from the *Los Angeles Times* about the effects the devolution of power from the federal government to the states is producing in terms of direct relationships between and among local communities across national borders. We see the impact right in Norman, the home of the University of Oklahoma, through its sister-city relationships and the expansion of local businesses into the international arena. Often Washington is being bypassed as the economy is being extensively internationalized at the local level. Very direct international links are being established and broadened between private businesses of all sizes, American cities, counties, and states with their counterparts in the rest of the world. We are engaging in international relationships in a very new and fascinating way, and we must learn how to manage and facilitate them and how to help our people benefit from them.

Part of the answer is in education and exposure to foreign cultures. In Utah one-third of the adults speak a language in addition to English. This is an outgrowth of the work of the Mormon Church around the world and the teaching of foreign languages to students who are going on overseas missions. Over the years this has resulted in Utah now having a large cadre of citizens with intercultural and language skills. Utah citizens' broad cultural experience and knowledge of languages have led to a very rapid economic growth rate in their state. Utah is the second-fastest-growing state economically in terms of per capita income of the country, and it provides an important lesson for all of us interested in economic growth and international affairs.

I repeat that we live in one of those incredible moments in history, rarely given to a generation, in which the peoples of the world have an opportunity to act constructively together. That was not possible for our parents or our grandparents. The world is no longer divided into warring or precariously balanced power camps. The great powers have the chance to work together to secure a better world. President Bush spoke after the fall of the Berlin Wall and after the Gulf War about the opportunity to create a new world architecture that will allow us to pool our talents, make the world safer for our children and grandchildren, and usher in an unparalleled period of peace and cooperation in the world. Will we take advantage of that opportunity for cooperation and partnership? How long will this window of opportunity remain open? How quickly could it close if, for example, the passions of nationalization and ethnicity exacerbated by economic difficulties turned areas of the former Soviet Union into chaos and conflict? How quickly could it end if mistrust and misunderstandings of national pride fueled sensitivities into flames about issues of human rights and national sovereignty between the United States and the People's Republic of China—two great nations whose relationship is critically important as we enter the next century?

That the United States–Chinese relationship is crucial to determining what will happen is an opinion shared by many thinkers about foreign policy, and it is evident in this book. The answer to the question of whether existing U.S.-Chinese problems can be managed depends on how well the United States and China learn to understand each other, respect each other as great nations with very different cultural backgrounds, and cooperate for the mutual benefit of both countries and the rest of the world. Together, these two countries represent a very large portion of the world's economic power, cultural power, and population, and they control a large percentage of the world's resources. In the next ten to twenty years into the twenty-first century, these two countries can make this planet a very different and much better place. If we do not understand these truths and if we do not find a constructive partnership, the danger of world destabilization could be far greater than that experienced during the cold-war rivalry between the Soviet Union and the United States.

There is no reason why the fundamental, long-range national interests of these two great countries cannot coincide in the kind of world we want to create. That does not mean it will be easy. It is a tremendous challenge. It is a challenge particularly for us Americans to equip ourselves with the understanding we need to make it work. We are far behind the Chinese in doing our part. As pointed out by Vice President Walter F. Mondale and by Professor Mikael S. Adolphson in Part II of this book, there are many more students from Asia—China, Japan, India, Southeast Asia, Korea—who come to the United States each year to study us, live with us, and come to comprehend us than there are American students who go to Asia to learn about and understand that critical part of the globe. Moreover, Asian students most often remain in the United States for four or five years, whereas most American students' study-abroad experiences are for a year or less.

I recently discussed with the class I teach on American government the Chinese perspective on what is going on in Hong Kong. How can we understand China if we do not know the history of the Opium War? How can we understand contemporary Chinese sensibilities to the threat of disorder within their own society if we do not know the history of the relatively recent Cultural Revolution in that country and the actions of the Red Guard during that period? And yet if we were to poll Americans, even those in university communities, how many would be knowledgeable about the last fifty or seventy-five years of Chinese history, let alone be acquainted with the last 5,000 years that form the perspective of today's China leaders? Dr. Kissinger makes clear in chapter 22 the need for this knowledge if we are to understand, respect, and be empathetic to the role of China as a great nation in the world.

We in this country face enormous challenges and responsibilities with respect to China. For a partnership to work, each partner must know, understand, respect, and trust the other. All of us hope that as we go into the next millennium, as we pass this world on to our children and grandchildren, the United States–China relationship will be based on reality, mutual respect, and friendship. For this to happen, we as a people, our government, and our key institutions, especially the educational system and the media, have much to do.

We are living through times that some have called the "sound-bite" culture, but as a nation we need to deliberate seriously about the problems we confront in foreign policy. Many of us feel a deep hunger to get together as a community to discuss the challenges that face us, to deal with substance, to collect our best thoughts, and to listen to those people with the greatest expertise in our society.

We yearn for substance, not images and slogans. We desperately need serious, substantive conversation and more dialogue in our country. With this book we are trying to help our country get on that path. We focus attention on preparing our country, indeed on preparing ourselves, to enter a new century, to enter a new millennium.

As I have studied history I always have wondered if the people who lived through remarkable times knew they were living through them. Were those people living through the Renaissance aware of the fact that they were in a period of transformation that historians would judge to have been a renaissance? Did those who lived through the industrial revolution realize they were experiencing rapid and fundamental changes that would alter the ways in which society was organized and have profound sociological implications? Did husbands and wives come down to breakfast in the morning, turn to each other, and say, "Just think! We are living through the industrial revolution!" I doubt it. Martin Luther King once said, "One of the great liabilities of history is that all too many people fail to remain awake through great periods of social change. Every society has its protectors of the status quo and its fraternities of the indifferent who are notorious for sleeping through revolutions. But today our very survival depends on our ability to stay awake, to adjust to new ideas, to remain vigilant and to face the challenge of change."[3] Perhaps our generation is different. We understand that we are living through a period that is unprecedented in terms of the encapsulation of so much change in the world in such a brief period.

Knowing that we live through this period of enormous change, and realizing that historians who follow us will judge this period as one of the watershed periods of history, we confront this question: Will we make decisions that are better and wiser than those who, without realizing it, slumbered unconsciously through other great periods of history? Our challenge is to make decisions now that will make this world a safer place for our descendants tomorrow.

Abraham Lincoln warned us that none can escape history. Our generation will be judged by how decisively we seize the moment of opportunity that has been given to us.

Admiral William J. Crowe in his foreword, Ambassador Edward J. Perkins in his preface, and I in my comments have stated that the purpose of this book is to contribute to America's essential task of developing a new paradigm for the conduct of United States foreign policy as we enter the twenty-first century. Perkins describes the conference on which this book is based, and provides a brief overview of the University of Oklahoma's goals and activities to "internationalize" education to prepare students to live and work successfully in what is a rapidly changing and increasingly global community.

In Part I an astounding cast of practitioner authorities who concisely and keenly depict the current state of the major regions of the world will challenge and inform you. Launched by an insightful overview by Yale Professor Gaddis Smith, Pulitzer Prize–winner Jim Hoagland analyzes Europe. Our recent ambassador to Mexico, James R. Jones, emphasizes the importance of the Western Hemisphere. Our last ambassador to the Soviet Union before its collapse, Jack Matlock, puts Russia and the former states of the USSR into proper perspective. Edward Perkins cautions that the United States leaves out Africa only at future loss to the world.

Asia has emerged so rapidly in the economic field and looms so large geopolitically that Part II is dedicated solely to that region. Perkins' overview sets the stage on which former Chinese ambassador to the United States Li Daoyu presents his country's view of its place in the world. Complementing him is Chinese Professor Zhou Dunren's insightful essay and advice. In chapter 4, veteran China hand Jan Berris of the National Committee on U.S.-China Relations and preeminent American China scholar Michel Oksenberg expound the American view of China at this stage of history. Although China seems predestined to be the major Asian power, Japan will continue to have the second most powerful economy in the world for some time to come and cannot be left out of the equation. Former U.S. Vice President and ambassador to Japan Walter Mondale brings enlightenment by expositing in chapter 5 on Japan and its vital role in U.S. foreign policy and Asia's stability. Ably backing him up is former ambassador Francis McNeil, a Japanese-language officer and specialist, who also comments on the futures of the countries of Southeast Asia, South Asia, and the Korean Peninsula. Dean of American Asia scholars Robert A. Scalapino rounds off treatment of the region with a *tour d'horizon* of countries and issues in chapter 6. Provocative comments by OU Professors Mikael A. Adolphson, Marlan Downey, and Edwin G. Corr, who was also ambassador to several Latin American countries, end Part II.

Following the survey of the current world in Parts I and II, the book focuses in Parts III through VII on components that as a whole constitute American foreign policy, and then moves to Part VIII for proposals of overarching strategies and paradigms. Part III examines the military challenge. After an overview by Corr, former senator and chairman of the Senate Armed Services Committee Sam Nunn leads off in chapter 8 by discussing national security in a world with weapons of mass destruction, residual issues from the cold war, and the growing security threats of cyberspace warfare. Former ambassador Robert Oakley draws on his Somalia experience and knowledge of contemporary conflict to describe evolving American doctrine and policy for the employment of military force in the post–cold war era.

Attention centers on the intelligence function in Part IV. Drawing on my experience as chairman of the Senate Intelligence Committee, I provide the initial overview. The reader can entertain the views and wisdom of four former directors and the current director of the Central Intelligence Agency. Robert M. Gates evaluates intelligence during the cold war in chapter 10, and Director George J. Tenet takes a strategic look in the next chapter at intelligence in the future. In chapter 12, Professor Stephen Sloan, from the University, and I comment on Gates and Tenet's presentations. These more conventional chapters are followed in chapter 13 by a roundtable discussion on the role and organization of intelligence in the twenty-first century, moderated by John Milewski of *Close-Up* for C-Span. Former directors Richard Helms, R. James Woolsey, and Judge William H. Webster are participants, along with Professor Robert H. Cox, from the University of Oklahoma, and myself.

Part V deals with trade and foreign economic policy. The dean of the

University of Oklahoma Michael F. Price College of Business, Richard Cosier, provides the overview. Former secretary of agriculture and U.S. trade representative Clayton Yeutter uses chapter 14 to dissect and make recommendations for U.S. trade policy in the twenty-first century. In chapter 15, the presidents and CEOs of two major oil companies—Archie Dunham, of Conoco Inc., and Luke R. Corbett, of Kerr-McGee Corporation— express their views on unilateral trade sanctions as an instrument of U.S. foreign policy. John S. Wolf, U.S. ambassador to the Asia-Pacific Economic Cooperation forum, addresses trade liberalization in chapter 16, focusing on regional trade organizations. Views on what is needed to strengthen the United States for international competition are covered by well-known value investor Michael F. Price and trade attorneys W. DeVier Pierson and Max N. Berry in chapter 17.

The environment in international relations is the topic of Part VI. Professor Zev M. Trachtenberg, of the University's Department of Philosophy, sets the stage with the overview. Dr. Richard L. Sandor, creator of the use of markets as a major element in U.S. foreign policy to protect the environment, discusses and puts forth a model for containing greenhouse-gas emissions. In chapter 19, political economist Rajeev Gowda, with Trachtenberg's help, raises possible difficulties for the model from the point of view of lesser developed countries.

In Part VII, chapter 20, former presidential adviser and current editor of *U.S. News and World Report* David R. Gergen provides the set piece for thought about the media in international relations. David Dary, director of the University of Oklahoma's School of Journalism and Mass Communications, provides the overview. Joining him in chapter 21 are Lee Cullum, columnist for the *Dallas Morning News,* and Lois Romano, regional correspondent for the *Washington Post,* for a lively discussion of the media in the making of foreign policy.

In Part VIII, foreign-policy authorities follow the experts' analyses on the regions of the world and on various components of foreign policy to put forth more comprehensive policy and guidance for America's conduct of foreign affairs in the twenty-first century. I provide the overview. Former Secretary of State and National Security Adviser Dr. Henry A. Kissinger's contribution in chapter 22, "The Architecture of an American Foreign Policy for the Twenty-first Century," is the cornerstone around which the book has been built. His survey of the major regions of the globe gives special attention to China as we look to the next century. Kissinger's views are both the heart and spine of this book, and the reader will find his thoughts and analysis playing a major part again in the book's conclusions in chapter 29. The highlighting of Kissinger's presentation is in no way meant to detract from the ideas and opinions of our other distinguished contributors, many of whose views expressed in this book are compatible with those of Kissinger.

In chapter 23, Dr. Zbigniew Brzezinski, National Security Adviser under

President Jimmy Carter and a noted Russian scholar, proposes a geostrategy for Eurasia, which is in essence a proposal for America's global foreign policy. Former U.S. ambassador to the United Nations and cabinet member Jeane J. Kirkpatrick analyzes a vital aspect of American strategy in chapter 24, in which she insists that nations emerging as world actors must be taken into account in our thinking and actions. In chapter 25, President of the Center for Strategic and International Studies (CSIS) and Ambassador David M. Abshire calls for an "agile strategy" in the implementation of global policy. Rounding out Part VIII is Ambassador George C. McGhee's optimistic statement, in chapter 26, of his view of America and the world's future.

In Part IX, "Epilogue and Conclusion," Perkins and I attempted to provide greater historical perspective to deliberations on a new paradigm for American foreign policy by asking Colleen McCullough to extract from the history of Rome lessons for the United States as a superpower at the turn of the millennium. A noted writer of works of fiction, including *The Thorn Birds*, McCullough has just completed the fifth novel of her *Masters of Rome* series. J. Rufus Fears and Alfred S. Bradford add perspective by critiques of her presentation. Perkins and I then close the book in chapter 29 with summary comments and observations.

A final note about the structure of the book: Although many presentations were made separately, we have attempted to organize them in a logical sequence and to group them so that they are coherent to the reader. We also have sought to tie them together and to provide a unifying thread through the text by the preface, foreword, and concluding chapter. We have purposely included commentary and some questions and answers from the conference, because we believe they contain valuable information and insights, and they are for the most part related directly to the theme of this book. In the few instances where they stray from the main flow of the study, they are refreshing and thought-provoking.

I cannot think of a better group of practitioners and thinkers than the contributors to this book to discuss and help us to understand the necessity of vigorous, responsible, innovative leadership by the United States, the world's only superpower. The contributors help us to understand that although the world is more complex and intellectually challenging than it was in the last half century, it does not relieve us of our responsibilities to create security, stability, economic and social development, and enhanced freedom and social justice.

We understood who we were a few years ago. We were the leader of the free world. Our job was to contain the spread of the Soviet empire and to make the world secure from it. Who are we now? What is our role? What is our place? What is our purpose? There is not yet any new prism through which we can view the world with all its complexity and seek to understand it and bring order to it. That is the task of our generations—the older and the younger—armed with the wisdom that we are living through incredible times. That is the challenge we are addressing at the University of Oklahoma and in this book.

NOTES

1. Dean Acheson, *Present at the Creation: My Years in the State Department* (New York: W.W. Norton and Company, 1996).

2. Henry A Kissinger, *Nuclear Weapons and Foreign Policy* (New York: Harper, Inc., 1957).

3. James M. Washington, ed., *Testament of Hope: The Essential Writings of Martin Luther King, Jr.* (San Francisco: Harpers, 1991), p. 619.

Chapter 2

The State of the World

Overview

Gaddis Smith

Aprofessor of mine once said that anything after the Renaissance is journalism. I do not want to go back to the Renaissance but I would like briefly to look at the last 250 years. We are in the fifth global postwar era, going back to the middle of the eighteenth century. The first was after the Seven Years' War, which ended in 1763; the second after the Napoleonic Wars, ending in 1814–15; the third after World War I, ending in 1918; the fourth after World War II, ending in 1945; and now, of course, we are in the post–cold war era.

These five eras have at least four things in common. First is great uncertainty over how the winners would treat the losers and even greater uncertainty over how the losers would behave. I think if we look at all those postwar eras, the answer to that question was very important in determining whether a postwar era was almost simultaneously a prewar era for the next conflict or whether a period of reasonable stability intervened. The second common characteristic is the appearance of powerful political ideologies—currents running much more strongly than they had before the war that was just ended. Sometimes these were constructive, stabilizing currents; sometimes they were very destabilizing, revolutionary, or reactionary. We see them after every great war. Third, we see ever-escalating change of a technological nature in each postwar period: the technologies of weapons, of industrial production, and of communication. And fourth, the nature of these postwar eras was absolutely crucial for the history and well-being of the United States.

The outcome of the Seven Years' War, as every student of American history knows, contributed to the birth of this nation, to American independence. The outcome of the second, the Napoleonic period, created a century of security vis-à-vis Europe. In the three twentieth-century postwar eras, the capacity of the United States to shape the future was greater than that of any other nation. After 1918, we blew it. After 1945, we saw the creation, referred to in Dean Acheson's memoirs, of security and relative stability in the face of unimaginable danger.

The first four eras differ, though, in one significant respect from the present, fifth postwar era. In the first four you see either one great power or a group or groups of great powers developing coherent international policies. Sometimes these policies were sharply diametrical and clashing. Indeed, they led to other wars, but these eras had clarity and coherence. Clarity and coherence did not necessarily save leaders from mistakes, however. They often led to poor outcomes, but at least the issues were well defined. They provided guidelines for handling a specific crisis.

Today, we have all the characteristics of the earlier eras without any agreed-upon goals by any individual governments, societies, or groups comparable to goals in those previous eras. Those goals included France's determination to redress the balance of power after the defeat of 1763, Germany's determination to do relatively the same thing after 1918, and American determination after 1945 to avoid the irresponsibility of the previous generation and to contain the dangerous tendencies of the Soviet Union, as the United States had failed to do after World War I with respect to Hitler. This absence of clarity is not entirely a bad thing. Napoleon was clear; so was Hitler; so was Stalin. We do not need their likes again. But navigating in a fog of uncertainty is dangerous too.

This chapter covers all the major areas of the world except Asia, which is treated in Part II.

Europe

Jim Hoagland

Henry Kissinger rightly says that Europe has no address and no telephone number. He means that no single system or single power dominates Europe in a way that would enable a true continental power like the United States to appeal to or order around a European entity and get a unified response. That is both the joy and the frustration of dealing with Europe. After all, we in the United States have spent the better part of this century trying to make sure no single power that could be hostile to our interests dominates Europe, and we have succeeded. Will we be able to succeed in this period when, in the leading geopolitical bromide of the day, the disappearance of the Soviet threat has dissolved the glue of Western unity?

Today, we watch political Europe struggle to achieve European monetary union and to build something that Europeans call common defense and foreign-policy identities, which would seemingly be in contradiction to their history and to our interest. I think it is safe to predict that the relationship between America and Europe, which is much older and much bigger than NATO's and the collective response to the Soviet threat, will continue and will in some ways deepen.

After all, American colonials adapted European political and social models to the frontier. Today, Europeans have adopted many bits of Americana, from M.B.A. programs to MTV programs, from Big Macs to computer Macs. I think the sense of common traditions and common long-term interests will survive deeply into the twenty-first century, as Russia becomes a functioning democracy and strong political partner for the West. For the purpose of our discussion, let us assume that will be the case. I will leave it to Jack Matlock to describe it otherwise if he believes that to be so.

In these circumstances, I believe the main threats to continuing an effective global partnership could lie in American politics and in European economics.

In many ways, it will be much easier to get the military part of the new transatlantic equation right. To this point, the focus has been on NATO's recent expansion. The objective now, I believe, should be to make NATO expansion irrelevant to big-power politics. That should be no problem with the Czech Republic, Hungary, and Poland, which Russia has now acknowledged to be outside its sphere of influence and area of immediate concern. The problems will emerge, of course, as we get to the Baltic States and Ukraine. But it should be within the power of mankind to arrange a diplomatic formula that will extend NATO-sponsored security guarantees—rather than NATO membership—to those countries while allaying Russian fears.

Assume that this is done in the next ten to fifteen years. The process will have to be accompanied by a significant revision of American-European military relations within NATO. That revision is, in fact, already beginning. One of the unavowed but clear purposes of NATO expansion is to provide a new basis for the continuing presence in Europe of a militarily significant American force deep into the twenty-first century. Currently, that is defined at about 100,000 soldiers based in or near Germany. By extending the alliance to the east and thereby relieving Germany of the demanding duty of being NATO's eastern frontier, both Germany and the United States have a clear rationale for continuing an American military presence that began as an occupation and continued as a cold-war necessity. That, in some ways, is the covert little secret at the heart of NATO expansion. The fact is, Europe continues to need an American presence and capability even if Russia remains quiescent, and even if European states have given up warring among themselves.

This has been amply proved in the Persian Gulf War and in Bosnia—the two types of conflicts that Americans and Europeans are most likely to face together in the next quarter century.

In each theater, European troops were ineffective without American logistical and intelligence capabilities and clear political support. If Europeans are to protect their interests in the resource wars and in the ethnic upheavals likely to disturb global stability in the future, they will need to do so with the Americans. That is the reality that lay behind the debate about extending the stability force in Bosnia beyond June 1998 and Europe's hope for finding a defense identity within NATO.

Current military trends will sharpen European dependence on the United States, which now spends more on defense than do all of its European allies combined. Defense budgets in France, England, Germany, and elsewhere are shrinking while our military spending stays relatively constant. Moreover, the last European armies are now being shrunk and professionalized. France is abandoning conscription. Germany will be forced to do so within a decade or less.

As the forces are restructured, they give up the primary mission of defending the homeland and its borders against outside invasion and they shift to what the military likes to call power projection—intervention in areas outside or on the fringes of Europe. France's recent decision to reduce and redeploy its forces in Africa is basically a decision that France can no longer project military power alone, even into Africa. That requires help from the United States. The French will not go into a conflict like that in the Congo without American support. When they did not receive U.S. support in 1997, they did not go. Germany can use its military force abroad only in the context of NATO. The United States, of course, sees it is in its interest to have Europe join in military operations when feasible.

Clearly, this is not going to happen without friction. Serious debates will occur about NATO expansion involving the old burden-sharing problem. I think we can overcome those because the mutual interests are so clear.

More worrisome for the long-term prospects of the transatlantic relationship is economic stagnation in Europe, which has unemployment levels not seen since the depression years of the 1930s. Perhaps more disturbing even than those levels, however, is the phenomenon that economic growth and favorable trade balances, when they can be achieved in Germany or France or other countries (always with the exception of Britain), do not translate into significant decreases in unemployment. Germany has wrestled with the enormous financial, economic, and social problems of unification and so far is losing. The rest of Europe has been straitjacketed by the Maastricht Treaty, which provides for European economic and monetary union. As John Newhouse puts it in his new book, *Europe Adrift*,[1] monetary union has been a massive distraction. The only unifying force in Europe today is unemployment.

The forces known in shorthand as "globalization" have thus far not been kind to European economies and welfare states. Europe has not been able to take advantage of the enormous productivity increases that the information revolution is powering in the United States. As you talk to executives and analysts in engineering, finance, and information-related fields in Europe, you get the sense that Europe risks being left behind permanently in key areas of the new global economy. Europe lags significantly in Internet applications such as E-mail, a key measure of new economic adaptability.

Such concerns have been expressed and overdone in the past, as in the Europe-pessimism fad in the early 1980s. Those proved to be cyclical problems rather than structural ones. The current Euro-stagnation seems more serious because it is more structural. It may be beyond the reach of the fiscal changes that European monetary union will bring when it enters in effect on schedule, as I believe it will. What is amazing is that countries such as Germany and France remain significant economic competitors for the rest of the world even with their staggering social-welfare costs and exorbitant hourly wages. They remain significant exporters. They remain competitive because of their social infrastructure, which creates something that the late Nicholas Colchester called "collective productivity"—a value added by a populace working smoothly together to create wealth and quality.[2] Out of that experience and commitment to diversity, Europeans may find a way to blend their collective productivity and social responsibility with the labor-market flexibility and the technology focus that Anglo-American societies have used to forge ahead in the 1990s. I think it is in our interest, for the sake of a healthy partnership, that they do so.

Finally, we must look at the danger that the United States' complete dominance of the international scene poses for this partnership. Only the United States—by badly misplaying its hand—can do what the Soviet Union could never accomplish: turn the Atlantic into a gulf of misunderstanding and mistrust between Americans and Europeans. My concern about this is a concern about unilateralism and arbitrariness in U.S. policy toward the rest of the world. I think it is a trend that is surfacing increasingly, driven by two main forces. One is the growing assertion of the U.S. Congress that American law, religion, and family values—as defined by Congress—should prevail everywhere as the international norm. Some legislation embodies that idea. The second force is the ever-growing influence of ethnic organizations on the making of American foreign policy. These two forces produce a trend toward arbitrariness and unilateralism. Conflict with Europe is certainly not the intent of the legislators who signed up to support the Helms-Burton and Iran-Libya Sanctions Act (ILSA) bills. However, their lack of recognition of how the rest of the world is reacting to American assertiveness on these issues is a measure of declining U.S. attention to experience with the rest of the world, particularly by members of Congress.

Time and the learning curve may do much to resolve this problem. The store of goodwill and of influence the United States has accumulated by half a century of standing guard against the Soviets and being an honest broker in European problems will be difficult to squander so quickly. Europe and America have a unique ability in international affairs to learn from each other's mistakes and problems. That should continue to tie us together far into the twenty-first century.

Western Hemisphere

James R. Jones

As we look at the past half century of our foreign policy, we have to be pleased. Although it was described by many names, such as "the policy of containment," the real underlying vision of our foreign policy has been one word—*freedom*—that is, a freedom defined by open, democratic political systems and free-market economic systems. We have won. That is the trend. That is the goal. That is virtually the objective of countries all over this world. Nowhere has the pursuit of freedom and market economics been more impressively and effectively put into effect in such a short period of time as in our hemisphere, in Mexico and Central and South America. That was evident to me in Mexico.

I have had dealings with Mexico for more than thirty years. The four years when I served there as ambassador were truly a time of great change— one of the two most important transitions in Mexico's political and economic history. If one considers what has happened in our hemisphere in less than ten years, it is truly remarkable. Ten years ago, Mexico and virtually all the countries of the hemisphere had very closed economic systems. They also had very closed political systems. Today, the hemisphere is characterized by the most open and vibrant economic and political systems in the world.

This fact was evidenced in December 1994 when the Summit of the Americas Conference was held in Miami. It was the first meeting of our hemispheric nations since 1967, in Punta del Este, Uruguay. I think I am the only person who was part of the official delegations of both those summits—in 1967 as a young assistant to President Johnson, and in 1994 as ambassador to Mexico. What a difference that period of time had made! In 1967, as I recall, eighteen nations attended the summit at Punta del Este, ten of which were headed by military dictators. In 1994, thirty-four nations were present, all of whom had presidents democratically elected by their people. In 1967, the United States clearly wrote the agenda, and it centered around foreign aid and development assistance, government-to-government assistance. In 1994, Latin leaders themselves essentially wrote the agenda, and it centered around two things—trade and investment.

A true change has occurred in our hemisphere, and it has gone almost unnoticed in the United States. We should pay more attention because the Western Hemisphere, Asia, and eastern Europe especially are areas of emerging markets that are absolutely vital to U.S. foreign policy and economic growth in the twenty-first century. As much as we may identify with our traditional trading partners of Europe and Japan and as much as we identify with our domestic markets, if we are to continue dynamic economic growth and opportunity for our children and grandchildren, we have to be fully engaged in the emerging markets of this hemisphere, Asia, and eastern and central Europe. That is where the growth will be in the twenty-first century.

The growth opportunities in our hemisphere will be more promising in the next couple of decades than what has occurred in Asia in the past couple of decades. The projected growth rates for Western Hemisphere countries are 4 to 8 percent in real growth. This will be better than those projected for the Asian tigers, which will continue to grow, but at a slower pace. All this change is occurring in a context in this hemisphere that is motivating leaders to make their places in history by developing fully respected, recognized First World status for their particular countries. They are doing it by building the three major pillars of First World respectability.

First is economic reform. In less than ten years, country after country has gone from state-owned and -dominated industries to privatizations; from hostility to foreign investment to attracting outside private investors; from closed trading systems to free-trade agreements. This is manifest in the North American Free Trade Agreement (NAFTA), in MERCOSUR (the Southern Cone customs agreement), in the Andean Pact, in the Central American Common Market, and in many bilateral trade agreements among and between various countries. It is especially seen in the Declaration of the 1994 Miami Summit that the hemisphere should be a free-trade zone by the year 2005. Strong winds of free-market economics are blowing throughout the Latin nations.

Economic reforms set in motion the second important measure of First World respectability, the demand for and progress toward the second pillar—political reforms. Competitive party systems are in place. The media display significantly more open expression and criticism. Political and economic reforms have complemented and reinforced each other significantly.

Now, the third pillar of First World status is beginning to be constructed in countries such as Mexico, Argentina, and Brazil. This is legal and judicial reform. In many ways this pillar is the most difficult. Corruption is endemic in many institutionalized ways. To get around the strictures of the Napoleonic Code and the overcentralization of the legal structure, alternative dispute-resolution mechanisms are being developed, especially as they deal with the new free flow of commerce. In the past, bribery of corrupt officials was virtually necessary to do business in these countries. In Mexico and some other Latin nations, change in this area is beginning. Mexico has adopted a major reform that if a solicitant to a government agency has not been given an answer within a certain short time period, the petition is automatically approved. This removes the need for paying someone to move papers from one desk to the next. Those kinds of subtle reforms are aimed at making the legal system one that the First World can respect.

With all this, we have to ask ourselves what our foreign policy toward Latin America should be. I would say first of all that we have to maintain our leadership. At the end of the cold war we, the United States, stand as a beacon of the values we have been espousing worldwide during this last half century. Yet many people in our country say global leadership is not important, or they want to shrink from that responsibility. Leadership is extremely important. In the area of trade, for example, we have to maintain the leadership in opening up trading régimes around the world and keeping them open. In this hemisphere almost one billion consumers await doing business with the United States. For U.S. leadership, Congress must restore to the president fast-track negotiating authority for trade, an authority Congress has bestowed on presidents for the last quarter century. This is essential to negotiate freer and more open trading systems around the world. I would hope that people who attend conferences such as this would express themselves positively to their elected representatives in Congress.

I was in Brazil and Argentina in 1998 on business. It was alarming that Brazilians are pleased with the United States' inability to exercise leadership on trade in the hemisphere. This is because (1) our lack of leadership allows Brazil to become more important in defining what free trade will be in the hemisphere, and (2) it allows Brazil to keep its markets more closed to American commerce during this period when we are unable to lead. For our benefit and the hemisphere's, we have to maintain our leadership.

Second, our foreign policy has to be centered around commerce more and more. We made that the number-one objective of the six major objectives in Mexico while I was ambassador there. To me, the competitive field of the twenty-first century increasingly will be economic as opposed to military. I have found in Mexico that commerce and investment are perhaps the United States' most important foreign-policy tools for persuading another country to accept our views and values. Commerce must be highlighted even more in our foreign policy during the twenty-first century.

With respect to legal reforms, we have to give more help to those countries that are trying to change their legal systems and that have endemic criminal problems. This is so for criminal situations such as exist in Russia, or for narcotics trafficking in certain parts of Latin America. Many countries are trying to make their legal structures honest and reliable so people can have confidence that the law will be evenhanded. American-sponsored administration of justice-assistance programs is very important. We have much to offer in terms of training, technical assistance, and even internal surveillance methods for use on police forces. We have started such a program in Mexico, and we should do a lot more.

Another part of our foreign policy has to do with our overall attitude. One of the big reasons we are doing so much better in Mexico and parts of South America is that we have fundamentally changed from paternalism to partnership. It is a much more effective way to achieve our foreign-policy goals.

Finally, we should also be aware of what I consider the biggest problem in South America and in certain other emerging markets. It is what I call the opportunity gap. There is not only the problem of a huge rich-poor division with very little middle class that exists in Latin America society today, but there is also the lack of opportunity to close that gap during the next generation. It is like the Great Depression in Oklahoma. Even though I was not born until after the depression, our families talked to us about it. They realized that their opportunities had been lost, but they believed their children and grandchildren would have a chance for better lives.

We as Americans have been successful in preaching the twin gospels of free markets and democracy. But a look at the emerging markets shows that not more than 50 percent of the people are benefiting from the wealth and changes these new markets are generating. If the situation that 30 to 50 percent of those populations that have no opportunity to benefit continues without improvement for another ten years, this will constitute a political constituency waiting to be led by some demagogue who will want to roll the clock back on economic and political reforms. To prevent this, the moral and pragmatic leadership of the United States must promote public-private partnerships for things that can make a difference in closing this opportunity gap in developing countries—education and training, health care, and the development of infrastructure. It is very important.

Another important thing is the educational exchanges themselves. The biggest difference in dealing with Mexico from my first trip in 1966, as a member of President Johnson's staff, to my going there in the 1990s as ambassador was that in 1966 I did not meet a single person in government or business who had received any education in the United States. Today, it is hard to find leaders who have not had some part of their education in the United States. It is not so much the education itself—it is breaking down the barriers of distrust. It is students living with one another, debunking stereotypes, and developing a network of trust and friends who can do business together. The student exchanges should be a major part of our foreign policy.

Those are the things that are going on in the Western Hemisphere.

Mexico and China are the two most important countries in terms of our foreign policy. These two nations will lead the economic and political development in the twenty-first century of the two regions that comprise 60 percent of the world's population. How we handle foreign policy with these two countries and these two regions will largely determine our global position in the next century.

Russia and the CIS

Jack F. Matlock Jr.

As I was thinking about our current relations with the states that once were part of the Soviet Union, there came to mind a story that a prominent Russian politician, Grigory Yavlinsky, told in Washington in 1996. He had lost in the presidential election by a pretty wide margin but he probably is the best educated and the most Western-oriented of the Russian politicians. He tells a story of two hunters who loved to seek big game and had, for several years, hired a fellow with a small plane to fly them to a remote area to hunt bears. They arranged their annual trip. The pilot dropped them off and told them he would be back in a week, but they should remember that the plane was small and could take just one bear. He returned in a week and one of the hunters said, "We shot two bears." The pilot replies, "I told you we only have room for one." But the hunters insisted, saying, "Ivan, calm down. Last year you told us the same thing, but we shot two and you managed to stuff that second one in. We gave you $100 then; this time we'll give you $200." The pilot grumbled a bit but finally agreed. He stuffed both bears in the plane and they took off, but in twenty minutes they crashed. They were all dazed, and one turned to the other and said, "Where the hell are we?" The other one responded, "Gee, I don't know for sure, but it's pretty close to where we crashed last year."

Russia has something of a habit of making the same mistakes over and over. When you think about it, not only the Russians do that. Sometimes you can make a mistake by continuing to do the same thing even if it was right the previous times. If circumstances have changed and you do not recognize the change, the momentum of the way you did things in the past can carry you into policies and actions that do not serve your interests. This is one of the things that worries me today about at least some of our approaches to this area. The most important prerequisite for a sound foreign policy is to recognize the changes that have occurred in the past few years. They are as significant as the earlier ones that Professor Smith mentioned in his overview. In some respects they may be even more profound.

Actually, what we witnessed and experienced in the last few years of the 1980s and the first two years of the 1990s was no less than three major revolutions. *Revolution* may not be the right word because these were not bloody revolutions, but they were seismic events in a geopolitical sense. Three major changes occurred, but we often merge them in our minds. And when we merge them we sometimes come up with the wrong conclusions. What were these key events or transformations?

(1) The cold war ended. You can argue about just exactly when it ended. Was it when the Berlin Wall came down? Was it when the Soviet government agreed to a reunified Germany in NATO, or was it when we signed the treaty to reduce conventional arms in Europe? Well, it ended somewhere between 1989 and 1990. It ended definitively.

(2) Within a few months, the power of the Communist Party within the Soviet Union was shattered. That is, Communist rule over a sixth of the earth's land surface in what then was in many ways militarily the most powerful country in the world, collapsed—not suddenly, but very rapidly.

(3) Before we had a chance to recognize how profound that change was, the Soviet Union itself broke up. These three events were clearly interconnected, but they were also distinct.

The relationship of the West and the United States to the three events was different. We wanted to end the cold war. As a matter of fact, it was ended almost precisely on our own prescription. We set out from the beginning what to do, and we did it. We could not have done it if the Soviet leadership with Mikhail Gorbachev and Eduard Shevardnadze, his foreign minister, had not come to understand that it was in their interest to end the cold war. As far as ending Communist rule in the Soviet Union is concerned, we did not do that. We contributed to it by our pressures to open up society—by many of the things that we did, by communicating, by simply being ourselves. Stalin had understood that the greatest threat to the system he perfected as a totalitarian system was exposure to the outside world. He had to cut the country off if he was to rule in the way he did. Gorbachev's opening of Soviet society made that system of rule impossible. Gorbachev, Shevardnadze, and the others did not fully understand what they were doing or what the consequences would be. They thought they could manage it. It turned out that they could not. But we should understand that we did not bring the end of Communism there; they did.

This is even more true when it comes to the collapse of the Soviet Union. In that case, once the Baltic states were free, we would have been, to be quite honest, happier dealing with one country making up the twelve remaining republics, if their remaining in the Soviet Union could have been voluntary and democratic, than with the twelve separate ones that resulted. We saw that in President Bush's speech on August 1, 1991, in Kiev. Bill Safire called it his "Chicken Kiev" speech. What Bush said was very significant. He said, "Freedom is not synonymous with independence." Is not that true? I think it is true. Since they gained independence some of the Soviet Union's successors have been finding out exactly that. Several of the successor states have been notably less free than they were in 1991 when Communist rule was collapsing.

Why do I go back into this history? For one thing, it is not that far back. We are talking about events within the last decade. Yet sometimes when we make our policies we either think in the stereotypes of the past without realizing it, or we project the present situation back to a previous one. For example, I am often identified as having been ambassador to Russia. I was never ambassador to Russia. I was ambassador to the Soviet Union. The Soviet Union and Russia are two different phenomena, not just in theory, but in practice. Russia was by far the largest but was only one of the fifteen republics in the Soviet Union. I will tell you the truth: When I took the oath of office as ambassador to the Soviet Union in 1987, it never occurred to me that it would take fifteen people to replace me.

In any event, the fact is that today's Russia is different from the Soviet Union. When I think back, I understand the reasons we won the cold war. But the cold war we won was against the Soviet Union, not Russia. In 1990 and 1991, prior to the collapse of the Soviet Union, when we were dealing with the elected leaders of Russia, then a constituent part of the Soviet Union, they saw winning the cold war in exactly the same way we did. They wanted to throw off Communist rule. They wanted a more democratic system. They wanted an end to it. When the Soviet Union dissolved, they felt Russia also had won against the Soviet Union, and objectively speaking, it had. Yet some say that we won and Russia lost. This confuses Russia with the Soviet Union and distorts history. In fact, the end of the cold war brought immense benefits to both Russia and the West. That is one thing we should bear firmly in mind as we look at the future.

Now, what was the source of the conflicts of the cold war? Was it that Russian interests conflicted with American? A lot of people thought so. One very perceptive observer, Louis Halle, wrote a book in the 1960s, when the cold war was really just getting started, called *The Cold War as History*.[3] He said it would have happened because of geopolitics whether or not there was Communism in the Soviet Union. I think that is quite wrong. If you look back at Russian history before Communism, you can see very clearly that there were very few conflicts of basic interests between Russia and the United States. The cold war was about ideology and the political system based on it. It was not about Russian national interests. If you look at interests today you will find that Russian national interests are fully compatible with American national interests. We often do not recognize that, and the Russians certainly do not always recognize it. But it is important because it means we are not dealing with the sort of intractable territorial disputes or other basic problems which in history have been almost impossible to solve. The problems we have now stem from a Russian feeling of weakness and the difficulties in Russia's economy and political development.

As for our security interests, the overriding security interest of the American people is to keep weapons of mass destruction under responsible control and to reduce them as rapidly as possible. It seems to me we have to question any policy that tends to make that more difficult and to say, "Is it really necessary?" In this respect, I feel that the present policy of moving the borders of NATO eastward is unwise. This is not just a matter of NATO's sponsored security guarantees; if that were all it were, it could probably be handled. Clearly, as NATO moves eastward, it is going to be much more difficult to persuade the Russia Duma to act in a rational manner on weapons of mass destruction and ratify START II, and to ratify what I hope would be a START III. We need to move much more rapidly to reduce stocks of nuclear weapons. Politically, this is going to be much more difficult if NATO takes in new members.

NATO is essential for European security and particularly for the future of Germany and the United States' role in Europe. NATO expansion will tend to distract our attention from what the two major security issues really are in Europe—weapons of mass destruction and instability in the Balkans. The most palpable threat to security now is in the Balkans, not in the NATO area at all and not east of the NATO area. Bosnia is still an unsolved problem although, thank goodness, it is under temporary control. So far as I know, we still do not have a common NATO policy regarding the future. What happens after next year? Do we simply continue to keep troops there? How much intervention can there be? Can outsiders, in fact, encourage something like a civil society in a nation as divided as Bosnia? These are first-rate problems, and spending so much attention on which countries should be members of NATO is bound to distract the alliance.

It seems to me that by bringing countries into NATO before they are in the European Union, we put the cart before the horse. The countries in eastern Europe need the European Union and the economic integration more than they need the security protection of NATO, because their security is not being threatened. They still have very fragile economies. But it is extraordinarily difficult for west Europeans to accept them, to open their markets to them. I am afraid our west European allies, although they do not often say so openly, really are pushing NATO expansion as a surrogate for what east Europeans really need. It would be most unfortunate if we find that in moving NATO eastward, east Europeans will be denied what they need even more, which is membership in the European Union.

In May 1997 I was in the Republic of Georgia and had a long talk with President Shevardnadze. I think he is one of the heroes in bringing an end to the cold war and, during the post-Soviet period, in pulling Georgia out of a civil war into some coherence. I asked him, "What do you need most of all from us?" He surprised me. He said, "We need the European Union to take in Turkey." We are talking about a very strategic area—in other words, the stabilization of the Turkish economy by Turkey being brought into the European Union, which would calm a lot of problems in the region. It would also give countries in the region a more secure flank and be of great use to people such as Shevardnadze in dealing with his Russian problem. We need to think more carefully about these things and what our policies should be.

I hope we will not be too distracted over a secondary issue, that is, precisely which countries should be members of NATO. We must devote greater attention to real security threats and to the economic dimension of security. The fact is, we cannot have stability in Europe without stability in Russia. We cannot have European security unless Russia pulls itself together and feels secure. That is a fundamental truth. We cannot create security for Russia, or national unity, or national purpose. The Russians themselves must do that, but we can have an influence on Russian decisions because our actions feed back into their political system. Even though our interests are compatible—not identical, but compatible—if we begin to fight over secondary and tertiary issues it could lead us to split on matters more important to both countries. It would be a great tragedy if this were to happen.

Africa
Edward J. Perkins

As America searches for a foreign-policy framework suitable for the twenty-first century and prepares an architecture for operationalizing its leadership role, it must include the African continent. America's policy must be proactive, not benign; it must include shared values, shared ideas, and a genuine sense of equality. The United States and the developed world of nations, it seems to me, would do well to actively promote worldwide partnerships among the several African nations, and to see clearly, without altruism, that a stable, prosperous, contributing African continent is in their collective national interests. Our assessment of African nations and any plan for policy development must start with a holistic vision of a stable, growth-oriented continent with increasing acceptance of and adherence to representative government and human rights. Such an approach must first acknowledge the changes taking place across that continent. They include a policy for representative government, eschewing state-controlled economies, sensible investment codes, and acceptance of a market economy.

America's policy must take note of countries such as Ghana, Côte d'Ivoire, Uganda, South Africa, and Zimbabwe, for example, which are working hard to get things right. Clearly, ethnic strife is still a big problem. Human-rights abuse is still practiced in some countries, and one-person government is still present in certain countries. AIDS, refugees, inadequate delivery systems, hunger, and infant mortality are still present and are increasing in some cases. However, the United States cannot walk away from Africa even if it wanted to. Rather, Africa and the nations that make up that continent will affect our national interest, our potential for world leadership, and our ability to grow politically, economically, and socially.

Policy Formulation

Formulation of the United States' Africa policy begins by explicit recognition that the continent is made up of many nations—forty-eight of which are in sub-Saharan Africa. The relationship with each nation must be active, contributing to an objective of continentwide development based on well-conceived economic-development plans, on the order of those put forth by the Summit on Africa[4] and the recent study on Africa by the Council on Foreign Relations.[5] The United States has the opportunity to cultivate a series of big markets in Africa, resulting in new challenges and the creation of new market potential. U.S.-Africa policy formulation must urge international economic integration with the underdeveloped world, resulting in increasingly greater political stability, assuring a positive outcome economically. The Africa Summit deliberations conclude, "The joint efforts of every country in the African continent will be required to build cooperation in

Africa–United States relations," an important statement. Three suggested routes for policy makers arose from that conclusion:

(1) reinforcing internal democracy with concomitant economic expansion in each country

(2) building free trade throughout the continent

(3) restructuring and strengthening regional institutions such as the Southern African Development Community, known as SADC, and the Economic Community of West African States, ECOWAS

As a policy is formulated and implemented, trade models in place should not be overlooked. Although the Asia-Pacific Economic Cooperation forum (APEC), North American Free Trade Agreement (NAFTA), and Free Trade Agreement of the Americas (FTAA) are considered stepping-stones to the new World Trade Organization (WTO), APEC would seem to be a good model as workable plans are developed to enhance trade and economic stability on the African continent. Acceptance of APEC as a model also assumes, and perhaps ensures, a holistic involvement of essential players such as business and nongovernmental activities in the process. A proactive Africa policy is essential to the good economic health and continued prosperity of the United States. An increase in the health of the global economy will also result.

If the United States is to have a successful policy of cooperation with African nations in line with its national interest, promoting sustainable development must be part of that policy. In a leadership role, the United States must engage the international community in promoting this eventuality.

The world must see its involvement on a quid pro quo basis; that is, it cannot afford not to involve itself in assuring sustainable development on a long-term basis. Promoting sustainable development assures broad-based economic growth across all levels of respective populations. At the same time, attention must be given to protecting the environment and other essentials. Sustainable development and trade go hand in hand. The United States must take the lead in establishing a playing field which promotes greater cooperation among African nations and within the international community, which will promote free trade. The continent has experienced and continues to experience successes: Ghana, Benin, South Africa, Angola, Zimbabwe, Uganda, and Mozambique each manifest growth achievement and stability and a drive to overcome obstacles in their paths. Three reasons suggest themselves as to why sustainable development makes sense:

(1) The economic well-being of Africa adds to the well-being of the United States.

(2) Hunger, pestilence, and refugees will affect all economically well-off nations.

(3) The African continent, like others, except perhaps Antarctica, provides potentially great market areas.

The Concept of Leadership

Any approach to foreign-policy making inevitably must include the concept of leadership. The United States is in a primary leadership position in a nonbipolar world. Exercising that leadership is a requirement for developing methods of cooperation, assuring regional balance-of-power arrangements, determining the national interest in relationship to the entire world, and determining how to engage the community of nations. That challenge must include Africa. In fact, Africa is at the doorstep of all nations. The leadership challenge to the United States is to develop foreign-policy models which embrace business, the private sector, private voluntary groups, state and local governments, the media, and future education directions. A successful U. S.-Africa policy must have the support of our nation at large. Accordingly, support for the efforts of the ongoing Summit on Africa, plus efforts of the Council on Foreign Relations, is essential. Africa must become known not as a failing geographical entity without connection to the world at large, but rather as an essential part of the world that promises enormous benefits resulting from sustainable cooperation. Essential community activities such as these can help in the development of a real-time futuristic foreign policy toward Africa.

A Sustainable Approach to Trade

First off, the United States must make a viable trade policy with African nations a priority. Formerly beset by wars and many other setbacks, some African nations are now experiencing relative peace and experiencing economic stability and gradual growth. In 1996 the southern region of Africa experienced an average 6 percent economic growth rate. Privatization schemes are now in place in countries which seemed unlikely candidates just five years ago. Mozambique and Zambia are leading the way. According to the latest reporting, Mozambique has sold many of its state-owned enterprises; its national airline is next in line. Zambia plans to sell off 145 state-owned enterprises. Ethiopia, Ghana, Eritrea, and Uganda are also out front in applying sensible market policies. For such programs to continue and to spread across Africa, trade policies must be developed which promote trade in cooperation with African nations. The United States must play a central leadership role here. Congressionally mandated fast-track authority would permit the United States to engage African nations in free-trade discussions in a credible manner. Such authority would also permit the United States to exert its leadership across the developed world, urging a universalistic approach to Africa trade. A campaign for fast-track authority must also include meaningful participation by the business sector of our country.

A government and business partnership will enormously enhance U.S.-led efforts for overall trade policy. The African continent already has SADC and ECOWAS. Using these two established economic-related organizations, the United States should work in partnership with Africa to create a trade organization embracing all of sub-Saharan Africa and perhaps North Africa as well. As noted earlier, the Asia-Pacific Economic Cooperation forum could be a likely model for such a trade organization. It should have as little bureaucracy as possible while also permitting periodic meaningful exchange among member African states, business interests, and nongovernmental organizations.

The Challenge to Business

U.S.-African foreign policy must envision business as an integral part of the policy. No foreign policy is possible without the private sector playing a part. This is especially true for Africa, where market sectors must be developed by the nations themselves with the active encouragement of the global community. The African continent poses a special challenge to American and international business. Africa is potentially a world market area. Business must view Africa within the context of a new model. Business should take the potential for big emerging markets as a given. Business can reap huge benefits if it assumes responsibility for helping in overall African development. The first requirement of business is to make a profit. That must be accepted and indeed enhanced by the African community. Business reasonably could be expected to assume a role in helping the community to develop itself, enabling the community to buy more goods and services for itself, including education. When business leaves part of its profit in the community, it should expect community representation to work with it to put that profit into sustainable development addressing education needs, medical delivery, health conditions, and community infrastructure, to name a few. Business does have a role in the making of foreign policy, whether it accepts it or not. If it accepts it in a proactive sense, it will potentially reap benefits consistent with sustainable development. In this sense, the concept of community capitalism encapsulates the model above and puts business in the role of a change agent. A cooperative business paradigm includes making a profit, letting part of that profit work toward community change, and generating a turbulence of ideas to support sustainable U.S. development.

Africa in a Global Context

A sustainable U.S.-Africa policy will support and enhance the movement of Africa onto a more visible global scene, interacting with the developed world of nations. It is noteworthy that only one sub-Saharan African nation is a member of the new World Trade Organization. Without in any way suggesting what should already have taken place, it seems that a concerted effort should be made to ensure membership in WTO by an additional sub-Saharan African nation as soon as possible. The United States, in cooperation with Africa, should support a likely candidate for early entry into the WTO. We should also work toward that end by once again bringing the international community membership in WTO into such planning. A policy that includes a push for added WTO membership, consistent with meeting the requirements for membership, will be psychologically enhancing. African nations should be considered equal partners in a global context in fact as well as in theory. Neither will happen automatically or quickly. However, the extent to which a positive discussion takes place resulting in global policy intent, such as that reflected in preparing other African nations for membership in the WTO, will increase confidence among these nations.

Change Agents

Sustainability can be enhanced only by cooperation within Africa and among the nations of Africa. The entire sustainable development model lends itself to the use of a nation or nations as a change agent in Africa. Such a country would be one already taking actions that affect other nations in an upward-growth sense. The United States should recognize that another nation can be a "change-agent nation" in its Africa policy, and should work with and support such nations.

United States–Africa Policy for the Future: A Summation of Recommendations

As noted earlier, the United States must have a sustainable proactive policy toward the nations of Africa. It is a fact that we cannot withdraw from Africa, nor can we afford to treat Africa paternalistically. In fact, the United States must look to a partnership with that continent assuring equality on both sides. A review of recent studies on Africa (most notably the Summit on Africa, and the Council on Foreign Relations Task Force on Promoting U.S. Economic Relations with Africa, plus other studies) leads to the following policy suggestions:

(1) Promote vigorously U.S. two-way trade with and direct investment in African countries.

(2) Increase U.S. development assistance in a partnership arrangement that emphasizes macroeconomic policies aimed at improving the business climate and attracting investment.

(3) Work with those African countries to reduce their debts and to improve their international creditworthiness if they are taking actions to develop and strengthen their markets.

(4) Help African countries become members of the World Trade Organization and work in concert with other WTO members to help the most likely candidates meet admission requirements as soon as possible.

(5) Encourage African governments and businesses to promote and develop products in which they have a comparative advantage, remove U.S. and European trade barriers to such products, and enable their access to global markets.

(6) Promote and support conventions leading to an African regional trade organization.

(7) Emphasize and enhance greater regional economic integration to (a) assure that Africa is not further marginalized, (b) globalize trade, finance, and telecommunications, (c) encourage aggressive competition, and (d) integrate African nations into the global economy.

(8) Support the creation of enabling national political environments that include (a) decentralized political activity, (b) accountable and responsible government, (c) respect for human rights, and (d) a free press leading to the free flow of ideas.

The United States should pursue these specific objectives in concert with countries in the Organization for Economic Cooperation and Development and other nations, to strengthen international cooperation and coordination in support of African development and integration into the global community and market. Not to do so could be a tragedy for the long-suffering African people and an economic and cultural loss to the world. The most urgent and imperative step to the pursuit and implementation of the objectives I have outlined for U.S. foreign policy toward Africa is for the executive branch to implement the African Growth and Opportunities Act, which embodies many of the ideas advanced in this chapter.

Middle East

Peter W. Rodman

Every region seems to have its folk wisdom, so I will relate a story that people tell in the Middle East. It is about a scorpion that wanted to cross a river. The scorpion goes up to a turtle to try to persuade the turtle to give him a lift. The turtle protests, "You'll just kill me. Why should I do that for you?" The scorpion replies, "If I kill you, we'll both drown. Why would I do that?" So the turtle agrees, and they set out. Midway across the river, sure enough, the scorpion stings the turtle. As they both sink beneath the waves, the turtle cries out, "Why did you do that?" The scorpion replies, "This is the Middle East!"

The Middle East today is a paradoxical and frustrating mixture of destructive trends and hopeful trends. How it will look at the beginning of the next century will depend on the outcome of this race against time, or this contest, if you will, between the positive forces and the negative forces.

Positive Trends

First, the positive trends. The collapse of the Soviet Union transformed the region to a degree that is not always fully appreciated. It deprived the leftist, secular radicals of their Soviet patron and its diplomatic, military, and financial backing. The strategic position of Syria and the PLO, for example, was transformed overnight.

In a sense, a forty-year struggle between pro-Western moderates, on the one hand, and Gamal Abdel Nasser and his heirs—the secular radicals who based their power on socialist ideology and whose anti-Western foreign policy was backed by the Kremlin—was over. The Gulf War of 1991 only confirmed the new balance of forces in the Arab world. Moderate, pro-Western Egypt and Saudi Arabia were now ascendant. It was a condition that American policy makers could only have dreamed of five or ten years before. The PLO also lost its Gulf Arab backing because of its stance in support of Saddam Hussein.

It is no accident that during this period Egypt was welcomed back into the Arab fold, without sacrificing its peace treaty with Israel. It is no accident that Syria accepted direct talks with Israel at Madrid. It is no accident that the PLO essentially sued for peace, and the ever-cautious Jordan (always a bellwether of the Mideast balance of forces) signed a peace treaty with Israel without waiting for Syria. It was the change in the geopolitical context that made this possible.

Negative Trends

Now, the negative trends. The most important negative trend is Islamist radicalism. (I do not mean Islam as a religious faith; I mean the political movement, hostile to the West, based on an ideology that invokes Islam.)

In much of the Third World, the discrediting of the Marxist-Leninist left has opened the way to normal politics. When there is no radical, absolutist challenge to the existing system, politics is no longer a matter of life and death; pluralism and the alternation of parties are conceivable. So on every continent—Africa, Latin America, East Asia—we see normal politics resuming. We see a wave of democratization.

The tragedy of the Middle East is that just as the Soviet collapse discredited the radical left, a radicalism that came from the opposite direction, namely Islamism, filled the vacuum. For years after the Iranian Revolution, there was fear of its spread to the Arab world. It did not spread, because of the gulf between Arabs and Persians, Sunni and Shia. But now it *has* spread—in part, as I said, because of the vacuum left by the collapse of the left. It is a by-product of the end of the cold war.

I consider Islamism an antidemocratic, indeed totalitarian, phenomenon. It espouses cultural hegemony, wholesale changes in the institutions of society that exclude opposition. If Islamist movements come to power, I do not see this as democratization.

In foreign policy, we see the phenomena of terrorism and the pursuit of weapons of mass destruction. But these are really symptoms of a deeper problem, namely that Islamism embodies an anti-Western, ideologically hostile foreign policy whose targets in the region are precisely the pro-Western moderate Arabs in North Africa and the Arabian peninsula (especially Egypt and Saudi Arabia), on which the U.S. strategic position depends. That is the strategic problem.

How Will It Turn Out?

How will it turn out in the twenty-first century? I do not want to cop out after just describing the competing trends. I will venture an optimistic view.

First, the Israeli-Palestinian issue. It is remarkable how far we have come. The Oslo Accords, in my view, are irreversible, whatever the mess the region is in now. Ninety-eight percent of the Palestinian population already lives under self-rule. If the immediate mess can be overcome—and I expect it will—the negotiation is rather hopeful. Prime Minister Benjamin Netanyahu essentially accepts a Palestinian state, and others in his party, such as Ariel Sharon, have said the same. Oslo, they say, already gave this away because the Palestinians really already have a state now, whatever one calls it. The main issues left are its geographic extent and some limits on its sovereignty in the security sphere. That is how a Labour government would have described the issue too. This shift in Likud doctrine may have been the most important—if underreported—development in the Middle East in 1997. So we have the partial domestication of Likud, to go along with the partial domestication of the PLO.

Economic change will occur also. Of course, economic and social hardship underlie the Mideast malaise and provide the fertile soil for radicalism. But the rest of the Third World seems to have figured out that market reform is a way out of the economic morass. Oil has been a curse for the Middle East, permitting some countries in the region to evade real economic choices. The socialist legacy and the big bureaucracy that goes with it are a burden. But I refuse to believe that with bureaucracy off their backs, Arabs do not know how to be traders. Paradoxically, Egypt, one of the worst cases, has launched some impressive economic reforms in the last two years, which experts are taking seriously. If change can come to Egypt, it can come anywhere.

What about political change? I think an evolution will happen here too. But it will depend first on a subsidence of Islamist radicalism.

All revolutions have a life cycle, and this one is clearly running out of steam. Even less than Marxism does radical Islamism have a real answer to the economic and social grievances it exploits. Egypt and Algeria seemed about to go under a few years ago; today, they do not seem so susceptible to Islamist takeover. In Iran, the election of Mohammed Khatemi may be a sign of the Iranian public's disillusionment and of possible change, down the road, in that régime. So the Islamist "tide" is not what it seemed to be a few years ago.

The traditional monarchies in the Arab world also may be more resilient than many people had thought. During the Gulf War, there was great anxiety about their survival. But it turns out that they always had roots in their tribal societies; they always had a social compact of their own, and often good religious credentials. King Hassan of Morocco and King Hussein of Jordan have good relations with the Muslim brotherhood because they shielded it during the Nasser period, when secular leftism was in the ascendant. It turns out that collapse of "Arab socialism" has created more of a crisis of legitimacy for the secular "progressive" régimes, such as Algeria and Egypt, than for the monarchies.

In the meantime, I am not eager to push friendly moderate governments (which are also key strategic allies) into risky political-science experiments that could open the door to what is essentially an antidemocratic—and certainly anti-Western—movement. But it is clear in many ways that civil society is evolving in the Middle East as elsewhere, and when the radical Islamist enthusiasm runs out of steam, political pluralism will come to that part of the world too.

Conclusion

Much depends, I have to add, on a strong Western presence, especially the U.S. presence, and especially including a U.S. military presence. This helps to deter radicals, to give confidence to moderates (who are taking risks for peace), and to back up our mediation of the Arab-Israeli conflict. Our role is indispensable if the positive forces are to prevail. As in so many other areas of the world, the United States is the pivotal factor for stability, and the future depends on whether we have the political will to remain so.

NOTES

1. John Newhouse, *Europe Adrift* (New York: Pantheon Books, 1997).

2. Nicholas Colchester and David Buchan, *Europower: The Essential Guide to Europe's Economic Transformation in 1992* (New York: Times Books/Random House, 1990).

3. Louis Halle, *The Cold War as History* (New York: Harper & Row, 1967).

4. "The African Summit Deliberations," in David H. Dunn, ed., *Diplomacy at the Highest Levels: The Evolution of International Summitry* (New York: St. Martin's Press, 1996).

5. Study on Africa by Council on Foreign Affairs, "Statement of an Independent Task Force, *Promoting U.S. Economic Relations with Africa*," Frank Savage and Peggy Dulany, Co-Chairs, and Salih Booker, Project Director (Washington: Council on Foreign Relations, 1997).

PART II

The United States and Asia in the Twenty-first Century

Overview

Edward J. Perkins

The Asia–United States relationship compels the United States to make more than just an interested review of where our foreign policies are going now and well into the twenty-first century. Because parts of Asia have grown so powerfully— politically and economically—since the 1960s, it is imperative that we give special attention to this region as we prepare America's foreign policy for the twenty-first century. We therefore dedicate all of Part II to understanding United States–Asia relations—from both the American and Asian points of view, and with special emphasis on China and Japan. Good relations with Asia are absolutely essential to the lifeblood of the United States and to our continued improvement as a people.

Seasoned diplomat Li Daoyu, ambassador of the People's Republic of China to the United States (and China's former ambassador to the United Nations, where we respectively represented our countries and became friends), presents, along with Chinese Professor Zhou Dunren, the view from China in chapter 3. Experienced China hands Michel Oksenberg and Jan Berris look at China through American eyes in chapter 4. In chapter 5, former vice president and U.S. Ambassador to Japan Walter Mondale addresses Japan, the nation with the world's second-largest economy and awesome economic impact. Complementing him is Japanese specialist Ambassador Frank McNeil, who not only offers views on Japan in Asia but also comments on the importance of other Asian nations and where they fit into the regional dynamics and American policy. Professor Robert Scalapino, respected and veteran scholar, provides in chapter 6 a prescriptive *tour d'horizon* of the region and its impact on the future. Finally, questions from the audience at the University of Oklahoma conference and presenters' answers, followed by comments of Professors Michael Adolphson, Marlan Downey, and Edwin Corr, wrap up Part II.

You are in for a treat as you read and contemplate sage and experienced experts' views on the region and its implications for American foreign policy.

Chapter 3

The View from China

Li Daoyu

We are at the threshold of a new millennium: The twenty-first century is only a year from us. You all know that Chinese President Jiang Zemin paid an official visit to the United States at the invitation of President Clinton in the fall of 1997. This was the first state visit by the Chinese president since 1985. Obviously, it had important historical significance, not only to the China–United States bilateral relationship, but also to world peace and prosperity as a whole. What kind of China–United States relationship will be brought into the twenty-first century? This is the question facing each and every one of us. Whether this relationship is characterized by equality, mutual respect, and cooperation or by confrontation will have an important bearing on the world scene. I will share with you my views on this important bilateral relationship.

With the end of the cold war, we find a complicated world undergoing profound changes. Despite the fact that there are still troubles and conflicts, the international situation is, on the whole, moving toward greater relaxation. Working for peace, development, and cooperation has become the mainstream of our times.

China is the largest developing country and the United States is the largest developed country in the world. We share a common responsibility in maintaining peace and stability in both the Asia-Pacific region and in the rest of the world. We also share an important responsibility in promoting global economic prosperity, including human environment and many other important matters. The need for both countries to stay engaged with each other is increasing, not decreasing. The potential for both countries to cooperate in various fields is expanding, not dwindling. We should firmly bear these common interests in mind, and conduct our bilateral relations in the spirit of increasing mutual trust, reducing troubles, developing cooperation, and avoiding confrontation to bring a stable and healthy China–U.S. relationship into the twenty-first century. We should also work with other countries to bring a peaceful, stable, and prosperous world into the next century.

We are glad to see that since the beginning of 1997, China-U.S. relations have maintained the momentum of improvement and development. High-level official exchanges have increased steadily. More senators and congressmen visited China in 1997. Bilateral economic relations and trade are expanding. Military-to-military exchanges have made remarkable headway.

On top of these visits and exchanges, Chinese President Jiang Zemin's state visit to the United States in 1997, along with President Clinton's return visit to China in 1998, provided a good opportunity for bilateral relations to set a new landmark and enter a new era. China is ready to work with the United States to seize this important historic opportunity to establish a long-term, stable, and healthy relationship geared to the next century on the basis of the three Sino–United States joint communiqués.

Both in terms of China's current development strategy and its foreign-policy agenda, China regards its relationship with the United States as one of the most important bilateral relationships in the world. We strongly believe that a healthy and good China–United States relationship not only serves the fundamental interests of our two great nations, but also holds the key to peace and stability in Asia-Pacific and the world. Therefore, both China and the United States should handle their bilateral relationship from a strategic perspective. Although the two nations differ in social systems, culture, and other aspects, our common interests far outweigh our differences. In many areas, we have a huge stake to work together.

(1) Both China and the United States want to maintain global and regional peace and stability and wish to see the continued strengthening of forces working for peace and the prevention of new wars. Both sides want to strengthen their strategic dialogue and cooperation. As permanent members of the United Nations Security Council, our cooperation holds the key to the success of all United Nations endeavors. This has been demonstrated by various United Nations peacekeeping operations and such regional conflicts as the Gulf crisis and Cambodia. As China's permanent representative to the United Nations between 1990 and 1993, I witnessed our active and fruitful cooperation in all these areas. The two sides must continue their consultation and cooperation on these and other United Nations endeavors.

(2) Both countries are key players in promoting peace and stability in the Asia-Pacific region and have collaborated effectively on many of these issues. China played and will continue to play a constructive role in maintaining peace and stability on the Korean Peninsula.

(3) Both countries share largely the same final objective of preventing proliferation of nuclear and other weapons of mass destruction. We have worked together for the extension of the Nuclear Nonproliferation Treaty and the conclusion of the Chemical Nuclear Biological Treaty (CTBT) negotiation. The two countries issued a joint statement concerning the Missile Technology Control Régime (MTCR) in October 1994. We also reached an understanding on the transfer of nuclear technology and related materials in May 1996. Both sides continue to hold talks on these issues on a regular basis. Recently, Premier Li Peng signed an executive order setting up strict regulations on export control of nuclear material and equipment.

(4) Our cooperation has contributed to the evolution of regional security forums such as the ASEAN Regional Forum (ARF). We have also worked

closely together in the Asia-Pacific Economic Cooperation (APEC). Together, we have helped to promote regional stability and economic prosperity.

(5) As big powers dedicated to environmental protection, China and the United Missile Technology Control Régime (MTCR) States share common interests in strengthening cooperation in this area. Leaders of our two countries have already taken the initiative to create the forum on environmental protection and sustainable development. The two sides are discussing cooperative projects on protecting the environment and developing energy.

(6) Both countries have been engaged in good cooperation on other transnational issues such as international terrorism, drug trafficking, and illegal immigration. China will continue to cooperate with the United States on these important issues.

(7) Both sides attach importance to their exchanges and cooperation in such fields as education, culture, and science and technology.

(8) Last but not least, I want to stress a most important, if not *the* most important, aspect of our common interest—economic and trade ties. In the past twenty years, our booming economic cooperation and trade have brought tremendous tangible benefits to our two peoples. The United States is now the largest investor by country in China. By the end of 1996, the United States had committed more than $35 billion to the China market with a paid-in volume of $14.29 billion. United States–funded projects and ventures in China had exceeded 22,000. In terms of trade, the United States is now the second-largest trading partner in China, whereas China is the number-four trading partner for the United States and one of the fastest-growing markets for United States exports. Both countries' statistics suggest that between 1990 and 1996, United States exports to China grew by more than 16 percent annually on average, far exceeding the overall United States export growth in the same period. United States exports to China support more than 20,000 high-paying, high-tech jobs in the United States.

Although more and more people have come to realize the importance of a close China–United States relationship, from time to time we still hear discord. For instance, some people say that with the end of the cold war, there are no longer any common interests between China and the United States, but only confrontations. From the above eight areas of common interest I have just mentioned, one can see that such an argument is totally wrong. Some of the people in the United States are spreading the "China threat" theory. According to their argument, China has replaced the former Soviet Union as the main threat to the United States. They predict that China and the United States will move toward confrontation, even conflict, and therefore they call for containment against China. They believe that as its economy and national strength grow, China is bound to pursue external expansion. These views, I must say, could not be more wrong.

A review of China's history shows that China does not have a tradition of expansion. On the contrary, it was the victim of repeated foreign aggression, domination, and bullying. China has never occupied a single inch of foreign soil, nor has it stationed a single soldier abroad. China's defense policy is completely defensive in nature. Its defense spending is the lowest among the big countries in absolute terms. In per capita terms as well as in terms of the share of gross national product, it is among the lowest in the world. According to statistics, the United States' 1996 defense budget exceeded $260 billion, averaging $996 per person. China's defense spending was only $8.7 billion, averaging $7 per person. We have reduced our armed forces drastically in recent years. China has announced its intention to cut the size of its armed forces further, by half a million men by the year 2000.

China is still a developing country. It is faced with the gigantic task of improving the livelihood of its 1.2 billion people. This can be accomplished only by concentrating on economic development. Therefore, what China desires most is a peaceful international environment so it can focus on economic development. China has firmly adhered to an independent foreign policy of peace and has worked to maintain and develop friendly relations and cooperation with other countries.

On trade issues, because of imbalances in China–United States trade, some people fear that China will become "another Japan." In fact, China's trade surplus with the United States has been greatly overstated. Once we put this issue in the right perspective, we can see easily that China is not and will not be another Japan in trade.

(1) More than 46 percent of China's exports are made by foreign-funded enterprises or joint ventures. Such exports not only benefit China but also our foreign partners, including the United States. Many Chinese products on the shelves in the United States still carry U.S. trademarks and, to a large extent, are U.S. products.

(2) Most of China's exports belong to those low-valued labor-intensive goods that the United States stopped producing ten or twenty years ago. Such exports do not cost U.S. jobs; rather, they bring tremendous benefit to American consumers. According to a World Bank report in 1994, American consumers would have had to pay $14 billion more if the United States had imported the same products from other countries that year.

(3) China is a developing country with a weak industrial base, while Japan is a highly developed, industrialized economic superpower. Japan is the United States' strong competitor, but China is not. The Chinese and U.S. economies are in fact highly complementary. We sell what you need, and you produce what we want.

We are living in a diverse world. China and the United States differ in social systems, historical backgrounds, cultural traditions, values, and levels of economic development. It is therefore not surprising that they have different views on human rights. Some people in the United States use American standards of human rights to judge whether democracy exists in China. This is not the right way to look at it. China has its own national circumstances, just as the United States does. Under China's democratic system, the Chinese people enjoy extensive freedoms and human rights, although they are not expressed in the same ways as in the United States. China's form of democracy is that chosen by the Chinese people, just as yours is the choice made by the American people.

The Chinese government attaches great importance to promoting human rights. In keeping with the principles of universality of human rights and China's specific national circumstances, China has made great efforts to ensure the rights to survival and development for the Chinese people. At the same time, China has stepped up the development of democracy and the rule of law to advance the civil and political rights of its people. China also takes an active role in United Nations efforts to promote and protect human rights. It has become party to seventeen international human-rights instruments, two more than the United States has. As another step forward, China has decided to sign the International Covenant on Economic, Social, and Cultural Rights.

It should be pointed out that Taiwan is the most important and most sensitive issue in China–United States relations. If it is handled wrongly, it can be the biggest obstacle to the sound growth of relations.

The Taiwan question is at the heart of the three Sino–United States joint communiqués, namely, the Shanghai Communiqué of 1972, the Joint Communiqué on the Establishment of Diplomatic Relations between China and the United States of 1979, and the joint communiqué of August 17, 1982, concerning United States arms sales to Taiwan. In these documents, the United States explicitly acknowledges that there is but one China, and Taiwan is part of China. It explicitly recognizes that the government of the People's Republic of China is the sole legal government of China, and that within this context, the people of the United States will maintain cultural, commercial, and other unofficial relations with the people of Taiwan. The United States reiterates that it has no intention of infringing on Chinese sovereignty and territorial integrity, or of interfering in China's internal affairs, or of pursuing a policy of "two Chinas" or "one China, one Taiwan." It also states that it does not seek to carry out a long-term policy of arms sales to Taiwan and pledges to gradually reduce its sales of arms to Taiwan, leading to a final resolution. On many occasions U.S. government leaders have reaffirmed the United States' commitment to the "one China" policy and to the three Sino–United States joint communiqués. It is our hope that these commitments will be truly honored.

To put an end to the current separation between the two sides of the Taiwan Straits and to achieve Taiwan's reunification with the motherland are the strong aspiration and unshakable determination of all the Chinese people, including the Taiwan compatriots. It is also an irresistible historical trend.

For Taiwan's reunification with the mainland, the Chinese government proposed well over a decade ago the principles of "peaceful reunification on the basis of one country, two systems." In 1995, President Jiang Zemin further made an eight-point proposal to advance the process of peaceful reunification. As the first step, under the "one China" principle, leaders of the two sides should conduct talks on formally ending hostility. At the heart of these proposals is the principle of "one China." It is the basis and premise of peaceful reunification. The Taiwan authorities, however, are using various means, including squandering money to engage in activities aimed at creating "two Chinas" or "one China, one Taiwan." This constitutes a serious challenge to our sovereignty and territorial integrity. We can never tolerate this. We hope that the Taiwan authorities will come back to the "one China" principle so that the cross-Straits relations can be relaxed and developed.

The whole world has witnessed a momentous event that will go down in the annals of history: China resumed the exercise of sovereignty over Hong Kong, and the Hong Kong Special Administration Region (HKSAR) of the People's Republic of China was officially established.

China's basic policies toward the HKSAR—namely "one country, two systems," "Hong Kong people governing Hong Kong," and "a high degree of autonomy"—have become a reality. The HKSAR enjoys a high degree of autonomy, including executive power, legislative power, independent judicial power, and the power of the final trial. Events have shown that these policies work well in the HKSAR. Tung Chee Hwa, the first chief executive of the HKSAR, made a successful visit to the United States in 1997. Hong Kong's successful return to China is not only in the interests of China, including Hong Kong, but also in the interests of other countries and regions, especially the United States, which has extensive economic trade links with Hong Kong.

The year 1997 marked the twenty-fifth anniversary of the Shanghai Communiqué. A quarter century ago, with courage and statesmanship, Chinese and American leaders reopened the relationship between our two countries. Today, the China–United States relationship once again faces a historic opportunity for improvement and growth. We should once again show strategic vision and courage, just as our leaders did in those days.

We should expand our common ground, increase that trust, reduce differences, and create the future together. We should join hands and press forward toward our goal—that is, to bring a stable, healthy China–United States relationship into the twenty-first century. Our accomplishment will not only bring concrete benefits to our peoples, but will also help create a safer, better, and more prosperous twenty-first century for the whole of mankind.

Zhou Dunren

The United States today remains the strongest and wealthiest nation in the world. We in China, both in and out of government, know and appreciate this fact. United States foreign policy exerts direct impact and causes indirect repercussions on most issues in the world. It is timely to deal with the foreign policy of the twenty-first century, which is coming to us faster than expected. This coming hundred years are going to have their own nature and style, and we can expect them to be very different from the century that is ending. By looking back and imagining ourselves on the eve of the twentieth century, we would find how inadequate our visions and understanding of the twentieth century had been as against what has actually happened. For example, who then had foreseen and therefore prepared himself for the cold war that dominated almost half a century after World War II?

As a Chinese scholar, I would like to address Sino–United States relations, or the foreign policies involved. I firmly believe that for the coming century, a stable, friendly, and mutually respectful relationship between China and the United States is strongly needed. Call it whatever you like, for example, the "constructive strategic partnership." The three elements in the relationship are indispensable—stability, friendliness, and mutual respect.

It is not too difficult to see why such a relationship is needed, if we look at the issue from two angles. One is the absence of such a relationship. This could result in tensions, conflicts, and even wars. China does not want to produce tensions and conflicts with the United States, let alone wars. The past two wars that occurred in the 1950s (Korea) and 1960s–1970s (Vietnam) between China and the United States, even though proxy in form, were most unfortunate. Hundreds of thousands of lives were lost and enormous wealth was wasted. China paid dearly but gained little, nor did the United States gain more. The wars pushed the two nations apart and the ensuing estrangement and hostility lasted too long. The two wars, including the "debt" China owed the USSR for weapons and ammunitions it supplied, set China back in its economic development for at least one or two decades. Were such wars avoidable? One has to seek answers from the historical context, but the lessons must not be forgotten. And so the two nations should strive in the coming century to avoid future tensions, conflicts, and especially wars, which would be much more costly and deadly.

China's paramount goals are to develop its economy, raise the living standard of its people, and protect its ecology. It does not take much to be convinced that these are China's primary goals today if one comes to China and spends of bit of time touring the country. A peaceful and friendly international environment is absolutely indispensable to China. This overrides any possible scenarios suggested by those who set or want to set China up as a challenger or an adversary to the United States. It is not in China's interests to provoke tensions or hostilities with the United States.

The other angle is the presence of a stable, friendly, mutually respectful relationship, which will benefit not just the two nations but the world in general. China, being the largest developing nation in the world and therefore the largest potential market left in this century (and perhaps in the century to come), offers almost infinite potentials in economic exchanges and cooperation with the United States. Whereas the United States, being the largest and wealthiest developed nation with the most advanced technology and management in the world, could help China *and* itself, more than any other nation. The economic complementarity between these two nations is unmatched in the world. Along with the development of trade, investment, and other economic cooperation, many other things of importance will follow on a positive track. These will include international and regional security, environmental protection, social and humanitarian causes, non-proliferation of mass-destruction weaponry, drug and disease control, and other issues. Recently, the fact that China has managed to stay relatively untouched by the financial storms sweeping Southeastern Asian and Eastern Asian nations and regions shows that China is a good player, worthy to work with. The successful state visit to the United States by China's president, Jiang Zemin, has proved again what a good and friendly relationship with China can accomplish.

Of the three elements in the relationship of stability, friendliness, and mutual respect, the third needs to be stressed. Without mutual respect, the first two elements would come into doubt, now that the United States and other nations want China to be a responsible member of the world community. Yes, China should be a responsible member of the world community. At the same time, China should be respected as a member of the world community. Being responsible and being respected are two aspects of one thing in international relations. If China wants to be duly respected, it has to show it is a responsible member. It is also true that if the United States and the world want China to be a responsible member, they have to pay due respect to China.

Due respect necessitates adequate understanding. Unfortunately, adequate understanding of China does not yet exist on the part of United States policy makers toward China. Scant understanding or misreading could lead to disasters as a consequence of the wrong policy or actions. History does not lack such instances. One example was whether China would come into North Korea to support it while it was engaged in the war with South Korea and the United States in the early 1950s. Another was China's reactions to the about-face change in granting a visa to T.H. Lee to visit Cornell University. At first some Americans could not believe that the return of sovereignty over Hong Kong from Britain to China would be peaceful and smooth. The presumptions were all proved to be wrong. Today, an average Chinese person knows more about the United States than an average American knows about China. The following are some of the things that need to be understood.

There has been a national sentiment that can be called the "Chinese dream." It began as an aftermath of the Opium War in the 1840s, when Western powers bullied and ravaged China, when British gunboats forced opium trade on the weak and senile Qing dynasty of China. China's doors were stormed open to the outside world for the second time, with mostly very bitter experiences. In contrast, China's first encounter with the outside world was a happy one in the Tang dynasty about a thousand years before, when camel caravans came to and from China along silk routes. (Now we know marine silk routes also existed at about the same time.) There were no opium and gunshots, and no unequal treaties and ransoms. That was a great time for China and its foreign trading partners; both benefited a great deal from the encounter, not just economically but also scientifically and culturally. Today, some artifacts, fauna and flora, music and food that we call Chinese actually came from the geographic West. However, the second encounter was very different.

Since the 1840s, the Chinese have had a dream for China to be strong and rich and thus respected, and to stand unashamedly among the nations of the world. On an equal footing, China can conduct friendly and cooperative exchanges with the rest of the world. One must not misread the Chinese dream. China does not want to be rich and strong to take revenge by humiliating nations that unjustly humiliated China. The return of Hong Kong was conducted in peace and decency. China does not want to be rich and strong to gain the power of hegemony. Imperialist expansion is not in the Chinese culture, and in today's world, such expansionism is totally anachronistic.

The Chinese dream does breed national sensitivities, natural to the Chinese but not readily understood by other peoples. That is why a woman student of a major university in Shanghai stood up and, after expressing her good feelings about the United States, said she could not understand why NBC should single out the Chinese Olympic swimmers, as they achieved excellent records in the contests, and attribute their successes to use of drugs. "Is it because the NBC people think the Chinese are still the sick men of East, wearing pigtails?" she asked. The earliest Americans that came to China were mostly merchants and missionaries. Modern "missionaries" are welcome if they respect the Chinese national feelings and if their "missions" contribute to the Chinese dream.

There is a lot of talk about the fast economic growth in China since the early 1980s. Some people worry about the economic superpower status China will soon attain to become a viable challenger and threat to the United States. The worries are groundless, and China's economic strength is inflated. The gross domestic product figure, cited in estimating China's strength, can be very misleading if exchange rates other than the market rate are applied. Right now, the gross domestic product of China is a bit less than $1 trillion U.S. dollars, according to the official and market exchange rate of roughly one to eight. Thus China's GDP is about one-seventh that of the United States. With the Chinese population five times that of the United States, the GDP per capita of China is only one-thirty-fifth that of the United States. However, if the ratio of one to one or one to two is applied, then China's GDP could instantly jump eight or four times, which is absurd. Talk of China's soon becoming a matching economic superpower is nothing but irresponsible.

Yes, the growth has been phenomenal, but that growth rate cannot be sustained indefinitely without incurring serious problems in finance, environmental protection, and social instability. Fast growth, although needed for a period of time in developing nations, is not necessarily the best formula. Sustainable and stable growth is best. If this was not recognized earlier, China is now beginning to see the wisdom of it. Much more moderate growth will be seen. Fundamental reform of the big state sector, which increasingly drains the newly created national wealth, represents tremendous tasks for the Chinese government and people. These tasks include the restructuring of finance, the creation of dozens of millions of jobs to absorb people laid off from downsizing the government sector, the urgent pollution control and environmental protection, the provision for the aging population as the inceptional affluent society of China comes into shape, and the corresponding social readjustment and political reform.

This third encounter with the outside world is, in fact, a historical mandate and challenge for China. The historical mandate demands that China needs friends but not enemies, and China needs to be friendly but not confrontational in its international affairs. China needs friends and trading partners in its efforts to meet the historical challenge. Any objective person could see that more often than not the actions China takes are defensive rather than offensive. The Chinese people will remain busy with themselves, if they are allowed. It is obviously unwise and even dangerous to set China up as another "evil empire" and try to push it into a narrow corner. The time is gone with the cold war when a nation could expect other nations to rally around itself against an "evil empire." One of the things about globalization now is the emerging and changing matrix of interests between and among the nations of the world. China needs to be seen and treated at the right positive point in the international matrix of national interests.

It does not follow that China understands the United States adequately. Owing to cultural and ideological differences, the Chinese, including policy makers, need to make more efforts in understanding America. China has stayed too long in feudalist dynasties, in which whatever the emperor said went. But that is definitely not the case with an American president. China should not expect an American president to decide and conduct China policy as consistently and smoothly as China wishes. The three branches of U.S. government are constructed to effect checks and balances. One powerful check and balance against the executive branch is the United States Congress. Each of the 535 members of Congress is accountable to his own constituency. In international affairs, they could become 535 "secretaries of state." Even the individual departments of the executive branch have their respective constituencies and do not always speak in the same voice as the White House. Whether China likes this system or not is beside the point.

The system is admittedly not perfect, but it was built that way and it is working. China has to learn to deal with and work with this system. Chinese foreign policy should not be based on or respond to one or two voices from such a vast number of U.S. government institutions or policy makers. What is more important is not what these American policy makers say but what the relevant institutions do. Therefore, judging American policy and "American intention" based only on one or several similar or divergent voices can be very misleading.

China has to understand the consequences of political influence in the United States, although it is not always effective and efficient. The president reads the polling results in the press and listens to the people in the entire nation, but the members of Congress listen mostly or even almost exclusively to their own constituencies. Given the lobbying interest groups, the average people that form the constituencies are in turn influenced by the omnipresent media to varying degrees. This is especially so in foreign affairs, which ordinary people understand and concern themselves with much less than they do immediate domestic issues. The image of and message from a visiting Chinese head of state have to go through the media to reach the average American citizen. That is why the media in the United States are called the power-to-be. If China wants the United States to be friendly with China, whether the government or the people, or if China wants to convey an important message to the United States, it should not ignore the U.S. media. And the chain of political influence grows stronger before and during any election campaign.

There are things in America that can be regarded as cultural which China does not have to accept, or at least, not accept without reservation. One is "human rights." Americans regard human rights, in most cases overlapping civil rights, as sacred because they form part of the American politico-social value system. Most ancestors of Americans today came to the New World to escape tyranny and persecution in their home countries. The broad idea of human rights was written into the United States Constitution. And so Americans are very sensitive to such issues, although this does not mean all human rights are well protected and guaranteed in the United States. Similarly, the issue of religious freedom is also part of the American value system. Even for Americans who do not go to church, defending religious freedom is a matter of course. Cultural values do not change, or do not change easily. So the Chinese need to understand Americans' reactions to what they term violations of human rights and religious freedom, and to check the facts. In the meantime, the Chinese cannot allow the value standards of any foreign nation to be imposed on them.

If China wants to be a responsible member of the world community, it has to "play the game by the rules" of the community. Most basic rules reflect the common interests of the community members, and no member should be an exception to its observation of its rules, even though not all rules are equitable and impartial. China has to play by the rules. So does the United States. If the United States, which is a major rule setter, does not respect the rules, say in the World Trade Organization (WTO) or the United Nations, it cannot expect China or any other nation to abide by the rules. Because the United States is almost always the major, if not the dominant, member of international organizations, negotiations for China to enter such organizations may take on the look of bilateral discussions. In these cases both nations have to be very careful.

In the final analysis, there are hardly any fundamental conflicts of interests between China and the United States, be they territorial, economic, or religious. Much of today's difficulties between them derive from leftovers of the cold-war mentality or ideology. Such an ideology is becoming more and more incongruous with the historical trend of the information society and the global village. Nevertheless, the cold-war ideology still sticks in people's heads and can be as dramatic as the case with a young Buddhist monk in an ancient Buddhist parable.

Once upon a time, a senior monk and a junior monk on their way home came to a stream crossing. There they encountered a pretty woman crying for help. She told the monks her leg was seriously injured and she could not cross the stream by herself. "Could you kindly carry me across the stream?" she pleaded. It was against Buddhist rules to touch the female body, and the young monk refused, saying this would be against Buddhist teachings. But the senior monk said, "Here is my back. Get on." He carried the woman across the stream and let her down to go on her way. The young monk burst out, "Elder, how can you do this?" The senior monk replied, "Son, I have already put her down, but you are still carrying her." In our understanding of this story, we see that modern policy makers should have the wisdom and courage to get rid of obsolete prejudices so they can accomplish what is truly good.

Chapter 4

The American View of China in the Twenty-first Century

Jan C. Berris

Avery heated and intense debate is going on in the United States about China. Where one comes down in this debate—how one perceives China, what one thinks about it—depends a lot on when one first began to interact with China or to study its extraordinary culture. I have been involved with China since 1962, when I began to study the language, history, and culture as a freshman at the University of Michigan, and my defining associations with China came during three important historical periods:

- as a student just a few years after the disastrous Great Leap Forward, when some people estimate as many as twenty-seven million peasants died of malnutrition and other causes

- as a foreign-service officer based in Hong Kong during the height of the Cultural Revolution, where I was surrounded by people fleeing from a society so out of kilter that children were denouncing their parents and intellectuals were considered the scum of the earth and forced into such degrading acts that for many of them suicide was the path of least resistance

- as a staff member of the National Committee on U.S.-China Relations when, in 1973, I took the first of what have now been about forty-five trips to China. This was a period when the Chinese people had absolutely no control over the very basic issues of their lives—where to live; what school to attend; what job to take; when, or even if, they could divorce. It was a time when everyone parroted the Chinese Communist Party line, even on innocuous questions, and certainly no one would express any negative sentiments or even joke about the Party or the leadership.

Contrast that with today. Although parts of the country, as in the past, are still incredibly poor (especially the remote regions), most of China (especially, but not solely, limited to the urban, coastal areas) is experiencing enormous economic growth. It is estimated that 180 million people have been lifted out of absolute poverty in the last two decades. During that time, China's average annual growth rate has been more than 10 percent; if one measures just the industrial sector, it is closer to 20 percent. According to the World Bank, no nation in history has moved greater numbers of people forward in a shorter period of time in terms of poverty alleviation, improved health care, literacy, and education.

This means millions no longer die of malnutrition. The urban life expectancy and infant-mortality statistics in Shanghai are now as good or better than in parts of some American cities.

The Communist Party can no longer mount mass campaigns such as the Great Leap Forward or the Cultural Revolution. People have control over their own lives (with, it is true, some exceptions, such as how many children to have). And just about any subject, including the government—certainly in private and increasingly in public—is fair game for discussion.

In the 1970s China seemed to be a society that never changed. When I would come back from those early visits to China, friends would ask how this trip had differed from the last. In fact, it never did. China looked the same. It felt the same. It was a static society. The only thing that changed from year to year was the name of the bad guys. First it was Liu Xiaoqi, then Denq Xiaoping, then Lin Biao and Confucius, then Deng Xiaoping again, then the Gang of Four.

Today, China is in constant flux. Even if I go once every two or three months, I still see changes. Certainly, the physical changes are the most obvious. Take Shanghai, which is in the middle of an extraordinary building boom. The claim, although probably apocryphal, is that three of the world's five largest building cranes are currently in use in Shanghai. However, some profound changes are going on in the society itself. I want to focus on just a few, those that are in areas of great concern to Americans.

The first of these changes is in the rule of law. Throughout China's history, law has been an instrument of the ruling power, whether that power was the emperor or the Communist Party. However, recent developments suggest that the Chinese are very serious about trying to incorporate Western legal concepts and making the rule of law something more substantial than it has been in the past. The first moves in that direction came—not surprisingly, for a country eager to promote foreign investment—in commercial law. In the early 1980s, at the insistence of Deng Xiaoping, new legal codes were written and law schools were opened after a thirty-year hiatus. (The country which used to pride itself on having no lawyers began to train them in earnest, and the Ministry of Justice plans to train 100,000 new lawyers by the year 2000.) The increased activity in this area can be seen by one statistic alone: Between 1983 and 1994 the number of commercial cases that went to court rose from 90,000 to 900,000.

Increased activity in the courts is not just focused on commercial issues. More and more, it is manifesting itself in other areas, such as the environment. Even fairly powerless local environmental-protection agencies, at provincial or municipal levels, are increasingly taking polluters to court and winning cases, forcing offenders to pay heavy fines or close their operations.

In 1997 there was a major revision of the criminal code. This is not yet a society that presumes innocence; however, the revised criminal code makes it a much more adversarial system. The new law institutes major changes in the way criminal cases are investigated, prosecuted, and tried. The focus on training lawyers came fairly early on; recently, attention has been paid to the training of judges, which is extremely important. In China, judges have very little power, primarily taking orders from the Party, but it now seems there is an awareness that judges need to be given more training and more independence. This training is taking place in China as well as abroad. For example, the National Committee on U.S.-China Relations is hosting groups of judges coming to the United States to look at our court systems, judicial independence, and the rule of law, and is sending American federal judges to China to hold judicial-training workshops.

One of the most surprising and interesting developments vis-à-vis the new emphasis on rule of law in China—and one which has great potential political repercussions, including on Sino-American relations—is that the highest court in Jilin Province in 1997 overturned a ruling against four Tiananmen dissidents who had been jailed for counterrevolutionary acts. The Jilin high court reversed that decision and released the two prisoners still in jail. This was the first time a court had overturned one of the Tiananmen verdicts. It could give some credence to rumors that the Chinese leadership has discussed the reversal of Tiananmen verdicts. Such a decision could never have been made while Deng Xiaoping was alive. Since his death, however, some Party leaders have begun to use terms other than *counterrevolutionaries* to describe the people involved, and some observers believe this case might be a trial balloon. Pressure for legal reform and increased emphasis on the rule of law in China is certainly coming from the outside, but it is encouraging to see that it is coming from inside the country as well.

Another important change is the gradual emergence of civil society in China—that is, the emergence of economic and social organizations that are increasingly independent of the state and the Party. The Western term for these organizations is NGO (nongovernmental organization). That does not quite fit the Chinese model, because in China, by law, NGOs must have a close relationship with a government organization. Some people in the West have thus given them a new title: Instead of NGO, it is GONGO (government-organized nongovernmental organization). Organizationally, GONGOs were set up primarily in the area of poverty alleviation, and were like our United Way and similar charity organizations. However, they are beginning to spring up in several other areas—particularly the environment, legal reform, and women's issues. In the past few years we have seen the emergence of what could almost be called real NGOs. They are quite small, their relationship with the government is minimal, and they are primarily founded and run by one or two very dynamic and highly motivated individuals deeply committed to their causes. A few of them have begun to push the envelope by branching out into advocacy activities. Whether GONGOs or NGOs, they all offer Chinese citizens greater space and the means to be involved in shaping their own lives and, eventually, the means to be involved in politics.

Indeed, another change in China is that citizen involvement in politics is now possible. Since 1988, with the passing of a law a year earlier by the National People's Congress, local elections in China have been held at the village level. Estimates of how many of China's one million villages have held elections range from the Government Ministry's claim of 80 percent to that of a magazine on township affairs that puts the number at no more than 10 percent. The point is that competitive elections are taking place. Where they have taken place, 20 percent of incumbents have been booted out of office. In several provinces more than 50 percent of the people who head villages are not Party members.

Unfortunately, not everyone responsible for the implementation of such elections is enthusiastic about them. Elections have the potential to increase the accountability of local leaders and to establish meaningful democratic reform. Therefore, local leaders who worry about being removed from office by the election process are less than enthusiastic about assuring that elections are held. What is interesting and encouraging is that the efforts to implement elections have largely been driven by grassroots demands, by unhappy villagers wanting to get rid of unpopular, corrupt leaders.

A key question is whether such elections will move up the government hierarchy. My belief is that eventually they will. But as with the other changes I have mentioned, it will take time. Although the opening of the political process has not yet been replicated at the top, it is clear that something resembling coalition building has been developing in the Party's inner sanctum. Because President Jiang Zemin does not come from the generation of older leaders who earned their positions and the unquestioned obedience and loyalty of others through participation in some of the defining periods of modern Chinese history (i.e., the founding of the Party, the Long March, the Civil War), he has had to consolidate his base somewhat like a modern Western politician by appealing to various groups within the Party elite. He has become quite good at it.

Another encouraging change is that during the lead-up to the Fifteenth Party Congress, political advisers and analysts close to the leadership called publicly for more popular participation in politics, for direct elections of China's highest leaders, for the loosening of controls on the media, and for structural reforms in the economic and political arenas to proceed at the same pace. In fact, at a private meeting I attended in 1997, Premier Li Peng, considered to be among the most conservative of China's senior politicians, stressed the importance of political reform—not economic reform.

Thus, to return to my main thesis, those of us who have been long involved with China, who have seen so many, many changes take place—changes that have made the lives of most Chinese much freer and better than ever before in China's history—see the Chinese glass as half full, with the water level inexorably rising. However, those who began to deal with China since the Reform Years (from 1979 to 1984 in the countryside and from 1984 to 1988 in the urban areas), or with 1989 Tiananmen China, or with China in 1994—when most-favored-nation trading status and human rights were delinked and human rights seemed to be deteriorating—may have a very different perspective. To them the changes in China have been much less dramatic, and the Chinese glass looks half empty, with the water level inexorably falling.

Those of us in the first category recognize that China has enormous problems and faces major challenges, nor are we shy about raising these issues—including human rights and Tibet. We do, however, tend to do so in private, direct conversations with the Chinese, where we feel it will do the most good. No one likes being scolded, especially when that scolding is done publicly or when it is seen as condescending.

Let me highlight very briefly some of China's major problems. One is corruption. My Chinese friends tell me that corruption now is even greater than it was during the period of the Kuomintang (KMT) in the 1940s. That must give tremendous pause to Chinese leaders, because corruption was one of the causes that led to the downfall of the KMT on the mainland. And fury over corruption was one of the key factors that led people in 1989 to demonstrate in Tiananmen Square. China has tried to punish corruption swiftly and harshly. Crackdowns have come mostly at the local level, but there have been some high-profile cases at the central level, such as that of the former mayor of Beijing. The severity of these sentences seems, however, to have done very little to deter those who seek shortcuts to wealth. The average Chinese citizen does not believe the government has done nearly enough to squelch this endemic disease that is eating away at society.

How to privatize China's inefficient state-owned enterprises (SOEs) without causing massive unemployment and social disruption is another huge problem. The biggest news from the Fifteenth Party Congress so far has been the proposal that about 10,000 of the country's 13,000 largest and medium-sized inefficient SOEs be privatized in a sense—although that politically sensitive word is not used. Instead, Chinese leaders speak about people buying shares of stock of companies as "public ownership." This enables lip service to China's socialist underpinnings to continue. In the United States, public ownership is the government; in China it is the private sector. Whatever the semantic juggling, the key fact is that by selling off SOEs, China is abandoning a central tenet of Communist rule—the state as the dominant owner of industry.

Although the announcement has been made, it is likely that the implementation of this policy will be slow, at least slower than some here would like. It is estimated that resolving the current SOE problems could mean lay-offs or job terminations for fifteen million people. That is a huge number, especially in an economy where underemployment has always been a prob-lem, where unemployment recently shot up to levels of 20 to 30 percent in some cities, where there is a floating migrant labor force of about 150 mil-lion (people who have left the land to find work in cities where the economy is booming), and where SOEs provide for almost every social need of their employees. (This includes crèches for nursing mothers, nursery schools and kindergartens, primary and secondary schools, canteens, hospitals, housing, social halls, and entertainment.) So when SOE workers lose their jobs, they lose their cradle-to-grave protection and are left without benefit of a social safety net.

Finally, a long-term problem, but potentially China's most threatening, is the environment. China has five of the world's ten worst cities in terms of air pollution. The number of suspended particles in the air in some cities is as much as ten times higher than the World Health Organization deems acceptable. One quarter of all deaths are attributed to lung disease. Eighty-six percent of the water that flows through rivers in cities is polluted. There is a huge problem with water scarcity that the Chinese have not yet begun to address, and which will require massive restructuring. A whole city in the north China plateau is packing up, lock, stock, and barrel, and moving twenty-five miles north because its groundwater has become too polluted to be used.

The government has gone from thinking that the topic is an eccentric obsession of visiting Westerners to the realization that China does have very real environmental problems. China now has some of the strongest environ-mental laws of any nation. The problem comes in implementation. But again, a key role has been played by a long-silent Chinese public—embold-ened by reform, enlightened by education, and spurred on by an increasingly well-informed and vocal media.

Although China faces a huge array of staggering problems, only a few of which I have been able to touch on, I believe it is going to get through them. The historic and well-grounded fear of chaos and instability has kept China on the path of doing things "yi bu, yi bu," one step at a time. Eventually, in its own way, through its own process of, as they say, "crossing the river by feel-ing the stones," China is going to be an extraordinarily powerful country. We have it within our power to make sure that when that does happen, China and the United States come out as friends and not as foes.

Michel Oksenberg

I want briefly to discuss four topics: (1) Asia's rise and American response to it; (2) China's importance to the United States; (3) China's current situation; and (4) American strategy toward China.

Asia's Rise and the American Response

No more important geographic development of our era exists than the rise of Asia in world affairs. With earlier antecedents, beginning in the 1960s, a wave of economic development began in Japan and has been moving inexorably south and west ever since, engulfing Taiwan, Korea, and Hong Kong in the 1960s and 1970s, moving to China and Southeast Asia in the 1980s, and hitting the south Asian subcontinent in the 1990s. More than three billion people live in this arc from Japan to India. The industrialization of Asia is as significant for human beings as the Italian renaissance or the industrial revolution.

Some Americans do not understand the significance of this rise of industrial Asia. Instead of embracing it, they seek to protect us from it. Instead of joining it, they seek to isolate us from it. Instead of stimulating it, they wish to halt it. The protectionists and isolationists among our politicians and pundits—they exist among both Democrats and Republicans, among both liberals and conservatives—are simply running against the tide of history. Asia's economic development is occurring at the rate of roughly 6 percent per year, with ebb and fall in the inevitable business cycle. The rest of the world is growing at 2 percent per year. Asia's urban centers are joining those of North America and Europe as centers of intellectual, economic, and political strength.

What posture should the United States adopt for responding to this major change in world affairs? Some Americans would literally seek to halt this development, if not toward Japan, which would be impossible, or toward Southeast Asia, because it is friendly to us, at least with respect to China. To be blunt, some Americans prefer to keep a significant portion of humanity—the Chinese portion of it—poor and underdeveloped. Our country and the world will be more peaceful and prosperous when all humanity prospers. The United States should not seek to block developing countries from attaining higher living standards and improved quality of life.

But we must deal with reality too. How do we help? How do we participate? How do we attain our own security in that process? Central to that are military strength and a military presence in Asia. America's bilateral military treaties with Korea and Japan have been central in creating a framework that has enabled the rest of Asia to enjoy unprecedented peace and prosperity. Crucial here too is our reaching to China. Let us remember that the United States fought three tragic wars in Asia in this century—World War II, the Korean War, and the Vietnam War. One of the major reasons those wars occurred was the underlying tension and animosity between China and Japan. Those two had been rivals until President Richard Nixon and Secretary of State Henry Kissinger's opening toward China. In the context of Sino-Japanese animosity, the United States faced the unpleasant choice of having a good relationship with China and hence a bad relationship with Japan, or a good relationship with Japan and hence a bad relationship with China.

For the past twenty-five years, we have successfully had simultaneously constructive relations with the two indigenous giants of Asia. That is the fundamental strategy our country has pursued. It is the fundamental strategy our country must continue to pursue. It is that triangular relationship that has brought stability to the entire region. Our bilateral treaties with Korea and Japan undergrid that triangular relationship. Taiwan benefits from it; so does Southeast Asia. Our task in the decades ahead, as part of America's foreign policy in the twenty-first century, is to make that structure more durable and more multilateral, and to ensure that the United States has greater economic entrée into Asia's increasingly prosperous economies.

The Importance of China

We cannot speak about an Asian policy without a China policy. China policy must be integrated into an Asian policy, and that policy must be supported by Japan, Korea, and the countries of Southeast Asia. Some Americans advocate pursuit of a hostile policy toward China that no other Asian government would support. That is not a policy for national security; that is a policy for national suicide.

Why is China important? Usually, the argument goes that it has 1.3 billion people with a rising economy and it is going to be increasingly a major actor in the world scene. China's continued development is not foreordained. The leaders of China face enormous problems of economic development. It is by no means assured that the Chinese can overcome pressing environmental problems. Moreover, the inadequacies in the educational system have left China with a poorly educated populace, although with many brilliant people in it. And it is not clear that Chinese institutions can cope with the challenges of development. Thus, American policy cannot be based totally on the premise that China will be increasingly powerful.

In addition to the economic opportunities China offers and its obvious strategic importance, two other factors make China important.

(1) In an increasingly interdependent world, humanity simply cannot address the real problems of the twenty-first century without the cooperation of China. By real problems, I mean global climatic change, illegal population migration, narcotics trafficking, terrorism, nuclear proliferation, and the spread of weapons of mass destruction. Humanity cannot address any of these problems without the active, cooperative behavior of China.

(2) We are dealing with 1.3 billion people who twenty-five years ago were impoverished. Today they are improving their standard of living. In the

twenty-first century, perhaps one of the biggest underlying problems the world will confront will be the disparity between the rich and the poor, between the developed and the developing world, not only internationally but within countries as well, between the advantaged and the disadvantaged. The globalization of our economy benefits some people earlier than others. Some are being left behind. That increasing gap is a source of instability and tension.

In the long run, creating a more equitable world is a major item on the global agenda in the twenty-first century. That is what is really entailed in thinking about China or the Middle East as well as Latin America and South Asia. How do we move toward a more stable world, in which the bulk of humanity lives with dignity? After all, roughly 90 percent of the increase in the world's populace in the decades ahead will occur in countries with only 20 percent of the world's gross national product. That disparity underlies illegal population migration and narcotics trafficking. How do we deal with this big problem? It is a huge challenge. And if—and it is a big if—China can be brought into the existing world's structures and be encouraged to become a constructive member of the world community, in one fell swoop 1.3 billion people will have hope and will have incentive not to disrupt the international system but to become a force for stability and for the status quo. That is what is at stake and why China is important. It does not make China more or less important than India or indeed Africa or Latin America, but it must be put in this global context.

The Chinese Condition

It is easy to criticize the leaders of China for their inadequacies. For example, Han Chinese rule in Tibet has been harsh and it merits condemnation. The Chinese leaders deserve to be chastised for their human-rights record, particularly toward some of their ethnic minority groups.

At the same time, the challenges and problems that China's rulers face must be recognized. China must feed four times the population of the United States on 60 percent of our cultivated acreage. If the United States had the same population density on all of its tillable land, if all our front lawns were turned into rice paddies or wheat fields, the population of the United States would be between two and three billion people. Can you imagine what the United States would be like having ten times our population, trying to sustain our standard of living, and coping with the environmental consequences of that?

China's leaders and entire population are also in the midst of four enormous transformations.

(1) One transformation involves the rapid movement from a rural and agricultural society to an urban and industrial society. Every year since 1979, 1 percent of China's population—more than ten million people—has changed occupations from rural-based to industrial-based employment.

(2) The Chinese are managing a transformation from a planned command and nonmarket economy to some form of market economy. That transition is evident in all the other former Soviet-style economies. That path has not been clearly charted by anyone yet.

(3) China is in the midst of a generational transition of leadership from revolutionaries to bureaucrats—revolutionaries who derived legitimacy from accomplishments in their lifetime and were the founders of the political system they ran. Now, there is a new generation of people who grew up within that system, with very different orientations and without necessarily having a vision of where they desire to take their country.

(4) China is changing from a largely monolithic society to a diverse one, with a middle class beginning to emerge.

Empathy and understanding are required in thinking about the problems the leaders of China confront. And the many domestic challenges that China's leaders confront mean that we are not central to their concerns. Sometimes when they rebuff some of our demands, it is not because they dislike or oppose us; rather, they have other problems on their minds.

American Strategy Toward China

So we must understand the Chinese. The United States has major interests with China that we must pursue in a hardheaded manner. We need to have a strategy for coping with China, recognizing the opportunities and the challenges. In that regard, there are several dimensions to a China policy that this administration, after a halting performance at best in its first three years, is beginning to put together. The policy has returned to the policies of the previous several administrations, begun by President Nixon and pursued by every president since—Ford, Carter, Reagan, and Bush. Initially the Clinton administration departed from that policy, but it has now returned to it. That policy has the following components:

(1) Develop a shared strategic perspective with the leaders of China concerning the direction of world affairs. It is sometimes asserted that China's rise inevitably will mean that it will challenge the United States. That view is based on a particular theory of international relations that a rising power challenges the status quo power. That is what happened with Germany, Japan, even America in the nineteenth century, and with Russia's rise in this century. But that theory merits modification in two regards. Namely, it is possible to change people's perceptions of the world. It is possible to alter people's perception if you talk to them, to get them to understand the world in different ways. That is what Henry Kissinger did and continues to do through his extensive and frequent discussions in Bejing since 1971. No American has played a bigger role than Kissinger in trying to affect the way the Chinese leaders see the world. When he was the president's national security adviser and then secretary of state, he journeyed to China on eleven occasions. He sat with China's leaders for five and six hours at a time, on three or four consecutive days. It had an intellectual impact.

From the end of the cold war until the late 1990s, the United States government gave little attention to that task, but thank goodness, that process has begun again. It is hoped that in the Clinton administration and those to follow there will be persons who carry out that kind of intellectual dialogue with the leaders of China concerning the future of our world. Crucial to that is some very tough-minded talk to Chinese leaders about why a continued American military presence in the western Pacific and why America's bilateral treaties with Japan and Korea manifestly serve China's interest by maintaining stability in the region. If they cannot understand that, we will have a difficult relationship with China. Our presence deters the reappearance of age-old conflicts in the region, particularly between China and Japan, but also between Korea and Japan.

(2) Help bring China into the world economy. We should do that through the World Trade Organization. We should be bargaining hard, stressing to the Chinese that an open, international system is at least as much in their interest as in ours because they are major beneficiaries of it. This should be a very high priority on our agenda with China.

(3) With respect to Taiwan, our policy has been that any peaceful resolution of the issue by the two sides themselves is acceptable to us. Three documents—the 1972 Shanghai Communiqué, the 1978 Normalization Agreement, and the 1982 Joint Declaration on U.S. arms sales to Taiwan—established America's "one China" policy. The United States is not prepared to encourage Taiwan independence, but we expect the People's Republic of China to adopt a peaceful strategy toward the resolution of that issue. We should encourage the Chinese to recognize that a bear is attracted by honey, not vinegar. The Chinese policy toward Taiwan in 1995-96 had too much vinegar and not enough honey. But we should also emphasize to Taiwan that it should not needlessly provoke Beijing.

(4) Human rights must be an element of American foreign policy, not only toward China, but globally. It is part of our country, of our very essence. We should be confident that our values will ultimately prevail. We need not force them on anyone. We should be patient. Above all, human rights will be best advanced through institutional development: the development of the rule of law in China, the strengthening of Chinese parliamentary systems, the introduction of elections at lower levels. All these developments are now under way in China. We should work constructively with the Chinese. We should not preach at them.

Conclusion

I am a lifelong student of China, but I would not pretend for a minute that I understand China. It is too big, too diverse, its history too long, its culture too complex for any one person to grasp. The study of China is a little bit like entering a swamp. Now, our nation must prepare itself for an extensive, intensive, and enduring relationship with China. Clearly, our nation is ill-prepared intellectually and conceptually for dealing with an active China on the world scene. We need to greatly expand our capacity to understand China and Asia as a whole. We need to improve and expand our foreign-service and intelligence-community capabilities on China. We must not allow ourselves to become reliant on insights provided from that side of the Pacific. We have to assess our own interests. To do this we must expand and improve our educational system from that point of view to meet this challenge.

Chapter 5

Japan and Other Nations of East Asia

Walter Mondale

The relationship between the United States and Japan stands as one of the great international success stories of the past half century. In a short time, once-bitter enemies became close allies, partners, and friends. Our destinies have become inseparable. At the close of the twentieth century, the U.S.-Japan relationship is poised for continued success in the next century.

Despite the barriers of geography, history, culture, and language, the United States and Japan have a great deal in common: We are free and open societies; we have democratically elected governments; we are successful, advanced economies; and we are committed to international cooperation to secure a peaceful world.

Because the United States and Japan are the world's two largest economies, what we do literally affects every other country in Asia and throughout the world. It is clear that our relationship will only grow in importance in the future and, more than ever before, we will need to act as partners in international leadership. This is consistent with both America's changing role in the world and Japan's own aspirations for global responsibility.

The positive working relationship between the United States and Japan is a reassuring anchor in a world that has been shaken by waves of change in the final decade of the twentieth century. It is astonishing to consider the transformation that has occurred in the world: The countries of eastern Europe achieved their freedom from Communist control; the Soviet Union ceased to exist; and the bipolar world of the cold war vanished. Gone is the mortal standoff between the superpowers which dominated the world.

For more than four decades, the cold war exerted a chilling effect throughout the world. America's international relations in Asia were not immune. But today, America stands in a unique position. We are the world's only remaining superpower—an unchallenged global leader economically, militarily, and culturally. The American economy is more than half again as large as the world's second-biggest economy, Japan. The American military stands alone in being able to project power on a sustained basis anywhere in the world. American-made cultural products flood the world's media, carried by the advanced communications technology in which the United States holds a commanding lead.

But without the cold war, we now also lack a clear enemy—something which used to both reinforce our relations with other nations and induce them to follow our lead. As a result, our abundance of power does not necessarily translate into international deference to our values and priorities. In fact, many countries both admire and resent our success. Therefore, we now must work harder to nurture cooperation with major countries in each region of the world.

In Asia, fortunately, we have deep, long-standing economic and security ties with Japan, which have served us well and will continue to do so. Our alliance with Japan remains the foundation of stability and our most important strategic connection in the Asia-Pacific region.

The enduring stability and strength of the U.S.-Japan relationship gives us much-needed continuity during this time of change. But we must also be willing to adjust and adapt this relationship to the changing realities of the post–cold war world and the global economy. The many changes which are now reshaping the international environment also present important challenges for the U.S.-Japan relationship. Strengthening America's partnership with Japan will require long-term vision, mutual respect, and mutual responsibilities.

The United States has traditionally looked more toward Europe than toward Asia. We now find our trade and investment shifting toward the Pacific. Despite the financial crisis that hit Asia in 1997, this trend is likely to continue. Therefore, the United States is now giving unprecedented attention to this region. As a matter of history and geography, the United States has been a Pacific nation from among its earliest days as a nation. But the Asia-Pacific region will be the dominant economic force in the twenty-first century. With this economic strength will come political and strategic influence which is sure to be felt throughout the world.

Therefore, as we enter the twenty-first century, no region in the world is more important to the United States than Asia—and no relationship more crucial than that with Japan.

The United States is trying to approach Asia not merely as a series of bilateral relationships alone, but also on a regional basis. New prosperity, economic integration, the information revolution, the spread of democracy, and a growing awareness of the need for regional action—all of these provide a basis for building common interests among the Asia-Pacific nations.

In a speech at Tokyo's Waseda University in July 1993, President Clinton said that the time has come for the United States and Japan, along with others in the region, to create "a new Pacific community" based on "shared strength, shared prosperity and a shared commitment to democratic values." These three pillars are mutually reinforcing: Security is essential for economic development; economic progress promotes democratic change; and prosperous democracies make for peaceful neighbors. Clinton emphasized that America's relationship with Japan must form "the centerpiece of our policy toward the Pacific community."

This chapter previews four major questions that will shape the U.S. role with Japan in Asia in the twenty-first century—economic openness, regional security, democratic development, and intellectual and cultural understanding.

Toward More Economic Openness

First, there is the question of whether Asia will continue to move toward greater economic openness or whether the mercantilism found so widely in that region will remain a serious problem. Our economic approach to Japan and the rest of Asia must be based on the dual reality that American prosperity now depends on global prosperity and that global prosperity depends increasingly on what happens in Asia. This means we need to work for a more open world trading and financial system, and we need to encourage policies in Asia that will help contribute to this openness.

The free flow of trade and commerce among nations is the best guarantor of regional and global prosperity. In the post–World War II period, Japan and the other Asian economies have been among the greatest beneficiaries of an open world system of trade and finance. Open markets in the United States have been the essential underpinning of this system. The United States remains committed to keeping its markets open, but there is also an expectation that other nations must open theirs.

As the leading economic partners for other nations in Asia, the United States and Japan bear a special responsibility for leadership. The most important leadership we can demonstrate is to make our own markets as open as possible—both to provide the markets that others need for their exports and to persuade them to open their own markets in return.

The good news is that, during the 1990s, many of the Asian nations liberalized many sectors of their economies. In addition, the Asia-Pacific Economic Cooperation (APEC) forum has developed into a promising vehicle for greater economic cooperation in the Pacific Rim. It is an important institutional mechanism to open regional trade and investment, strengthen the multilateral trading system, and anchor the United States firmly in the Asia-Pacific region. APEC members have made a good start toward reaching the goal of removing all trade barriers in the region by the years 2010 to 2020. However, without continued strong leadership from the United States and Japan, this historic effort could lose momentum.

The bad news is that many of the Asian economies continue to be based on government-controlled investments, opaque financial structures, and mercantilist trade policies that burden the world economy and that led to the financial crisis which hit Asia in the summer of 1997. The Asian economies are not identical, but variations on a dominant economic model can be found throughout the region (with only a few notable exceptions, such as Hong Kong).

Japan is the classic example. For many years, Japan offered an economic model that was appealing throughout much of Asia. It was a model of economic growth based on a mercantilist strategy of production for export and protection from imports. There is a major flaw in this plan, however. Its success depends on an open American market—because the Japanese market remains as closed to goods produced elsewhere in Asia as to imports from America.

The relatively closed nature of the Japanese economy is well documented. Although formal tariffs are low on average, a combination of excessive regulations and restrictive informal business practices impedes imports and investments. Japan's markets in key sectors are substantially less open than American markets or those of other advanced countries, hindering the ability of competitive foreign firms to gain access to its economy. As a result, Japan absorbs far fewer manufactured imports, relative to the size of its economy, than any other industrial nation.

Foreign direct investment in Japan continues to be minimal. Research has found that trade tends to follow investment; as a result, where investment is restricted, so is trade. On the macroeconomic level, Japan continues to run massive current account surpluses with the world which deny export and growth opportunities to other countries, including the United States.

Throughout the 1990s, the United States and the world's major economies have urged Japan to open its markets, deregulate its economy, and reduce its excessive global surplus. These steps would benefit the rest of Asia and the world. Most of all, they would benefit the Japanese people who, because of Japan's restrictive economic policies, must pay on average considerably more for tradable goods and services than do the citizens of other industrialized countries.

Fortunately, there are more voices for change in Japanese society, especially within the business community. They increasingly recognize the costs and disadvantages of an overregulated, closed economy. The economic stagnation of the 1990s and a general sense that overregulation is stifling the economy have combined to produce a growing domestic constituency for economic reforms.

As many Japanese themselves are pointing out, it is in Japan's own national interest to embrace market-opening reforms that will strengthen its domestic economy, expand consumer choice, lower prices, improve living standards, and bring Japan more in harmony with regional and global economies. Japan's ability to manage the costs of a rapidly aging society depends on improved productivity and innovation that will fuel continued economic growth. In turn, improved productivity and innovation depend on a more open, competitive Japanese economy.

But for all the recent talk about deregulation and reform, there is much evidence that Japan is still fundamentally wedded to its traditional policies. Previous attempts at economic reform in Japan have been repeatedly frustrated by the country's unique decision-making process—shaped as it is by powerful bureaucrats, "keiretsu" relationships among companies, and highly insular, group-oriented attitudes of decision makers which require consensus. The resistance to change from bureaucrats and entrenched interest groups in Japan is formidable. Change is coming, but it is likely to be incremental and agonizingly slow.

The Asian financial crisis of 1997–98 highlighted the important role Japan must play in promoting the region's return to economic stability and growth. Japan is, by far, the largest economy in the region. Indeed, Japan's economy is still more than twice the size of the other Asian economies *combined.*

Japan, with aspirations to greater international leadership, has a basic responsibility to the rest of the world to open its markets and to stimulate domestic economic growth. The United States is the most open economy in the world, and our commitment to free trade has been the engine of global economic growth for the past forty years. Japan can be a partner with the United States in strengthening and extending the open world trading system. A vibrant and growing regional and global economy depends on a vibrant and growing Japanese economy. An open and vital world trading system depends on a Japan whose own markets are more open.

The reality is that the United States cannot be the only engine of global growth or the sole buyer of goods to absorb the tremendous productive capacity of Asia. Even with our wide-open markets, the United States is simply not large enough to consume the ever-increasing production of the dynamic Asian economies. For these countries to realize their own aspirations for prosperity, they must have access to consumers in Japan.

Nonetheless, the basic economic challenge in Asia remains: Will these nations move ahead with market-oriented reforms and accept the discipline that comes from international competition and integration with the global economy? Or instead, will these countries simply tinker around the edges of the problem—leaving in place the old "crony capitalism" and government-dominated economies which led to their difficulties and burdened the world economic system?

This is not a minor question. Real reform will mean not only major economic changes, it will also require moving away from deeply entrenched political and cultural practices. But it would not only restore stability and ensure recovery from the present crisis, it would also set these nations back on the path to sustainable economic health and promote a more open system of global trade and finance.

The kanji character for "crisis" combines the terms for "danger" and "opportunity." That has been the case with the Asian financial crisis of 1997–98. It has posed real dangers to the Asian economies and to the United States. But it also offers Asia—and the rest of the world—the opportunity to rebound from this crisis with economies that are stronger, more open, and more stable.

"At the end of the day," Fred Bergsten of the Institute for International Economics has forecast, "the trade and investment climate should be considerably stronger throughout Asia as a result of the crisis and the policy responses to it."[1]

Sweet are the uses of adversity, Shakespeare once wrote. If Asia's financial crisis does lead to fundamental reform, it may well prove to be a blessing in disguise. Reform would not only restore stability and ensure recovery from the crisis, but it also would put these nations on the path to sustainable economic health. In turn, this would promote a more open system of global trade and finance that would be a boon for the United States and the rest of the world.

Toward More Regional Security

A second question that will be a major concern for the United States and Japan in the twenty-first century is the issue of regional security in Asia.

The United States and Japan share a vital interest in a peaceful, stable, and prosperous Asia-Pacific region. The threats to these shared interests have evolved over time, and our two nations have worked together to counter them.

This alliance was formulated at the height of the cold war to contain the challenge of international Communism. Our cooperation was essential to maintain peace and to promote economic opportunities in the region. We are now living with the benefits of these efforts—an Asia-Pacific region in which democracy has spread, trade has flourished, and standards of living have risen dramatically. Asia is today possibly the most stable region in the world. There are no significant military conflicts, and most of the countries in the region have experienced impressive economic growth and development.

During the cold war, the aggressive behavior of the Soviet régime—armed with nuclear weapons—made it relatively easy for both the Japanese and U.S. governments to explain to their citizens the basis for the alliance. Recent events have posed a new and fundamental challenge to the alliance. The collapse of the Soviet Union and the end of the cold war have caused critics in both Japan and the United States to argue that the rationale for our security alliance has evaporated now that there is no longer an immediate military threat.

The world remains a dangerous and complicated place, however, certainly more complicated than before—and in some respects, possibly more dangerous as well.

Asia has been a historically unstable and troubled region. This is a region where, in the past, great powers have maneuvered and battled and let loose their ambitions for regional dominance. The three major wars in my lifetime started in this historically unstable region. Although the Asia-Pacific region is now much more stable, the end of the cold war has not ushered in an era of certainty. The Korean Peninsula remains divided and tense. The internal developments and the external policies of key regional players could move in unsettling directions. There is a range of unresolved territorial issues. Many countries are also trying to increase their military spending. Competition for resources is likely to increase as these dynamic economies pursue ambitious development plans. In this uncertain environment, we cannot take stability for granted, and any reduction of U.S. forces would send the wrong signal about our commitment to the region.

Our security presence in Asia continues to rest on a network of bilateral relationships with individual countries. The process of regional cooperation in Asia remains much less developed than in Europe. Asia does not yet have a multilateral security structure to manage the shocks and tensions—or prevent a destabilizing power vacuum—of a diverse Asia-Pacific community. There are no European Union and no NATO, reflecting the complex history of this region with its economic, political, and cultural diversity. We are beginning to build such institutions through APEC, the ASEAN Post-Ministerial Conference, and the Northeast Asia Security Dialogue. But this process will take time.

For the foreseeable future, the American presence, based on the U.S.-Japan Security Treaty, will remain essential to stability and prosperity in the region. America's continuing presence in the region serves the interests of both the United States and Japan, as well as every other nation in the region.

According to scholar Daniel Okimoto, the U.S.-Japan security alliance is "the longest lived and most successful alliance that Asia has ever known. It is a watershed institution in a region historically inhospitable to the creation and maintenance of alliances." Okimoto writes,

> By almost any criterion of success—be it cost effectiveness, risk-reward ratio, multiplier effects or sheer longevity—the Japan America Security Alliance stands out as one of the most successful alliances in twentieth century history. . . . In terms of historic impact, the Japan America Security Alliance is comparable to the North Atlantic Treaty Organization (NATO), a multilateral alliance that restructured the European security landscape in 1949. For nearly a half-century, the Japan America Security Alliance and NATO have functioned as the bedrock on which the Cold War security systems of Asia and Europe have been constructed. . . . Never before in the chronicles of Asian history has there been an alliance of comparable staying power and effectiveness. Japan America Security Alliance's longevity is especially noteworthy given the absence of other enduring alliances in the region's history.[2]

One of the great virtues of our alliance with Japan has always been its adaptability. The fact that it is as relevant today as it was in the midst of the cold war shows the deep interdependence of American and Japanese national interests.

The U.S.-Japan alliance is not directed against China. It is not designed to contain any country, nor is it directed at a specific threat. The alliance is based on common interests, not common enemies. The United States and Japan share a wide range of strategic interests which transcend the end of the cold war and require an effective stabilizing force in the region. Indeed, the U.S.-Japan security relationship is widely perceived in Japan and the rest of Asia as essential not only for Japan's defense, but also for ensuring peace and prosperity in the entire Asia-Pacific region.

The international response in 1994 and 1995 to North Korea's nuclear program showed that the United States continues to be the principal source of balance in this region—a role it has had since the end of World War II. Free of historical animosities and rivalries, the United States can simultaneously maintain excellent relations with Japan, South Korea, China, Russia, and the other nations of Asia. No other country can assume this role.

Although there have been signs of Japanese movement toward an expanded role in Asia, Japanese foreign policy will continue to be anchored in the basic U.S.-Japan relationship. There is little prospect in the near or midterm (or probably in the long term) that Japan will seek major changes in the political and security aspects of our relationship.

In Japan, there is a consensus among the public and the political leadership that the U.S.-Japan security treaty serves Japan's interests and is a source of regional stability. Both governments understand that to ensure regional stability, the United States must continue to maintain a forward-deployed military presence in East Asia. The heart of this presence is our bases in Japan and the 47,000 American servicemen and women stationed there. Without these bases, we could not maintain the forward-deployed carrier battle group and the air force, marine, and army units necessary to meet our commitments. Japan's generous contribution to maintaining these forces, through its host-nation support, is vital. By any standard, it is a tremendous bargain for both the United States and Japan.

Security does not come without costs. It requires the forward deployment of forces, which means a substantial American security presence in Japan. Japanese support for American bases was put to a severe test in the mid-1990s by an outrageous crime when three American marines raped a twelve-year-old girl on Okinawa. This tragic incident revealed that although a substantial majority of Japanese continue to support the alliance, many question the need to maintain the current level of U.S. forces in Japan. People in Okinawa Prefecture in particular feel that the security burden has been disproportionately placed on them. Of the approximately 47,000 American troops in Japan, about 28,000 are stationed in Okinawa. The U.S. government has been working with the government of Japan to reduce the impact of the military presence on the people of Okinawa.

At the same time, it is important that any adjustments in Okinawa and elsewhere in Japan are done in a manner that is consistent with responsibilities under the security treaty. To do our job, we must have adequate bases and our forces must be trained and ready for immediate deployment. Both the American and Japanese governments must continue to do a better job of explaining publicly the rationale for our deployments in Japan and the key role our bases play as the anchor of America's commitment to the security of Japan and the stability of the region.

As we look to the future, we need to consider, with others in the region, ways to develop regional security structures to supplement, but not replace, the American military presence in East Asia. ASEAN and its dialogue partners have begun taking the first steps in this direction. But this will take time. Moreover, the prerequisite for building a multilateral security framework is regional stability, which can be maintained in the foreseeable future only by the U.S.-Japan alliance.

Therefore, American security commitments in Asia and the presence of U.S. forces there will continue to serve as the foundation of regional stability: We ensure the freedom of the seas. Our stabilizing presence helps to deter possible military confrontations among nations in the region. Our presence has prevented North Korea from using its huge military forces to attack South Korea. It has reduced the pressure for an arms race and, by providing stability, it has been the key ingredient in the region's economic success. In the future, this presence must remain strong, both to deter military threats and to provide reassurance against national rivalries which could undermine the region's hard-earned stability.

The critical importance of regional security in Asia is highlighted by the potential for instability as a result of growing energy dependency in Asia. Asia's rapid economic growth has already generated rapid increases in energy consumption. This trend will only accelerate in the years ahead as both industrial and consumer demands for energy resources rise with the growing prosperity of these economies.

In this context, Daniel Yergin and his colleagues at Cambridge Energy Research Associates refer to Asia's double miracle: ". . . the phenomenal economic growth most east and southeast Asian countries experienced over the recent decades has been doubly miraculous since it occurred despite severely limited energy resources in some of the fastest-growing economies."[3]

But scholar Kent Calder has also appropriately described the region's "profound energy insecurities" as "the dark side to the explosive economic growth of East Asia."[4] Asia's locomotive of economic growth depends on a reliable supply of fuel—which none of the countries in the region believes it can afford to take for granted. Asia is particularly dependent on outside supplies of energy. The region simply does not have the indigenous energy resources—whether oil, coal, or natural gas—to meet its dramatically increasing levels of consumption.

In 1990, the Asia-Pacific oil demand overtook that of western Europe, making it the second-largest oil-consuming region in the world, after the United States. Within the next twenty years, the region will become the number-one consumer of oil—with virtually all of this new supply coming from outside the region. Asia's continued growth and development mean that the region's energy demands are likely to grow at an annual rate that is double or more the annual global growth rate for energy.

China is already the world's second-largest consumer of energy. It has traditionally been a major energy exporter, especially to Japan. But since 1993, it has become an increasingly important net importer of oil, with rising dependence on the Middle East. China is also the world's dominant user of coal. Estimates differ about the scale of the projected increase, but China's coal use is expected to double in the first ten to fifteen years of the next century, adding coal to Asia's problems with acid rain and worldwide concern about global warming.

As China further develops its economy, the demand for energy there will soar. Similarly, questions about future energy supply and demand are facing virtually all other countries in the region. Estimates differ about how much more oil and gas Asia must import from the Middle East and Persian Gulf area. Estimates broadly agree, however, that Asia will more than double its oil imports from the Middle East within the first ten to fifteen years of the next century, and that China alone will increase its oil imports from the Gulf by a factor of four. By that time, Asia will be consuming roughly two-thirds of all the Gulf's oil exports.

There are already signs in Asian countries of increasing nervousness about their energy dependence and how to defend against this vulnerability. There will be increased tensions and the potential for military confrontation around conflicting territorial claims for areas in the South China Sea and East China Sea, where oil and gas deposits are believed to be located. Freedom of movement in the sea lanes of Asia, especially the waters around Indonesia, will gain even greater strategic importance than now exists.

Overlapping territorial claims and the region's dependency on outside energy supplies underscore the importance of an active American diplomacy and the presence of American security forces to ensure the integrity of open navigation and the safety of the high seas.

A continuing American presence is vital to the future stability and prosperity of Asia. Our presence offers everyone in the region the reassurance needed to seek cooperation instead of confrontation in handling international disputes. The alliance with Japan remains indispensable to the American presence in the region and, as we enter the twenty-first century, this alliance promises to remain the foundation of peace and stability throughout the Asia-Pacific region.

Toward More Freedom and Democracy

A third question on the horizon is political development to expand the boundaries of freedom and democracy in Asia.

There are already many democracies in the region, including Japan. But there are still many nations whose progress toward democracy and human rights remains in doubt. This question of political legitimacy is crucial because stable political systems are indispensable to sustained, healthy economic activity. Commerce depends on a fair, predictable system of rules. Economic actors can have trust in such a system only when a government is in place with the legitimacy to enact and enforce these rules. In several places in Asia, this legitimacy is either nonexistent or very weak.

Democracy and human rights are not only important values in their own right. They are also important to the possibilities of both peace and economic progress—because democratic nations tend to settle disagreements without resorting to war and because free people are better able to develop their talents and thus contribute more to the productivity and creativity of their societies.

Earlier in history, Asia was largely without any experience in democracy. But with prosperity and growing middle classes, we have seen—and will continue to see—greater pressure for more open and responsive political systems.

In China, the leaders may no longer speak much about Communism, but their government and their power descend directly from Mao and the Communist revolution. They have made it clear that they are willing to use government power to suppress dissent and enforce compliance among the Chinese people. Where this system goes—toward greater democracy and legitimacy or not—will be one of the most challenging questions of the next several decades.

Asian societies tend to reflect a different idea about the status of the individual. Confucian thought—emphasizing social hierarchy, harmony, and loyalty to the group—still heavily influences Japan, although it is a democracy. Variations on this principle are found throughout much of Asia.

Many Asian nations have succeeded in reconciling these cultural values with democracy and human rights—including Japan, South Korea, Taiwan, Hong Kong, and the Philippines. The appeal of democracy is strong and growing throughout the Pacific Rim. On the other hand, Asia is where we can find some of the most brutal, repressive régimes in the world—notably North Korea and Myanmar (formerly Burma)—as well as governments that are rife with corruption at the highest levels.

There is, in fact, a great debate throughout much of Asia about whether the American system of individual liberty is an attractive model. Apologists for authoritarian governments argue that American freedom really means selfishness and personal license, leading to violence and disorder. By contrast, they claim, government control is essential to stability and economic prosperity. Their ideal is what some call a "civilized despotism"—with order above freedom, duties above rights.

Lee Kuan Yew, of Singapore, is a determined and articulate spokesman for this view. He once said, "I do not believe that democracy necessarily leads to development. I believe that what a country needs to develop is discipline more than democracy. The exuberance of democracy leads to undiscipline and disorderly conduct which are inimical to development." He has argued that American freedom is the cause of "massive social decay."[5] He is not alone in this view. Prime Minister Mahatirbin Mohamad of Malaysia has said much the same thing.

The arguments are by now familiar: Democracy and human rights are alien to the "Asian" way of thinking; they are a form of cultural imperialism imposed by the United States; and they are incompatible with economic growth.

The reality is much more complicated. There are plenty of examples of people in Asian countries protesting and demanding freedom from their repressive goverments—living proof of the homegrown nature of human rights and democracy. In each of these cases, the claim that the repression of human rights is a good thing was not a popular mandate, but the self-serving excuse of dictators and autocrats.

The economic turmoil that struck Asia in 1997 also challenged the claim that authoritarian control is a superior route to economic development. Indeed, it became apparent that the economic problems in the region reflected a lack of openness and public accountability which permitted endemic, institutionalized corruption and massive inefficiencies.

New York Times columnist William Safire has put it very well:

> The great lesson of the financial meltdown of Asian autocracies is this: Freedom is indivisible. Economic freedom cannot exist without political freedom.
>
> For decades, Asian dictators claimed that they had perfected a higher form of capitalism. Those in power would determine which entrepreneurs would succeed, and these—related by blood or bound by kickbacks to the politicians—would maintain position by perpetuating the dynasty.
>
> The world was assured by such philosophers as Singapore's Lee Kuan Yew that a concern for individual liberty was merely a "decadent Western value," and that Asians had discovered that a one-party state with a strong ruler would better provide the stability for growth. . . .
>
> [But] the outstretched hand of local politics is no match for the invisible hand of global markets. . . . The dictatorial model, driven by mutual back-scratching of elites, rather than a profit motive open to all, rewarded despotism and nepotism at the expense of efficiency and transparency. Now eyes are opening all over the world to the realization that the gravy train does not run on time.[6]

In other words, dictatorship and repression are bad for business as well as for people. There is, in fact, a strong positive connection among open societies, democratically accountable governments, and sustainable economic development. No country in the world can enjoy long-term prosperity without allowing its citizens the freedom to participate fully in society.

Asia's recent economic crisis has provided an important opportunity for reform and progress, both in politics and in economics. The challenge ahead is to ensure that economic reforms in Asia will bring an end to the corruption and the so-called crony capitalism, while contributing to stability, openness, and democratic development.

With the growing wealth, power, and military strength of Asian societies, how they develop politically will greatly affect our own security and prosperity. We do not need to be reminded that this historically unstable part of the world has provided us with too many wars and too much bloodshed. A democratic, law-based Asia will help lead to stability, peace, prosperity, and ever-closer human and cultural ties.

Japan is an inspiring example for other nations in the region. It is, as Edwin O. Reischauer observed, "the one great extension of democracy the world has witnessed since the end of World War II. . . . Here, before the war, a shallowly-rooted, incomplete democratic system withered under the hot sun of militaristic nationalism. But now this new world giant is a flourishing, smoothly-operating democratic system ardently supported by virtually the whole nation."[7]

Although America helped Japan make this democratic transition, it would be an injustice to the dedicated efforts of the Japanese people to suggest that democracy in their nation is simply a "Western import." Nobody expects democracy in Asian countries to look exactly like democracy in the United States, Britain, or France. We need to be respectful of the different historical, political, and cultural realities in Asia. But we must also insist on our right to speak and be heard where our interests and values are involved.

For this reason, America must not mute its advocacy of human rights and democracy, despite suggestions that Asians do not want to hear about it. Tying human-rights policies to most-favored-nation trade status (recently changed by legislation to be called "normal trading relations") proved to be ineffective, even counterproductive, with China. But Americans should not "overlearn" the lesson from that experience.

Our message is not that everyone must copy the American system, but that there is abundant international authority to speak up for fundamental human rights. There is no "Asian ethic" that rejects such values, as is apparent when we observe the popular support for human rights in Japan, South Korea, Hong Kong, the Philippines, and elsewhere in the region.

In almost no other way does America reflect its uniqueness more than in the pursuit of human rights. No one can say that we do it for money or power. We do it because we want human beings to be fairly treated—wherever they may live. The espousal of human rights is a noble purpose reflecting the deepest instincts of the American people. History has already vindicated this support of human rights worldwide. We need only ask Nelson Mandela and the people of South Africa, or the citizens of the Philip-pines, or the people of Russia and eastern Europe, or the Argentinians and Chileans, or Aung San Suu Kyi, the Nobel Prize–winning woman who has long been confined under house arrest for trying to promote democracy in Burma. We need only ask them and millions of others yearning for freedom if they wish America's voice to be heard on behalf of human liberty. They have all made their support clear.

Much of America's strength and vitality as a society and an economy is to be found in our enduring dedication to individual freedom, opportunity, and openness and the accountability imposed on our leaders and institu-tions by democratic processes and the rule of law. But Americans also need to be careful about arrogance and complacency.

How America conducts itself will influence how people in Asia view the legitimacy and value of democratic freedom. People throughout Asia closely observe what happens in America. They read and hear about us daily. The American example of individual liberty under law has been spectacularly successful. Many Asians will grant much of this. But they are dismayed by the spectacle of violence in America. They look at it all—from the daily cata-log of murders to the wanton use of guns to the Oklahoma City bombing. Young people in Japan and throughout Asia are attracted to the United States. Many want to come to the United States to visit, study, or work. But they often express fear about coming here and are deeply troubled by a nation that permits violence of a kind unknown in their own countries.

The critics of America—and of democracy—have a field day with this. When I was in Japan, the rape of the Okinawa schoolgirl did enormous harm to our relationship with Japan. Shortly before I arrived in Japan as ambas-sador, a bright young Japanese high school exchange student had been shot to death in Louisiana while trick-or-treating on Halloween with a friend. Then in the spring of 1994, two Japanese college students were gunned down in a Los Angeles parking lot.

Increasingly, it is the youngest in America who are victims of the vio-lence. It has been reported that nearly three-quarters of all the murders of children in the industrialized world occur in America. As a result, violence in America is no longer solely a domestic scandal. It has become a direct assault on the moral authority of the United States. It gives aid and comfort to those anywhere in the world who oppose freedom and promote tyranny.

The United States carried a similar burden in the 1950s. I remember how propagandists for the Soviet Union would point to racial discrim-ination in America. They demanded to know how Americans could speak for the liberty of others when they denied basic rights to millions of Ameri-ca's own citizens. The civil-rights movement, with the legislative and legal revolution it helped to produce, enabled Americans to remove this national dishonor.

Likewise, Americans must now respond to the epidemic of violence in our midst—not only for the good of the nation, but for all humanity. This may not be a traditional foreign-policy issue, but it has enormous implications for American influence abroad. Perceptions about crime, violence, and the wanton availability of guns in America badly damage our credibility with the Japanese and others in Asia—indeed, the very validity and attractiveness of our nation. This widely held perception that America is unsafe and falling apart as a society seriously impairs our ability to lead worldwide. Just as with civil rights a generation ago, this is not only a domestic issue for Americans. It is a growing impediment to American leadership in the world.

America's moral authority is a priceless asset that we must protect and use with care if we wish our ideals and values to inspire people throughout the world.

Toward Greater Intellectual and Cultural Understanding

A fourth question facing the United States is the need to expand our intellectual and cultural understanding of Japan and the rest of Asia—and the need to build greater human and institutional connections across the Pacific.

In the last half century, the bonds between the United States and Japan have expanded substantially. At the grassroots level, Americans and Japanese now have a broad base of successful relationships—not only academic and cultural, but also scientific, political, and economic. Nonetheless, the reality of our interdependence has outpaced our mutual understanding as people. Language, distance, cultural differences, and some insularity in each of our countries interfere with communication. There is still a broad gap to be found in our societies between the importance of the U.S.-Japan relationship and the level of knowledge and scholarship underpinning it.

I returned to the United States from Japan convinced that one of the most important things the American people need is a deeper understanding of Japan's importance to America and to our future. So much flows from this relationship—our economic prosperity, our security, and our ability to meet global challenges.

America and Japan are both modern, prosperous, democratic countries. But we also remain profoundly different societies. Many Americans admire Japan's wonderful qualities: the rich history and ancient culture; the highly educated, industrious people; the social stability, spirit of cooperation, and absence of violent crime; and the nation's impressive technological and economic achievements.

Inevitably, there are also features of Japanese society that Americans find difficult to comprehend because they are so different from our own experience. There are, for example, the cultural homogeneity and insularity; the priority attached to group over individual rights; and an economic system which tends to favor producers over consumers.

There is no doubt that Japan remains a very different society from the

United States and other Western nations. These differences often cause misunderstandings on both sides.

The American image of Japan sometimes oscillates from one extreme to another. One day many Americans see Japan as an economic miracle, with some even fearing it as an economic juggernaut that threatens our national security. The next day many Americans see Japan as an economic basket case, while they shout triumphant about the American economy. Or one day we see Japan as an exotic realm of cultural mysteries—with tea ceremonies and Shinto shrines. The next day we see Japan as basically "just like us"—with McDonald's and the Winter Olympics.

Americans need to be careful about slipping into these extremes, through which we project our own wishes or fears onto Japan rather than trying to see the nation and the people on their own terms. Over the long term, personal contact—especially by young people through educational exchanges—will help to reduce these misunderstandings.

Fortunately, the number of Americans studying overseas has been growing steadily—almost doubling in the past decade. But the large number of international students who come to the United States every year still dwarf this number. According to the Institute of International Education, nearly a half million international students attend American colleges and universities. By contrast, fewer than 100,000 Americans study overseas each year.

The disparity is especially stark in American exchanges across the Pacific. Asia sends more than half of all the international students currently in American colleges and universities. Japan alone sends more than 45,000 young people each year to study in the United States. The problem is that the United States still sends only about 2,000 American students to Japan—and fewer than 6,000 to *all* of Asia. This total is just one-tenth the number of American students who go to Europe each year.[8]

This disparity is worrisome. America's single best hope in the long term is for young people to travel, to live and learn, and to become friends with their peers in Japan and elsewhere in Asia. The United States still needs to do a much better job of reaching across the Pacific—building the intellectual, educational, and cultural bridges necessary for the future vitality of its relationship with Japan and the other nations of Asia.

Since the end of World War II, under the Fulbright and other programs, the U.S. government has helped thousands of Japanese to study in the United States. These programs have proved to be among our wisest investments, and the graduates have gone on to become leaders in Japanese society and have formed a core of solid support for our overall relationship.

Likewise, our two nations have a shared interest in increasing the number of young Americans who travel to Japan. As former U.S. Senator William Fulbright once said, "Educational exchange can turn nations into people, contributing as no other form of communication can to the humanizing of international relations."[9]

Historically, the United States has thought of itself more as an Atlantic nation than an Asia-Pacific nation. Although this self-image is beginning to change, it still lags behind the profound changes that have taken place in Japan and throughout Asia in the past fifty years. Therefore, additional efforts must be made to promote greater understanding among Americans about the Asia-Pacific and our stake in the region.

The answers to these four questions about Asia's future—on economic openness, regional security, democratic development, and cultural understanding—will have much to say about the future of the United States.

Understandably, the hard work of diplomacy often focuses attention on the daily list of compelling problems, with attention distracted from long-term planning. But we must learn to look down the road ten and twenty years. If we do more of this strategic thinking, we will be better prepared to lead the Asia-Pacific region toward becoming a model of peace, stability, and prosperity.

The United States is now in the unique position of being the world's only military superpower; the world's most open, largest, and most productive economy; one of the world's most stable democracies; and above all, the nation to which the world looks for leadership—leadership across a broad range of security, economic, and political concerns, as well as leadership to advance the cause of human liberty, social justice, and human progress.

Even with the recent Asian financial crisis, America's future remains in the Asia-Pacific region. This fundamental reality means that our future depends on the continuing success of our partnership with Japan. The United States is essential to Japanese interests; Japan is essential to American interests; and together, our two nations are essential to the interests of the Asia-Pacific.

The United States and Japan cannot build the kind of world we want in the twenty-first century unless our two countries cooperate across the full range of issues we face. The foundation of this cooperation has been carefully built up during the past fifty years and it remains solid, with the leadership in both countries committed to enhancing our ties. If the United States and Japan can work together, then practically every problem in Asia and the world will get better or, at least, become much easier to handle. But if our relationship deteriorates, then every one of these problems will get worse or become that much harder, even impossible, to solve.

As we move into the next century, it is reassuring to know that the U.S.-Japan relationship—the most important on earth—is solid and productive. Working with Japan and our other neighbors in the region, the United States can help lead the way in building new levels of security, prosperity, and freedom for Asia and for the world.

Francis J. McNeil

To paraphrase late Speaker of the House Tip O'Neill, all international relations are local, and the American people have a pretty big stake in what is going on in the rest of the world. There is no region about which this is more true than the Pacific. Seven or eight years ago, the only country in Asia that mattered to American elites was Japan. We were worrying about the trade deficit and about the Gulf War. All these things were proper issues to talk about. But in all those years there was more to Asia than Japan. I owe Paul Volcker, whom I had the honor to work with on Japan, for the wisdom to see that Americans and Japanese alike had to consider the U.S.-Japan relationship in a larger context.

In fact, after experimenting with a single-minded focus on trade with Japan during the last part of the Bush administration and the first Clinton administration, the United States and Japan at last began to deal with each other in a wider Pacific and global context. There will continue to be economic frictions, including the prospect of an increasing trade deficit, but we have to put all the economic issues in a proper framework. With that in mind, I would like to highlight four matters and then address each of them briefly.

The first is that the United States is a "pendulum country." Does anyone today remember Nicaragua? I do, but for reasons not relevant here. Our interest shifts intensely toward one problem in one part of the world and all but loses focus on other places. We swing wildly from one issue to another.

Second, just as there was more to Asia than Japan, today there is more to Asia than China. I will assert, and others may disagree, that in point of fact the United States cannot deal intelligently with China, nor can China deal intelligently with America, without placing the relationship in a larger Pacific and global framework. A narrow focus on bilateral relations with China is a recipe for permanent neurosis and could become dangerous in the years ahead. Since there is more to Asia than China, let us talk about Japan.

I have lived for ten years in Japan and used to speak the language well. I first went there in 1957 when it was still struggling out of the ashes of the war. I last lived there after teaching international relations in a graduate school in northern Japan in the spring of 1996. Japan today still occupies 60 percent of Asia's gross domestic product (GDP), and its economy is seven times larger than China's. Japan is the world's second-largest economy, even in times of stagnation.

Japan is also America's most reliable long standing ally in Asia. I say *reliable* in the political sense. I do not want to downgrade the difficulties we have had with opening Japanese markets and making economic institutions more transparent, or the feeling among the Japanese that we have pressed them on the wrong issues. We have to get used to disagreement. But in a political sense, Japan has been a very reliable ally from the 1960s, when it first had international choices. Previously, it did not, obviously, in the shadow of the occupation.

There is also Southeast Asia to think about. I just got back from three weeks in Southeast Asia, starting in Vietnam in the north and ending south of the equator in Indonesia. I do not see how the United States (or China, for that matter) can craft intelligent Pacific policies without taking into account the dynamism, the structural difficulties, and the long-term potential for contributing to a Pacific century (i.e., the twenty-first century) that Southeast Asia has.

Then there is Korea. Some of you must have seen the latest guesstimates about the number of people who have died or are starving in North Korea. Pyongyang, at this moment, probably is the single largest challenge to American foreign policy. And it involves, very directly, a trilateral relationship among the United States, China, and Japan. Korea is not an issue that can be handled in isolation. I will assert that this applies to most issues that the United States is dealing with in Asia today, especially the economy.

The third point—having said that we are a pendulum country and now we are overfocused on China, as we were previously overfocused on Japan, and that there is more to Asia than China—is that we need a new structure of peace for the region. As Henry Kissinger argues, we need a new structure of peace in the post–cold war Pacific to replace that which died with the cold war. You can call this a new balance of power, but it is a peaceful balance and a durable balance that we seek. In that context, a close relationship between Japan and the United States is indispensable and will remain so.

The fourth point is that the United States needs to pursue a policy of engagement, not only with China, but with the rest of the Pacific. I would remind you that there is a school of thought in the United States, as David Gergen indicates in his chapter, that suggests that retrenchment is the preferred strategy for the United States. Simply articulating the word *engagement* as a mantra will not suffice if we are going to continue to remain part of the Pacific economically and politically. So the elites that Gergen speaks of so eloquently are going to have to do a better job of explaining to average American citizens why it is important for their future prosperity and their safety for the United States to retain a strong position of engagement, including, I will assert, a substantial military presence in support of building this structure of peace I have spoken about.

We ought to look—and I hope our Chinese friends will look—at the continuing military presence of the United States in the western Pacific as a reasonable hedging strategy, not some sort of "containment," an irrepeatable phenomena which was applicable to a singular period of world history, the long twilight struggle with the Soviet Union. I assert, and so do many Asians, that the American military presence in Japan and the naval presence deployed elsewhere in the Pacific are, in fact, a force for peace and stability. I know that the Chinese government disagrees with that position. But in point of fact from the perspective of the United States and Japan and most Asia countries, and perhaps eventually China, a structure of peace must include military understandings and confidence-building measures designed to keep the Pacific a peaceful place.

Let me turn to Japan per se. The images of Japan, as you can imagine, have changed a great deal during my short lifetime. Shortly before I arrived there for the first time, Japan's image was wreathed in swords. In the late 1950s and the 1960s one might say it was wreathed in chrysanthemums, and then more recently in Toyotas. For many Americans, Japan had become a state of mind. I fear that China has, too.

Fortunately, I think Japan has now become a real country in American eyes. I am happy to see that. There were years of bizarre transpacific discourse. For example, a book called *The Coming War with Japan,* written by two American academics, pretended to describe a future war with Japan, which was in fact a rerun of 1941. This sort of froth commanded attention during the highest point of the trade tensions. There were similar books in Japan.

Now, the governing concept for relations between Japan and the United States for the next few years is likely to be rather prosaic, in the absence of an explosion on the Korean Peninsula. The focus will be on managing the relationship in its economic and political dimensions—and it will be punctuated by flare-ups over economic and trade issues. But I would argue that there is enough real work, contentious, irritating, and important, in dealing pragmatically with these economic matters and with fleshing out new security arrangements described under the rubric of the Guidelines for Cooperation and Security Emergencies Between Japan and the United States.

In these vital matters, there is work enough for intelligent people without moving to the recommendations from members of the "theory class"—notably some analysts in Washington, New York, and certain academic centers—who are advising the United States government and publishing in intellectual journals that the U.S.-Japan security relationship must be fixed immediately. If it ain't broke, don't fix it! No president is going to casually launch off into an unknown new relationship even if it is argued by self-described brilliant minds of the century. We have something that works reasonably well, is good for the United States and, currently, in Japanese eyes, is good for Japan.

Finally, I want to make a point about militarism. It is true, of course, that Japan has not come to terms with what it did in World War II in the way that Germany has. On the other hand, the Japanese people are recognized in Southeast Asia and elsewhere as being of a peaceful temperament.

It is interesting to pose a question about whether Southeast Asians see Japan as a threat. From Hanoi in the north to Jakarta in the south, uniformly the answer I have heard was "no," but only so long *as there is a close political and security tie with the United States.* That is a useful thing to keep in mind.

I do not know if the Japanese are going to change their constitution with respect to defense and their armed forces. I think it is their business.

I will make a final point, which is very important if you believe, as I do, that it is vital to maintain as an element of our Pacific security a strong relationship with Japan, to maintain with Japan a civil argument (dialogue) over economic issues, to cooperate in such matters as the environment and scientific investigation, and to work together in the United Nations context. If you believe these are important, then it is also incumbent on the United States government to pay a great deal of attention to the size of the American military footprint in Japan.

That is going to be particularly true after peace comes to Korea, as I assume it will in some manner in the next ten years, perhaps sooner than we think. Right now, we occupy a large part of land on Okinawa—about 20 percent of the land area. Much of that land is not useful for anything else, but it is necessary for the United States and Japan together to pay more attention to reducing the footprint to that which is necessary.

It is a rather orthodox view that I have presented here in most respects. I end on an unorthodox note by saying that surprise is going to be with us during the next ten years. There are going to be discontinuities and there will be a need for institutional change in Asia. My sense is that Asian countries need and do not have a "just-in-time" system for delivering institutional change. Almost all these countries are going through or will go through major political change. One of the important effects of this that we are beginning to see, fortunately, is the end of the recent argument about "Asian values," "clash of civilizations," and "the end of history." As soon as that strange argument dies, we will all be better off.

NOTES

1. C. Fred Bergsten, *Statement before the Subcommittee on Trade, Committee on Ways and Means, U.S. House of Representatives (*Washington, D.C.: Institute for International Economics, 1998).

2. Daniel Okimoto, *The Japan-American Security Alliance: Prospects for the Twenty-first Century (*Stanford, California: Asia/Pacific Research Center, 1998), p. 3.

3. Daniel Yergin, Dennis Eklof, and Jefferson Edwards, "Fueling Asia's Recovery," *Foreign Affairs (*March/April 1998), 34-35.

4. Kent Calder, *Pacific Defense: Arms, Energy and America's Future in Asia* (New York: William Morrow and Co., 1996), p. 43.

5. Lee Kuan Yew, "Democracy and Growth: Voting is Good for You," *The Economist,* 17 August 1994.

6. William Safire, "Gravy Trains Don't Run on Time," *New York Times,* 19 January 1998.

7. Edwin O. Reischauer, *The Japanese Today: Change and Continuity* (Cambridge, Massachusetts: Harvard University Press, 1988), p. 289.

8. Todd Davis, ed., *Open Doors 1996-97* (New York: Institute of International Education, 1997).

9. J. William Fulbright, *The Price of Empire* (New York: Pantheon Books, 1989), p. 205.

Chapter 6

Asia-Pacific: Looking to the Twenty-first Century

Robert A. Scalapino

All transitional eras harbor paradoxes, and ours is no exception. This is a time when almost everywhere, individuals have a greater opportunity to know more about the world in which we live. The informational revolution is still unfolding in an awesome fashion; mobility has never been more extensive; and cultural infusion is universal. Yet rarely in recent times have individuals been concentrating so intensely on those "close-in" issues such as livelihood, crime, congestion, education for their children, and similar concerns involving everyday life. For the overwhelming majority, foreign relations are a very secondary, spasmodic concern.

This situation is understandable given the all-encompassing revolution into which we have been thrust, but it is the responsibility of leaders to constantly reiterate the fact that foreign and domestic issues are inextricably intertwined. None of us can be secure in a chaotic regional or global environment; all of us are neighbors in an ever-shrinking globe.

Another seeming paradox with special relevance to Asia-Pacific is now in evidence. Generally speaking, this region has been characterized by economic dynamism despite the current crisis, a crisis caused by excessive exuberance and tightly knit govermental-financial-industrial relations marked by favoritism, corruption, and lack of transparency. Nevertheless, no region in the world has shown such strong growth rates in recent decades. On the political front, however, fragility has been commonplace. Asian cultures are old, but Asian political institutions are relatively new, at least in formal terms, and are still being tested and amended. Can economic dynamism be regained if political fragility continues?

There are two further generalizations that warrant attention. One is widely recognized, namely, the fact that economics dominates both the domestic and international stage today. Virtually all political leaders are dedicated to economic development, and equally important, they are dependent on it for their legitimacy. Governments rise or fall in accordance with the economic fortunes of their people, and in the day-to-day relations between and among nations, economic issues generally take precedence over all else. In this period of economic uncertainty, especially in Asia, these facts are all the more important.

A second broad trend is less well recognized. Today, we are witnessing the simultaneous rise of three somewhat conflictual forces: international-ism, nationalism, and communalism. The accelerating growth of interna-tionalism is strongly in evidence in all parts of Asia-Pacific, both in institu-tional and noninstitutional forms. In the past thirty years, we have seen the emergence of the Association of Southeast Asian Nations (ASEAN), on a broader front, the Asia-Pacific Economic Cooperation forum (APEC), and most recently, at the global level, the World Trade Organization (WTO).

At the noninstitutional level, perhaps more important developments have occurred. In recent decades, we have witnessed the emergence throughout Asia of natural economic territories (NETs), economic entities cutting across political boundaries, combining resources, manpower, capi-tal, technology, and managerial skills to optimal advantage. NETs testify to the importance of economic interaction among regions at different levels of development, with different assets to offer and needs to be met, under con-ditions of geographic proximity and, often, cultural compatibility. Hong Kong–Guangdong province of China, Taiwan-Fujian and, more recently, South Korea–Shandong province are but a few examples of a phenomenon that is rapidly spreading throughout the region, based on solid economic logic.

Similarly, we witness the rising international flow of capital and, with it, technology, and the internationalization of various economies such as that of Japan. An increasing number of products have multiple sources of origin. Intra-regional trade and investment, moreover, have reached major proportions, making the quest for an open regional trading system ever more important.

In the political-security realm, Asia-Pacific internationalism has pro-gressed more unevenly and less rapidly. There is no counterpart to NATO, nor is one likely in the near future. Continuing disputes and important polit-ical or developmental variations stand as barriers. However, the ASEAN Regional Forum (ARF), involving some twenty-one participants at present, is a useful mechanism for discussion, with leaders exchanging views and crucial issues brought forward for examination. Moreover, advances with respect to confidence-building measures (CBMs) in the security realm and progress on specific issues are generally moving through less formal chan-nels. A growing number of treaties and understandings on such matters as chemical weaponry, nonnuclear zones, and safety at sea are also being reached. In addition, in an effort to reduce or prevent conflict, ad hoc coali-tions have been formed among states having a perceived national interest in a given problem. The intensive discussions among the United States, Japan, China, and the two Koreas over the thorny issues of the Korean Peninsula are a prominent example.

Bilateralism will remain a prominent factor in international relations, and on occasion, when national interests are considered vitally involved, unilateralism as well. But the broad trend is toward multilateralism in vari-ous forms, and that too signals the rise of internationalism in this era.

Yet at the same time, nationalism is again in ascendance, as is patently clear in virtually all parts of the Asia-Pacific region. In some cases, heightened nationalism may serve as a partial substitute for ideology—now in steep decline—as a means of cementing allegiance and loyalty to the state. It may also be a product of pride in the success of rapid growth, yet with a residue of insecurity or resentment over past treatment, or in other cases (among them, the United States) a feeling that costs and risks are now unequally apportioned. Whatever its roots, nationalism is a powerful force in the contemporary Asian scene, benign in some cases, militant in others, and certain to play an important role in the politics of the coming century.

A third force, that of communalism, also shows no signs of decline. When individuals' moorings are threatened by continuous, rapid socioeconomic change, when their values and lifestyle are shaken, it is natural to search for a closer, more meaningful community. This may take the form of stronger ethnic consciousness; a renewed affiliation to religion, especially fundamentalist religion; or more intensive identification with one's particular locality. These are all powerful influences on Asian-Pacific politics today, and they will remain so.

The capacity to balance these three forces, reducing the conflicts among and between them, will play a key role in determining our chances for a more harmonious global order in the coming century.

Let me now turn to the principal Asian-Pacific nations, exploring briefly their key strengths and weaknesses, and their prospective role in the decades ahead. It is appropriate to commence with China because the future of this huge nation will impact the entire region. At present, China is approaching a population of 1.3 billion people, with the prospect for steady increases to at least 1.6 billion before the middle of the next century. The rising needs for energy, food, and water will constitute a challenge not only for the Chinese but for others as well. Environmental degradation is an interrelated problem. If technology is to be harnessed to these tasks, vast sums of money will be required, along with an army of technical experts.

To draw up a balance sheet on China's strengths and weaknesses is a difficult but necessary assignment if one wishes to contemplate Asia's future. On the positive side, the economic reforms that have been under way for nearly two decades have resulted in growth rates averaging about 10 percent per annum, with inflation increasingly under control, and an economy sufficiently attractive to induce rising amounts of foreign investment accompanied by the transfer of more advanced technology. The livelihood of hundreds of millions of Chinese has been improved, especially those living in eastern and coastal China.

The role of the market has been steadily enhanced and a higher degree of autonomy permitted for the various regions of this very diverse country. A new group of managers and entrepreneurs is emerging, along with an increasing number of technocrats in government, replacing the old ideologues. Moreover, the evidence strongly suggests that there can be no turning back to the old order.

On the other hand, many economic problems remain. China is still part socialist, and the state-owned enterprises are in deep trouble in many cases. They account for about 40 percent of productivity, and as many as half of them have been operating at a deficit. Outdated management, a surplus labor force, obsolescent equipment, and the production of redundant or unwanted items are the chief causes. Reform efforts have been under way for some years, but there are no easy answers. Management can be replaced with new types only gradually. To dismiss workers when the plant has been responsible not only for wages but also for housing, medical care, and children's education is to risk social disorder, although that risk is now being taken. A more adequate state social-security system is urgently needed. The capital for modernization is lacking, and coordination among and between plants is slight. The willingness to take bolder measures—including encouraging mergers, more privatization, and permission for bankruptcy—is growing, but the problems will not be resolved quickly or easily.

Another difficulty is the vast under- and unemployed rural work force. About 800 million Chinese are still village dwellers, and as many as 150 million of these have insufficient work opportunities. The expansion of township enterprises has been helpful, but even so, millions of rural people pour into China's towns and cities each year in search of at least temporary employment. Another aspect of the picture is the sizable gap between west China—still weakly developed—and east, or coastal, China where resources and efforts have been concentrated. Despite current exhortations to help the west, investors have responded cautiously, given infrastructural and other problems.

Corruption is another serious matter, omnipresent both at official and unofficial levels. We should be very cautious in advancing cultural generalizations, but one with a certain validity is this: After centuries of arduous effort and some continuing transgressions, Western politics is based essentially on legalism, whereas despite changes under way, Asian politics is based on reciprocity—"You do this for me, and I'll do that for you." The difference is profound.

Corruption bridges the economic and political realms. And other complexities are on the political front. On the positive side, the earlier concerns about the possibility of China disintegrating, prevalent especially during the Cultural Revolution, have subsided. This is a society that has shown a capacity to live with considerable turmoil. Further, the transition from the Maoist era appears to be advancing relatively smoothly. The military constitutes a significant interest group and an important political force. Yet current signs indicate that it is integrated into the party in such a manner as to inhibit separatism or any disposition to seize power.

However, several important political challenges face the party and government. First, can China move toward a more collective leadership and some type of institutionalized federalism? No all-powerful figures such as Mao or Deng loom on the horizon. The third and fourth generation of Communist leaders, now in authority, are better educated than their predecessors, more technologically inclined, and more experienced in urban administration, but none has the total political reach of Mao or Deng at his zenith. Thus, the trend toward a greater sharing of power must be preserved if recurrent factional struggles are to be prevented, despite the fact that collective authority runs against the grain of China's political traditions.

Equally important is the need for the construction of a federal system whereby power is officially allocated among center, region, province, and locality rather than constant fluctuations dependent on strong personalities. With development has come ever-greater diversity, and this fact must be recognized through system alteration.

Another challenge has potential regional as well as domestic implications. Despite valiant efforts by China's leaders to sustain ideological faith, the appeal of Marxism-Leninism has steadily waned. Materialism dominates the scene; citizens concentrate on making money and getting ahead. Various new slogans and themes are advanced in an effort to stem the tide, such as "socialism with Chinese characteristics." The strongest trend, however, is the revitalization of Chinese nationalism. Today, one again hears about China's "five thousand years of glorious history"; Confucius is being restored, and Sun Yat-sen is being elevated.

Not surprisingly, many of China's neighbors are wondering where the nationalist thrust will lead. Will another era of China as "the Middle Kingdom" ensue, with all others considered barbarians, good or bad, and treated accordingly? Will attitudes and policies on such issues as territorial disputes or economic controversies be conducive to compromise or militancy?

Renewed nationalism, combined with the drive for military modernization, has led some observers to define China as an inevitable future threat. In the opinion of this author, such a position is overly deterministic and takes insufficient account of certain new factors on the international stage. Clearly, China will have a greater military reach in several decades, although it will not approximate the power of the United States. Other Asian states, moreover, will also have advanced their military power, especially in defensive terms, although current economic problems will slow the pace of military modernization in some cases.

Equally important, the combination of continuing domestic challenges and growing interdependence, both economic and strategic, will constitute a strong inhibition against the resort to force. Today, China asserts that its priorities are firmly attached to development, that it intends to live by the five principles of peaceful coexistence, negotiating all issues and treating others as equals. It has made strenuous efforts in the recent past to improve its relations with every nearby state, with some success. On the other hand, numerous unresolved issues remain. With the United States, for example, economic concerns, human rights, weapon transfers and, above all, Taiwan continue to be divisive matters.

What are the appropriate policies for the United States and for China's other neighbors at this point? The dominant attitude should be "wait and see," avoiding any premature judgment and, meanwhile, adopting policies that seek the maximum involvement of China in a wide range of official and nonofficial dialogues and negotiations, bilateral and multilateral, encased whenever possible in a regularized, institutional structure.

Where does this China's future lie? Put succinctly, China in the twenty-first century will be a major power with major problems. In both economic and political-strategic terms, its impact on the Asia-Pacific region will be as great or greater than that of any other nation, including the United States. Economically, China will represent both an opportunity as a market and a source of major competition as an exporter of low-labor-cost goods. It is essential that those with whom China interacts press an evolution toward a more open market, with tariff and nontariff barriers reduced. There is reason to believe that despite recurrent cycles, China's overall economic progress will continue, and the market will play an ever more critical role.

In the political realm, the Leninist system will continue to undergo major alterations, but China will not move to democracy in the foreseeable future. The evolving system will be that of authoritarian-pluralism. Politics will remain constrained, with freedoms restricted in varying degrees. However, a civil society apart from the state will continue to emerge, with some degree of autonomy, and the economy will be mixed, with the market an increasingly key factor, as noted. In this manner, the effort will continue to be that of welding together stability and rapid development.

No one, including China's current leaders, can predict with certainty that nation's future role in the region and world. Amid the torrent of rhetoric currently heard, encouraging and pessimistic, one fact is clear: China is emerging from centuries of backwardness and defensiveness, and its voice will be more powerful. Thus, efforts must be made now to encourage a moderate, constructive role for China while retaining certain hedges in the form of balances—strategic as well as economic—if defenses should be necessary. The issue is not "engagement" versus "containment," but an intricate mixture—subject to change—of incentives and deterrents.

Turning next to Japan, we are again confronted with a complex picture, present and future. Measured against the conditions at the end of World War II, Japan stands out as a striking success story. Today, it is Asia's only global economic power, with remarkable growth rates in the past, yielding very high and relatively equitable living standards for its people. Indeed, some decades ago Japan became a model for other Asian developing societies. They widely copied mercantilist policies of state-managed planning and development and import substitution followed by export orientation.

Yet today, Japan stands as testimony to the fact that no economic strategy, however successful, is good for all time. If it is to continue to thrive, Japan must undertake far-reaching structural reforms, including deregulation, expanding its domestic market, and taking other measures to open up its economy. It must increase the flexibility of the system so that it can adjust to rapid changes, encourage innovation through expanded internal competition, and respond constructively to external pressures which otherwise will intensify.

Japan has paid a price also for a lack of financial discipline, a price now being exacted elsewhere in East Asia. The cozy relationship among the bureaucracy, the politicians, and the financial-industrial community has been conducive not only to corruption but also to serious economic overreach. The pledge of the Hashimoto government is that significant reforms will be carried out in the next five or six years—but there remains serious resistance rooted in the basic political-economic structure. Thus far, the alterations have failed to satisfy external observers and many Japanese as well.

On the political front, weakness continues to be a worrisome problem. In the early 1990s, the Liberal Democratic Party's dominance of national politics was challenged as the conservatives split. Coalition politics ensued. The so-called 1955 system had been based on a one-and-one-half-party operation, with one party always in power and all other parties continuously out of power. This system has been at least temporarily ended. Will it return, or will an alternative be established, either a genuine two-party system or continued coalition politics? At present, there are no strong parties—or leaders—although the LDP is not as weak and divided as others.

Whatever the outcome, Japanese politics is likely to be dominated by center-conservative forces despite modest gains for the Japan Communist Party, the only genuine opposition. Meanwhile, interest in politics among the electorate has declined and cynicism has risen sharply. As multiple scandals unfold, some of them engulfing such powerful agencies as the Ministry of Finance, the so-called party-bureaucratic-business iron triangle has been brought under growing pressure. Yet stability in the most fundamental sense does not seem threatened. Incrementalism, not upheaval, is likely to be the course.

Meanwhile, Japan will continue to wrestle with the question of its future role in Asia and in the world. Here too, nationalism is on the rise. Should not the patron-client relationship with the United States be modified? Is there not ample reason for Japan to have the same range of options—strategic as well as economic—as are available to other major nations? In sum, has the time not come to set aside the issue of past transgressions and restore to Japan the rights of a "normal nation"?

On the other hand, has Japan not benefited enormously from having had its security underwritten by the United States, thereby being relieved of the costs and risks of conflict, even of peacekeeping? Further, given the legacies of the past, how can Japan move upward in military power and strategic reach, taking on new responsibilities, without stimulating the embers of resentment and suspicion that still glow in the region, especially among Chinese and Koreans?

The probabilities are that the internal debate over Japanese foreign policy will intensify in the years ahead, with a more active policy gradually taking shape, but not necessarily one highlighting military power. Yet polls indicate that a majority of the Japanese people are willing to consider constitutional amendment to advance responsibilities in self-defense and military contributions to peacekeeping. Should an external enemy be perceived and should there be a U.S. retreat from its strategic commitments in Asia, including the security treaty with Japan, Japan's moves in these directions would unquestionably be accelerated.

Meanwhile, Japan's relations with its two immediate big neighbors—China and Russia—will continue to be of critical importance. Sino-Japanese relations, although likely to expand on the economic front, will remain complex, with cultural and political differences overlaid on specific problems such as that of the Senkaku (Diaoyu) Islands. In this relationship, history is no asset. And with China's rise will come ever closer Japanese scrutiny of its giant neighbor. Cooperation on certain issues is likely, but periodic tensions on other fronts are probable. Can the relationship be encased in a broader, multilateral framework, with a Northeast Asian Security Organization handling a wide range of outstanding issues, thereby softening bilateral problems? This is the broad direction required, and with the resolution or reduction of certain current controversies, it will come to pass, with only its timing in question.

Japan's future relations with Russia are also vitally important. With the restoration of Russia as a great power, an event that will take place in the early decades of the twenty-first century, this nation will again be a global player, with special interests in Central and Northeast Asia, the latter region critical to the Russian Far East. The basis for a close Japan-Russia relationship is limited, with a long history of enmity and great cultural differences. Yet accommodation with respect to the resources of the Kurils and the rich Siberian region is in the long-range interests of both nations. Through joint development, both can benefit, and recent trends are encouraging. Japan has pledged financial aid and investment to Moscow. Moreover, an agreement to seek a peace treaty between the two nations by the year 2000 has been reached.

As noted, current signs point to the likelihood that Japan will promote its interests internationally through economic and political activities. Its own economic health is intimately connected with that of the rest of East Asia, as its extensive investments make clear. On the political front, its role in advancing a formula for peace between the rival Cambodian factions of Hun Sen and Ranariddh—successful or not—is an illustration of the enhanced role that Japan intends to play in the region. Thus, it will put an ever-greater premium on multilateralism, but without abandoning its bilateral ties with the United States. It will also seek to maintain relationships with China and Russia that are, on balance, positive, looking toward the time when stronger, more institutionalized channels for decision making as well as dialogue exist, especially in the multilateral arena.

These activities do not signify an indifference to its strategic status. Japan will seek with increasing vigor to be accepted as a major state in regional and global councils. To achieve this status, it will take on additional strategic as well as economic and political responsibilities. Already, it has accepted an expanded interpretation of "areas in the vicinity of Japan" for which it is prepared to assume certain responsibilities. Many factors, however, including populational trends, will inhibit a unilateral, high-posture military stance.

Increasingly, Japan will take the lead with respect to environmental and resource issues, which are so vital to its interests. Given its resource needs, its aging process, and the memories of its past, Japan must count on being a team player, not a solo performer. It will seek to be part of several teams, partially overlapping, serving as funder, stimulant and, occasionally, mediator. Perhaps its greatest challenge will be to overcome those introverted, exclusive propensities innate to its homogeneous society and island status, and thus achieve true internationalism.

As noted earlier, Russia is destined to reenter the Asian scene more extensively in the decades ahead, especially in Northeast Asia. As President Boris Yeltsin once said, the Russian eagle has two heads, one pointing west, the other pointing east. Signs accumulate that the Russian economy is close to turning a corner, with productivity scheduled to rise soon, inflation curbed, and trade increasing. As time passes and events unfold, a reversion to Stalinist-type socialism seems increasingly improbable. The tasks will continue to be arduous, however, especially in regions such as the Russian Far East where the current signs are far from promising. A constructive economic relationship between center and region has not yet been rebuilt, and capital needs, along with a modernized infrastructure, are vital for this area.

Politically, the Russian scene is less certain. Will democracy, now so precariously positioned, survive? What leaders will emerge in the coming years? And how will Russian nationalism influence political decisions? The West has taken a major gamble in enlarging NATO, thereby potentially challenging Russia's urge for a protected buffer-state system. Can the compromise that brings Russia into dialogue with the new NATO hold? Or will events encourage that xenophobic nationalism recurrent in Russia's history at some point in the post-Yeltsin era?

Whatever Russia's relations with the West, its relationship with China is likely to be that of mutual accommodation, not alliance. The ideological glue is gone, the cultural differences are vast, and the major discrepancy in populations, especially with respect to the Russian Far East, will continue to underwrite Russian worries. However, good opportunities exist for enhanced economic ties and for confidence-building measures on the border, which have commenced.

Similarly, a Russian-Japanese alliance in the future is unthinkable, but as noted earlier, a mutually beneficial economic relationship is well within the range of possibility, along with agreements on a range of matters relating to nuclear waste, safety at sea, joint exploitation of resources, and similar issues. Within a few years, moreover, a formal peace treaty may be signed, with territorial issues resolved or set aside for the future.

Russia will remain a nuclear power second only to the United States, and at some point, it will begin the costly task of rebuilding morale and equipment in its military forces. It is thus essential that we push ahead with the START program, with multilateral CBM agreements, and with regularized dialogues, military as well as civilian.

Meanwhile, two issues continue to plague the security scene in East Asia—both involving divided states. One of these relates to the Korean Peninsula. It is widely assumed that Korea will be reunited at some point in the future, but when and how? Will it come quickly, through the collapse of North Korea, or slowly, as a result of a gradual evolutionary process? Will it come peacefully or through renewed conflict?

With the variables many and the data scarce, flat predictions regarding the future of the Koreas is very unwise. At least five scenarios for North Korea have some degree of plausibility: rapid collapse; gradual, irreversible decline with rising domestic tension; a hunkering down, with military dominance and minimum change; conflict; or an evolutionary process leading to peaceful unification at some point.

Rapid collapse does not seem likely at this time despite the huge economic problems and some signs of social unrest. The elite, with the military in priority positions, appears supportive of Kim Jong-Il, and there are no visible signs of rebellion at the mass level. Irreversible decline has a higher probability, and it could be dangerous if domestic struggles induced external involvements, thereby regionalizing the crisis. Hunkering down can be only a short-range option, given the environment around North Korea. The DPRK of the 1990s is not the Albania of the 1960s–1980s. Conflict is possible, but how often does an elite commit suicide on behalf of itself and its people (and such an action would be suicide, given the combined military power of the United States and the ROK)? Evolution is the one scenario that evokes greatest support from all outside nations, and although success certainly cannot be predicted, efforts in this direction are showing some signs of progress.

Meanwhile, South Korea has been facing its own problems, both economic and political. Overexpansion on the domestic front, combined with sweetheart political-corporation relations, created a financial-banking crisis that has proven costly. The ROK economy is still, on balance, a success story, and current problems do not appear to be system threatening, but a period of genuine pain lies ahead. As in Japan, fundamental reforms are now required if satisfactory growth is to be resumed.

South Korean democracy has made great strides in the past decade, and there is very little risk of a return to military coups and authoritarian régimes. Nonetheless, as in several other Asian societies, a gap exists between the democratic institutions and the authoritarian personalities at the political helm, or between formal and informal politics. Further, regionalism inside Korea remains a powerful factor, generally more important than issues.

The Republic of Korea serves to illustrate certain broad challenges to democracy in Asia and in the West as well. In addition to the need for a comprehensive, enforced legal structure, effective democracy demands that rights be accompanied by responsibilities. The right to govern must be protected as well as the right to oppose. The responsibilities of the civil society, moreover, are critical. For example, if the media engage mainly in promoting hype, a combination of cynicism and indifference on the part of the citizenry will rapidly grow. And money-politics born of the costs of elections and party maintenance can also induce progressive disillusionment. If these problems have plagued South Korea in recent times, they should also sound familiar to Americans.

Despite the difficulties, South Korean democracy will survive. The form of Korean reunification, however, can have a decisive effect on the nature of a new Korea. If some form of collapse occurs, the costs—both economic and political—will be huge, and the ROK will need assistance from key external sources. If the protracted decline of the North ensues or if conflict occurs, the risks of external involvement in addition to large-scale ROK military costs are real. Would China intervene if one faction in North Korea requested help? Would South Korea? How would massive migration be controlled?

In case of a conflict commenced by the North, it is questionable as to whether China would support Pyongyang, as it did in 1950. On the other hand, it would be enormously unhappy with a Seoul government on the Yalu River, across from a region heavily populated by Chinese Koreans.

In case of peaceful reunification, some form of federation might be feasible, at least in the initial stages, to ease the enormous economic and political differences between the two Koreas. Moreover, the thrust in the period ahead should be toward the creation of a commonly accepted peace agreement, progress through dialogue on all North-South issues, and the gradual strengthening of the North's economic relations with its immediate region as well as on a broader front.

With respect to Korea, a crisis could come soon. With respect to Taiwan, the time horizon is longer. China is not prepared to challenge Taiwan frontally in a military sense at present, both because of the severe economic and political costs of such action and because of the current status of its military force. However, it is also not prepared to accept an independent Taiwan, and on this issue, it refuses to pledge a nonuse of force. With Chinese nationalism strong, no leaders who gave up Taiwan could survive. Thus, the "one country, two systems" formula currently being applied to Hong Kong is offered as well to Taiwan. Indeed, it is Beijing's "final proposal," with "one China," at least in the past, being defined as the People's Republic of China.

The problem is that such a formula is not acceptable to the great majority of Taiwan citizens. Taiwan has not been a colony but a society with a separate government and socioeconomic system. Moreover, it has combined economic success with political openness in recent years, acquiring a favorable image in many quarters abroad. To add to the complications, the present government has actively sought to advance its role in the world by achieving membership in various international organizations; building stronger ties with many nations, informally if necessary; and continuing to modernize its military force. Taiwan's leaders have ranged far and wide, seeking to strengthen their contacts, often using economic instruments to that end.

To further complicate the picture, it is entirely possible that the Kuomintang, long in power in Taiwan, will lose control in the next few years to the Democratic Progressive Party (DPP). KMT internal factionalism, discontent over corruption, and uncertainties as to leadership make the governing party's position more precarious than it has been at any time in the post-1945 period. Should that occur, it might pose very complex problems for Beijing. However, the DPP has modified its initial stance of advocating legal independence. It now proposes a plebiscite on the issue and also asserts that because Taiwan is independent, there is no need to focus on this matter. Indeed, the positions of the KMT and DPP on the independence issue have come closer together in the recent past.

It remains to be seen whether some new formula can be advanced, such as that of confederation, with the matter of sovereignty set aside for the time being. Efforts to get semiofficial talks resumed have been stepped up recently, and the PRC may be prepared to leave "one China" undefined. It is clearly anxious to open a dialogue. Yet among the threats of the early twenty-first century, the Taiwan issue is likely to be the most dangerous. Unlike Korea, this issue produces tension among the major powers, notably, between the United States and China.

The future of Southeast Asia, taking into account the ten states that comprise this region, requires attention. In the economic sphere, the case for optimism over the long run can be made. Certain economic and social fundamentals are strong. Moreover, the current crisis is inducing corrective measures, and it is hoped that in addition to a stronger, more transparent economic order, a lesson regarding economic discipline will have been learned. The prospects are for a period of stress, then a resumption of growth, albeit at a lower level than in the past. Further, foreign investment will rise again in most parts of the region, and with it, opportunities for technological advances.

Corruption will continue to be a problem, and in some areas, wide disparities in income exist, especially between rural and urban citizens. Moreover, a few states such as Laos and Cambodia will be laggards because of a combination of economic and political reasons. As a whole, however, the ASEAN community will resume its economic advances well into the twenty-first century.

The political situation is more cloudy. Three basic political systems will probably continue to coexist. Two states—Vietnam and Laos—will define themselves as people's democracies—i.e., Communist. However, there, as in China, Leninism will slip downward despite efforts, and a gradual transformation into authoritarian-pluralism will take place. Indeed, it is already under way. Moreover, this system will characterize politics in Myanmar, Indonesia, Singapore, and possibly Cambodia for the foreseeable future. The Philippines, Thailand, and probably Malaysia will be democracies, with the strengths and imperfections of that system constantly being tested.

Ideological or systemic differences are less of a barrier to subregional discourse today than in the era of rigid Communist–non-Communist divisions, and that will be even more true in the decades ahead. Yet within ASEAN, consensus on certain issues is likely to be far more difficult than when that organization had six members rather than nine or ten.

Nonetheless, the new ASEAN has potent reasons for seeking to act as a unit with a maximum degree of solidarity. Only through a collective voice can it play the role it desires in East Asia and on the global terrain. And because it confronts several giants in its immediate vicinity—especially China—unity is of the essence.

As noted earlier, for the present, China is displaying a very accommodating demeanor, with numerous visits and pronouncements of the desire for a peaceful settlement of disputes. At the same time, periodic incidents have occurred, especially relating to the South China Sea atolls. ASEAN's best chance of keeping China in a conciliatory mood is to present a united front and to work through organizations such as APEC and ARF. A collective voice may also moderate U.S. pressures for quick action regarding economic liberalization or the advancement of human rights.

Southeast Asia will continue to face problems related to the heterogeneous and disparate nature of most societies in that region. Ethnic Chinese living in the area, for example, constitute only about 15 percent of the population, but they control as much as 85 percent of the economic productivity. Race relations in such countries as Indonesia are very delicate, as was demonstrated again in the 1998 protests. There are further divisions between hill people and valley people, long a source of conflict in Burma (Myanmar) and certain other countries. Yet none of these problems is likely to be régime threatening.

One cannot rule out the periodic breakdown of governments so highly dependent on leaders rather than institutions, Cambodia and Indonesia being recent examples. In the decades ahead, failed or failing states are far more likely to be the source of regional tension and conflict than major state confrontations.

A few final generalizations seem in order. First, Asia-Pacific will be a region critical to the global economy and to stability throughout most, if not all, of the twenty-first century, given the concentration of economic potential and the presence of four of the world's major nations (with India in a nearby position, also steadily increasing its reach).

The commanding issues of the future will shift from those centering on territorial control to those relating to survival in terms of resources and environmental conditions. Asia-Pacific, given its population and rate of growth, will again be central to these global concerns.

Agreements on a wide range of security matters are within reach, ranging from transparency and safety at sea to arms reduction, control of weapons of massive destruction, and weapon sales. The agreements will be partial, not complete, and compliance will remain a critical matter, but the next several decades will see progress on these fronts. Moreover, military strategies will continue to undergo radical changes, with the emphasis on information technology, theater missile defense systems, lift capacity, and rapid deployment. Close-in, permanent deployments by foreign (U.S.) forces will be less critical.

Nationalism—especially the type of militant nationalism that simultaneously supports xenophobia and isolationism on the one hand and aggressive attitudes and actions involving limited compromise on the other hand—will require constant surveillance and counteractive measures. This threat supplants the ideological cleavages of the past fifty years, and may be more difficult to confront and contain.

Cultural differences, however, will continue to be diluted as the informational revolution unfolds and mobility and affluence spread. No society will have a pure culture; rather, a huge range of cultural differences within every society will exist, some running along generational lines, others economic or subregional in character. Thus, the "clash of civilizations" is largely a myth.

Multilateralism in its many forms will continue to rise, but it will not supplant bilateralism. Further, the role of advanced scientific expertise will be enhanced as the issues involving our future center ever more deeply on highly technical factors.

Finally, the prospects for periods of domestic instability in many societies are strong, and most violence will stem from such conditions. We are not entering a period of universal stability and quietude. The most profound revolution in human history continues, and for leaders, the time to react is shortened even as the charisma once surrounding many of them is removed by the white-hot glare of an inquisitory media. Yet violence in the decades ahead is likely to be more local than regional. The prospects for avoiding a major-power or global conflict are very good as a result of a combination of factors: the massive destructiveness—hence, unwinnability—of such a conflict, the priority on domestic issues, the heightened interdependence, and the rising availability of alternate routes to dispute settlement. These combine to move us away from the global disasters of the past century.

Cautious optimism should thus be our mood, combined with heightened efforts to come abreast of the requirements that lie ahead.

Chapter 7

The United States and Asia: Commentary and Discussion

This chapter consists of answers to two questions posed to Ambassador Li Daoyu and Professor Zhou Dunren by participants in the University of Oklahoma foreign-policy conference of September 12–16, 1997. It also records the selected critiques and comments of OU professors who served as discussants at this conference for presentations on the status of the world.

Q: This question is for Ambassador Li Daoyu. I am a retired missionary, Southern Baptist. The *Reader's Digest* had an article about the global war on Christians, including one by China. The *Daily Oklahoman* had an editorial that we should shatter the silence and all speak out. I would appreciate Ambassador Li Daoyu addressing the matter of religious freedom and persecution in China.

Ambassador Li Daoyu

Yes, thank you very much. I think we need to do a lot to promote and reach an understanding between the Christian churches of China and the United States. I would like to invite you, your Adventist colleagues, and other Christian churches, especially the Southern Baptists, to China to talk with our religious people and to see what is really going on there. They will show you what they have achieved and, of course, they will not be totally content. They are making progress. You can critically exchange views. We need dialogue and not confrontation. Thank you.

Q: Do you see the United States during the next 100 years becoming a country—not unlike Singapore, Malaysia, Thailand, Indonesia—which has a large population of overseas Chinese that have worked their way up to political leadership, economic leadership?

Zhou Dunren

The United States is a nation of immigrants and is blessed by that. No matter what their ethnic backgrounds may be, all those citizens of this country are Americans. Americans of Asian extraction may not look like Caucasian Americans, but they think and act as Americans. This is especially true with the second and third generations of the immigrants. Sometimes, I even find them more American than the average Americans.

I just came from Washington, D.C., where there is an exhibition about the Japanese-Americans during the Second World War in the Museum of American History. Their loyalty to the United States and bravery in fighting against the Japanese militarists impressed me deeply. I myself am from China and have visited your country many times, and I see this is a great country, a country with great confidence in itself, and I see the melting pot working.

What if the United States were to have an American president or a secretary of state of Asian ethnic background? It should be no different from an American president who is female, black, or American Indian. That is the America that we from outside admire, and that is the America that Americans can be proud of. If one day the United States ceases to be able to deal with ethnic differences in skin, look, language, and food, this country, excuse me, would be in trouble domestically, and externally it would not command respect and admiration.

Mikael S. Adolphson

Obviously, there is no end to the many important insights that have been raised in the foregoing presentations on Asia. I would like to point out, however, that diplomacy is only one means of interaction. We must realize that we are not dealing only with foreign political and economic systems, but also and above all, with a foreign cultural system. Thus, we must focus more on a general change of perception, as Michel Oksenberg so perceptively noted.

We have many experts on Asian politics, economy, and history, but on another level, the general understanding of Asia's present cultural environment in the United States has in fact been so bad that it has caused severe problems in intercultural communication. To give you some examples, failures to establish lasting business relationships, poor political and economic negotiations, and the trend toward isolation here in the United States are all part of that poor understanding. In short, I would like to agree with Professor Zhou. They know a lot more about us than we know about them.

Very recently, the Institute of International Education published a report which provided some scary numbers pertaining to this cultural imbalance. Let me just give you some examples. In 1996, more than 40,000 Japanese students spent time here in the United States. We sent 2,000 to Japan, and that figure has not changed very much in the last five years. If you look at China it is even worse—40,000 Chinese here in the United States, as opposed to about 1,000 Americans in China. In addition, these exchanges are very different in character. Americans are usually satisfied with going for a couple of weeks or a couple of months, while Chinese and Japanese students spend at least a whole year over here.[1]

At the corporate level, the imbalance is very much the same. Many companies emphasize the importance of the global market. However, they have not put much effort into educating their own employees to enhance their understanding of the foreign markets and the foreign cultures, nor have they made enough contributions to a growing awareness in general of what East Asia is. By contrast, when Sony was still a small company in the 1950s, it made an effort to hire engineers with international experience in order to achieve its goal of becoming a competitive company in the international environment. I think we all know what happened to Sony and to the Japanese economy.

Unfortunately, our own government seems to be equally uninterested in improving our transnational competence. In his 1997 State of the Union Message, President Clinton focused heavily on education, but he did not say one word about our weak international curriculum. What is the problem here in the United States? It is clear that we have a number of experts who are very knowledgeable about their specific regions, but that is not enough. China and Japan are becoming very active and very competitive in the field of global science and technology, while the United States in fact is losing in that same area. Japan's share of the market has gone from 4 to 8 percent, whereas the United States has a diminishing share, going from 42 to 35 percent. What we need, in other words, is experts from other fields who are also masters of Asian culture and language. I would like to quote here former Senator Paul Simon, who said, "You can buy in any language, but you can only sell in the language of the consumer." To this insightful comment I would add that you can only sell with sufficient knowledge of the consumer's cultural setting and mind-set.

To conclude, we must learn to learn from other countries. We cannot do it in English only. If you do not speak the native language, they will only let you know what they want you to know. We need engineers, computer specialists, pharmacists, doctors, high school teachers, economists, and businesspeople who understand the cultural practices and languages of Japan, China, and all of Southeast Asia. The University of Oklahoma has taken some very important first steps toward correcting the educational imbalance with East Asia, thanks to the efforts of our international program and to President Boren. This is only a beginning and by no means enough. We need changes on the national level, and we need, above all, more resources to be able to accomplish our goal of achieving a higher level of transnational competence and of becoming more involved and competitive in Asia's cultures.

Marlan Downey

What I would like to do is briefly present my interest and my opinions about the economic growth of the Asia-Pacific region and most specifically about consequences to energy demand and national policy of the Asia-Pacific countries. Many of you are probably aware that it has been suggested that in twenty years, six of the ten largest economies of the world will be in the Asia-Pacific region, with China the largest. The consequences of that to the energy demands of the region are such that in present-day dollars there will be a transfer of about $250 billion a year from the Asia-Pacific into the Middle East. That is a lot of nickels. That transfer of energy for money requires a much closer relationship between those Middle Eastern producing countries and the Asia-Pacific area. The problem becomes the stability of those Middle Eastern countries (which we are accustomed to worry about), and the fact that there is an 8,500-mile sea lane—an avenue of energy transport—that Korea, Japan, and China will need to have protected. Much of the route is not over open ocean. Much of it is within easy flight from land, within easy attack by small ships. I merely pose a question: Who is going to continue to guarantee the safety of that transport lane for the next fifty years?

Edwin G. Corr

The presentations on the regions of the world in Parts I and II have been superb. The real challenge is how to take the concerns for each of the regions that have been discussed and put them into an overall, prioritized, coherent, and viable strategy that the American public is willing to support and pay for. This is a challenge the United States has been grappling with since the end of the cold war and for which the answer will emerge rather slowly.

In our search to create a much-needed new paradigm to guide our actions, I suggest to you that as we nostalgically look back on the policy of containment—and at the certainty and direction that paradigm seemed to give us—much of what is commonly presumed about the certainty and direction of containment is myth. The policy of containment was not fully accepted when George Kennan articulated it and President Harry Truman pronounced it in 1947. A few years later, it was debated strongly in the presidential election campaign of 1952, as Dwight Eisenhower and John Foster Dulles advocated the "rollback" of Communism, rather than containment. Acceptance of the policy of containment was forced in 1956 when the United States decided it was too risky to go to the rescue of rebelling Hungarians and other East European nationalists as they struggled to throw off the yoke of the Soviet Union. This consensus was short-lived. Containment policy was again attacked and questioned repeatedly during the seemingly endless ordeal of the Vietnam War. Afterward, the policy continued to show major fault lines, and it was only the collapse of the Soviet Union that forestalled a crisis over U.S. foreign policy.

Notwithstanding this caution about the degree of consensus on the policy of containment, it did give us an architecture for the conduct of foreign policy, and we do need to find a new paradigm or conceptual framework to help us cope with our international relations as we enter the twenty-first century. It is doubtful it will be as neat and simple as containment, which was predicated on the imminent threat of the Soviet Union and the Communist world to engage the United States in a nuclear holocaust, conventional war, and surrogate wars in the Third World. Today the world is not so dangerous but it is more complex.

As we seek a new paradigm, we should comprehend that no overall conceptual architecture can relieve our nation's president or senior foreign-policy decision makers from tough judgments. The policy of containment did not do so. Decision makers still must analyze the threat and the extent to which our national interests are at stake in particular ambiguous situations. They cannot escape the responsibility of judgments of whether conditions and possible consequences are such that the commitment of significant resources, intervention, and risking of our nation's youth are warranted.

This completes the review of the state of the world as we enter the twenty-first century. We now move, in Part III, to an examination of the component parts of foreign policy, prior to entertaining proposals of experts on a comprehensive foreign policy in Part VIII.

NOTE

1. *Towards Transnational Competence: Rethinking International Education,* a U.S.-Japan case study (New York: Institute for International Education, 1997).

PART III

The Military Challenge at the Beginning of the Twenty-first Century

Overview

Edwin G. Corr

We live in a time in which a number of our basic assumptions about geopolitics and military power have been rendered obsolete. In just a few short years the nature of the international system and the verities that shaped U.S. national purpose have undergone fundamental changes. The United States emerged a victor from the cold war, but success has undone more than one champion; and unlike the end of a game, having won the cold war has only made the playing field more crowded. The intellectual and political coherence of policies that saw stability, security, and peace as indivisible—and thus provided a sound foundation on which to plan, to structure requirements, to build campaign plans and force structures, and to sell to the public the need for sacrifice through taxes and service—ended when the cold war ended. The playing field, rules, and actors are more complex, and identifying the objectives of the game is more perplexing. Many new challenges at home and abroad now emerge, demanding immediate attention and action at a time when what we should do is unclear and when resources for foreign-affairs programs are constrained.

Perhaps the greatest threat to U.S. national security is the danger that we Americans do not change our thinking to coincide with the changes in the world around us. America's principal defense priority for more than forty years was the management of low-probability, high-intensity nuclear conflict, with a primary focus on Europe. Yet ironically, nearly all the armed conflicts during that time took place in the Third World and were classified as low intensity. With the exception of Korea and the tragic Vietnam experience—and in large part because of it—we Americans during the cold war were slow to adapt our thinking, organization, and resource allocations to high-probability, low-intensity conflict, in which our military's role is usually relatively small and indirect, and extraordinary support is required for civilian authorities in their development efforts. In the national-security establishment the planning focus has been on the high end of the conflict spectrum, while for some years U.S. forces have been increasingly engaged in military operations at the lower end of the conflict scale, such as peace operations, humanitarian and disaster assistance, and counternarcotics and antiterrorism operations. World leadership now and in the future depends on a different set of assets and resources than it did during the cold-war era of superpower confrontations. In the national-security establishment, policy makers are searching for new strategies.

One message is unmistakable. The end of the cold war–era conflict did not signal the end of all global conflict. Indeed, just the reverse is proving to be true. The absence of the relatively straightforward bipolar struggle left a power vacuum, an unstable environment, in which the potential for low-intensity conflicts and chaos is greater than ever before. Tribalism, extreme nationalism, religious fundamentalism, and holdover Marxist ideology all create situations in which governance is difficult and provide fodder for small-scale and internal wars. Perhaps most alarming is the threat of proliferation of weapons of mass destruction to rogue states and criminal groups.

Considerable form and structure, institutional habits, and ways of thought remain. Indeed, some people now long for the "good old days" when the enemy was obvious and the terms of reference simple. It is daunting, and at times overwhelming, to think about the nuances of a complex multipolar and partly anarchic world. U.S. policy makers must now consider which of the large number of potential and existing conflicts and chaotic situations warrant our attention. To what extent should the United States go to prevent proliferation of weapons of mass destruction? What criteria should be used in deciding whether to employ U.S. direct or indirect force in world-wide peacekeeping, insurgencies, and regional wars? How, as a great power, do we weigh our own narrow national interests against a broader responsibility to promote international order and stability? How much is chaos itself a threat? Our armed forces seem sometimes to be cast more as police and social workers than as soldiers.

We face a challenge to change perspectives. The definition of U.S. interests and power is clearly undergoing a fundamental transformation. This trend will continue unabated. We may be engaged for some years in sorting through the current bewildering world disorder in search of an organizing paradigm to assist us in clarifying our purposes and courses of action. In that process of sorting, the question of national security and defense is an essential component in shaping a new paradigm for the conduct of American foreign policy.[1] Senator Sam Nunn and Ambassador Robert Oakley, in chapters 8 and 9, respectively, help to clarify our thinking by defining and discussing threats and issues and setting forth our current thinking and preparation to meet threats to our national interests.

NOTE

1. For a greater elaboration of some of the themes mentioned in this overview, see:

(a) Edwin G. Corr, introduction and conclusion in Max G. Manwaring, ed., *Uncomfortable Wars: Toward a New Paradigm of Low Intensity Conflict* (Boulder, Colorado: Westview Press, 1991), pp. 1–5, 127–36.

(b) Edwin G. Corr and Stephen Sloan, eds., *Low-Intensity Conflict: Old Threats in a New World* (Boulder, Colorado: Westview Press, 1992).

(c) Edwin G. Corr, introduction in Max G. Manwaring, ed., *Gray Area Phenomena: Confronting the New World Disorder* (Boulder, Colorado: Westview Press, 1993), pp. xiii–xx.

(d) Max G. Manwaring and Edwin G. Corr, "Confronting the New World Disorder: A Legitimate Governance Theory of Engagement," in Max G. Manwaring and William J. Olson, eds., *Managing Contemporary Conflict: Pillars of Success* (Boulder, Colorado: Westview Press, 1997), pp. 31–48.

Chapter 8

Protecting and Defining our National Security in a Changed World

Sam Nunn

The emphasis these days is on defining. Defense policy is very difficult to define, and defense budgets today are difficult to relate fully to specific threats, because we are really dealing with the residue of the cold war. We are dealing with some severe hangovers from the cold war while living in new worlds of information, warfare, and cyberspace. We are now straddling more than one world, and it is very difficult to define precisely the threats that face our defense and national-security establishment.

During the cold war, we had a long period of very high risk. If there had been a war, it would have been a catastrophic event, with much of this country and much of the Soviet Union being destroyed. No one can really predict the effect of nuclear war on the environment and the planet. So the risk was very, very high. But stability was also very high because the risk was so high. Everyone knew that the stakes were enormous. Both the Soviet Union and the United States leadership understood that if there were a war between the two superpowers—or if there were a war between other countries that were our friends and proxies and it escalated up the ladder to a war between the superpowers—it could have been a disaster. So we had very high risk and very high stability.

Today the risk has gone down enormously. I think we have a better opportunity to have a peaceful and prosperous world than at any time during the whole history of our nation. Our young people have the best opportunity for peace and prosperity than any generation of Americans has had.

We have much lower risks, but we also have much lower stability, because we no longer have two superpowers with proxies of countries around the world that we control, furnish arms to, and basically influence. We have very little influence on so many countries in the world today, and there is no Soviet Union to restrain its "clients." So there is much lower risk with much lower stability. The world is more fragile in many ways because of ethnic and racial animosities.

Weapons of Mass Destruction

The risk for nuclear war is much lower, but the risk of a nuclear explosion or a chemical or biological attack has gone up. That is a real paradox and it is hard for us to understand. The Soviet empire collapsed with more than 30,000 nuclear weapons, 40,000 tons of chemical weapons, a very formidable arsenal of biological weapons, and tens of thousands of scientists and technologists who know how to make these weapons. At the same time these scientists cannot support their families during a very rough economic transition in Russia.

In 1996 I was in Moscow, where we had a briefing on the Nunn-Lugar Cooperative Threat Reduction Program. An American corporation, Hewlett Packard, was presenting a computer-technology seminar to those Russians responsible for maintaining the safety of their nuclear arsenal and nuclear weapons. A Russian colonel who had been taking part in the seminar told us how grateful he was that we were helping him because with this new technology, he could now understand in a matter of minutes or hours whether there was a missing nuclear weapon, whereas before it would have taken weeks or even months. After that discussion, which was very positive, I asked him, "How long has it been since you and your troops have been paid?" This is the man responsible for protecting nuclear weapons in Russia. He said it had been three months since anybody in his units had been paid. About two weeks after our visit, the head of a Russian nuclear city—one of the closed cities—committed suicide because he said he could not pay his people. The cities where they have their nuclear weapons and production have populations of approximately 100,000 people. Now that is the kind of world we are in today, and I think we have not yet fully comprehended that.

The aftermath of the Soviet Union's collapse is staggering. Fifteen independent states have emerged with no law-enforcement experience, no export-control régimes, and no real expertise in border control. Several civil wars have broken out and all sorts of racial and ethnic animosities exist in the region. In short, I believe preventing the spread of weapons of mass destruction—nuclear, chemical, biological, and the means to deliver those, including missiles—is the number-one national-security threat we face today, and it will be the number-one security threat for the next ten or twenty or perhaps even thirty years. You can label this nonproliferation or you can label it cleaning up the cold war, but nevertheless it is, I think, a fundamental security challenge that we do not focus on nearly enough.

We have had our warnings. No one can say we have not been warned. We have had the Twin Towers bombing in New York City. The trial judge there found there was a chemical component in the explosive that did not go off. If he is correct, we would have had our first chemical attack in the United States by terrorists. The people of Oklahoma, very courageously, lived through the terrible tragedy of the McVeigh bombing; and, of course, if there had been a chemical component in that, the tragedy would have been compounded many times over. And in Tokyo, we had the Aum Shinrikyo cult (which had never appeared on the screen of our intelligence community) that carried out an attack in downtown Tokyo intended to wipe out much of the Japanese government. They launched the attack before they had acquired a fully effective delivery means for their gas attack. They wounded some 15,000 people, but there would have been a much more horrible tragedy if it had happened a couple of months later.

This is clearly a series of warnings. What are we doing about it? We are doing a great deal, but not nearly enough. We have legislated the Cooperative Threat Reduction Program. It is also known as the Nunn-Lugar Program and should be called the Nunn-Lugar-Boren Program because Senator David Boren stood up on the floor of the Senate after the sentiment was overwhelmingly against that program and helped reverse, in a matter of about six weeks, overwhelming Senate opposition to the program. It was the most remarkable turnaround I have ever seen on a bill. We passed it in 1991. We have appropriated $400 million a year from the United States defense budget since that time (for a total of about $1.6 billion) to help the Russians and the citizens of other former Soviet Union countries to secure, safeguard, store, and destroy the most dangerous parts of their arsenals. There was a very slow start because of a lot of bureaucracy and distrust on both sides. The program is now rolling along with some staggering achievements, but it still has far, far to go.

The achievements: We have had a consolidation of all the nuclear weapons of the Soviet Union into Russia. Kazakhstan, Belarus, and Ukraine have all transferred their weapons to Russia—so instead of having four countries with their hands on the nuclear trigger, we only have one. We have seen the destruction of 3,800 nuclear warheads. We have seen the destruction of 276 submarine-launched missiles. We have seen the destruction of 597 ICBM silos and launchers. We have seen the destruction of fifty-three bombers.

We have also seen an unusual event in which the leaders of Kazakhstan informed us, very quietly, that they had discovered a large store of weapons-grade matériel, and they were worried about it leaking across the border and being sold to some of their southern neighbors, perhaps Iran or Iraq. The Kazakhis called on the United States to help. We used Nunn-Lugar funds to purchase that matériel and bring it to the United States, where it is now safely stored. We have also, very importantly, employed approximately 19,000 former Soviet weapon experts, scientists, and engineers who know how to make weapons of mass destruction and who are now engaged in constructive commercial endeavors. These are all achievements of the Nunn-Lugar Program.

What can we do about all this? One suggestion is to hire former Soviet weapon scientists to come to the United States to do constructive things. They could be from any of the former Soviet states. These people really are, in many cases, without a means to make a living. We had a great contest after World War II as to who was going to get the German scientists, whether it would be the Soviet Union or the United States. We got more of them than the Soviets did, and they had a lot to do with our weapons production during the cold war. There are countries all over the world that could constructively use these scientists now, and we need to give them gainful employment.

We also have passed legislation on the domestic side. This is known as Nunn-Lugar-Domenici II. In essence, without going into detail, it recognizes that our state and local "first responders"—policemen, firemen, health officials—are simply not prepared or equipped for possible chemical or biological terrorist attacks in this country. The legislation provides a pool of funds from the federal government to help our state and local officials, particularly fire departments, police departments, and health officials.

We have a formidable task in front of us. There is a pressing agenda of international issues we must address. We must strengthen the international nonproliferation régime. The tool to do that is the Nonproliferation Treaty. We also need to strengthen the organization known as the IAEA, the International Atomic Energy Agency. The IAEA provides the experts who inspect countries to make sure they are not developing nuclear weapons. We also need to strengthen the implementation of the missile-technology and -control régime. And we need to greatly improve intelligence gathering in this area, including our pattern of cooperation with foreign intelligence agencies. This is enormously important.

In summary, I visualize a tiered defense: (1) Safeguard the materials and the weapons at the source, if at all possible. That is the most efficient and most effective. (2) Help the former Soviet countries develop effective export and border controls. (3) Secure our home borders. We need to do a lot of research so we can recognize particularly when chemical and biological weapons are being imported into this country. (4) We must be able both to identify and protect our local governments and our own citizens against any attack here.

One quick example—you all remember when the bomb went off in Atlanta at the 1996 Olympic Games. We had the greatest array of chemical and biological specialists there that we have ever had in any American city—from every branch of the military service and from all of our intelligence and law-enforcement agencies. When that bomb went off, they had an extremely difficult decision to make. They had to decide whether to put on protective gear. Several hundred thousand people were cordoned off in downtown Atlanta. If the specialists had gone in with their protective gear on—which they had every justification to do, because they had no idea whether it was a chemical or biological explosion and they could not find that out for several hours—there might have been several hundred more people killed in the panic. You can imagine the fright of people had they seen these officials wearing chemical protective gear. Atlanta illustrates the need for early detection of these kinds of destructive devices in every city, and we have a long way to go to achieve that.

Regional Wars

Let me shift now from the threat of weapons of mass destruction to the threat of regional wars caused by rogue states. The Korean Peninsula is perhaps the last military challenge of the cold war. It is the place most likely to engage American land troops in warfare during the next few years. In late 1997 former U.S. ambassador to South Korea Jim Laney and I took a trip to North Korea. This trip was private, not official, but we had the encouragement and support of President Clinton and the National Security Council. It was brief, but we had intensive discussions. Our mission was to listen, to observe, to respond, and to report.

Just a few observations: The streets of Pyongyang, the capital, were deserted. It appeared more like a city of 200,000 than the city of 2,000,000 that it is. I saw nothing for sale. We rode all over the place. We did not see anyone buying anything or anyone eating anything—not one single person. I saw no visible starvation, but the people were clearly without energy. They were listless. And of course, the crops were very poor. The country had gone from floods to droughts. It looked as if the harvests had been devastated by droughts. We did not see a heavily armed group of military people, as we had anticipated. In fact, most of the military people we saw were out in the fields. I suspect most of the country's military power is on the border with South Korea.

We did not meet with Kim Jong-Il, who was then commander in chief and expected to succeed his father as president, which he did in 1998. He normally does not meet with foreign visitors. We had approximately thirteen hours of intensive discussions with three North Korean leaders. Let me briefly tell you what their message was to us, because this is indeed a very heavily armed, dangerous country. The North Korean officials said, number one, that they were grateful for our food aid. They said several times that they desperately need more. They are clearly seeking a large-scale U.S., Japanese, and South Korean food package. They also demanded that the United States lift economic sanctions. The United States did agree to lift economic sanctions when we signed the nuclear agreement getting North Koreans to pledge to curb its nuclear developments. Third, the North Koreans said over and over again, with a great deal of passion, that the South Korean government is illegitimate and that it is a puppet of the United States. North Korea's strategy is to isolate South Korea as a puppet and to talk directly to the United States. Fourth, they said that they had almost rejected but finally agreed to the four-party talks which President Clinton proposed among the United States, South Korea, China, and North Korea. They clearly are very puzzled about the Chinese role. They said repeatedly, "We see it as three against one." In their eyes China is more related to South Korea now than to North Korea because of the huge trade that has grown up recently between the two countries. Finally, they did pledge cooperation on clearing up questions on American prisoners of war from the Korean conflict.

They said several times, "We're ready for war." They did not say they wanted a war, but that they were ready. If there were war—and it would be an act of suicide on their part—we would clearly prevail, but hundreds of thousands of people would be killed. The North Koreans have eight or nine thousand artillery tubes buried in caves along their border looking down on the South Korean capital of Seoul, thirty miles away. Even employing our best military capability, it would take several weeks to dig them out. I asked the North Koreans to take us down to the subway. They have quite a subway system! We went down and down and down and down and down, 500 feet belowground. There is no telling how many military installations the North Koreans have underground. That is the kind of preparations they have been making for a long, long time. A war would likely cause huge devastation for both sides.

Is there a glimmer of hope? A cynic would say, with some justification, that to save themselves, the leaders of North Korea will continue to doom their people. But there is a glimmer of hope. They are willing to talk. They said they are ideologically wedded to their system and insisted that they will not make any basic changes, but they said they would make adjustments. They indicated that there could be a summit conference once there is a new South Korean election (which there has now been).

What was our message to the North Koreans? The number-one message I repeated over and over was that if there were a war—whether by accident or by miscalculation or by intent—the United States would stand with South Korea 100 percent, and the North Koreans should not have any illusions about that. Number two, in response to their statement that the sanctions should be lifted, we said to them clearly, yes, we did agree that the economic sanctions would be lifted on North Korea, but only if they agreed to have a dialogue with the South. We told them they had not carried out the agreement and, until they did, our recommendation to our government would be to not lift the sanctions. We told them that if they started talking to the South, if they had substantive discussions with the South, they would have carried out their pledge and we could carry out ours.

We said to them several times that there are two dangers on the Korean Peninsula. One danger they were acutely aware of was the economic deterioration and food shortages in the North. But there is also the second danger of war. And one of the reasons you have such a hard time economically, we told them, is because you have put all your money into your military, put all your forces right on the border to threaten the South Koreans. I said to them that we have to deal with both of those dangers at one time, not simply one at a time.

On food aid, we said to them, the American people do not want to see innocent people starve to death—particularly children and women. We have great sympathy for your citizens, your innocent people. And yes, we will help with food, but the American people's patience is finite. You have to change your structures or you will continue to have food shortages year after year.

We told them it is clear there are two roads. One is the old road—the road of huge military forces; trying to get your way by threat, intimidation, and terrorism; keeping a very large posture at the border, which threatens everyone on the Korean Peninsula; and generally causing isolation and hardship for your own people. That is one road you have tried, and it does not work. There is another road, a road of cooperation—reducing military presence at the borders; putting more money in your own economy rather than the military; and holding direct talks with South Korea. That new road can lead to the lifting of the sanctions and to trade and cooperation.

There is a long, long road ahead between now and the time we determine whether there can even possibly be a soft landing on the Korean Peninsula. There are a lot of different recommendations we made that I will not go into now. Suffice it to say that the cold war is not yet over on the Korean Peninsula, and it remains a dangerous place. The North Koreans are highly ideological, they are isolated, they are paranoid, they are hungry, and they are dangerous.

Cyberspace Warfare

I move now from the world of hangovers from the cold war to the world of cyberspace—two very different worlds, but our Defense Department and our intelligence agencies are caught between them. It is reconciliation of our national-security establishment and policies between these two worlds that is so difficult. I have been briefed time after time, as was David Boren in his position as chairman of the Senate Intelligence Committee—and many of you saw some of it on television during the Persian Gulf War—on what the United States can do to others in the world of information warfare.

We have fantastic capabilities. The United States is the best in the world in information warfare. There are all sorts of things we can do that are classified and will remain classified. After several of these briefings, I asked, "What can other people do to us in this age of information?" That is the side of the coin we have not thought about nearly enough. We must start thinking about it. We are much better at offense than we are at defense.

Our nation's infrastructure—all those key lifeblood components of our society—is increasingly involved in information and computer systems. By *infrastructure* I mean the lifeblood of our economy: the financial sector, the telecommunications sector, the energy sector of economy, the transportation sector of economy, the pipelines, water supplies, and emergency human services. These sectors are increasingly dependent on computers, computer technology, and networking, and they are increasingly interconnected. They are also increasingly vulnerable. The same things that are making us more efficient are making us more vulnerable to new kinds of attacks, and we have not yet started to concentrate adequately on that vulnerability. So we have a great blessing in the information age, but we also have an increase of dangers that we need to think about.

The infrastructure of a nation has always been a physical target in the case of war. We have always worried about saboteurs and spies. There is nothing new about that, but we must ask ourselves, "What is different today?" Why are we more concerned today than in the past about our infrastructure? Let me tell you a few things that give us concern. One, as stated, is that we are more interconnected. Our telecommunications depends on energy. Our transportation depends on telecommunications. Our finance depends on telecommunications. Even the defense of our nation—our ability to fight on the Korean Peninsula if a war should come, God forbid—depends on our telecommunications capability. Ninety-five percent of all defense information flows over open lines, only 5 percent over closed (coded or protected) lines of communication. That tells you a little bit about our dependence.

Why else are we worried? In the information age, our potential enemies' most lucrative targets are elements of our infrastructure, and they are also our most vulnerable targets. Moreover, for the first time, our most likely and vulnerable targets for terrorism and sabotage are owned principally by the private sector. Private-sector ownership is our strength. We do not want to change that. That is the reason we are more productive and have a stronger economy than any other country. Private-sector ownership of most of the infrastructure is what makes our system work, but we have to understand that the government has responsibilities along with the private sector to make sure our infrastructure is not disrupted.

The tools for distribution of information and the tools for its disruption are literally in the hands of millions and millions of people via the Internet. A whole series of hackers' pages on the Internet shows how to disrupt the basic communications that are so vital to our economy and our defense. All an enemy has to do is go to the hackers' pages to find the prescription for attack. So the lifeblood of our society, owned by private hands, is increasingly vulnerable. We are increasingly dependent on this infrastructure, and we are more dependent on it than any other nation in the world.

There are plenty of bad actors around. Among these are rogue states, terrorist groups, militias, disgruntled employees, hackers, and competitors who do not draw the line at the right places. The low risk of being caught for disrupting or even taking down a whole sector of our infrastructure is another reason we should worry. Moreover, even if the person is caught, the risk of being prosecuted is very low.

The question of how you deal with this, from a governmental point of view, is immensely complicated. Before it can be determined which U.S. agency has jurisdiction to investigate a violation, the culprit must be caught.

The problem is further compounded because the National Security Agency (NSA) does not have jurisdiction over any domestic crime.

Let me give you one example that happened in the mid-1990s. Two hackers in Great Britain seized control of a computer in Latvia. From that computer they seized control of a computer in the northwestern United States. From that computer they seized control of a computer in Chile. From Chile they captured control of a computer in Colombia. Then they hit and seized ultimate control of a computer at Rome Labs at Griffith Air Force Base in New York. From there, they launched attacks against and downloaded a huge amount of information from Goddard Space Center, U.S. military bases, a major defense contractor, and the South Korean atomic-energy laboratory. Two hackers did all this from Great Britain.

What do we do about it? The first thing we should do is meet the very serious challenge of getting all our computers adjusted to the year 2000. We ought to take advantage of this systemic and litigious problem to have every business ask: How can we improve our security while we are taking care of our year 2000 adjustment? The government has to get its own house in order. We need a set of standards within government. We do not have any now. We have to tell the U.S. government agencies to meet those standards and, if they are good standards, we need to share them with the private sector. The government-and-business partnership is absolutely essential. The encryption question is a source of great tension between the government and the private sector, and it must be solved in a spirit of partnership.

The government, in partnership with the private sector, needs to increase greatly its research and development in this area. We need a government–private sector partnership and information sharing. Currently, there is no trust on either side. Major competitive factors enter into this. Banks are reluctant to report on banking attacks. In one attack on Citibank, it lost several million dollars. Its competitor started to advertise that Citibank was not secure.

We have to have educational awareness, and we are going to have a different culture. All our young people and the rest of the world are going to have to understand that intellectual property is property. It is not simply out there. It is property. Everybody who has charge of a critical computer in the government or the private sector has to understand the importance of doing his job as a systems operator. We need intensive training for systems operators on the security side. In short, we are in a new paradigm in the information age, as some people would say. We know that the information age has changed our offensive warfare capability. We have not yet comprehended that it has changed the whole definition and framework of how we have to defend this nation. A twenty-three-year-old with a personal computer can do as much harm from his own living room today as hundreds of saboteurs and spies planted carefully around the country.

There are a lot of things we have to do. We have to update our laws because the old rules have changed and technology has gone far in front of our ability to deal with it. A single-agency or government-alone approach is not sufficient. We have to have a cooperative public-private partnership. Moreover, the old distinction between classified and unclassified information has to be reexamined, because tens of thousands of people without security clearances in the private sector are dealing every day with a lifeblood of our national security system. This is a huge challenge.

Questions and Discussion

Q: I was wondering if you happen to know if the Department of Defense was ever regretful of unleashing "Arponet" on the world?

Sam Nunn

No, I think overall that what we have done with the Internet is fantastic, but I want to put it into an overall framework. We have the greatest opportunity for spreading education, culture, knowledge, peace, and human values around the world than we have ever had. And the Department of Defense will be a beneficiary of that. But there are big challenges. The Internet is very fragile. We are more and more dependent on it, and most people do not yet understand it. A big challenge is that the CEOs of organizations—the people at the very top—many times are not plugged in to the security people, and this exacerbates vulnerability. It is also a generational gap. This is one of the challenges we have to deal with in this wonderful period of opportunity.

Q: Do you believe the United States is willing to use its conventional, special-operations, and intelligence capabilities to combat nuclear proliferation?

Sam Nunn

Well, as I said, I think it is our number-one national-security challenge. Our relationship to China over the long haul and the way the Russians develop out of the cold war are enormously important, but for the next ten to twenty years, how we handle the nuclear, chemical, biological, and missile technology will be the greatest vulnerability of the people in this country. The intelligence community is aware of that and is making it a higher priority. I think the Department of Defense is making it a high priority. Are we doing enough? No—far from it. Many citizens and congressmen still see the program by which we are trying to help the Russians get rid of nuclear weapons aimed at *us* as if it were foreign aid. It comes under attack every year as foreign aid. This program costs $400 million a year to get rid of missiles pointed at us and consolidates nuclear weapons into fewer hands for greater control. It would be worth $4 billion a year! We must have the cooperation of people around the globe. We cannot do it alone. It is very much in our national-security interest to use all our capabilities to control the proliferation of weapons of mass destruction.

Q: Could we ever expect the United States to conduct a strike like the Israelis did against the Iraqi reactor?

Sam Nunn

I certainly do not think we can rule that out. We have to have that capability. It would be employed as a last resort, but there is more than one place where it could become necessary.

Q: Do you think we have thought enough about what we ourselves are willing to do in terms of what kind of inspection régime we are willing to accommodate in order to lead the world in stopping the spread of dangerous weapons?

Sam Nunn

I think we have started on that debate with the Chemical Weapons Treaty, because it is one treaty that everybody knows cannot be fully verified. Chemical weapons can be made in a basement. The question basically is whether the treaty helps us more or sets us back. I think it helps us more, because there will be more people cooperating. But yes, to achieve the treaty we will have to open for inspection areas that we would prefer not to open in order to make similar inspections of other countries in the world. We have not yet gotten into detailed discussions, but we will have to in the future. You can also smuggle in a small package of nuclear weapons that can take out most of a city. Nuclear weapons are easier to detect at borders than are chemical and biological weapons, so an attack from chemical and biological weapons is more likely.

Intrusive inspections will be extremely difficult to reach agreement on, but all the civilized nations of the world have a common stake in them. It is in the Russian interest to fight terrorism. It is in the Chinese interest to fight terrorism. It is in the Chinese interest to begin to help curb missile technology instead of spreading it. These countries, if anything, are more vulnerable to attack than we are, and that is particularly true of Russia. We must reach a situation in which each country understands that it has a stake in controlling the proliferation of weapons of mass destruction. There will be rogue countries that will not cooperate, and we will have to bring down world scorn on those countries and isolate them.

Q: Senator Nunn, you wrote quite passionately in an essay for a book on farewell addresses of your concern about family breakdown, community breakdown, our civil-society breakdown. I wonder if you see the strength of our culture as somehow related to our position of leadership in the world.

Sam Nunn

I absolutely do. I think if you look at the components of national power—whether you are talking about information or resources or education—when you get down to the bottom line, i.e., whether or not a society can maintain a position of power in the world, the morale of the people is enormously important, and that relates to the strength of a nation's culture. Power is not simply military. Power and the morale of the people involve values and culture. When you get into maintaining American values and power there is nothing I am more concerned about than the breakdown of American family. School problems, drug problems, teenage pregnancy problems—all of these are complicated and serious, but if I had to name one factor, I think the most important is clearly the breakdown of the American family. We are all going to have to start talking about it without preaching, because people do not want to be preached to.

There are enormous numbers of very successful people brought up in one-parent homes, and God bless those who are bringing up children by themselves, but the odds are overwhelming that if you are brought up in a two-parent home, your chances of succeeding and avoiding problems go up astronomically. That is just an overwhelming fact of life. Someone did a statistical analysis about the question of pupil-teacher ratio and came to the conclusion that it was important, but the *most* important ratio in determining scholastic achievement in America is the parent-pupil ratio. And that is, I think, what we have to start talking about and thinking about.

Q: Under the Nuclear Nonproliferation Treaty the five permanent members in the [UN] Security Council can have nuclear weapons and continue to develop them while the rest of the world cannot. How do you expect emerging nuclear powers, such as India, Israel, and Pakistan, to comply with that? *(Note: This question was posed and Senator Nunn's reply was made before India and Pakistan exploded nuclear devices in 1998.)*

Sam Nunn

Well, in the first place, it is in their fundamental interest. If it is not in their interest, they will not comply. Just because the United States and Russia have huge arsenals of nuclear weapons built up over the last forty years, during the last thirty years of which we have had terrible headaches trying to get rid of them, is that a good reason for India and Pakistan to repeat the same costly experience? It seems to me that it is against India and Pakistan's interests to have a nuclear arsenal that could lead to nuclear war.

And beyond the Nuclear Nonproliferation Treaty, do we need to do more? Yes. Do we need to ratify START II? We have done so; the Russians need to. Do we need to go to START III? Do we need to get all weapons farther down? Absolutely. We need to do all of that. We can do much better in setting an example. But India and Pakistan have a fundamental interest in avoiding a war, and if they keep going the way they have gone the last twenty years, there could be a nuclear exchange there at some point in the future. India and Pakistan have to change. That is enormously important.

When I was in India and Pakistan, I came to a conclusion about one thing that those countries could do, and perhaps the United States could help here. It is to have a series of confidence-building measures so they do not have an accidental war, because both sides are jumpy. Each side is afraid the other one is going to launch some kind of attack. The United States could perhaps use its intelligence resources to help both sides by setting up some kind of joint center there, with the United States sharing intelligence so that nobody gets surprised. I came away from India and Pakistan believing that the greatest chance of war there was probably an accidental war.

Q: Do you expect the five superpowers to eliminate all their nuclear weapons?

Sam Nunn

I do not expect it to happen in the next ten years, probably not within the next twenty years. I think India and Pakistan have to solve their own problems before the elimination of all nuclear weapons from the face of the earth. If they are waiting on that, they are waiting on universal salvation. It is not going to happen any time soon. So I hope they will see eliminating their own nuclear weapons as in their own interest. And I hope that the superpowers will simultaneously be able to lower the number of their weapons to get them down, down, down to a *safe* level. You do not want all the weapons put in one little pile, saying all that is left are four on each side. If you do, the likelihood of war will go up, not down. So we have to work our way out of this, but there's no sense in India and Pakistan working their way into it, as we do so.

Q: Is the deployment of U.S. troops as peacekeepers a wise use of resources?

Sam Nunn

I think in some cases it is and in some cases we have to be very cautious. I worry about the United States getting spread too thin in Bosnia, Haiti, and all these places of conflict around the world. We are wanted everywhere, and our allies never want to go anywhere without us. We are unique. We are the only nation in the world that can help deter nuclear war. We are the only nation in the world that can patrol the sea lanes and assure the free flow of commerce, including strategic oil. We are the only nation in the world that has the kind of communications and intelligence to assist others to avoid wars. We are essential in helping to prevent a war on the Korean Peninsula. We are the only nation that can be the leader in making sure that the Chinese and other countries do not end up moving in the wrong direction. There are a lot of things we can do that nobody else can do.

At the same time, if we get spread into every place in the world and suffer casualties, the American people will ask, why are we there? Is this really a strategic interest of ours? The answer in cases like Somalia is no, it is not. Well, why are we doing it? We must be careful not to erode the willingness of the American public to act in cases crucial to our vital interests. I worry about the tendency of getting involved in too many places. You can make a case for each one of these, but when you put a cumulative total of all of them together it could be counterproductive.

Q: How in foreign policy do we deal with what seems to be a confederation of organized crime, ranging from the Russian Mafia to the drug cartels in Colombia with huge amounts of money and superior weaponry and equipment?

Sam Nunn

Well, it is very much a part of the proliferation problem and it enormously complicates matters. That is why we worry about the former Soviet Union—not just Russia but other countries too. As organized crime becomes more and more international, will these criminals turn to buying and selling nuclear weapons, materials, and know-how? The answer is, if history tells us anything, they will. What worries me now is not the ones we have caught; it is the ones we have not caught. We have all sorts of controls and coordination on Russia's western borders, but we have very little on the southern borders of the former Soviet Union; and those borders lead to Iran and Iraq, countries that would like these weapons. So is it a major problem? Yes. How do we deal with it? All the ways that I have talked about, plus a big effort to coordinate law enforcement.

Now, the difficulty in coordinating law enforcement is that many times you do not know who the honest people are that you can work with. Sometimes you are greatly disappointed, but that does not mean you do not keep on trying. Our FBI now has liaison offices in parts of the former Soviet Union. We are going to have to increase them. We are going to have to do what we can wherever we are asked to use our good offices to help others strengthen their own law enforcement—not just border controls but their own internal law enforcement. The Communist Party basically was the enforcer for years over there. Now they have lost the Communist Party, thank goodness, but they do not have institutions to take its place. And so we have sort of a "Wild West" going on in much of the former Soviet Union. This is a major problem.

But again, in perspective, we are safer today than we have been in the last forty-five years, and I hope our young people understand that. I want to close by saying again, that, in spite of these problems, there is no generation of young Americans that has ever had as great an opportunity to help promote peace and prosperity here at home and to help spread it abroad.

Chapter 9

The Direct Use of Military Force: Criteria of Intervention

Robert Oakley

Background

In the world of today and tomorrow—even more than in the past—there are several categories of use of United States military force in protecting/promoting very important (or vital) U.S. interests. These go beyond the most vital, immediate interest of defending the physical security of the United States. During the cold war this was correctly construed as encompassing the defense by the North Atlantic Treaty Organization (NATO) against conventional Soviet attack in Europe as well as deterring Soviet nuclear attack. It was sometimes extended to include the struggle against command-supported régimes or rebel movements and to protect the free flow of oil, but these were debatable in terms of truly vital interests.

Since the collapse of the Soviet Union and its conventional military power, the end of the Warsaw Pact, and Russian adherence to arms-control treaties, debate has raged over what U.S. interests can rightfully be considered vital, ranging from access to strategic resources and markets and keeping sea lanes open, to the defense of the Korean Peninsula and Japan, and preventing/containing the proliferation of Weapons of Mass Destruction (WMD), to protecting allies and friendly states and applying pressure to "rogue states." Although not usually described as such, the maintenance of the spirit of the Monroe Doctrine can be said to be a vital interest, given the various and frequent uses of military force by the United States in this hemisphere during and after the cold war. Perhaps it would still be so, but there is no short-term or long-term external threat. Today, some would stretch the definition of very important (if not absolutely vital) interests to include promotion of basic U.S. values, particularly democracy and human rights ("expansion"), and humanitarian assistance.

For the purposes of this chapter, we will use a restricted definition of vital interests to cover direct defense of the United States' security, including its territory, people, and armed forces. This is without debate, and it would be a criterion that would almost automatically trigger the direct use of U.S. military force. For the rest, we will use the phrase *important interests,* recognizing that they tend to be both subjective in nature and variable.

For a given time and place, a strong majority of U.S. public and congressional opinion may support the use of U.S. force for what is, at the moment, considered the important interest of humanitarian intervention, as in Somalia in December 1992, and in Eastern Zaire in August 1994. At another time, the public will oppose such use as not important and therefore not warranted, as in Somalia after October 3–4, 1993, and in Eastern Zaire between October and December 1996. The use of U.S. military forces, including ground forces, against Iraq to assist friendly states and to protect access to oil in the Persian Gulf was formally approved (but barely) by the U.S. Senate and strongly supported by the U.S. public in 1990–91, but only after Kuwait had been conquered and Iraqi tanks were lined up on the Saudi border facing south. (Had Iraq withdrawn quickly after taking Kuwait, or had it taken only half the country, it is unlikely that U.S. forces—particularly ground forces—would have responded and that they could have used Saudi facilities.) In 1994 there was general approval of a buildup of U.S. naval, air, and ground forces to protect Kuwait against Iraqi military movement. However, the use of U.S. military force in late 1997 and early 1998 to somehow deal with the Iraqi régime and its Weapons of Mass Destruction was much more controversial, dependent on varied and fluctuating public and political perceptions of the support available from other countries, the type and amount of force to be used (ground forces were seemingly ruled out), the objectives sought, and the likelihood of achieving them. Ultimately, no military attack took place despite massive buildup. Another hypothetical situation that would be extremely controversial would be the use of U.S. military force to go to war to defend Taiwan from Chinese attack. The public and Congress did support the dispatch of two carrier battle groups to the Taiwan Straits in 1996 in response to Chinese military exercises. Whether this was considered an important U.S. interest might well depend on public and political perception of whether it was Taiwan or China that provoked and initiated the attack and what our regional allies and friends were willing to do.

Because of the difficulty in arriving at a widely accepted definition of very important U.S. interests, this chapter does not set forth a set of precise criteria for the use of military force. Instead, it will examine the various ways in which U.S. military leadership currently conceives of the use of force (and what kinds of force), discuss how these forces have been applied or might apply to various situations, suggest what conditions should be satisfied before a decision to use force is taken, and discuss what the realistic outcomes might be.

The *National Military Strategy* (NMS) of 1997[1] conveys the advice of Chairman John M. Shalikashvili and the Joint Chiefs of Staff on the strategic direction of the armed forces in implementing the guidance in the president's *National Security Strategy for a New Century*[2] and the secretary of defense's report, the *Quadrennial Defense Review* (QDR),[3] both issued in 1997. We shall use NMS as the basic structure for this chapter on the direct use of U.S.

military force. It adopts three basic elements of strategy for use of U.S. military forces:

- Shape the international environment and create conditions favorable to U.S. interests and global security;
- Respond to the full spectrum of crises in order to protect our national interests (e.g., Small-Scale Contingencies [SSCs] and Major Theater Wars [MTWs]);
- Prepare our forces now for an uncertain future.

Shaping

Because the topic is the direct use of military force, we will cover only briefly the category of shaping, which the NMS defines as having two principal components, namely the inherent deterrent qualities of U.S. forces and their use for military engagement. An inherent deterrent quality does not qualify for discussion as direct use. Engagement does involve the use of military forces, but in a passive manner that does not include actual use of weapons.

Institutionalized in doctrine and assigned as a major mission for the first time because of the vision of former Secretary of Defense William J. Perry, military engagement or preventive defense is the deliberate use of U.S. military assets to "shape" the international security environment. Although Perry correctly described it as our first line of defense, it involves the use of military capabilities for peaceful, essentially political, purposes such as training or educating and exercising with foreign military forces. The purposes are to promote awareness of and positive attitudes toward U.S. values such as democracy and human rights; enhance commonality of doctrine, technology, procedures, and attitudes to promote military cooperation with the United States; and prepare the way for actual coalition operations. It also increases potential U.S. influence in certain countries on significant political and economic policies and decisions, given the major influence of military establishments in these countries (e.g., Indonesia, Pakistan, Chile, Rwanda, Egypt). Important as this is, however, it does not constitute the direct use of military force, despite its proven long-term, substantial, but indirect contribution to the defense of U.S. interests. The maintenance of NATO as an effective military alliance responsive to U.S. interests falls under the rubric of shaping the international environment of military engagement. So does NATO's deliberate use of military exercises, seminars, training, etc., with the non-NATO Partnership for Peace countries, which has proven its value. The Perry initiative of promoting intensive U.S. military-to-military contacts with the Chinese People's Liberation Army (PLA) is also beginning to bear fruit, as the latter has become considerably less anti–United States in its publications and attitudes in the past year, and more interested in good relations with the U.S. military.

Small-Scale Contingency Operations

Nature of Operations

The Bottoms Up Review of 1994 recognized the end of the threat of a major U.S.-USSR, NATO–Warsaw Pact war, and was instead predicated on the primary objective of the United States' being able to fight and win two simultaneous Major Regional Conflicts (MCRs), or Major Theater Wars (MTWs), for example, in Korea and the Persian Gulf. The ability of the United States to do this in one theater, supported by allies and friendly states, was clearly demonstrated during the Gulf War of 1990–91. Its ability to do so in two theaters at one time is debatable.

The years following the Gulf War showed that crises smaller and arguably more complicated than an MRC were apt to be the norm. The 1997 *Quadrennial Defense Review* recognized the international political, military, and economic trends since the mid-1980s. In that time, U.S. (and international) military action has often been required to resolve or limit lesser conflicts—sometimes totally internal upheavals—and to respond to humanitarian emergencies, even when no vital interests of the United States were threatened directly. The use of military force as one element of response was predicated, in U.S. military doctrine, on the belief that inaction can be too costly over the long term or unacceptable to U.S. ideals, broad interests, and public opinion. It is also seen as an element in U.S. strategy to cope with proliferation of Weapons of Mass Destruction, terrorism, and narcotics trafficking, and to promote regional and international stability, important for U.S. global economic as well as security interests.

Therefore, the QDR raised the level of U.S. commitment to employ military forces to assist in meeting these challenges. Rather than continuing to regard them as incidental or secondary activities, it explicitly established a broad category of military operations, labeled the Small-Scale Contingency, as a new mission for military operations and a major consideration in deciding on force structure:

> In general, the United States, along with others in the international community, will seek to prevent and contain localized conflicts and crises before they require a military response. If, however, such efforts do not succeed, swift intervention by military forces may be the best way to contain, resolve, or mitigate the consequences of a conflict that could otherwise become far more costly and deadly. . . . Therefore, the U.S. military must be prepared to conduct successfully multiple concurrent smaller-scale contingency (SSC) operations worldwide, and it must be able to do so in any environment, including one in which an adversary uses asymmetric means, such as nuclear, biological and chemical (NBC) weapons. Importantly, U.S. forces must also be able to withdraw from smaller-scale contingency

operations, reconstitute, and then deploy to a major theater war in accordance with required timelines.[4]

Although SSCs are not precisely defined in the 1997 *Quadrennial Defense Review*, they encompass a very wide range of combined and joint military operations beyond peacetime engagement and short of Major Theater War. The primary rationale is to protect United States citizens and interests, support political initiatives, facilitate democracy, and promote other fundamental ideals (e.g., human rights, rule of law), or to disrupt specified illegal activities that could constitute a serious, if not vital, threat to the security of the United States as well as its interests. SSCs may include:

- reprisal strikes and other limited intervention
- noncombatant evacuation operations (NEOs)
- counterdrug operations
- counterterrorist and counterproliferation operations
- shows of force
- maritime sanction and "no-fly" enforcement
- peace-accord implementation and other forms of peacekeeping (under United Nations [UN] or outside UN command)
- support for humanitarian operations and disaster relief

The chart on the next page depicts the SSCs in which the United States participated during the period 1991–97, with a purely illustrative projection for the next ten years based on the previous six years. (This is not meant to be predictive. The tendency of U.S. participation over the last few years is down.) The variety of operations ranges from limited but opposed large-scale intervention in Somalia, to large-scale, no-fly-zone enforcement over Iraq, to short-term humanitarian assistance for Rwandan refugees in Eastern Zaire, to NEOs for Liberia, Sierra Leone, and the Congo (Zaire). One might add Panama (1990–91) and Grenada (1983) as unilateral intervention operations—in contrast to Somalia, Haiti, and Bosnia, which have all been multilateral. The duration of SSCs has ranged from a few weeks to several years, the size from several scores to tens of thousands of personnel.

SSCs are difficult to define because they include subcategories that vary according to the type of mission, size and type of forces deployed, and rules of engagement (ROE). Yet they share some characteristics that distinguish them from MTWs. Decisions to intervene tend to be made quickly and unpredictably, often with little time for planning, preparation, and deployment. They can extend well beyond the initially envisioned duration, increasing projected strains on military forces. (Operation Provide Comfort in northern Iraq, 1991 to present, for example, was projected to last two to three months; Implementation Force/Stabilization Force [IFOR/SFOR] in Bosnia, 1995 to present, was projected to last one year.) Few established

DYNAMIC COMMITMENT
ILLUSTRATIVE VISION OF THE FUTURE

UNCLASSIFIED

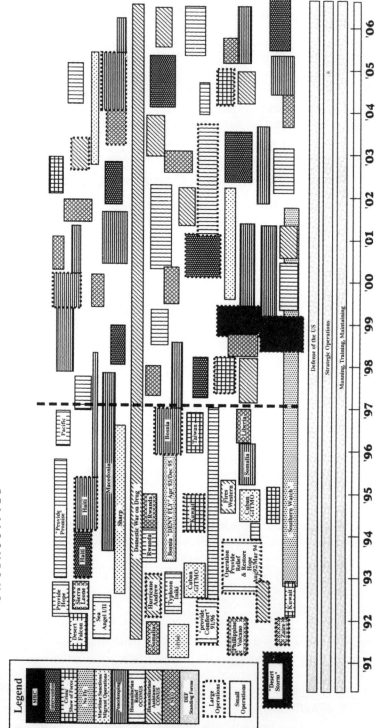

facilities in the deployment area may be available, and the operation may need to rely on lighter forces organized in a less than conventional manner (e.g., greater mobility, less firepower, and less use of airpower and standoff weapons). The commanders' objectives and the ROEs emphasize avoiding casualties on all sides, along with a need, when possible, for dialogue and cooperation with local power groups.

SSCs are not "fight-and-win" operations designed to inflict maximum damage on the enemy, and the "enemy" is often ambiguous by virtue of its shifting attitudes and actions toward the United States. This calls for a distinct change in attitude, conduct, and interpretation of the ROE, with an emphasis on restraint whenever possible, while ensuring force protection and carrying out the usually more limited actions involving the use of firepower. One particularly difficult decision is whether to use deadly force and, if so, against what target. Given the high level of public and political attention focused on theater operations, there is a potential for an individual incident (e.g., inadvertent killing of unarmed civilians) to become a "defining moment" that can undermine U.S. domestic support for military operations, as well as create a much more dangerous indigenous and regional environment for U.S. forces. (This is one of the motivations behind increased interest in development and use of nonlethal weapons.) To achieve success, SSCs must put more stress on understanding local culture and politics and the combined use of political, diplomatic, humanitarian, and economic and information programs. The variety of the challenges posed by SSCs, the number and type of forces required, and the relevant foreign-policy considerations often result in the involvement of combined (or coalition) military forces and of civilian personnel from governments as well as nongovernmental organizations (NGOs) and regional and international organizations (IOs):

- Some SSCs may require only a few military personnel for non-combat military observer missions (e.g., the Military Observer Mission, Ecuador, Peru [MOMEP], in the Peru-Ecuador border conflict, 1995, required only fifty personnel).

- Some require military forces ready for combat, on a widely varying scale (e.g., from 500 personnel for the Somalia NEO in 1991, through the Haiti Multi-National Force [MNF] of 8,000 personnel in 1994–95, to the Taiwan Straits show of force in 1996 — 18,000 personnel).

- Some are basically nonmilitary (that is, humanitarian intervention and disaster relief, as in Bangladesh, 1991) with, on occasion, limited military forces assisting large-scale civilian operations (as in Provide Relief, in Somalia, 1993, and Support Hope, in Rwanda, 1994).

- For operations in support of large-scale civilian efforts, international and nongovernmental relief organizations (e.g., United

Nations High Commission for Refugees [UNHCR], World Food Program [WFP], International Committee of the Red Cross [ICRC], CARE, Doctors without Borders, Oxfam, International Rescue Committee [IRC]) are usually present before, during, and after military intervention. For such operations, considerable liaison and coordination are required, much of it ad hoc because there are no firmly established U.S. or international procedures for command, control, communication, and intelligence (C^3I) in combined military-civilian operations and even fewer internationally codified procedures. This was the case for Somalia, Haiti, and Bosnia.

Because SSCs do not often call for a major commitment of military force or visibly serve vital U.S. interests (or have a widely accepted "enemy" such as Saddam or Qaddafi), such operations may require of any U.S. administration a sustained effort to mobilize and maintain public and political support at home. Because they are of small scale, limited duration, and low expense, and are visibly directed at an accepted U.S. interest (e.g., protecting U.S. citizens), NEOs most easily command public support. Similarly, short-term, peaceful disaster-relief operations tend to garner positive public support. In contrast, large, long-lasting, potentially dangerous, and expensive peace operations in remote regions with only limited visible relationship to U.S. vital interests have difficulty gaining support, although it is stronger for coalition operations in which friendly states are seen to be doing their fair share.

The likelihood of U.S. casualties and a high cost can decisively affect public and political support or the lack thereof. An excessive preoccupation with the public fear of any casualties—rather than proper concern for force protection—can constrain the response of commanders in the field facing unpredictable and rapidly evolving situations. It can also encourage potential enemies to conclude that, if they inflict casualties, public opinion will force the United States to withdraw (e.g., Vietnam, 1974; Lebanon, 1983; Somalia, 1993). With proper justification and explanation, public and political opinion can be brought to support prudently conducted, continuing operations for important objectives despite casualties (e.g., Iraq's attack on the USS *Stark* in 1987 and the Khobar Towers bombing in 1996, which killed more military personnel than the October 3–4 battle in Mogadishu). In addition to an effective explanation and justification by senior policy officials of the administration, public information provided by the media is a major consideration in sustaining indispensable support at home. Therefore, a successful operation requires, as a vital element, careful planning and execution of media relations in the field. (The most successful media-relations programs have usually been the most open and cooperative.)

Flexible Use of Capable Forces

The U.S. military is often called on to participate in SSC operations that involve civilian organizations or basically civilian tasks and to participate in multinational forces, either in ad hoc coalitions or UN peacekeeping missions, for two main reasons: its ability to deal with low-intensity dangers posed by local military, militia, or armed gangs and its unmatched lift, logistics, planning, and command, control, communications, and intelligence capabilities. These capabilities not only can protect and support civilian activities but also can enhance them by reducing time requirements for deployment, hastening the delivery of relief supplies, and improving coordination of disparate organizations. When large-scale humanitarian disasters strike, even a combined national and international civilian response often is not adequate, and military assistance becomes critical (e.g., Hurricane Andrew in Florida and the cyclone in Bangladesh in 1991). Extensive experience in training and exercising with almost all the world's armed forces makes U.S. forces very capable for coalition management. In general, skills honed for preeminence on the battlefield are readily adjustable to the needs of different missions and cultural settings and to the nuances of particular operations.

The modern U.S. military, although developed essentially in response to the cold war, has the personnel, weaponry, and supporting equipment to satisfy basic operational military requirements for all SSCs. In combined military-civilian operations, it has displayed a remarkable ability to adapt and improvise, often in an unplanned manner and in an unfamiliar operating environment, including the following actions which took place during the four-year period 1994–97:

- enforcing naval embargoes simultaneously on Bosnia, Iraq, and Haiti
- enforcing no-fly zones over Bosnia and northern and southern Iraq
- conducting a show of force in the Taiwan Straits, with two aircraft-carrier battle groups
- maintaining an essential carrier presence in the Mediterranean Sea, Persian Gulf and Indian Ocean, and the Pacific
- organizing and providing the core of highly capable MNFs in Haiti and Bosnia
- using Marine Expeditionary Units and Special Operating Forces for NEOs in Liberia, Sierra Leone, Zaire, Central African Republic, and Cambodia

Some U.S. combat-support units have proved themselves even more valuable for SSCs, particularly peace and humanitarian operations, than for regular combat. Specifically, in Somalia, Haiti, and Bosnia, the U.S. military used a combination of specialized units that resulted in effective planning, organization, and conduct of joint civil-military operations, including the coordination of programs by international and nongovernmental organizations and their protection. The most notable of these units were:

- Special Operations Forces (SOF) for Civil Affairs, Psychological Operations (PSYOP), and Special Forces units
- combat engineers and Seabees
- logistics and communication
- Military Police (MP)
- Civil Affairs personnel

Restore Hope, 9 December 1992–4 May 1993

During operation Restore Hope in Somalia, about 30,000 U.S. forces (plus 10,000 friendly forces under U.S. command) planned and initiated a military-humanitarian support-coalition operation within ten days after President Bush approved the idea. Within three weeks the operation achieved its basic objectives of ending a major conflict and providing large-scale food and health assistance to millions of Somalis. In nearly all aspects of this operation, U.S. forces were central to coalition C^3I and logistics and coordinated effectively with civilian agencies and nongovernmental, regional, and international civilian organizations.

In the Haitian operation, which included a UN force (United Nations Mission in Haiti [UNMIH]), U.S. forces provided much of the coalition C^3I and logistics. Augmented by Civil Affairs and PSYOP units, they also played a critical role in UN mechanisms for cooperation among the military force, U.S. civilian agencies, nongovernmental, regional, and international organizations, and the government of Haiti. For the strictly humanitarian operation (Provide Hope) in Rwanda in 1994, the U.S. European Command provided essential airlift for food, water-purification equipment, and medical supplies. It also coordinated the urgent large-scale delivery and distribution of assistance with the UNHCR, WFP, ICRC, and numerous NGOs and provided these organizations with limited engineering and logistics support. In all three instances—Somalia, Rwanda, and Haiti—the United States developed and adapted the Humanitarian Operations Center/Civil-Military Operations Center (HOC/CMOC) concept for coordinating civilian and military-humanitarian operations and communications.

This broad range of military capabilities—particularly effectiveness in supporting and conducting essentially civilian missions—constitutes a potential downside for the armed forces. Given the weakness of most U.S.

and international civilian organizations in rapid mobilization, surge capacity, planning, logistics, and rapid implementation of programs, it is all too easy for civilians to pass the burden to the military, not only at the outset of an operation when they are struggling to mobilize but even as it continues, simply because it is easier. Such an approach by civilian organizations places an unnecessary demand on military forces, and tends to delay the substantial effort required to increase basic civilian capabilities so they can respond more rapidly and effectively.

Current and projected total forces have adequate capabilities for the anticipated number and types of SSCs in the near future. However, continued deployment over the long term at the 1990s rate, with the existing force structure and organization, training, forward presence, and other requirements (e.g., especially the demands of a major presence in the Persian Gulf) will diminish capabilities to conduct SSCs as well as readiness to conduct MTWs. Since 1990, SSCs have imposed unexpectedly high demands on operations tempo (OPTEMPO), personnel tempo (PERSTEMPO), and deployment tempo on several units with specific capabilities, such as the Fleet Marine Force, Army Modified Table of Organization and Equipment (MTOE), and Special Operations Forces. These demands are expected to continue into the next century, with potentially negative effects on readiness, morale, personnel retention, and MTW capabilities. The units experiencing most of the demand are combat support, combat-support services, light infantry battalions, and those incorporating specific matériel such as helicopters and Airborne Warning and Control System (AWACS) aircraft. Because approximately one-third of combat support and two-thirds of combat-support service units are in the reserves, an additional strain is put on those particular units and on the reserves generally.

The longer an SSC lasts, the greater its negative effect on preparedness of forces that must be ready for MTW operations, the essential rationale for U.S. combat forces. This is particularly true for such units as light infantry and helicopter squadrons, which are deployed more frequently than other forces for peace operations, as well as combat support and combat-support service units. These forces would usually be engaged away from their home base at the outset of an MTW; after SSC duty, most of them will require considerable retraining prior to deployment to an MTW. An inexact rule of thumb has been that six months of retraining is needed after SSC operations lasting six to twelve months. The time required to retrain is an important consideration in force planning and force structure, as well as in deciding initially whether to engage in an SSC. Thus it is extremely important to assess carefully any situation that might require an SSC operation by the United States. Unless there is a clear need for action that involves important U.S. interests (and values) and a "doable" outcome is visible, the better part of valor would be to refrain.

Criteria for SSCs

Approved in May 1994, Presidential Decision Directive 25 (PDD-25) sets down useful guidelines for deciding U.S. involvement in peace operations, which can also be used for other SSCs. It came in the aftermath of what was seen, in late 1993, as a failed operation with shocking loss of U.S. life in Somalia (UNOSOM II) and what was also seen as a failed UN operation in Bosnia, as well as the unexpectedly high cost of peacekeeping. Congressional pressure and Clinton administration rethinking led to a policy directive that covered four major issues:

- making disciplined and coherent choices about which peace operations to support
- defining clearly the command and control of U.S. forces in peace operations
- reducing U.S. and UN costs and improving management by both for peace operations
- enhancing administration communication with Congress and the public

The guidelines in this directive have led to a much more systematic (and more realistic) U.S. approach to peace operations. Eight specific factors were identified as needed for U.S. support of a peace operation, and nine more for actual U.S. participation in a situation that could involve combat. Parallel reviews by the UN secretary-general and other member states reached similar conclusions. As a result, the management of the UN has significantly improved, the number of operations undertaken has been considerably reduced, and the UN has avoided operations that might involve large-scale conflict. It has shifted to a systematic policy of "subcontracting" operations to multinational coalitions organized and led by countries (e.g., the United States) or regional organizations (e.g., NATO) which have a coherent doctrine, proven C^{3}I, substantial logistics and transport capacity, and experience in military operations of the magnitude and complexity envisaged. IFOR/SFOR in Bosnia, starting in 1995, is a good example of a peace operation approved by the UN Security Council (UNSC) but operated outside the UN system, as was the initial Multi-National Force operation in Haiti in September 1994. PDD-25 was followed by PPD-26 on interagency planning and coordination in conducting complex peace operations. The two presidential directives have moved the United States closer to the same sort of systematic planning for peace operations that had been the practice for major conflicts, and they establish detailed, albeit illustrative, criteria for action. (If the guidelines had been applied literally, the United States would not have been able to mount either the Haitian or the Bosnian operation, given the uncertainty that prevailed before each began and during initial deployment.) They also provide for adequate preparation of a politico-military plan.

When there is a decision to intervene, U.S. strategy for larger SSCs, especially peace operations and complex humanitarian operations, should be premised on mobilizing a coalition to share political and resource burdens while ensuring capacity and credibility. That means getting on top of an opponent—politically, psychologically, and militarily—and staying on top, even while restraining the actual use of force and preserving an even-handed approach to minimize casualties and to avoid unnecessary armed conflict. Initial forces must have an overpowering edge in firepower, C^{3}I, logistics, and SOF, including Psychological Operations (PSYOP). They also must have political, diplomatic, and intelligence support from civilian agencies, and a combined knowledge of local culture, politics, and psychology, as well as potentially hostile military and terrorist capabilities. Military action must be linked to effective, early humanitarian and economic support from national and international civilian agencies. PSYOP and public-information programs intended to solidify political support on the ground and at home should be implemented from the onset as a vital element of the overall operation.

Political-military strategy should be premised on plans to exit completely. However, since the date cannot be accurately predicted, there also need to be plans for interim force-reduction measures (e.g., replacing active U.S. forces with reserve units, foreign forces, or civilian assets once initial stabilization has occurred, or replacing a U.S.-led operation by a UN operation.) Haiti is a good example. Such a strategy should include long-term, systematic assistance to the UN and regional bodies (such as NATO, the Organization of American States, and the Organization of African Unity), as well as selected governments, to improve their individual and collective capabilities for conducting peace operations. This will enable others to operate effectively without U.S. participation or with greatly reduced U.S. participation (e.g., transport, logistics, and equipment). Significant programs are under way to do just this with military forces from African, South American, and former Soviet-bloc states. Even when the forces of other nations have not been adequately prepared in advance, U.S. forces can make coalition operations more effective by providing last-minute training and some basic support, thereby alleviating the burden on themselves. International and military education and training (IMET), foreign military sales (FMS), and other forms of military engagement such as joint/combined exercises are being targeted for this purpose—which clearly falls under the policy of "preventive defense" articulated by the secretary of defense. Experience has proved that this approach enhances long-term military-to-military relations as well as the capabilities of coalition partners to conduct peace operations.

Major Theater Wars

Quality of Forces

U.S. forces are large, strong, and versatile enough to meet major warfighting requirements (MTWs) as well as lesser contingencies. The United States has a substantial military posture and defense budget to meet global responsibilities, but in numerical terms, its forces do not dominate the military balance in the three key theaters (Europe, Asia, Persian Gulf). Other countries have large forces in the theaters, but in wartime U.S. forces can concentrate because of their agility. Even so, they are designed to defeat the enemy not by outnumbering but by outfighting it. Their excellence is based on high quality. The following attributes account for this quality.

Global Power Projection

The United States has an overwhelming projection capability. Large U.S. forces are deployed in three theaters on a peacetime basis: 109,000 personnel in Europe; nearly 100,000 in Asia; and 25,000 in the Persian Gulf. This presence provides not only already deployed combat forces available on short notice in key locations, but also well-developed military infrastructure and reception facilities and prepositioned weapons and equipment for the rapid deployment of additional major combat units (e.g., enough for ten ground brigades). Initial defense operations can begin almost immediately, and reinforcements from the continental United States (CONUS) can begin to contribute immediately after arrival in these theaters. The effect is to reduce vulnerability to surprise attack while enabling the United States to amass large forces for decisive operations within a few weeks.

Most U.S. military forces are designed for overseas expeditionary missions. They are equipped with strong combat units and large logistics assets that allow them to deploy overseas on short notice, operate for lengthy periods in austere environments, engage in intense combat, and conduct a full spectrum of defensive and offensive missions. They have good strategic mobility forces, important because of the vast tonnages that must be moved in deploying large forces (e.g., a three-division corps has thousands of vehicles and can weigh nearly a million tons). The United States enjoys control of the air and sea lines of communication to the three key theaters, control provided in part by U.S. forces and in part by allied forces. In Europe, for example, NATO allies provide military bases and escort forces as support for the transit of U.S. forces through the Mediterranean toward the Persian Gulf. In the Persian Gulf and northeast Asia, allies provide local air defense and sea-lane defense for arriving U.S. forces, as well as sites for prepositioned weapons and equipment. In consequence, enemy forces would be hard-pressed to interrupt the flow of U.S. forces to key theaters threatened by war.

Superior Knowledge, Planning, and Information Dominance

Large military operations require defense knowledge, planning, and information dominance—areas in which U.S. forces excel. Within the Pentagon, civilian and military staffs develop coordinated plans, programs, and budgets for each service component and theater. Regional commanders in chief (CINCs) develop operational plans (Oplans) and associated time-phased force deployment data (TPFDD) to coordinate the flow of forces overseas for specific contingencies in their theaters. The effect is to accelerate the process by which U.S. forces are deployed overseas and to increase their effectiveness once they arrive. In addition, the U.S. intelligence community generally provides better information on each region than is available to any other nation, thereby giving U.S. forces an important advantage as they deploy and begin operations.

U.S. forces enjoy information dominance because of superior C^{4}ISR assets (command, control, communications, computers, intelligence, surveillance, reconnaissance). No other nation comes close to matching the United States in these assets, in strategic terms or on the battlefield. New intelligence assets and digitized communications systems increase the speed with which far-reaching decisions can be made and complex military operations launched. (Such data systems permit commanders to blend the operations of several army and marine-corps divisions, air-force wings, and navy battle groups.) They permit delegation of authority and initiative to lower echelons, enhancing force effectiveness. They also provide commanders with knowledge of enemy forces and operations. This ensures major advantages in concentrating U.S. forces and using maneuver and firepower.

Coalitions

The capability of conducting combined operations with allies and coalition partners is also very important. U.S. forces work closely with foreign military forces in all three theaters. This is true not only in peacetime but also in crises and war. In Europe, U.S. forces are embedded within NATO's integrated command and multinational formations to conduct a full spectrum of missions. The IFOR/SFOR mission in Bosnia is a classic example of a NATO operation in which the United States provides less than half the forces. In the Persian Gulf, Desert Storm was a combined operation in which Arab and European coalition partners provided as much as one-third of the total forces. (The presence of Arab forces was a major political plus.) Another Gulf war might witness a similar pattern. In Asia, a new Korean war might find the United States providing only one-fourth of U.S.-ROK ground forces, albeit the bulk of air and naval forces.

Robust Forces

Demanding battlefield campaigns and their missions can be successfully mounted only by robust forces. The more ambitious the campaign, the more robust the forces must be. Four pillars of strength are required: scale (i.e., sufficient numbers), readiness, modernization, and sustainment. Developing all four is difficult; most military establishments are strong in only one or two. U.S. forces today excel in all four areas.

Scale involves having enough combat and support units to carry out the required missions in adequate strength. The U.S. military possesses large and diverse enough forces to conduct almost any mission or combination of missions with considerable strength. They can carry out many types of campaigns, in many operating environments.

Readiness is a product of many factors: e.g., high-quality officers and enlisted personnel, full staffing by active troops, extensive training and exercises, well-maintained weapons and equipment, efficient procedures, and the capacity to operate at a fast tempo. Because U.S. forces emphasize all these factors, they have higher overall readiness than any other forces in the world.

Modernization requires high-technology weapons and munitions that match or exceed those of enemy forces. Since the early 1980s, U.S. forces have benefited from a sweeping modernization program, giving them the world's best weapons virtually across the board. Critics debate the extent to which certain U.S. weapons are better than those of others—selected West European or Russian weapons are often of comparable quality—but Desert Storm suggested that U.S. models are more superior in combat to Russian-made weapons than had been realized. In recent years, the United States has not acquired new weapons in large numbers but has produced and incorporated better munitions, C^4ISR assets, and other technologies, and has developed—if not mass-produced—many next-generation weapons. Economic pressures have obliged other countries, especially Russia, to slow their programs for developing new weapons. The effect has been to preserve a clear margin of superiority in overall modernization.

Sustainment can be surprisingly important, even in short wars of a few weeks. An air force that can fly each aircraft at a rate of one to two sorties per day will have a big advantage over an enemy that can sustain fewer than one sortie per day. Similarly, an army's effectiveness is heavily influenced by whether it can constantly resupply its combat forces with fuel and ammunition, repair damaged vehicles, keep roads open, and replace casualties with fresh troops. Overall, U.S. forces have better sustainment than almost any other military establishment.

Fighting MTWs

These high-quality U.S. military capabilities are basic assets for fighting wars, but the exact manner in which they are used and their effectiveness will depend on the specific situation. Mounting decisive interventions to defend U.S. interests requires deploying to the scene with the right forces at the right time, and then employing them effectively. The latter requires the right commanders, with proven leadership qualities, combat experience, and a breadth of vision encompassing cultural, political, and economic, as well as military, realities. It will also require, in most instances, the participation of allies and coalition partners, not only for the military forces they could provide but also for their support facilities and their political and economic contributions to the overall power of the operation.

An MTW could occur in several places. The *Quadrennial Defense Review* called for a U.S. posture that can respond to expected events while preparing for the unexpected, including two partially overlapping MTWs. For both wars, separate or simultaneous, the outcome would hinge on the ability of U.S. reinforcements to deploy in a timely manner. In the event of a single conflict with no worry of a second one, U.S. mobility forces could be concentrated on that theater, thereby easing the task of responding. In the event of a second conflict, U.S. air forces, light ground forces, and local naval forces could converge on the scene quickly, for essentially defensive purposes. Larger forces would follow later, strengthening U.S. or allied defense and enabling offensive operations to begin.

Either MTW contingency could pose serious challenges, particularly if one (or both) were to be sustained by an enemy determined to fight to the end (alien thinking) rather than recognizing his losses and surrendering (U.S. thinking). This is what took place in Vietnam. Prospects are still good that U.S. and allied forces would win both wars because they can rush large reinforcements and mount decisive operations with superior forces. The wars, nonetheless, could be costly, bloody affairs, although U.S. operations would aim to minimize casualties.

The main obstacle for the United States in winning an MTW would be political, not military. In the Persian Gulf, Saudi Arabia and other Gulf countries might not respond effectively because of internal weaknesses or fears of external attack (e.g., by missiles and Weapons of Mass Destruction), and a large multinational coalition might not form as in the 1990–91 Gulf War. This development could prevent the United States from deploying forces as quickly and efficiently as envisioned in current plans, and it would require more U.S. forces. This could also cause political and perhaps economic damage to U.S. interests in other (especially Muslim) countries. In addition, it could encourage the enemy to fight longer and harder. In Asia, a lukewarm stance by Japan or opposition by China and Russia to a war on the Korean Peninsula might have a similar effect.

The enemy might also employ WMD—if not nuclear weapons, then chemical and biological weapons. Even in purely conventional war, the enemy might show unexpected skill in employing asymmetric strategies that exploit Achilles' heels in the U.S. reinforcement plan, e.g., by destroying key airfields and mining ports or by inflicting casualties and exploiting the "CNN television factor" to increase the shock effect on U.S. public or political opinion of U.S. casualties—or to portray the U.S. military as slaughtering innocent noncombatants. War is inherently dynamic and unpredictable. The offense has the advantage of seizing the initiative, and sometimes the breaks go against the defender. Even a well-planned defense can be rocked back on its heels. The United States will need flexibility to respond effectively to different events, including the unexpected and unwelcome. If it retains such flexibility, the United States will be justified in having confidence in its military capacity to prevail. However, sustaining the political will to continue until victory has been achieved is more uncertain.

Criteria for MTWs

The principal criteria in deciding on the direct use of U.S. military forces in a situation that could become an MTW—to fight and defeat a regional enemy—are not dissimilar to those for more limited uses of military power, especially large-scale peace operations.

(1) Does the administration consider the situation of sufficient importance to U.S. interests to warrant expending hundreds of millions of dollars and risking scores or even hundreds of U.S. lives, and can Congress be convinced at least to acquiesce? An administration that is unified, confident, and credible on the issue can usually carry the day with Congress, which does not like to block proposed action in advance even if it is highly skeptical, but a strong case must be publicly made. The U.S. protection of shipping in the Persian Gulf, in 1987–88 (Earnest Will), and the Gulf War, in 1990–91 (Desert Storm), are two major, direct applications of military force that exemplify this point. The case was made by a cohesive, credible administration, and an uncertain Congress and public acquiesced. The operations continued; support was sustained.

(2) Is there a clear, achievable objective, satisfactory for U.S. interests, with an approximately perceivable end date and end state, which will not leave the U.S. military engaged in large numbers in a risky situation for an indefinite period? In light of experience in the past decade, one should not require a finite end date or a definitive end state, but a clear idea of general timing and outcome is critical—the more so if the situation is causing or very likely to cause U.S. casualties. Rapid final withdrawal is not necessary, nor is an absence of casualties. A phased reduction in U.S. force levels, with limited numbers of casualties and a perception of progress toward a satisfactory solution will usually suffice, particularly for a confident administration.

(3) There needs to be a reasonably accurate idea of the amount of U.S. military and financial resources required, both at the outset and over time; what resources will be available from others; and that these resources will be adequate for success. In operations of smaller scale or low risk for the United States, this consideration has been less important. But for larger, potentially higher-risk operations, it is critical. The means must match the objectives. (This was not true for UNPROFOR, in Bosnia, or for UNOSOM II, in Somalia,

when the UN Security Council, with U.S. pressure, approved tasks beyond the military means provided. In both cases, serious difficulties occurred, with casualties on the ground, followed by a severe U.S. political backlash. In the case of IFOR/SFOR, for Bosnia, resources were obviously adequate, achieving a rapid end to internal conflict with no combat casualties.)

(4) What will be the political, military, and financial support of other countries, starting with NATO nations and Japan, but including China and Russia and states in the region of the prospective operation? This is not as important as the first criterion, particularly with respect to initial actions by the United States, but it is an important consideration in enabling the United States to sustain an operation. If the operation should require economic and political suasion and/or sanctions as well as military force, and if the operation should move past the restoration of law and order to the reconstruction and redevelopment stage, the contributions of others will take on still greater importance to the United States, politically as well as in terms of U.S. resources required.

In the post–cold war world of today and tomorrow, the clear-cut, emotionally and politically satisfying fight-and-win war has, for all intents and purposes, disappeared. This is explicitly recognized in the 1997 statement by the chairman of the Joint Chiefs of Staff on *National Military Strategy of the United States of America:* "Decisive force is the commitment of sufficient military power to overwhelm an adversary, establish new military conditions, and *achieve a political resolution* favorable to U.S. national interests." The president's 1997 *National Security Strategy* postulates as the nation's enduring security needs "the protection of the lives and safety of Americans, maintenance of the sovereignty of the U.S., and provision of the prosperity of the nation." It calls for enhancing that security "with effective diplomacy and with military forces that are ready to fight and win." Clearly implicit in this statement, and in that of the chairman, is recognition of Clausewitz's theorem that "war is an extension of politics," that the best general or admiral is the one who understands and is able to achieve a political objective. Such an objective is unlikely to be the total destruction of another country or its total military defeat and occupation.

This has been evident in what has occurred in the Persian Gulf in the past decade. During the Gulf War the ultimate objective was to protect friendly states in the Gulf (and Israel) from Iraq, and to maintain the free flow of oil. The same objective had been sought between 1982 and 1988, except that the enemy was Iran, which was threatening oil shipping and friendly states. The means the United States applied were a combination of rallying international political support and using limited, direct military force to protect shipping and to reassure friendly Gulf states that they would be protected, indirect support for Iraq's war against Iran, and mobilization of global political and economic pressure on Iran. After the multinational coalition expelled Iraqi forces from Kuwait in 1991, the Bush administration decided that continuing to rain destruction on Iraq and going on to Baghdad to put an end to Saddam Hussein would not be in U.S. interests. The United States, its coalition partners, and the United Nations Security Council had all endorsed a proximate objective of getting Iraqi forces out of Kuwait, not getting Saddam out of power. If U.S forces had gone on to Baghdad, the United States would have lost most of its partners, notably, but not exclusively, the Muslim countries (in which there would have been a powerful anti-U.S. public backlash, echoed in varying degrees by the régimes). U.S. public and political opinion might have initially backed such an emotionally satisfying move, but once the United States would have moved into Baghdad—and probably became involved in a fierce fight with elements of the population as well as with the Iraqi army—the mood would have begun to shift. And once the Iraqi capital had been conquered, then what? Conquer the rest of the country and install direct U.S. martial law or a puppet régime and indirect U.S. martial law, with no end date in sight for withdrawal, with enduring violent anti-U.S. demonstrations throughout the Muslim world, sharp criticism from Europe, Asia, and Latin America, and possible guerrilla action and terrorism against U.S. forces in some parts of Iraq, with support from Iran and/or Syria? Installation of an inevitably weak régime followed by a quick withdrawal would not have led to a better result. Instead, Iraq very probably would have broken into pieces, with the Shia in the south and the Kurds in the north receiving assistance from across the border. The clash of interests and actions by various states would likely have thrown the entire Near East, stretching from Turkey to the Arabian Peninsula, Egypt to Iran, into serious tension and disorder, possibly into regional conflict.

Thus, the Bush administration's demonization of Saddam was not wise because it exacerbated domestic political pressure, but the policy decision to contain and seek to undermine with strong outside support, rather than forcibly remove him with little or no help, made sense. Iraq's threat to the oil supplies of the Gulf and to U.S. friends was managed by unprecedented sanctions and inspections—effective because the UNSC endorsed them under chapter 7 of the UN Charter, and they were therefore accepted globally—and by the presence and vigilance of U.S. military forces plus those of our friends in the Gulf. Relative stability and peace were restored to the region even though Saddam remained a threat. This showed the limitations of direct military force as well as its capabilities, and the need to continue military, diplomatic, and economic actions. It also showed that most MTWs come to an emotionally and politically unsatisfying end (as with Korea in 1953) rather than achieving total victory.

The 1998 confrontations with Saddam merely reinforce the point about these limitations. To the United States, Iraq's continuing to pursue modest capability to manufacture and perhaps to deliver Weapons of Mass Destruction and to avoid total UN inspection became intolerable, even though Iraq no longer had much capability to invade Kuwait and would be incapable of overcoming U.S. and Gulf states opposition. A major U.S. military buildup on the Gulf took place, with strong U.S. statements. Political pressure within the United States dominated military action, with many people calling for Saddam's removal. However, Saddam showed no threatening signs of invading Kuwait or of using WMDs on Iraq's neighbors (or the United States). The only way to be certain of removing the again-demonized Saddam was to invade Iraq on the ground, not to hurt Iraq from the air. However, the U.S Congress and public would not tolerate the costs in dollars and lives, most of our coalition partners of 1990–91 would have been opposed, and many Muslim states would have erupted in a frenzy of anger, so this was ruled out. Moreover, unilateral bombing could well have brought an end to future inspections and even to sanctions, thereby leaving Iraq freer in the future to sell its oil, obtain foreign investment, procure foreign weaponry and equipment, and thus be in a better position to regain strength over time than before, making Saddam a huge Nasserlike force in the Arab world for having withstood the United States. Because there was no serious likelihood of destroying from the air all Weapons of Mass Destruction and the capabilities to make more, why bomb? Only to relieve domestic political pressure and to respond to Saddam's provocative behavior by destroying Iraq's infrastructure, further weakening an already weak army and killing large numbers of civilians.

The combination of force and diplomacy as of July 1998 paid off at least temporarily in resumed inspections with more freedom to operate than in the past. Sanctions remain in place, tensions in the region are down, and U.S. military forces in the region have been reduced. Inspections will minimize future production of WMD and probably will ensure further reductions, but it will not eradicate all capabilities. The possibilities and limitations have been demonstrated regarding the direct use of military force plus diplomacy to deal with WMD and the capabilities to produce them, as have been (once again) the possibilities and limitations of direct military force in dealing with a regional rogue state.

Conclusions

Prepare for the Future

The United States needs and clearly can afford to maintain its current unparalleled range and quality of military personnel, education/training, doctrine, weaponry, and other technology, particularly information systems. It needs to continue to emphasize military engagement and coalition-enhancing programs vis-à-vis other countries and to improve significantly its attentiveness to their essential needs, playing down a tendency toward moralistic, quasi-hegemonic self-assertiveness and playing up the use of traditional diplomatic and new economic tools. It needs better intelligence collection and especially better analysts, rather than relying so heavily on technological means, and it needs to systematically combine private-sector information with that of the intelligence community. It also needs to have the political will to accept the costs, in money and possibly in casualties, of using direct force on carefully selected occasions across the spectrum, from NEOs, no-go zones, and humanitarian operations to major peace operations, deterrence, and shows of force to actual use of force if deterrence fails.

In most instances, with careful assessment and sound political judgment, this can be done in a coalition context, either approved by, but outside, the UN or as a UNSC operation. This maximizes support from others and reduces the extent of U.S. commitment, either throughout an operation or after more sizable U.S. participation and leadership reduce the difficulty and danger of the situation so that others will have the capability and will to participate. One must recognize that not all operations will be successful, that the Lebanons of 1983 and Somalias of 1993 will occur. But the lessons of Somalia were invaluable for the success of Haiti, which followed the same pattern of a U.S.-led MNF transitioning to a UN peace force—a transition well planned and well executed by the United States and the UN. The important thing is consistency, demonstrating the will and capability to act and the will to continue until success is achieved, rather than turning back because of temporary obstacles, assuming careful assessment of a situation provides a reasonable chance for success in enhancing U.S. interests. At present, a disconnection has developed between words and deeds on the part of the presidential administration with respect to the use of force, partly because of inadequate matching of realistic objectives and the military capabilities to achieve them. The partisan political attitude of many members of Congress also further erodes the world's perception of the United States as a powerful, firm, and confident leader.

Sustaining military excellence is not an exorbitant goal for the United States, although it will require an increase of 1 or 2 percent in annual defense appropriations, along with greater internal Department of Defense efficiencies and more restraint in producing high-cost, sometimes overlapping, advanced weapons and technology. One should look at the "peace dividend" already generated by cuts in defense appropriations in the past decade (including its contribution to a balanced budget, low inflation, and low interest rates). Then look at how the United States has benefited at home and abroad from the superior military establishment created and used effectively in the past fifty years. The conclusion is obvious: Maintaining a powerful military in the interests of both U.S. and global security is a small price to pay. The administration has not been willing to provide enough funds to sustain broad military effectiveness of all forces.

U.S. Leadership

Since the founding of the Republic, the United States has embraced several fundamental and enduring goals as a nation: to maintain the sovereignty, political freedom, and independence of the United States, with its values, institutions, and territory intact; to protect the lives and personal safety of Americans, both at home and abroad; and to provide for the well-being and prosperity of the nation and its people.

Achieving these basic goals in an increasingly interdependent world requires fostering an international environment in which critical regions are stable, at peace, and free from domination by hostile powers; the global economy and free trade are growing; democratic norms and respect for human rights are widely accepted; the spread of nuclear, biological, and chemical (NBC) and other potentially destabilizing technologies is minimized; and the international community is willing and able to prevent and, if necessary, respond to calamitous events. The United States seeks to play a leadership role in the international community, working closely and cooperatively with nations that share our values and goals, and influencing those that can affect U.S. national well-being.[5]

The capacity and will to use its military power to good effect—throughout the world, usually in concert with others, but alone if need be—has been perhaps the most important attribute of U.S. international leadership in the past half-century. That leadership, which has also included political insight, and generally intelligent use of bilateral and multilateral diplomatic and economic instruments, has had a very positive long-term effect in providing stability, enhancing the free-market system, and promoting U.S. and global economic growth as well as containing Communist expansion until it crumbled from within. As events of the past decade have shown, the challenge for the United States is to maintain its military power—more overwhelming than ever, relative to any and all potential adversaries—and to use it intelligently so as to encourage a continuation of presently favorable trends.

Clearly, this essential element of the future use of military force depends primarily on the ability of Congress to understand the need, and its will to join the administration in justifying it to the people. Without it, the wide-ranging, superior capabilities of U.S. military forces described above will soon erode. In addition to the increase in overall spending levels, there also needs to be a decrease in second-guessing and the imposition of tight conditions by Congress on the expenditure of defense funds, linking them too closely to political perceptions of what is best (for Congress) rather than to realistic appreciation of what makes sense for the military. Both the excessive domestic cuts in the defense budget and many of the conditions on its expenditure stem from an increasingly inward-looking tendency by Congress. Assuming that adequate levels of properly directed defense spending can be maintained, this tendency will impact more and more negatively on the intelligent use of U.S. military capacity. More rather than less flexibility, agility, and adaptability is needed for the U.S. military in an increasingly uncertain world. More cooperation and coordination with other countries is also needed. Cutting international and military education and training and other forms of engagement with foreign military forces, reducing the number of forces stationed and deployed abroad, imposing limitations on U.S. participation along with other countries in peace operations, and refusing to pay legally binding UN dues will significantly damage U.S. ability to deal with current and projected threats.

Looking to the future reinforces Clausewitz's basic doctrine that war is an extension of politics, that military action should be understood as subordinate to political objectives and direction. The 1997 *National Military Strategy* describes "decisive force" as the "commitment of sufficient military power to overwhelm an adversary, establish new military conditions and achieve a political resolution favorable to U.S. national interests." It goes on to lay out the requirement for U.S. forces to be able to operate not only jointly and in "concert with our friends and allies" but also "in consensus with other U.S. Government agencies, Non-Governmental and International Organizations, in a variety of settings."

Moreover, if one looks at transnational threats such as the proliferation of Weapons of Mass Destruction, the spread and power of narcotic trafficking and international crimes, and the continued but more fragmented and localized use of terrorism, one sees that military force alone has been able to make only a modest contribution to containing, much less removing, them, and that the unilateral use of U.S. military forces has made a very minor contribution. The combined use of force by U.S. and foreign militaries is an important element of a sustained international politico-economic effort to get at the causes as well as the symptoms. An additional important element is the development of reliable civilian internal security and law-enforcement institutions for foreign countries, and the capability of effective interaction among them. The United States and other countries are more aware than before and are doing more than before to assist countries with weak public-safety institutions, but it is not nearly enough. It requires a combined military-civilian effort plus funds. The latter are lacking. The same reasoning and the same development of capabilities of national institutions as part of an international effort apply to the problem of troubled or failed states. One must attack the causes as well as the symptoms of what has become a serious regional threat to political stability and economic growth. The value of the United Nations system and regional organizations must not be underestimated, particularly as a vital validating or legitimizing authority for most other states, as well as a coordinating mechanism.

Finally, the United States must learn to be much more realistic and patient in pursuing its objectives and in employing military forces intelligently, combined with diplomatic and economic instruments, almost always on a coalition basis, to achieve these objectives. Former National Security Adviser Brent Scowcroft explained this eloquently and succinctly in the *Washington Post* on March 1, 1998, not only replying to a February 26 article by William Kristol and Robert Kagan on U.S. policy toward Iraq but also addressing the broader, longer-term issues involved:

> The Kristol/Kagan analysis of containment as a policy (containment leads to détente, and détente leads to appeasement) calls to mind a debate that raged during the first half of the cold war. Critics insisted that containment would merely provide the Soviets the time they needed to build up their forces to the point at which they could destroy us. These critics argued that since a war was inevitable and containment only served to strengthen the position of our enemies, we should attack them preemptively and destroy them while we could. Our victory in the Cold War proved these critics wrong, and provides a powerful case that a policy of containment—implemented with strength, determination and patience—can serve core U.S. national security interests. And if containment could produce a peaceful end to the cold war on our terms, surely it can be sufficient to deal with threats posed by Saddam Hussein.[6]

The United States, as the world's preeminent military power, must act with firmness, patience, and resoluteness, and to do this, it must continue to act from a position of superior military strength.

NOTES

1. Joint Chiefs of Staff, *The National Military Strategy* (Washington, D.C.: U.S. Government Printing Office, 1997).

2. Executive Office of the President of the United States, *National Security Strategy for a New Century* (Washington, D.C.: U.S. Government Printing Office, 1997).

3. Secretary of Defense Report, *The Quadrennial Defense Review* (Washington, D.C.: U.S. Government Printing Office, 1997).

4. Ibid.

5. Ibid.

6. Brent Scowcroft, "The Power of Containment," *Washington Post*, 1 March 1998.

PART IV

The Intelligence Function in the Twenty-first Century

Overview
David L. Boren

Part IV of this book has special interest for me because of the years I spent as chairman of the Senate Select Committee on Intelligence and the tremendous amount of thought and time I have given to this subject, both then and since. I believe that in the world we have lived in and in the world of the twenty-first century the intelligence function will continue to be a vital part of the national-security equation and of our foreign policy.

The position of director of the Central Intelligence Agency is an extremely sensitive one. It is very hard sometimes to balance the values of an open and democratic society when national-security interests are at stake that demand secrecy and privacy in the conduct of those affairs. That kind of power, action, and information can be entrusted only to people of extraordinary integrity who have a deep personal commitment to basic American democratic values and who can be held accountable. As you will see in the following chapters, I believe that one of the most remarkable developments of the past two decades is the innovative adaptation of our institutions to assure the proper balance between our democratic values and effective intelligence gathering in accordance to law, and with accountability.

We have assembled an astounding amount of knowledge and experience in the contributors to this part of the book. Included are four former directors of Central Intelligence and the current director. I enthusiastically take part in the discussion, two knowledgeable academics are involved, and John Milewski of *Close-Up* and C-Span is superb in keeping the experts on track and engaged in provoking discussion.

Part IV begins with a review by former CIA Director Robert Gates about where we have been in the past fifty years, in chapter 10. Current Director George Tenet, who previously was the chief staff member on the Senate Intelligence Committee, tells us in chapter 12 where we are and where we are going in the intelligence field in the coming century. This is followed by comment and discussion by Professor Stephen Sloan and myself, along with an enlightening question-and-answer session that includes Directors Gates and Tenet with the audience of the 1997 OU foreign-policy conference. Treatment of the subject concludes in chapter 13 with a roundtable discussion moderated by John Milewski. Former CIA Directors Richard Helms, Judge William Webster, and James Woolsey, Professor Robert Cox, Milewski, and I cast light on intriguing subjects of importance to effective intelligence work and to our country in terms of our values and institutions.

Chapter 10

An Evaluation of Intelligence During the Cold War

Robert M. Gates

Asking me to evaluate the role of American intelligence during the cold war is a little like asking the barber whether you need a haircut. Even if I claimed to be objective, most listeners would be skeptical. However, I will try to be balanced, providing some observations on failures and shortcomings, as well as successes.

President John Kennedy, in a visit to CIA headquarters years ago, told his audience of intelligence professionals that "your failures will be trumpeted and your successes unknown." He was exactly right. There are few people in the world with access to television or newspapers who are not aware of the CIA's failures, real and imagined.

However, even as the failures have been trumpeted, the CIA has fought tenaciously to keep its successes secret. I believe this is a mistake. The public needs to understand better the nature and value of intelligence and its role in and contribution to American policy making. To this end, in the early 1980s I initiated a program with the Kennedy School of Government at Harvard University to declassify for student and faculty use CIA documents that could be used in case studies on the role of intelligence in U.S. decision making during key events of the cold war. Several dozen of these Kennedy School case studies are now available publicly. A decade later, as director, I announced in Oklahoma a new program to declassify all the national intelligence estimates on the Soviet Union, as well as materials relating to key covert actions, beginning with those in Guatemala and Iran in the early 1950s, the Bay of Pigs, and others. Several hundred of those estimates are now available, up through the mid-1980s, and the materials on Guatemala also have been released. As these and other materials are declassified—naturally, in a way that protects intelligence techniques and sources still alive—scholars can conduct more comprehensive, objective studies of the role of intelligence in the cold war.

For now, let me summarize my views on the strengths and weaknesses, accomplishments and failures of intelligence in the cold war, especially during its last thirty years.

First, you must understand that the CIA, like the presidents it served, was under political attack from both conservatives and liberals from the early 1970s on. Liberals generally opposed its operational activities, and conservatives its assessments of the Soviet Union, which they considered too soft and too supportive of arms control. The CIA was—also like the presidents it served—more or less constantly embattled through nearly all of the last half of the cold war. Yet its record, in retrospect, is far better than its critics of all political hues will admit.

Operationally, it had important successes in covert action. Perhaps the most consequential of all was the war in Afghanistan, in which, under CIA management, the United States funneled billions of dollars in supplies and weapons to the Mujahedeen. The resistance was thus able to fight the vaunted Soviet army to a standoff and eventually force a political decision to withdraw. Both the costs and the stalemate had significant and broad political impact domestically in the Soviet Union. Similarly, covert actions in Angola and even in Nicaragua produced sufficient pressure on Soviet clients to make them seek a political solution. Elsewhere in the Third World, the CIA worked successfully with governments friendly to the United States to combat subversion by the Soviet Union or its surrogates. We waged the war of ideas and a covert human-rights campaign inside the Soviet Union and supported the growing opposition in eastern Europe, especially in Poland. The CIA carried out a propaganda war against the Soviet régime, publicizing to the world Soviet abuses inside the USSR and aggressions beyond its borders. With our own surrogates, we challenged Soviet clients such as the Libyans, Cubans, and even the Vietnamese.

In short, after Vietnam made the use of American military in the Third World politically impossible at home, the CIA became the instrument of successive presidents—and acted at their direction—to maintain the decades-long policy of containment of the Soviet Union. It was a policy based on the premise that if the Soviet Union was denied the chance to expand influence and power outside its own borders, it would eventually collapse from its own internal contradictions.

The agency's clandestine successes went beyond covert action. We secretly acquired—by James Bondlike thefts, scams, and trickery—an amazing array of sophisticated Soviet military equipment for the U.S. military to dissect and study that enabled the preparation of countermeasures. We stole Soviet weapons manuals, recruited Soviet scientists and engineers who told us about weapons in research and development, and developed agents who revealed much about Warsaw Pact war plans and military capabilities. From the Berlin tunnel of the early 1950s to the very end of the cold war, the CIA developed astonishingly imaginative and advanced techniques, devices, and technical schemes that yielded much information on the Soviet military and its operations.

The operational record, although very strong—in fact, I would argue it was without peer in the world—was obviously far from perfect. We made significant mistakes regarding Central America, nearly all of them in Washington. We failed to dislodge Qaddafi in Libya. Double agents in Cuba and East Germany duped us. The Soviets penetrated us with devastating effect at least twice, and we suffered other counterintelligence and security failures. We never recruited a spy who gave us unique political information from inside the Kremlin, and we too often failed to penetrate the inner circle of Soviet surrogate leaders in Hanoi, Tripoli, Havana, Managua, and elsewhere. For too long, our support to U.S. military operations was not as good as it should have been, plagued by bureaucratic rivalries and turf wars on both sides, and by a cultural gap that grew too wide after Vietnam.

The agency was criticized from time to time, often after the fact, about the character of the individuals and the governments we helped, or who cooperated or worked with us. It is a sad fact of life that at no point in the cold war were there very many democratic governments in the Third World. As a result, during the global struggle with the Soviet Union, the CIA (and the United States, more broadly) ended up with some strange and often unsavory bedfellows. But especially after the mid-1970s, we told foreign agents and governments our rules, and if they did not play by them, our policy was to walk away. The agency's record in this respect was far from perfect, but it was better—and we worked harder at it—than is usually understood.

Similarly, on occasions our operations—for example, in Afghanistan—had lingering and dangerous aftereffects. Sometimes the paramilitary training and weapons we provided after the conflicts ended were put to unwelcome purposes and were even used in actions hostile to U.S. interests. We were always conscious of that likelihood and, indeed, had warned policy makers about it during the debate over whether to use Stinger missiles in Afghanistan.

All in all, the CIA—unique among the world's intelligence services—endeavored to conduct its operational activities, especially during the last half of the cold war, according to presidential directive, under the rule of law and, in every way possible, in a manner consistent with American values. No one can or will deny that there were lapses and failures—and the agency paid a high price for them. But in a shadow war that ranged across the globe, such failures were remarkably few and far between.

In sum, the CIA generally was successful in carrying out the operational missions assigned by presidents. I had differences with the clandestine service over the years and probably was regarded by many of its officers as overly critical. But their record of accomplishment in the cold war was unequaled, far surpassing that of their Soviet adversaries. They were the effective hidden hand of American presidents in the shadow wars of the cold war.

In the area of technical collection, the CIA and the U.S. intelligence-community scientists and engineers were brilliant. The American people—and indeed, the West in general—owe a huge debt of gratitude to the unsung technical experts of U.S. intelligence (and to those in industry who worked with them) who figured out how to obtain information from a distance of hundreds or thousands of miles; who designed and built unique technical systems to monitor Soviet missile testing and deployments; and who could make sense out of bewildering arrays of squiggly lines, rows of numbers and, at least at the beginning, fuzzy pictures. If ever legends and stories of American technological genius were deserved and not yet realized, they would be about the scientists and engineers—the wizards—of the CIA who pioneered reconnaissance aircraft such as the U-2 and the SR-71 Blackbird, and photographic satellites from the KH-4 to the KH-11, people who worked anonymously to serve their country. It is a tribute to these remarkable men and women that, after the 1960s, as they targeted one of the most secretive countries in the world, there were virtually no Soviet military surprises of strategic importance.

The continuing great strength and success of the analysts of CIA and the intelligence community were in describing with amazing accuracy, from the 1960s until the Soviet collapse, the actual military strength and capabilities of the Soviet Union. Liberals long argued that the CIA overstated Soviet military power, and conservatives argued just as stridently that it underestimated. But we located and counted with precision the number of deployed aircraft, tanks, ships, and strategic weapons. The executive branch (including the Defense Department), Congress, and our allies could rely on these numbers and capabilities with confidence, both in arms-control negotiations and in military planning.

Perhaps the intelligence community's greatest contribution was that during the last half of the cold war there were no significant strategic surprises—no more "bomber gaps" or "missile gaps," as in the 1950s. Further, our detailed knowledge of Soviet forces and capabilities after the mid-1960s made it virtually impossible for the Soviets to bluff us. And this helped prevent miscalculations and misunderstandings that could have destroyed the world.

Similarly, the CIA's work on the Soviet economy stands up far better than hindsight criticism suggests. The CIA's record—literally thousands of assessments, briefings, and monographs, public and classified, during a thirty-year period—makes it clear that the agency, from the late 1960s onward, accurately described the growing economic, political, and social weaknesses of the Soviet Union; accurately portrayed the futility of tinkering with the system; and pointed out how Mikhail Gorbachev was undermining the foundations of the old system without embracing a new one. By 1988–89, the CIA was warning of deepening crisis, the potential for a rightist coup, and the possible collapse of the entire system.

In analysis, as in operations, the record was not perfect. On the military side, the technical capabilities of specific Soviet weapons occasionally surprised us, for example, the speed of the Alpha-class submarine. We would, from time to time, both over- and underestimate specific characteristics of specific Soviet weapons. We were constantly revising our estimates of exactly how many Soviet troops were stationed in the Warsaw Pact countries. Further, during the mid-1980s—perhaps as a reflection of the criticism of our underestimates of future Soviet strategic forces in the late 1960s—our projections of the military forces we thought the Soviets would deploy five to ten years in the future were too high. Although we saw no slackening in military expenditures or the vigor of Soviet research-and-development and modernization programs, the already huge Soviet-deployed forces in the 1980s did not grow as quickly as we had predicted.

Even so, for a quarter of a century, American presidents and Congress negotiated and made strategic decisions with confidence in our knowledge of the adversary's actual military strength—a confidence that was justified. The existing Soviet military capabilities that we described were real, and those capabilities were created, to a considerable degree, at the cost of bringing an already fundamentally flawed economic system to its knees. It is one of history's little ironies that the Soviet military helped to destroy the system it was built to defend.

Finally, the CIA came late to the realization that the entire Soviet structure might collapse. Until early 1989, the CIA did not contemplate that a Soviet Communist *apparatchik*—Gorbachev—once in power would unintentionally set in motion forces that would pull the props from under an already declining economic system and bring down the entire political and imperial system in the process. To be fair, the CIA had a great deal of company in this regard—in the United States, elsewhere in the West, and especially in the Soviet Union.

Most important, though, by early 1989, the CIA was warning policy makers of the deepening crisis in the Soviet Union and the growing likelihood of a collapse of the old order. The gloom and doom of these assessments had two concrete results. (1) At the White House, I took them seriously. With President George Bush's explicit approval, because of these assessments, I established a top-secret, high-level contingency planning effort to prepare for the possibility of Soviet collapse. (2) By the summer of 1989 these reports persuaded the Bush administration to consolidate many accomplishments that were in our national interest.

Preventing surprise was the CIA's mission and, with respect to the Soviet collapse, it fulfilled that mission more than two years ahead of time. That was two years' more warning than Gorbachev got. Prophecy beyond that was not in the CIA's charter and, in the real world, speculation of a Soviet internal apocalypse much before then would have been ignored, if not ridiculed, by decision makers.

The CIA has been accused of failing in the 1980s to warn of Soviet limitations, vulnerabilities, and weaknesses. The facts and documents do not support the accusations. The agency's record of the Soviet economic and social crisis is well documented. In the military arena, after many a hard-fought debate, the CIA warned about Soviet shortcomings and the limitations of specific Soviet weapons systems. On issues ranging from the declining rate of growth in Soviet military spending in the early 1980s, to problems of morale and the unreliability of the USSR's Warsaw Pact allies, to economic crisis, we described Soviet problems and vulnerabilities, often providing analysis that policy makers did not want to hear. Although we reminded our government of continuing Soviet interest in opportunities in the Third World and the large sums Moscow was still spending to support Cuba, Angola, Nicaragua, Vietnam, and others well into Gorbachev's tenure, we also advised them of strains in those relationships and the dissatisfaction of Soviet clients with much of the aid they received.

In sum, I believe the CIA and the American intelligence community made an important contribution to victory in the cold war. Because of information provided by U.S. intelligence, President Kennedy had an accurate picture of Soviet strategic inferiority during the Cuban missile crisis. Because of U.S. knowledge of Soviet strategic strength and capabilities, there would never again be a similar U.S.-Soviet nuclear confrontation. U.S. intelligence information made possible the negotiation and then the ratification of all arms-control agreements. In short, U.S. intelligence, during a period of nearly fifty years, helped keep the cold war cold.

During the cold war, the CIA was the American sword in the surrogate wars of the Third World; a source of help and sustenance for dissidents and oppositionists in the Soviet Union and eastern Europe; worldwide purveyor of the realities of Soviet repression and subversion; gatherer of critical military information; accurate appraiser of Soviet military strength and weaknesses; chronicler of the growing Soviet crisis at home; and, by 1989, first herald in governments East or West of potential systemic collapse. Americans deserve to know more about this record, warts and all. Two generations of the brave men and women of American intelligence deserve acknowledgment of their sacrifices, their service, and their victories.

Chapter 11

A Strategic Look at Intelligence in the Future

George J. Tenet

On September 18, 1997, the Central Intelligence Agency celebrated its fiftieth anniversary. Before addressing the future, I think it is important to review history. At CIA headquarters there are two important monuments. The first is made of steel and concrete. It is a section of the Berlin Wall. For most of the first fifty years of the CIA's existence, tearing down the wall and defeating Communism were our consuming passions. There is another wall at CIA. It is made of polished marble and it is on the right side of the lobby near our front entrance. There are seventy stars carved into the wall. Each star represents a CIA officer killed in the line of duty. These seventy individuals, along with countless others throughout the cold war, paid with their lives to reduce the Berlin Wall to a museum piece. Their work tells a powerful story, one of tremendous accomplishment, of skill and determination, of covert operations and actions behind enemy lines, of ordinary people asked to do extraordinary things, ordinary people willing to put themselves in harm's way to serve this great country. These walls also tell us that our intelligence work was decisive in ending the cold war. Our people made a difference, from officers abroad to analysts at home, from scientists to engineers, from linguists to photo interpreters. Although Communism is nearly extinct, these two walls provide an enduring message to us: There can be no achievement without sacrifice.

The best way to honor these achievements and the sacrifices of the past is to prepare to meet the challenges of the future. The president, Congress, and the American people expect no less from us. They know and we know that there is an enduring need for intelligence as we prepare for the next millennium. No one with a responsibility to tend to the nation's security, no one with the responsibility to protect the American people would ever suggest that we could do so without intelligence. We are at a turning point in history, one that is full of both opportunity for increased global stability and the challenge of containing ethnic, religious, and regional disputes. If we in the intelligence business approach this turning point with the right stuff—with energy, with decisiveness, with conviction, with unity of purpose, and with an unrelenting focus on our mission—we will accomplish great things for the future.

I have not the slightest doubt about what the president and the American people and you expect of us each and every day. First and foremost, they and you expect the intelligence community to help protect the lives of Americans everywhere. They expect us to work to protect the lives of our men and women in uniform and to ensure that they dominate the battlefields when they deploy to remote parts of the world. The record in Bosnia and Haiti has been truly remarkable in this regard. They expect us to protect Americans from other threats such as those that come from terrorists and hostile nations with weapons of mass destruction. They expect us to provide our diplomats with the critical insights and foreknowledge to advance American interests and to avert conflicts. They expect us to anticipate and warn of major geopolitical changes in the world. They also expect us to focus not just on threats, but also on opportunities—opportunities to act before danger becomes disaster, opportunities to level the playing field so that American interests will always prevail. They expect our reporting and analysis to add real value to what they already know about the toughest problems facing the United States.

We know we exist because we offer unique analytic and clandestine collection capabilities that reside no other place in the United States government. Simply stated, we have the responsibility to provide the president with information he cannot get by any other means. The *Washington Post* does not provide it. The *New York Times* does not provide it. The *Daily Oklahoman* does not provide it. We do not just report on what happened yesterday. We try to tell the president what is going on, what is going to happen tomorrow, the next month, and the next year. We focus on issues such as the plans and intentions of terrorist groups that threaten to kill Americans; whether the North Koreans are refueling their nuclear reactor; how narcotics traffickers intend to flood the United States with heroin and cocaine; and when and how the Iranians will develop a nuclear weapon, and how they intend to deliver it. These are questions that only a secret intelligence organization and community can answer, and they are questions that we simply cannot fail to try to answer.

But we are not just observers. We also have to give the president the wherewithal to act. In late 1998 a team of very brave FBI agents and CIA folks brought a man home to justice from half a world away. His name was Mir Aimal Kansi. In 1994, he stood in front of the front gates of the Central Intelligence Agency and killed two of our employees and wounded four others. It took us almost four years to find this man and bring him to justice. One of the greatest things I have ever done in my life was to call the wives of Lansing Bennett and Frank Darling to tell them that we never gave up. We will never end in our determination to bring to justice on your behalf people who commit these acts.

Just as the intelligence community helped to bring about an end to the cold war, today we are helping to usher in and define this new world that I am talking about. If we look at the world before us, let me point out a few trends that are interesting and also frightening. Today, more wars are being fought within states than between them. The results of such ethnic strife have been all too apparent. From A to Z, from Albania to Zaire, humanitarian crises, large-scale suffering, and regional instability have been commonplace. Consider that states have become more interdependent economically and politically. Interdependence and more openness have helped increase global wealth. But at the same time, we confront lethal weapons, illicit drugs, and dirty money flowing more easily across porous borders. Consider that by the year 2010 the world's population will have increased by 1.2 billion, with 95 percent of that increase occurring in the developing world, further straining governments and societies. Consider that by the end of the next decade, the world will need as much more oil as the equivalent of one additional OPEC to satisfy growing energy demand. Consider that the communications revolution is adding fifteen new Web sites every minute. We live in an age in which ten-year-olds are creating Web pages. Yet just as the Internet has helped us to reach out to anyone with a telephone and a modem, new technology has also provided greater opportunities for terrorists, international criminals—and even hostile governments. Small wonder that these tools have been called weapons of mass disruption!

But in addition to telling you how busy we are and how demanding the global environment is for those of us in the intelligence business, I will tell you how we are going to prevail against these challenges.

(1) We will produce outstanding all-source analysis that is timely, prescient, and persuasive. To do that, we must be—and be seen to be—the nation's leading experts in a wide variety of fields. Through every means available to us, we will reach out to the rich body of expertise that exists outside the United States government in academia and in our private sector.

(2) We will mount imaginative and sophisticated clandestine human and technical operations to get vital information that our nation cannot get in any other way. I know this will involve risks, and not every operation will succeed. But next to integrity and objectivity, this risk-taking ethic is the most important part of the CIA's professional identity. Concentrating our attention on these hard targets, the most difficult targets that confront us, will demand the highest standards of professionalism, tradecraft, and innovation. To do what our country needs, we can be nothing less than the world's greatest espionage organization.

(3) We will be vigilant on the counterintelligence front. Our enemies, our competitors, and even some of our friends are trying very hard to steal our secrets. They want to gain a competitive edge in any way they can. We would do a great disservice to ourselves and to all that we hope to achieve if we neglected this arena. In the world we live in today, it is not enough to play strong offense. We must also play strong defense.

(4) We will sharpen the CIA's capacity to effectively employ covert action

on those unique occasions when our nation's leaders conclude that an important aim can be achieved through no other means.

(5) In all our endeavors we will use technology to advance our mission, not only to ensure that we have the support infrastructure we need to perform, but also to ensure that we develop the scientific and technological expertise that allows the CIA and our intelligence community to be a national center for excellence in technological innovation. The agency and community that brought our country the U-2 and imagery from outer space have no less an obligation today to push the technology envelope.

To succeed in these efforts in the future requires that we set a clear direction and keep an unrelenting focus on the most important threats to our country. Intelligence success demands the highest standards of personal integrity and professional performance. It requires that we be independent and forthright. It compels us to take risks to get information our leaders need to protect our interests. Intelligence success means not allowing the cloak of secrecy to stand in the way of an open and honest dialogue with the American people or with experts outside the intelligence community who can help us interpret this complex new world.

Intelligence success in the future means that we have closed the door on the cold war and are embracing the challenges and opportunities of the era ahead. Our mission is clear; our responsibilities are many; our determination is strong. Understanding this new world and interpreting it for our leaders remain consuming passions for the intelligence community. After more than fifty years and on the eve of the new millennium, we will continue to help our leaders to shape this new world and make it less threatening. We will continue to serve as the first line of defense, and we will work to preserve our country and its freedoms. This is our calling, and there can be no more important mission for the men and women of our intelligence community.

Finally, you should know that the people of the intelligence profession reflect the ideals of our country. Those ideals are embodied in the two monuments at our headquarters building. Hard work, achievement and, yes, sacrifice have been our hallmark for more than fifty years, and so they will be for decades to come. Our objective every day is to ensure that all Americans are safer because of how we do our job. I want the people of our country to know that we will honor the trust you have placed in us, and we will serve you with fidelity, with integrity, and with excellence.

Chapter 12

The Intelligence Function: Commentary and Discussion

David L. Boren and Stephen Sloan

Stephen Sloan

The issue I want to address is that we are in a much more ambiguous international environment now than we have been in the past. I do not minimize the dangers created by the cold war, as particularly illustrated by the Cuban missile crisis. But I also recognize the fact that there was a certain coherence in terms of the adversary during the cold-war period. There were relatively neat orders of battle in which you could identify the opposition. We were familiar with Soviet military doctrine. We were familiar with the tactics, strategies, and policies directed against us. The difficulty now is that the targets of our intelligence are much more ambiguous. We lack the cohesiveness that we had before. We also have the additional challenge that we do not, on the policy level, have a clearly enunciated strategic vision.

The policy of containment, with its bipartisan thrust for many years, did work, but increasingly one raises the question, "What policy, what bipartisanship?" That is a major difficulty that we all face.

In addition, although, as Robert Gates noted, prophecy is beyond the CIA's charter, we nevertheless face the demand of assessing global change in the long term. The issue that concerns a lot of us is the necessity of genuinely engaging in strategic intelligence. Do we really focus on strategic intelligence? Although I appreciate the current threats—although on occasion they appear to really be the threat du jour—what are the new threats over the horizon? What are the new challenges? What are the broader social, economic, and political movements which are already transforming this world and creating new demands for another generation of students, scholars, analysts, and spies? In essence, although Washington has to put out the current tactical fires, it cannot ignore the strategic implications of concentrating only on short-term, immediate threats.

I am very pleased to see—and I want to emphasize this—the growing efforts by the intelligence community to reach out to the academic community and beyond, to obtain assistance for new challenges, many of which are not even known today. It reminds me very much of the contributions scholars made in the Library of Congress in the very dark days of World War II. I think reaching out and breaching the barrier between the academic world and the intelligence community is very much a step in the right direction. That is one of the reasons we are concerned about educating our students to understand the international arena.

I would address another central concern. I deeply appreciate the inherent tension in regard to reconciling secrecy about clandestine and covert operations with openness and accountability in a democratic society. I know there is indeed a real and vital need for meeting this task. I hope the type of oversight process continues that we witnessed when David L. Boren, as chairman of the Senate Select Committee on Intelligence, provided leadership to establish an effective oversight process. Finally, there are profound issues about collection and analysis in terms of their constitutional implications.

More and more, what has been called seamless terrorism has blurred the line between domestic and international intelligence, where the boundaries between states have lost their meaning. Increasingly, the FBI is taking on functions that it had lost when the CIA was established. Director J. Edgar Hoover would have been very happy to see the expansion of the FBI's role overseas. On the other hand, the CIA and the military, because of the changing threats of terrorism and organized crime, are walking on that dangerous line which may involve them in the legally questionable area of domestic collection. Also, we see the military increasingly participating in law enforcement.

I end on three notes. (1) Although the line between foreign and domestic is increasingly being blurred, it is extremely important to keep that line in mind. (2) We are no longer living solely in the era of nation-states. We see the decline of states and the rise of a wide variety of nonstate actors, which are now also exerting greater influence on the global community. (3) I share Gates' concern that our intelligence community not engage in economic spying. This means corporate competitive intelligence and counterintelligence become more important, particularly as organized crime and governments—whether in the former Soviet Union or other places—seek to maximize their economic capabilities by the use of espionage.

I would note one last thing. I was very struck by George Tenet's comments about the Berlin Wall and the seventy stars memorializing those who lost their lives in the pursuit of their duties. The tradition of patriotism is one which the members of the intelligence community have perpetuated in the finest way. I am therefore very proud to say that some of the University of Oklahoma students have pursued and will continue to pursue careers in a very demanding and vital profession.

David L. Boren

Professor Sloan's remarks raise many questions, and I direct to Director Tenet and Dr. Gates two of them. The first is about the blurring line between the FBI and the CIA. The CIA obviously, by its charter, should not collect intelligence within the United States against American targets, but very often international drug traffickers, money launderers, and terrorists have relationships with domestic criminals. Some Americans are in league with unsavory people outside the United States. The FBI—which is mandated to act domestically under the constraints of our law, which requires such things as search warrants—is now operating overseas, where there are less restrictions. Could this affect the FBI's domestic conduct? The CIA is being pushed into greater cooperation with the FBI, and perhaps being pressed into action within the United States. What are the risks of this blurring line, and the increasing difficulty in delineating the missions of the FBI and the CIA? I direct this question to Director Tenet.

The second question relates to foreign economic intelligence. I can recall instances in which we found foreign intelligence services, not just foreign private companies, stealing secrets from American private companies to give their countries' companies the competitive advantage internationally. We also found foreign intelligence services paying bribes to influence decisions of other governments and thus shut out American companies bidding competitively to enter those marketplaces. I ask Director Gates to address the question of the use of counterintelligence and intelligence resources in the growing area of economic espionage.

George Tenet

Senator, I think one of the greatest successes we have had in the last three years is increasing the cooperation between the CIA and the FBI, coming to a firm understanding about the delineation of responsibilities, and entering into a working relationship that allows us to train together, to operate together, and to understand exactly where those lines should never be crossed.

The examples I offer are the Aldrich Ames betrayal, which was a tragic case for the Central Intelligence Agency, and the Nicholson case. Jim Nicholson was arrested after Ames. The difference in the level of CIA cooperation with the FBI on the Nicholson case versus the Ames case is palpable. The fact is that by statute the FBI has expanded its extraterritorial jurisdiction around the world. We have worked enormously hard in 1996 and 1997 across the world to ensure that law-enforcement powers are not expanded at the expense of intelligence powers, or that the respective communities do not suffer in the process. I believe at the end of the day this will be a significant enhancement to our country's security.

Returning to my theme of making Americans feel safer, I do not think they are threatened by the cooperation of the CIA and the FBI. We understand how each other operates. We understand what the distinctions are. The U.S. intelligence community has no interest in going after Americans, and we will not do so. But the fact is that terrorism does not stop at the water's edge. There needs to be a handoff between domestic and foreign assets, between what the FBI does and the CIA does. If the right hand and the left hand do not know what they are doing with each other, then the American taxpayer is getting a pretty bad deal.

We are putting a lot of this history behind us. J. Edgar Hoover would turn over in his grave if he knew that the director of the FBI actually swore me in on the day I was confirmed. The world has changed in a fundamental way.

Robert M. Gates

I have reevaluated my position that the intelligence community should not collect commercial intelligence to give individual American firms a competitive advantage, and I have decided it was right. There are, however, appropriate roles for the intelligence community in the realm of economic intelligence. The first of these is monitoring technological developments around the world that may pose some national-security danger to the United States, e.g., the ability of other countries to intercept or disrupt our communications, as George Tenet described. Second, we must be aware of other countries' technological developments that might produce new kinds of weapons that could be deployed against the United States. Keeping aware of these kinds of developments around the world is very important. Third, it is also very important to support American policy makers in their economic decision-making and negotiating process, to help our leaders be aware of the positions of other governments and the differences between what governments say and what they do. I know it will come as a big surprise to most of you to know that governments sometimes say one thing and do another. Finally, I think intelligence has an important defensive role to play. It is one of the areas, in fact, where CIA and FBI cooperation is oldest. We have told American companies that they are targeted by a foreign intelligence service or by some foreign entity that has either planted "moles" in their factories or is trying to acquire their technologies. I think we can work with such companies to help them defend themselves, and perhaps catch some of the foreign spies.

I have yet, during the last ten years, to have a single American CEO come to me to request the CIA's help in getting competitive advantage. Mostly, they want us to stay out of their way. I believe that is right. I believe we would march down a path that has all kinds of difficult legal, moral, and ethical questions were we to try to collect intelligence for competitive advantage. As Professor Sloan indicated, if we were going to target collection of telecommunications information, which communications company would we give that information to? How would we make sure we give it all to the right company, or all of it to all of the companies? The potential for litigation and so on is endless. I believe the goal of the American government should be to stop economic espionage by other foreign intelligence services, not for us to join them. I believed that ten years ago, and I continue to believe it today. I believe that my three successors have all followed that same view.

> **Q:** Do you think U.S. intelligence on narcotics activities in Mexico have been compromised to strengthen trade ties?

George Tenet

No, I do not. The nature of the drug problem is a very serious one and although people can pick out "lapses," there are many more successes. The CIA, along with our Drug Enforcement Agency and our law-enforcement community along the Southwest border, is doing all that it can to stem the flow of drugs from Central and South America and Mexico. One of the great successes in the last few years of U.S. intelligence, along with our law-enforcement colleagues, has been breaking the back of the Cali cartel in Colombia. The bad news is that these cartels are enormously agile, have a lot of money and, like an amoeba, they sprout in other places. Our government is working very carefully and closely on the policy level and on the law-enforcement level with the Mexican government to deal with these difficult problems.

> **Q:** Mr. Tenet, the CIA has experienced significant reductions in force and may have been compromised in its ability to collect secret information and to focus on strategic threats. You mentioned the possibility of drawing on the university community and different actors other than the CIA to provide analysis. Would reliance on actors other than the CIA lead to the CIA's inability to provide strategic intelligence and affect its ability to predict accurately what is going to happen and to analyze the information gained from intelligence?

George Tenet

You have asked me a number of questions. Let me see if I can parse them out in a way that is helpful. First, our intelligence community is smaller. The entire United States government is smaller. That is not a bad thing. It is probably a good thing from the perspective of getting our focus on things that matter the most. We know what our mission is. We know what our priorities are, and we have a very clear sense of the ten or fifteen things that will endure over a decade and continue to threaten American interests. We are focusing in a rather relentless manner on how to allocate resources against those problems.

You have raised interesting questions. Few people would have thought a number of years ago that Somalia would have been a problem. Few would have predicted the humanitarian crisis in the Great Lakes region of Africa. In those cases, U.S. intelligence surged to provide our policy makers and our military with the ability to do their jobs. I talked about outreach to the academic community. The CIA cannot afford to have an expert for every country in the world. As a manager who has fewer people and less money, every day I have to make strategic decisions about what threatens Americans. I have a responsibility to figure out how, in the most cost-effective manner, to access the best minds in this country to give me ground truth when I do not have it. That is the kind of program I am pursuing. I have to be mindful of the targets that matter the most. I also have to be mindful of the fact that as a great power, this country and its intelligence community are often asked to do things that no one thought we would ever do. In the crisis in the Great Lakes region of Africa, because of the way we were able to surge and provide information, U.S. intelligence was largely responsible for our not having to deploy U.S. forces there. These needs are real, and that is why I think we have to rely on the academic community to help us keep a database alive to attack these difficult problems.

Q: We were reminded very forcibly during the Iran-Contra affair of the difficulties of coordinating the different parties and agencies involved in national security and intelligence-gathering affairs and operations, and the difficulties of ensuring proper oversight and accountability of all the various operations. How much has changed, how much has improved with regard to some of the problems we saw at that time?

David L. Boren

This is a question I was asking when I was at the Senate Intelligence Committee—how can we avoid duplication, and should we not give more power to someone? I thought at the time that the director of the CIA ought to coordinate the budget for all of our intelligence efforts. Many people do not know that historically the military generally has spent more money on intelligence than the CIA. Are we making progress or does that problem remain? We will begin with Director Gates.

Robert M. Gates

First, there is a need to step back to gain a little perspective on the question of congressional oversight. Since the rise of the nation-state, intelligence activities have traditionally been the province of the sovereign or the president. It was true under George Washington. It was true under Abraham Lincoln. It was certainly true under President Franklin Roosevelt during World War II. What the country set out to do in the mid-1970s in creating genuine congressional oversight of intelligence was something that had never been tried before in any other country, had never been tried in any other democracy. What we have seen is an evolutionary process.

I believe the role of individuals in governments plays a huge difference. For example, it matters a lot in policy making if the secretary of defense and secretary of state are not speaking to each other. Similarly, relationships make a big difference in terms of congressional oversight. I think the structure that was put in place beginning in the mid-1970s was historically significant. We have evolved enormously from the fairly limited arena of congressional oversight at that time to where we are now, twenty years later. Among other things, we have a whole generation of intelligence professionals who have grown up in a world of congressional oversight, where the expectation is that you give the facts, the analysis, and the perspective that are needed. You do not hold back, you do not play games, and you are completely truthful. If you are being told by the president not to tell Congress something, as the director you go back to the president and say, "Either I tell them, or you get yourself a new DCI."

I think we made a decent start on congressional oversight in the Carter administration because Admiral Turner believed in it. President Jimmy Carter certainly believed in it. There were a lot of problems in those days, a lot of differences between a Democratic administration and a Democratically controlled Congress on the role of Congress and oversight, and there were a lot of fights over congressional prerogatives.

From 1980 to the end of 1986 there was regression. It is not sharing any particular secret to say that Bill Casey did not have a particularly forthcoming view of Congress or the oversight process. He basically regarded it as an unwarranted intrusion. This veteran of World War II, this creature of the OSS in an all-out war against the Nazis, in his war against the Soviets saw Congress as nattering at his heels and getting in his way. His relationship with Congress was always difficult, from within weeks of his confirmation until the day he suffered a stroke.

Since the end of 1986 and the beginning of 1987—which coincides with David Boren's taking the chairmanship of the Senate Select Committee on Intelligence and Senator Bill Cohen of Maine being the senior Republican and vice chairman—there has been a steady and very sharp acceleration and improvement in the quality of the relationship between the intelligence community and the congressional oversight committees.

David Boren should get a lot of the credit for that. When I was acting director, we sat down within days of his taking that job and laid out ways to cooperate, which included private meetings between us so that we could get a deal with things not on the public agenda. These procedures have continued. There has been a series of directors of Central Intelligence who have been committed to congressional oversight—from my period as acting director, through Bill Webster, then my term as director, and my successors' terms. I think that process, both from a personal level and from an institutional level, has now been established and grounded firmly enough that it is a part of our system. What is interesting now is to watch others in the world, particularly the British, French, and Germans, try to figure out for themselves how to have some kind of parliamentary oversight. It is very painful for them, as well. We can sit back and assure them it will be all right.

Regarding the question about the powers of the director, George Tenet is probably in a better position to answer this than I am. I think there have been a number of measures taken in the last five years or so to enhance the authority of the director within the intelligence community, to better allocate resources, to move resources around, to establish priorities, and to see that they are enforced. The fact remains, however, that the Defense Department spent—and I suspect still spends—85 percent of the intelligence budget. The secretary of defense is loath to give up entirely his authority over that money and how those military-intelligence institutions operate. A great deal depends on the personal relationship between the CIA director and the secretary of defense in terms of how that process works, and how much authority the director has. The statutory authorities of the director have not been significantly expanded, but I think his real overall authority within the community and vis-à-vis the Defense Department probably has been enhanced.

George Tenet

Two points to follow on Gates' comments: I believe the oversight process that we have is a real strength and net advantage for our country. Quite frankly, the British, French, and Germans are also thinking about this. From our perspective we want all of the former east European countries and all the newly independent states of the former Soviet Union to adopt similar kinds of oversight mechanisms. We believe this kind of oversight not only serves democracy, and therefore our people, but also provides an enormous advantage for our intelligence community. This is a relationship that is far different than it was in the early 1980s.

With regard to the power of the director, I could make some news by asking for more power, but I am not going to do that, because I think what Gates said is right. By virtue of my relationship with the secretary of defense and by virtue of the influence I exert over the rest of our community, I have enough power and about the right ability to influence how budget decisions are made, how we eliminate redundancies, and how we allocate money in a way that reflects real gain against the toughest targets we face.

Robert M. Gates

Let me come back with just one point on oversight that I think is important. One of the things that has happened in the last twenty years is that you now have a generation of American intelligence officers who understand that thorough congressional oversight is in fact a great advantage for U.S. intelligence. We now have a body of people in Congress, in both the Senate and the House, who have served on the intelligence committees and who understand the secrets of our business, the technical systems, and the risks and benefits of clandestine operations and covert actions. These people tend overall—while being critical and exercising their oversight judgments —to be very supportive of the idea of intelligence and of resources for intelligence. Intelligence professionals are smart enough, and have been for a number of years, to understand the benefits. That is another reason why I believe that the level of oversight and the institutional relationships that have evolved will endure.

David L. Boren

That certainly is true. Moreover, there are members of Congress who understand that as we cut the military budget and as we have fewer overseas military bases, we need even earlier warnings to be able to respond in a timely manner. Warnings come from the intelligence community, and this should be taken into account in a time of budget reductions. I think both directors would know instances, too, in which the fact that the intelligence committees had to be told certain information also helped to protect honest people in the intelligence community who might otherwise be put under pressure to do improper things, were it not for the fact that the congressional oversight committee existed.

Q: This question is mainly directed towards Director Tenet. A situation now in the Defense Intelligence Agency is that many, if not most, of its senior analysts are due to retire in the next four to five years. Is such a situation also occurring at the CIA and other parts of the intelligence community, and if so, where are new analysts going to come from?

George Tenet

This is a very good question. I told you before that we are getting smaller. In fact, we have created incentives for people to retire early. One of the great challenges, and I alluded to it in my chapter, is to maintain and build on the analytical depth we have had. This is a very difficult problem, because you do not grow an expert overnight. We are now maintaining and developing a system of training and education that guarantees that we recruit the best and the brightest. We give people educational and professional opportunities and try to convince them to stay for twenty- to thirty-year careers. In addition to people retiring, matters are compounded by our society having become much more mobile. Few people view government service as a career anymore. There has been a loss of historical perspective about the meaning of public service. Very few people remember what World War II was all about. It is very difficult to deal with.

To all young people, let me say that although somebody can pay you more money, you could never find a career that can provide you more fun and challenge than the Foreign Service, the U.S. military, or the Central Intelligence Agency. Just as Uncle Sam wanted you, "Uncle George" wants you desperately. I want you!

Q: With the demise of the Soviet Union, I have learned through the media there are suitcase bombs with tactical nuclear capability. I would like for the panelists to speak on that, please.

George Tenet

This is an issue and obviously a problem. The safety of the Russian nuclear arsenal and of the fissile material is something of deep concern to us. With regard to these specific reports, we are looking at all of them quite closely. This is an issue that, as Russia makes the transition, we care deeply about. We have a similar concern for the loss of fissile material. We have programs of cooperation in place with the Russians to ensure that we can account for their nuclear matériel and that in an economy that is struggling, people who have money—terrorist groups, rogue states—do not entice Russian scientists and nuclear matériel out of that country. I must say the record is generally much better than people perceive. It is something that we work on very, very hard.

Q: In the popular press, there has been a lot of discussion of the dissemination of strong encryption algorithms into both our domestic economy and throughout the world. I know that if those exist they make your job harder. How much harder is it and what can we do about it? Do we need more human intelligence instead of signal intelligence?

George Tenet

The problem of encryption is a very difficult one that our government is attempting to grapple with today. Obviously, U.S. industry has a great commercial advantage in terms of the products it wants to generate. We need to work out an equitable way to accommodate the needs of both our industry and our law-enforcement community. Think about the ability of the FBI not to be able to decrypt a conversation between terrorists planning a terrorist event against Americans in this country that could take the lives of hundreds of Americans. We are looking for an approach of cooperation between government and industry to design products that give U.S. industry a competitive advantage but also give our law-enforcement community the ability, when a judge provides a legitimate court order, to continue to do its job. This is a tension being played out on Capitol Hill through different pieces of legislation. This is a very tough problem, indicative of how technology can threaten the intelligence community and the law-enforcement community.

Q: Russia has vast oil reserves in eastern Siberia, and recently has shown its inability or unwillingness to cooperate on contracts with U.S. companies—Conoco, Exxon, Amoco. Dr. Gates mentioned the burgeoning needs of the world, particularly China, for oil. The reserves of eastern Siberia are a lot closer to Beijing than they are to Moscow. What is the potential for conflict, or a drive on China's part to access those reserves?

Robert M. Gates

We in the intelligence community say everything in our business falls into two categories—secrets and mysteries. We can find out secrets. The mysteries are when the people involved do not know themselves what they intend to do. My own view is that the likelihood of the Chinese acting in some forceful way to try to access Russian oil reserves in Siberia is very low. There is the potential, perhaps some years in the future, for cooperative business arrangements between China and Russia in which pipelines are built. In fact, the Chinese are already cutting deals in central Asia to build oil and gas pipelines to China. However, I think that for some indefinite period the Chinese will not have the technical and business skills to build the kinds of pipelines, do the kind of exploration, or develop oil and gas fields in a way that the Western, and particularly American, companies can. Farther down the road, there may be the opportunity for some kind of tripartite arrangement in which American companies, in a Russia that has finally gotten its act together, can develop oil fields for which the market is China. I think that is the most likely outcome in the next ten or fifteen years.

Q: During 1977 there were allegations, led by Congresswoman Maxine Waters of California, that the CIA in the mid-1980s may have introduced crack cocaine into the inner city of Los Angeles. I was just wondering what your views on that are.

George Tenet

We take these allegations very seriously. Our inspector general is working quite diligently on running all of these things down. The Department of Justice inspector general is launching a similar effort. The House and Senate Intelligence Committees are also looking at this. The allegations are being taken extremely seriously. I would also say that to the men and women of the Central Intelligence Agency who fight narcotics trafficking every day of their lives, it is inconceivable that the leadership of the Central Intelligence Agency could have consciously infiltrated cocaine into our inner cities and created this kind of problem. Those certainly are not the men and women I know. I will suspend my judgment until our inspector general comes forward to see what did or did not happen. But if any Americans believe that this in fact is true, then we have a responsibility to act in good faith, to alleviate their concerns and get to the truth behind it, and that is what we are trying to do today.

David L. Boren

I might point out again that this relates to the reform of the oversight process, because when Mr. Tenet was staff director of the Senate Oversight Committee and I was chairman, we did create statutorily an independent inspector general. The inspector general used to be appointed by the director of the CIA, in essence. Now the inspector general is independently appointed by the president, confirmed by Congress, and subject to independent reporting requirements. When situations such as the allegations about CIA involvement in narcotics arise, we have more opportunity now to make sure any kind of investigation will be purely objective and will be carried out in an appropriate way.

Chapter 13

The Role and Organization of U.S. Intelligence for the Twenty-first Century: A Roundtable

John Milewski

I want to welcome you to this very special edition of *Close-Up* on C-Span. We are in Norman, Oklahoma, on the campus of the University of Oklahoma for a discussion of the future of the United States intelligence community. It is part of a larger conference taking place here at the University over three days that is looking at U.S. foreign policy in the twenty-first century. In a moment, I will introduce you to our panel. Let me first tell you that we are also joined by hundreds of students, faculty members, and invited guests who are taking part in the conference. Later in our discussion, they will be asking questions and you will get to meet some of them.

In the meantime, let me introduce you to our panel. Joining us is David Boren, the president of the University of Oklahoma. He formerly served the state as governor and as a United States senator. During his time in the Senate, he was chairman of the Senate Select Committee on Intelligence. Also with us is Richard Helms. He joined the Central Intelligence Agency at its inception in 1947 and was director from 1966 until 1973, when he became ambassador to Iran. Two other former directors of that agency join us. Judge William Webster headed the CIA from 1987 to 1991 and, prior to that, he served as director of the Federal Bureau of Investigation, also part of the intelligence community. James Woolsey is the most recent former director of the Central Intelligence Agency. He served from 1993 to 1995, and he happens to be a native of Oklahoma—Tulsa, I believe. Also joining us is a member of the staff here at the University, a professor of political science, Robert Cox. Gentlemen, welcome, and, President Boren, would you please begin by speaking about the role of the intelligence community within the larger context of foreign policy?

David L. Boren

The intelligence community, of course, is mainly charged with gathering information and getting that information to the policy maker in a way that makes sense. Some people have said, oh well, now that the cold war is over why do we need a CIA? Why do we need an intelligence community? In my opinion we need intelligence even more than we did before. We need early warning. We need to know what is going on in the world. If there is trouble brewing, we need to know sooner rather than later. We used to have troops all over the world. We had huge numbers of troops in Asia and Europe that not only were strategically located for combat, if warranted, but also served as a trip wire of defense. Now we have pulled back most of these forces and have a much lessened military presence in the rest of the world than we used to have. We still need greater technological capabilities, but what we now require more than ever before is greater human intelligence.

How does one penetrate that terrorist cell that might try to bring a chemical weapon in a very small lipstick-sized container into the United States, and put it, say, in the air-conditioning system of the World Trade Center? We have a need for greater human intelligence because of the way in which the threats have fragmented. We now need the ability to penetrate the drug trafficker, the terrorist cell, and other threatening groups that are far less predictable than was the threat of mobilization of the Soviet Union, which we could pick up by satellite or electronic eavesdropping. So it is a world in which we still desperately need intelligence. It is a world that in some way is more disorderly and less predictable than ever. And that means we need particularly renewed emphasis on human intelligence, and early warning from that human intelligence.

John Milewski

Q: Gentlemen, I want to ask the three directors who are with us if you could provide some historical context for our discussion before we start to get too far ahead of ourselves. Perhaps you could each speak to your time in office. During your tenure as the head of the intelligence community in this country, what were the priorities and the challenges that you faced? Let's do it chronologically. Ambassador Helms, may we begin with you?

Richard Helms

At the end of World War II, I thought to myself, we are victorious and have eliminated this evil connotation in Europe. Now the United States will really get interested in the world out there and pay attention to other cultures, languages, and religions and to world developments. To an increasing extent, it did. To my horror, at the end of the cold war, almost a half century of successful global engagement, I discover that the United States seems to be withdrawing into itself more than it ever did before. At a dinner party or a conclave of any kind, one is much more likely to hear baseball talk about the Orioles or the Redskins than discussion about any foreign-policy issue.

And there are so many important and fragmented issues that demand the attention of the world's, for the moment, only superpower.

I want to go back to the beginnings of all this. The Congress established the CIA on September 18, 1947. In other words, 1997 was the fiftieth anniversary. The idea was to prevent another Pearl Harbor. After an examination of the evidence that was available before the start of the war, it was clear that if the available information had been put together, analyzed, and packaged in the proper way, and presented to the national policy makers in a fashion that they could understand, they would have seen what was coming. This is what the Central Intelligence Agency was set up to do. It was not set up as a cold-war organization. But as the cold war came along, obviously, the policy makers propelled the agency into the larger and compelling issues. Gradually, over time, the CIA has grown. And gradually, over time, that part of the intelligence community which is in the Department of Defense—and it is the largest element of the intelligence community—has also grown.

Returning to the CIA, I am astounded when I read in the Sunday papers that some writer has said the Central Intelligence Agency is an organization without a mission. These gentlemen here on this panel have spent much of their time trying to figure out in detail what the intelligence community's mission is, and they have been surrounded by a lot of very bright, well-informed, intelligent people who have also dedicated themselves to this. The mission is quite clear—it is to save all our skins! It is the national security and survival of the United States, which includes not only direct military attacks, but also ancillary things such as drug trafficking and proliferation of weapons of mass destruction.

Stop a minute and think. Proliferation—a bomb here and a nuclear device there—how do you find this out? One of the ways you find it out is by having friends in the world. If a terrorist in Amsterdam suddenly organizes a group and wants to attack something in New York City, is some American sent from Washington, from the CIA to Holland, likely to find that fellow? No, it is the police in Amsterdam who will be the first to find out about it. And if they are friends with you, they will pass it along and you will have some protection from something like this. So we need a vast network of friends in the world. Unfortunately, the United States, being by far the most powerful country in the world these days, has started to clomp around somewhat arrogantly and demandingly. A lot of our friends do not like this, and I cannot blame them. I am speaking of good friends such as the British, the French, and the Germans.

I will conclude with a Persian folk story. There was a small wise man in the ancient days of the Persian Empire named Mullah Nasradin. A terrible pestilence grew up in a small town out near the Dasht-e Kavir, a great desert. The city fathers called on Mullah Nasradin to come to the mosque on Friday to tell the people what he could do to help. The wise little man arrived and went up into the mihrab, a kind of a pulpit in a mosque. He looked at the crowd of people and said, "My friends, do you know what I'm going to say?" The crowd roared back, "No, Master." "Ah," he said, "if you do not know what I am going to say, there is no point in my saying it," and he left the mosque. A month later the situation had worsened. Mullah Nasradin was persuaded to return again to the mosque. He went up to the mihrab. The crowd was ready. When Nasradin asked the question, they said, "Yes, Master." He said, "Ah, then if you know what I am going to say, there is no point in my saying it," and he left. Six months later, the place was about to collapse. The city fathers once more persuaded Nasradin to visit the mosque. This time the crowd was ready for him. When he asked the question, half of them said, "Yes, Master" and the other half said, "No, Master." He said, "Ah my friends, those who know tell those who don't know." And he again left the mosque.

John Milewski

Q: Judge Webster, do you remember what the major issues were in 1987 when you were sworn in?

William H. Webster

I can, because we were about to go into a major series of changes. But before I do that, I would like to say that we have tried to be true to the intelligence community's mission as Dick Helms has described it. He said it is to save our skins. I would like to modify the statement only to say that *we* do not do the saving, but we do provide the information upon which our policy makers can make wise decisions in the interest of our country. Every military officer in our history, starting with George Washington, wanted eyes and ears. Robert E. Lee lost his eyes and ears when Jeb Stuart went off somewhere looking for treasure trove at Gettysburg. And as Dick pointed out, it is very important that we get wind of a possible Pearl Harbor before it happens. This has been a major responsibility.

In the period of the cold war after World War II—right up to and through part of my directorship—in many respects, intelligence officers were listening for hiccups. The two bipolar great powers and their allies were confronting each other. Each side was convinced the other would engage in a stand-up, start-up, sudden offensive against them. We had NATO forces on the ground in Europe which were inadequate to confront the Warsaw alliance without reinforcements. We needed to know ahead of time! As General Jack Galvin, the NATO commander and commander of U.S. forces in Europe, impressed on me, we needed to know in time to develop the political will at home and get the reinforcements there.

This began to change as the Soviet Union began to crumble economically. President Reagan's support for the Strategic Defense Initiative (SDI) helped change the dynamics. I believe that the prospect of the Soviet Union having to spend so much money to contest us as we engaged in such a major undertaking drove Gorbachev to make a number of unilateral decisions and changes. These changes brought us to a different level of engagement: his withdrawal of troops to behind the Urals; his unilateral discontinuance of certain intermediate ballistic weapons; and his willingness to negotiate. In the United States all of these things had to be analyzed. Information had to be collected accurately to access the intentions and capabilities of our major adversary.

While this was going on, we had the Panama incident, the Philippine insurrection, the closeout of Iran-Contra, and then Desert Shield and Desert Storm. In each case it was exceedingly important that current intelligence be marshaled to guide our armed forces in the selection of targets and the choices of decisions to be made. Simultaneously, we were seeing something very important happening in East and West Germany, as those two countries suddenly came together in a very dramatic way, and the end of the Warsaw Convention, which ended Soviet hegemony over Poland, Hungary, and Czechoslovakia.

All of this had an impact on how we focused our resources, but basically our mission was the same. It was to collect timely—not old, but timely, useful, and hopefully accurate—information about what was going on in the world so that our president and his principal policy advisers could judge what kind of action—military, economic, or diplomatic—would best serve the national-security interests of this country.

To say that the "eyes and ears," i.e., the intelligence community, were unimportant would be to ignore history. As Senator Boren pointed out, today intelligence is all the more important because the ordinary sources of forward power projection are not present, as our military draws back. If our intelligence assets did not exist, someone would have to invent them. What is important is that that information be absolutely objective, absolutely divorced from any political agenda, and dedicated to the essential mission described by Dick Helms as the saving of all our skins.

John Milewski

Q: Mr. Woolsey, your tenure occurred at a time when the most dramatic change in the world's maps since World War II occurred and you were one of the constructors of this new architecture. Will you comment on this?

R. James Woolsey

Let me say quickly that the issues Senator Boren pointed out and Directors Helms and Webster have too—the proliferation of weapons of mass destruction, terrorism, rogue states, narcotics cartels, and still keeping an eye on Russia and China, which are far from being stable capitalist democracies—are a reasonable summation of what the CIA and U.S. intelligence as a whole were looking at during my tenure and are looking at today. But I think there is a more interesting point. Many people who ask about the role of intelligence in the post–cold war era often assume that we have to scrap everything and start over. The answer to that, briefly, is: nonsense. When thinking about intelligence it is useful to look at the distinction the military draws between force planning and operational planning. Force planning is deciding what to buy—how many aircraft carriers, and so forth. Operational planning is deciding what to do with what you have.

The intelligence structure of the United States now consists largely of three worldwide networks: (1) reconnaissance satellites; (2) National Security Agency capabilities for the interception and decryption of foreign communications; and (3) espionage, operated by CIA stations and case officers overseas. Each of these networks is somewhat smaller than it used to be. Much of each of those networks, although they were used during the cold war to focus on the Soviet Union, is still extremely useful and quite adaptable to doing what needs to be done today. The same reconnaissance satellites that were keeping track of Soviet silo construction in Siberia can do a perfectly fine job of mapping poppy- and cocaine-growing fields, for example. Case officers need to be trained more in Arabic and less in Russian. There are changes one has to make. But many of the changes are in a difference in focus rather than scrapping things and starting over.

During periods such as the one we are in now—the 1990s, with our booming stock market and our prosperity, and just having won the third world war of this century, the cold one—we in this country tend to lapse into a sense of naïveté about the outside world. The closest parallel I can think of is the period of the 1920s. We had just won World War I. The United States, in terms of its being the principal power that survived the war intact, essentially bestrode the world like a colossus, in some ways almost like we do today. In several ways we became very foolish. The general line was that we had made the world safe for democracy. We were going to rely very heavily on arms-control treaties. We felt we did not need much of a military anymore. We cut back our military too much, and we were even more extreme in the intelligence arena. A public servant as able as Henry Stimson, who was twice a very fine secretary of war and during the Hoover administration was secretary of state, closed down the State Department's code-breaking office, saying, "Gentlemen do not read one another's mail." We were very lucky that there were people in the U.S. Navy who were less than gentlemanly with respect to Japanese codes during those years, because their work came in very handy at the Battle of Midway and other battles during the war in the Pacific.

The point is that during the good and easy times—whether it was the Roaring Twenties or, you might say, the Roaring Nineties—this country tends to pull back into itself, tends to relax, tends to think it has made the world safe for its own way of life, and tends to do things such as close down code-breaking rooms and cut back intelligence capabilities. Therefore, although we in the

1990s do not know for sure (and they did not know during the 1920s) what will come in the future—who the enemy will be, who the real threat will be— we have to keep an eye on a number of things, and we must be far more prudent than Stimson and his colleagues were in the 1920s.

John Milewski

Q: Has the current budget-cutting climate in Washington had a negative impact on the intelligence community?

R. James Woolsey

I think budget reduction has gone a bit far on intelligence. I think some rebuilding is necessary. Certainly there are some ways in which we can shrink, and have shrunk, the number of people in the intelligence community. We have reduced the number of reconnaissance satellites, closed down a number of National Security Agency facilities for intercepting communications, and so forth. So the community is going to be smaller. But it needs to be more flexible. Just as the navy is going from fifteen aircraft carriers down to about ten, we want each aircraft carrier to carry highly capable aircraft and, with their increased capacity, be able to do what is needed in an emergency. In the same way, we need to spend enough funds to have a very flexible ability to collect and analyze intelligence in these various areas that Senator Boren and others talked about.

David L. Boren

One thing about that is we can less afford duplication. In the past, there has been a lot of duplication within the intelligence community. Perhaps the community was, with the end of the cold war, a little bloated. A lot of people think only of the CIA when they think of intelligence. But there are also the National Security Agency, the Defense Intelligence Agency, and the Reconnaissance Agency. The Department of Defense spends considerably more on intelligence than does the CIA. And there is not anyone that is really in charge of all U.S. intelligence organizations. Some of us at one time talked about creating a director of national intelligence. I have somewhat backed off from that proposal, because I am not sure that someone working without an agency would have sufficient backing and support. But I do think we need an intelligence czar and that it probably should be the director of the CIA; at a minimum there is a need for someone within the whole intelligence framework who has the budgetary power to prevent duplication. Giving the director of the CIA that authority would be good. There is still too much spent on intelligence by our government—the exact amount is still not public, but it is a very high figure. It is larger than the budget at the University of Oklahoma by about forty or fifty times. It is a considerable figure, and too much of it is still caused by duplication.

John Milewski

Q: Bob Cox, I want to ask you about public perception as it relates to covert activities, or intelligence activities in a free society. Can you talk about the tension that exists in the United States between the need to have an intelligence community that from time to time operates in a covert manner, and a tradition of openness and the right to know?

Robert H. Cox

I think in an open and democratic society, especially in American society, the biggest problem in the public mind is about where the CIA fits. Perhaps there are three problems that are involved here. One is the public's legitimate right to know, which means that information ought to be available and that public officials ought to be able to provide the information, almost on demand, when people want to know what is happening. This is necessary to hold officials to necessary levels of accountability, which is the second and related problem. In a society where the rule of law dictates people's behavior, and especially the behavior of public officials, there is a concern that no public officials violate the laws that exist. Indeed, they should be expected to uphold the law. A third concern, more important than merely observing the letter of the law, is a sense that moral behavior itself must hold to certain standards that rise above the minimal expectations of the law. Those, I think, are three important dimensions of the tension between democratic societies and covert operations.

William H. Webster

I agree with what you have said, but one must remember that a covert action is what it says it is. It is secret activity, necessarily secret if it is going to be successful. To deal with your concerns, our government has put in place surrogates, both for the Congress and for the American people. The Senate Intelligence Committee, which President Boren headed, is one of those two major surrogate organizations, along with its counterpart committee in the House of Representatives. They have a right to know, and the intelligence community is obligated to report to the committees on all covert actions. I think that was a very healthy thing.

I think, too, that the public does not always understand that covert action is not something in which the CIA or other members of the intelligence community sit around and dream up ideas to create trouble for our enemies. Covert action results from requests from our government, our executive branch, to address specific problems where diplomatic measures have failed and where military measures are inadvisable. The executive branch asks the Central Intelligence Agency to come up with some other effort to force our foreign policy forward in a useful way.

The procedures in place today are very sound ones. When a request comes to the CIA, the Covert Action Review Group reviews it to decide whether the particular project can be developed and will work and whether it is lawful—permitted by our laws. The group also examines the project to see whether it is logistically sound and whether it is consistent with our overt foreign policy, not an effort to do something different from the policy objectives that our public figures are espousing. In addition, I used to ask the Covert Action Review Group to consider whether the project, when it becomes public, will make sense to the American people. The information is then provided to the National Security Council, which includes the president and all of his principal national security advisers. The report is given with all of the council members present, and the president makes a final decision. If he certifies the action, it goes to Congress with a written document called a "finding." Congress then has an opportunity to weigh in. I have to add also that covert action represents only about 3 to 5 percent of the CIA's resources and about 95 percent of the CIA's problems. So there are many people who would just as soon that the army or somebody else took over covert action.

But no one has found a better place than the intelligence community for directing and controlling covert activities. Some such operations have not worked. Most of them are in the propaganda arena, which have been amazingly effective. An example is when the CIA insinuated *The Federalist* papers and copies of our Constitution in local languages into democracy-hungry countries that were deprived of freedom. Paramilitary actions, such as in Afghanistan, Central America, Angola, and Cambodia, had varying degrees of success. As Senator Boren pointed out, helping the Mujahedeen drive the Soviets out of Afghanistan had a far-reaching impact on the internal politics of the Soviet Union, as well as depriving the Soviets of the domination of a country they very much wanted to have. Covert action is going to be there. No president will ever deny himself the opportunity and the need to use it, but it should be realized that covert action represents a very small part of the CIA's principal mission.

R. James Woolsey

I also wish to make one quick point. First of all, Lech Walesa, Poland's great democrat and labor leader, once said that the most important thing the United States did during the cold war was Radio Free Europe. Radio Free Europe, for most of its existence, certainly during its early existence, was a CIA covert action. Covert action does not consist entirely of overthrowing governments or the crazy attempts to assassinate Castro that took place back in the early 1960s. The second point has to do with morality and intelligence collection on the one hand and covert action on the other. In selecting foreign individuals (who, by the way, are called "agents" in intelligence parlance; do not confuse them with CIA case officers)—the Americans who are full-time U.S. employees—to be used for a covert action to influence events abroad, there are some very reasonable ethical questions that should be asked. For example, one does not want to overthrow one government of thugs only to see it replaced by a worse group of thugs.

Now, consider some 99 percent of what the CIA and the intelligence community do—intelligence collection, not covert action. If one is trying to collect intelligence through informants inside terrorist organizations, narcotics cartels, and the like—organizations that can really harm the United States—there are not many democratic idealists in those groups who are going to decide to be American agents out of some sense of public-spiritedness. Sometimes that does happen inside foreign governments. We had some wonderful Soviets who were anticommunists and worked for the United States out of a sense of idealism, but inside Hezbollah and the Cali cartel such persons are few to nonexistent. When you recruit agents to get information from inside organizations of that sort, you are buying information from very unsavory people. And if we are not willing to do that, what that would mean is, in the Mideast, we might do a dandy job of, say, spying on the churches and the PTAs of Beirut, but we will not be able to learn what is going on inside terrorist organizations. Dealing with immoral agents in foreign organizations is no different than what the FBI does in dealing with informants inside the Mafia—namely, buying information from some very unattractive and immoral folks.

John Milewski

Q: Mr. Boren, do you want to weigh in on this?

David L. Boren

I want to comment on this because, in a way, my job was to oversee what some of these gentlemen did when I was chairing the Intelligence Committee. I provided oversight to make sure they were doing what they were telling me they were doing. And particularly that relationship was with Judge Webster, who was the director during the time that I was chairing the Senate Select Committee on Intelligence. I think Professor Cox makes a very important point. We must strive to achieve the proper balance between being an open society—a democratic society with certain fundamental values, a certain set of ethics by which we live—and still having the capability of doing things that have to be done to protect us each day. As Jim Woolsey just said, we need that information from inside terrorist groups. We may also need to pay unsavory characters inside a narcotics cartel to get information, and pay them enough that even though they are scoundrels, they give us information that may save lives of young people in the United States from being corrupted by drugs.

So we need information. We need to have covert actions occasionally. For example, I do not think the Mujahedeen would ever have been successful in Afghanistan without our help. And without telling secrets I should not tell, I remember one briefing in which we were told how the Mujahedeen had used a handheld, relatively inexpensive, American-provided missile that probably cost about $10,000 to blow up a $200 million Soviet ammunition depot outside Kabul. Now that had an impact! That had an impact on driving the Soviet forces out of Afghanistan. It even had an impact on weakening the Soviet Union ultimately. Very interestingly, at the time of the attempted coup against Gorbachev, Yeltsin holed up in the so-called Russian White House. The KGB and others were plotting his assassination, and the military also was moving in. There were many "freedom fighters" along the route to the Russian White House that blocked armed-forces tanks from getting to Yeltsin. Had the army been successful the course of history might have changed. The cold war might not be over. The people who were running the KGB and others might still be in power in Moscow today. Moreover, a lot of those persons opposing the military—the young people that were organized, throwing the Molotov cocktail, and stopping the tanks—were led by disgruntled Soviet military officers who had been disillusioned by what had happened in Afghanistan. They were an important part of the movement to bring greater democracy to the Soviet Union. So all of what happened in Afganistan had an enormous impact on what happened in the Soviet Union. And if we ourselves had tried to intervene in Afghanistan directly with our military, we would have had to ask permission of Pakistani officials to move an army across Pakistan and they would have said no. They would not have wanted to openly provoke the Soviet Union. Further, would the American people have given us permission to intervene directly? I am not sure.

So what happened? We used a covert action in Afghanistan to help arm Afghans to fight for freedom and expel the Soviets from their territory. We did it in a covert way. I happen to think that was right. We now have a unique institution in our country in that the Senate and House Intelligence Committees provide oversight. The new Russian Parliament is looking at it. The Polish legislative body is looking at it. The British are looking at it. Some of our other European friends are looking at it.

In the Congressional review process, the CIA does not tell the whole Congress the names of all of our secret agents. We all know that would be foolish. There used to be a saying that the most dangerous place to be in Washington was between a television camera and some of my colleagues in the House and Senate, or between a newspaper reporter and some of my colleagues. They could not keep secrets. So the Intelligence Committee set up a small group of people who were kept informed by the CIA about what was going on, so that we would not have a covert action going on without some responsible people who had been elected by the American people knowing about it, and having a chance to control it through the Congress—through control of the budget. The Senate created its own independent audit unit so it could audit the CIA account without notice. Once or twice we found some things we should not have. To his credit, the minute I brought those items to Judge Webster's attention, those programs were stopped immediately. We Americans have again created a unique institution to assure control and accountability.

I viewed my role on the Senate Intelligence Committee—and I think other members felt the same way—unlike my service on any other committee. On the Finance Committee I would try to logroll for votes, that is, try to trade votes to get something that might be important to Oklahoma. On the Agriculture Committee I would do the same thing, to help Oklahoma farmers. But on the Intelligence Committee I did not try to push my own views or more narrow interests. I asked myself, as Judge Webster said, what if every single American knew what was going on? What if they knew about this secret program? Is it in keeping with American values or not? And if I could not answer that question in the affirmative, I would lead an effort to try to block that program, because I think we should be involved only in intelligence operations that the American people would approve if they knew about them. Now that is unique. That is an innovation for democracy—and my hope is that the newly emerging democracies and some of the older democracies around the world will develop similar kinds of procedures. It is an American way of answering the dilemma that Dr. Cox posed—how can we have secrets actions, covert actions, in a democracy without violating our principles? The intelligence committees carry out a unique process that has been developed to try to strike that balance.

John Milewski

Q: Mr. Woolsey made the case that the assumption that all has changed with the end of the cold war and the fall of the Soviet Union is a faulty one, but you have said that consequently, some things do need to change. Would each of you please briefly mention one or two things you think must change in the intelligence field in response to the new world order?

David L. Boren

I talked about the importance of increasing our human intelligence capabilities. I also think one of the things we have to do is to evaluate our ability to analyze what is going on in the world. It used to be that the most important thing for us to understand was what was being said inside the politburo, or what did it mean when one Soviet general sent a message with a certain code in it to another Soviet general? Today, we need to understand such things as what is happening within Islamic fundamentalism. What kind of impact is it going to have on our interests? We need to understand also what is happening inside China—its new nationalistic fervor, the impact of a reincorporated Hong Kong, the views and influence of Chinese young people. We think back to Tiananmen Square, where it was our Statue of Liberty the youth raised as a symbol. In a recent poll young Chinese now view the United States as the greatest enemy of China. When they were asked why, they said things such as, "Because the United States did not let us have the Olympics," or "The United States was siding with the Japanese, who took Taiwan away from China." We need to understand these things because China is a country that is so big and has an economy growing at a rate that will make it bigger than the total European economy early in the next century. If we were to have a new cold war with the Chinese it would be far more dangerous than it was with the Russians. We need to understand these things. A lot of that has to do with analysis. It has to do with the same kind of skills that an academic uses to try to find out what is going on, or a reporter uses, or a political officer in an embassy. We have to put more emphasis on analysis, and we need to use more open sources. We need not be too secretive. We need more diplomats and people who can overtly get outside the embassies, not operating as spies, but to attend dinner parties, to visit university campuses, to listen to what people are saying, and to look carefully at what public-opinion surveys are showing.

I would like to see the CIA create what I would call the world-class think tank. People could be drawn in from the academic community and from other areas where there is expertise. They would be clearly distinguished from the covert intelligence function, because they would be separate and apart. They would not become spies—no one would suspect them of using their credentials to collect information covertly. This would allow America to benefit from some of the country's best analytic talent. Our technology improved so quickly during the six years I served as chairman of the Intelligence Committee that I would guess the amount of technical data flowing to the CIA headquarters probably went up ten to twenty times—some have even suggested a hundred times. However, I am not sure that the quality of the intelligence product got better. It may have gotten worse. There was so much raw data that it overwhelmed our ability to separate what was important from what was unimportant. Ultimately, it is human ability and analysis that must determine what is important from what's unimportant. So I think that something we need to do is to use people with great analytical capabilities, even if they are not organizationally a part of the intelligence community.

Richard Helms

I want to add something to that. When the Central Intelligence Agency was established, and through the years, it was segmented. Over on one side were the spies and the covert-action people that we have chiefly been talking about. In the middle was the large core element of the agency, whose task was to take information from overseas, no matter in what form, analyze it, collate it, and come up with the final answer to give to the policy makers. Then there was a third element dealing with reconnaissance, science, and technology that was segmented from the other two. For many years you had to have a special pass as an analyst to get into the part of the agency that conducted covert operations. Senator Boren has put his finger right on the most critical part now, and that is that analysis has to improve. How we improve analysis is by training people better and getting more and better graduating scholars to enter the Central Intelligence Agency. The CIA has scores of Ph.D.s in all kinds of specialties who could teach at colleges anyplace in the United States. Analysis is really the core element for the success of the Central Intelligence Agency. One of the purposes of the Senate in writing the National Security Act of 1947, which set up the agency, was to be absolutely certain that the director of Central Intelligence was to oversee and guide all intelligence entities of the U.S. government.

William H. Webster

I think it all comes down to one simple word: *relevancy.* For an organization like the agency—and for the intelligence community—to be useful and important, it needs to be relevant to the times. It needs to understand where the problems are. We have described for you a very changed world from the world that preceded World War II and the world that immediately followed it. We have to have both scientific apparatus and trained analysts to deal with today's world. At the end of the Gulf War, when we evaluated it, we had done some mighty fine things in identifying targets and providing postbattle damage assessments, but we had done so by borrowing for periods of time satellites designed to cover the Soviet Union. We could not dedicate them to just covering the Gulf. We had to run them on a cyclical basis, and like a good navigator at sea, we brought the sweeps together. After the war, the generals told us that what they need now is synoptic coverage, so that they can see the whole battlefield. This would give us an advantage that no potential enemy could possibly have at this time. We should be working now to assure that if there is another regional war in which we are involved, we will have that kind of coverage.

We have identified pretty well the things that could cause upheavals and potentially involve our men and women of the military in warfare and casualties. Terrorism is a problem that we also have been addressing reasonably well but need to address better in the future. When I was director of the FBI and we dropped the annual number of terrorist incidents in this country from a hundred to five in nine years, I said that the key to that success was intelligence—getting there before the bomb goes off, not afterward. One can chase the bombers, but how much better to head them off beforehand! The same thing is true to a degree in the drug area. Information warfare is a threat for which we have not yet really marshaled ourselves to deal with, including prevention of the tremendous damage that can be done by manipulating financial transactions on the Internet. There are other targets that can be seriously manipulated or damaged, such as the military assets we control in the sky. If anybody devises the way to do this to *us,* just as we already know how to do it to other people, we will be in serious trouble.

The last thing I would emphasize is a subject that over the years has been underaddressed, both by the FBI, which has responsibility for protecting us here in the United States, and by the CIA and other agencies, and that is counterintelligence. It is our shield against spies who are coming against us. We are not the "Great Satan," but we are the "great target." Everyone wants to steal our intellectual secrets, know our military secrets, learn about all the things that they think we have that they do not. Unless we build up our capability to recognize and head off these kinds of intelligence activities against us, we will pay a heavy price. It is important to protect funding for counterintelligence.

R. James Woolsey

There are a lot of ways to answer your question, John, and I agree with virtually all of what has been said. Let me use a good word at a modern, hard-charging institution like the University of Oklahoma: *interdisciplinary.* As Dick Helms pointed out, there was in the past a rather sharp division among the functions of (1) collecting intelligence, (2) analyzing it, and (3) doing the scientific and technical work. But to collect intelligence of the sort one needs today—for example, from a network of companies and countries that is proliferating ballistic-missile components from someplace in Russia to someplace in the Middle East—requires what the military would call a combined-force operation. It is not just satellites; it is not just spies; it is not just electronic intercepts—it is all of them combined. The satellites tip off the spies and the spies tip off the satellites. So what one wants now is imagery engineers, analysts, and interpreters who understand something about espionage, and case officers, managers, and division chiefs within the Directorate of Operations of the CIA who know something about how satellites work. Case officers in the world of espionage need enough technical training and background to be able to appreciate and understand why it might be much more valuable to recruit as a spy, let us say, the computer-network administrator of a rogue régime's communications network than the special assistant or the secretary of the dictator himself.

To be able to analyze all the data which reconnaissance satellites and other intelligence collection soak up, and to deal with the great flow of information that David Boren so well described—one way to do that for some types of information is to use artificial-intelligence programs, and to have computer systems that can sort through reams of data. To use one example, when I was the DCI, I made a speech at a conference on mammography. The way one analyzes reconnaissance satellite photographs these days is to do a digital map. A year later, you put another digital map of the same area on top of the previous map by lining up the roads, and anything that is new is high-lighted by software programs. The same thing can be done with mammograms by lining up veins, and thereby the software discloses new tumors. An excited Harvard Medical School radiologist said he thought that using the algorithms and software the CIA had developed for reconnaissance satellite technology probably would result in something like a 35 percent improvement in mammography diagnosis and save thousands of women's lives annually in the United States. This is only one case dealing with a societal benefit derived from intelligence-community technology, but the important point is that both for intelligence analysis and for many other important endeavors, an interdisciplinary effort obtains better results. It is also an important way to reduce costs. It is an important way to multiply the effectiveness of the individuals who are involved. It is an important way to find new ways to contribute to society's needs.

Robert H. Cox

Building on what I have heard just now, one of the words I would add to the list is *cooperation*. In the academic community one of the big discussions right now centers on the question of the possible demise of the nation-state. Agencies such as the Central Intelligence Agency have been crucial components of the long-held notion that the nation-state as a sovereign, territorial unit is the major actor on the international stage. Today, the argument among academics is whether entities such as multinational corporations, drug cartels, or Mafias (such as the Russian Mafia) are acquiring such great power that they are starting to take the place of nation-states, or at least rival them for importance on the world stage. At the same time, states themselves seem to be working together a lot more. Things such as the NAFTA Agreement or the European Union mean that states are starting to recognize that they have common interests for which they can join together, that they are not just competitors. If this is the case, perhaps the intelligence community is one of their common resources that they can pool. I wonder if cooperation among national intelligence agencies might be an important focus for the future.

William H. Webster

Cooperation among national intelligence agencies is already a present focus. It is not widely advertised because, for example, in the United Kingdom, the MI6 did not officially exist until a couple of years ago. No mention of it was allowed. Until then the response in Parliament was, "Her Majesty's government does not respond to questions of intelligence." But they finally acknowledged it. The term they used was *avowal*—they avowed it. I think Colin McColl was the director of MI6 at that time. Because he was so secret and unknown he did not require security. After he was avowed, he had to move out of his home and into a secure place. We have worked closely for a number of years on intelligence with English-speaking nations around the world that share our common values and our common defense needs. It is also no secret any longer that the Poles helped extricate some of our agents and officers from Baghdad during the Gulf War. I may not elaborate in too much detail, but those nations with whom we work in common causes do share the products of their intelligence services to our mutual advantage. This must be done in a way that does not compromise information supplied by yet another nation without their approval.

John Milewski

Let us now go to our audience.

Q: Theoretically, how can the CIA use its tools, such as propaganda, to help bring stability to the new Russian and eastern European democracies?

William H. Webster

The CIA has used propaganda—and I use that term in its best positive sense—in the past to introduce new ideas and to strengthen ideas that might capture the imagination of people. They were used largely to develop and support people who had democratic ideas and visions and wanted to share them with others of their country to build a solid democratic base. I do not think that it serves our foreign policy as we understand it today to undercut the structures of government that are there in the fifteen former Soviet states. Those countries are potentially unstable but not presently at a stage of repression that requires us to create instability. Covert propaganda in a covert way must always, always support our overt foreign policy.

David L. Boren

Some of the things that can be done in the intelligence area to help stabilize democracy are worth noting. I had discussions with the chief of Polish intelligence after Poland had achieved independence and democracy, and he wanted our help. He was charged with cleaning up his own agency, in which many officials had been involved in the Communist repression in Poland. They had spied on and terrorized their own people. He wanted to know how the CIA might help the Poles weed out the rogue and bad actors to assure a dependable intelligence agency. We have had appeals from the Russian government for help in containing organized crime and its impact, and intelligence is vital in the war against narcotics trafficking. Requests for help in these areas have been open and voluntary by established democratic governments. These new democracies have asked us for help and we have been acting to help them gain information and to restructure in ways that could make their countries more stable.

William H. Webster

In the past there were either democratic and/or noncommunist countries being challenged by a Soviet surrogate insurrectionist organization against which we engaged in covert actions to help the existing governments preserve themselves in power, or there were repressive governments against which we helped democratically oriented insurgencies maintain and improve their positions. That was the approach. We ran operations in many parts of the world, including Central America, Cambodia, Angola, and Afghanistan, where the Soviets had puppets. We used covert action to help democratic-inclined insurgencies regain control of their countries.

Q: My question is directed to Mr. Webster. To what extent can we trust information from recruited agents within Middle Eastern terrorist groups about those groups?

William H. Webster

Their "information" must be considered with great caution. Throughout this whole business of intelligence tradecraft, there is the issue of the double agent, or the person who is simply looking for money and will tell an intelligence agency what he thinks would be regarded as valuable in order to get paid. Spying for greed has unfortunately been evident in some recent cases involving American officials. In earlier days, American spies operating in this country were spying principally for ideological reasons. Now it is for money. And I think that is generally true in most parts of the world. One has to be very careful about information provided only for money. Also, terrorist groups are quite cellular, and one must be satisfied that the informant is in a position to know about what he is reporting, because often they are not. But by gathering bits and pieces of information and turning them over to very skilled analysts, judgments about particular pieces of information and their importance to the whole picture can be made. We must improve our efforts. We have had some unique successes, and some of those successes have involved the apprehension of terrorists in other parts of the world as they move around in other countries.

John Milewski

Q: Without embarrassing anybody or giving away national-security secrets, is there anything panel members can share anecdotally about some vital information you received that turned out to be incorrect, that someone was purposely trying to feed to the United States?

William H. Webster

Most of our Cuban operations were compromised, and most of the information that came from there was from double agents and was not true.

R. James Woolsey

Let me suggest a spy novel that might be instructive on this. It is modeled on the exploits of a wonderful man, a very successful case officer, someone Dick Helms knew well, Bob Ames—the good Ames, not the one convicted recently for betrayal. Bob Ames was killed in Beirut in the early 1980s. David Ignatius works for the *Washington Post* and writes spy novels on the side. In his first one, about ten years ago, *Agents of Innocence,*[1] he essentially fictionalized a version of Bob Ames' career, which involved penetration of terrorist organizations in the Middle East. It is the best thing I know in literature for an accurate picture of what a case officer actually does overseas, and it is modeled on real circumstances, as distinct from some of the really crazy fictionalized things found in movies and other spy novels.

Q: Mr. Woolsey, generally an analyst within the Central Intelligence Agency is asked a question of what is country Y or group X doing now and what does it intend to do the next week, in the next six months, or maybe as far out as the next two years. Should the CIA or other parts of the intelligence community look at the farther-range perspective, say the next five to ten years? Does the CIA now have groups or units that do that?

R. James Woolsey

It is a good question. The evolution over the last few years has been away from doing very detailed, lengthy, thick analytical studies—which often were not read very much by consumers of intelligence inside the federal government—and more toward briefings and shorter analytical papers focused on specific issues. Some of those specific issues deal with events a number of years away. However, there is an issue buried in your question that I want to say something about. It is not always or exclusively and sometimes not most importantly the purpose of intelligence collection and analysis to predict the future. Some things are mysteries, not secrets. The CIA can steal secrets and give them to the president and maybe he can use them to figure out what he is going to do. But often people in other countries do not know what they are going to do. There is no secret to steal: It is a mystery. In that case the job is to analyze what might happen, and thus make it possible for the president to make better judgments.

Nevertheless, often the most important part of intelligence work is trying to steal secrets from others to give our country an edge. If I could use an analogy from baseball, imagine the scout who sits down quietly next to the manager of the Orioles, let's say on the opening day of the season against the Yankees. He says something like this: "We were able to get into their spring training camp. Their second baseman is half a step slow going to his left this year. That may open up the hit and run a little bit. Their left-handed relievers cannot get their breaking stuff over when they are behind in the count. And by the way, we stole their signals and here they are." That is what intelligence is for.

Q: Ambassador Jeane Kirkpatrick and others suggest that part of our foreign policy for the twenty-first century should be the elevation of trade and seeing that countries like the former Soviet Union are sound economically, because democracies do not go to war. Small businesses often have the problem of finding potential business partners in a foreign country and in obtaining good information on the people, the businesses, and even the governments they are dealing with. What do small businessmen do to find this kind of information?

William H. Webster

There is a major cottage industry out there offering such services for all parts of the world. Generally these businesses are focused on perhaps half a dozen countries. They have recruited experts, some of whom are former intelligence officers from those particular areas for which they are offering services. Their information is available and can be bought to review and evaluate. It may be helpful. Some have better reputations for probity than others. If you look in your Internet, you will see all kinds of people offering this service, and at prices you can generally afford.

R. James Woolsey

Just to be explicit about it, it will not be the CIA. U.S. intelligence agencies do not do industrial espionage. We do not go steal the secrets of Japanese automobile companies to give them to the Big Three American automobile manufacturers. Some of our friends and allies do that against us. We do not. We do spy on people overseas who may be bribing someone to land a business deal, so that we can tell the State Department. The U.S. embassy there can go to the government of the country involved and say, "That contract's about to be awarded by a bribe," and thus maybe keep it from happening. We also follow abroad so-called dual-use technology, e.g., supercomputers and certain types of chemicals, because those can be used in weapons as well as in commerce. And we do analysis for the president and the National Security Council of broad economic trends and a lot of economic issues, including such things as potential famines in Africa. But the U.S. government's intelligence community does not work for American business in a direct sense, in the same way that some of our closest friends and allies' intelligence services work for their businesses.

David L. Boren

I think that we should be able to count on our intelligence agencies to help assure that our businesspeople have a level playing field in terms of competition in open and fair markets. If people from another country—I will pull a hypothetical example out of the air, for instance, the French—are using their intelligence service to spy against an American business, our intelligence service ought to be there. It ought to let our business know that it has a penetration problem. And if the intelligence service of another country is bribing government officials of a Third World country to obtain a sale for one of the bribing country's firms against a U.S. firm—for instance, the sale of telephone parts for a national telephone service—we ought to use our intelligence capabilities to find that out. Our embassy can then go to the host government and say, "Well, wait a minute, why isn't AT&T or Southwestern Bell or some other American company having an equal shot, Mr. Minister? It is because your two deputies are taking bribes, and you had better stop it or we will expose it." So I think there are areas, particularly of counterintelligence, where our business community deserves the protection of our intelligence community.

Q: I have a question for Mr. Helms. How do you think the election of the new government in Tehran in 1997 is going to influence the relations between Iran and the United States?

Richard Helms

I would think very little. The conventional wisdom seems to be that the new president is more moderate than his predecessor. However, I do not think the powers that be in Iran these days are going to permit him to be more moderate about foreign affairs, particularly toward the United States. There are a lot of hardheaded mullahs in Iran who are convinced that the United States is the great Satan. Ayatollah Khomeini made it starkly clear to them that Iran should have nothing to do with the United States, because to do so could ruin Iran's religion, customs, history, and everything in society. So this new president, Mohammed Khatami, may be able to be more sensible on women's issues and certain local domestic problems, but I do not see much change in the foreign-policy field, at least in the near future.

Q: This question is directed to Judge Webster. Drawing on your experiences as director of both the CIA and the FBI, do you think that the acts of gathering information foster suspicion and noncooperation or help encourage trust?

William H. Webster

For me, at least as far as the activities in the United States are concerned, trust is everything. The FBI cannot function without the understanding, support, and trust of the American people. It is an organization one-third the size of the police force of the city of New York. It operates not only in the United States but around the world. There was some concern that extending its counterintelligence activities to gather information abroad might cause other law-enforcement and intelligence units not to cooperate. That has not been the case. The centers—the Counter-intelligence Center, the Counter-narcotics Center, and the Counter-terrorist Center—that have been developed within the intelligence community that implicate the FBI have provided new, unique ways through which the CIA and the FBI work effectively together. There seems to be no lack of trust because of them.

You give me a wonderful opportunity to make the point that neither organization is permitted to operate outside U.S. law. My friend Tom Clancy wrote a book of fiction in which an FBI director was blown up in Latin America and the next day the president called in Jack Ryan to tell him, "You have a blank ticket to find out who did it and retaliate." Well, we do not have a blank ticket. We have never wanted a blank ticket. U.S. laws control the CIA and the FBI. True, when we are operating in other countries—I am talking about the CIA now—every country has rules against espionage that we cannot observe, but when a U.S. executive order says "no assassinations," that means no assassinations. When a law requires us to have a court order for an electronic surveillance, that means *we have* to have one before we can act. It has been my experience that almost all of the men and women in both organizations are absolutely dedicated to doing their work according to our law. There should never be any thought that somehow CIA and FBI officers are on the loose out there and can do anything they want. We had Senator Boren looking over our shoulder, and I hope we have other people equally as competent who can assure the American people that although we cannot talk about the details of our work, we are within the law and are accountable. We need this to have the trust and support of the American people.

Q: With the proliferation of high-tech intelligence-gathering capabilities, what protection do we have as citizens against the invasion of our privacy?

William H. Webster

That is another good question. It reminds me of what General Vernon Walters—who was our distinguished ambassador to the United Nations and to West Germany, and was a deputy director of Central Intelligence—once said about intelligence. He said, "When the American people feel threatened, they want a whole lot of it, and they do not much care how they get it. And when they do not feel threatened, they think intelligence is somehow immoral." So in between those two, we have to strike a balance. I believe that applicable rules of law are the balance. Clearly, private technology—not official technology—is running far ahead of any rules to control it at the present time. Congress and state legislatures have to consider revising the rules to meet current needs. If a new system of intrusion is not covered by existing laws, it must be addressed. But at the same time, we must be careful not to throw out the baby with the bath water, because inside the baby is our national security.

Q: In the global environment where China is making the transition to a blue-water navy, how is intelligence dealing with incidents at sea to prevent future "Kitty Hawk" incidents?

R. James Woolsey

China is, I think, principally interested in a blue-water navy for two reasons. One is to pose a more effective threat to Taiwan, and the other is its oil interests in the South China Sea, particularly around the Spratly Islands. It has a long way to go to create a modern, powerful navy—probably decades, not years. I served as undersecretary of the navy back in the late 1970s, and I know that the naval side of U.S. intelligence is quite seized with this issue. It is principally the technological trends they are worried about, not so much about immediate Chinese naval construction.

The U.S. Navy normally does not engage in the kind of occasional close-up games of chicken that we did from time to time with the Soviet navy during the height of the cold war. There is much less of a risk of Kitty Hawk–type incidents with China. Moreover, China does not really have the capability to be long at sea far from its shores, the way the Soviet navy did, and we are probably some years away from seeing serious risks of the sort of thing you described.

But China is an increasingly wealthy country—a country that has one major clear ambition that has been a challenge for American policy—namely, acquisition of Taiwan, possibly, someday, by violent means. And it has another interest that is at odds with a lot of its neighbors in Southeast Asia, namely expanding its influence there. So I think later in the twenty- first century we will start to see increasing risks of exactly the sort of thing you described.

Q: President Boren, during your time overseeing the CIA, did a time ever come to pass when American values came into conflict with our national concerns? And if so, how did you respond to this?

David L. Boren

Yes; in fact, more than once. One started with an audit. I mentioned that the Senate Select Committee on Intelligence established an independent audit unit to have the capability to spot-check how money was being spent out of some of the CIA's secret bank accounts around the world. In two instances we found money we felt was being spent inappropriately. That led us in one case to believe that the agency, at least indirectly, might be interfering in the democratic process of another country. We did not think that was wise. We met in a closed, hermetically sealed room in the new Senate office building and heard testimony. People from the agency testified about exactly what was going on with this program, and we used the power of the purse to cut off funding. To their credit, when the audit information was taken to the agency, I am convinced that the highest officials and the director of Central Intelligence did not know what had been occurring. The person at the top of a large, complex organization does not always know everything that is going on. The director recognized our right to cut off the funds and immediately gave orders to halt the operation. The president recognized the committee's right to cut off the funds and confirmed the director's action. Those stories can be told someday through the new program for release to the public of intelligence documents. After a certain period of time, certain documents are declassified. They prove that the system worked.

John Milewski

We are out of time. That will have to be the final, upbeat word on this discussion. Gentleman, it is a rare opportunity for us to share in your unique experience and wisdom. Thank you very much.

NOTE

1. David Ignatius, *Agents of Innocence* (New York: W. W. Norton & Co., 1987).

PART V

Trade Policy and Preparing America's Economy for the Twenty-first Century

Overview

Richard A. Cosier

One of analysts' and government leaders' constant themes since the end of the cold war has been that economics and trade have become the major area of competition among states, replacing the power politics and the threat or use of military force that dominated states' decisions and priorities during the cold war. This certainly seems to be the case to date. Any consideration of the major components of American foreign policy must give close attention to trade policy and the preparation of America's economy for the twenty-first century.

It is safe to say that the health of the U.S. economy over the next century will strongly depend on the strength of the global economy and, vice versa, that the health of the global economy will depend greatly on the strength of the United States economy. Higher growth rates of the United States' gross national product (GNP) will depend significantly on exports. Fortunately, even with a strong dollar, there has been a high, even record-setting, demand for U.S. goods and services during the 1990s, and that demand seems likely to continue.

Part V leads off with former secretary of agriculture and former U.S. trade representative Clayton Yeutter addressing the subject of U.S. trade policy, in chapter 14. In chapter 15, Archie Dunham and Luke Corbett, the presidents and CEOs of two major American corporations, put forth their views on unilateral economic trade sanctions as a tool of U.S. foreign policy. Ambassador John Wolf then leads us on a tour of regional trade organizations, in chapter 16. Part V concludes with Wall Street money manager Michael F. Price and Washington inside-the-beltway attorneys DeVier Pierson and Max N. Berry taking a look, in chapter 17, at what American entrepreneurs expect from their government in the global economy and voicing concern about the pendulum within the United States moving back toward protectionism. Please enjoy reading about the future of U.S. trade policy, trade sanctions, trade liberalization, and the strengthening of the U.S. economy for the twenty-first century.

Chapter 14

United States Trade Policy in the Twenty-first Century

Clayton K. Yeutter

Space does not permit a comprehensive discussion of trade policy, but I will attempt to focus on some of the key challenges that lie ahead over the next few years.

Short-term Priorities

The first, and immediate, challenge is to obtain negotiating authority for the president of the United States. This is the so-called fast-track battle within the U.S. Congress. One must wonder why this is an issue at all, for it should be apparent that one cannot open up additional market opportunities for American exporters without negotiations. Occasionally a nation will voluntarily reduce its import restrictions, but those occasions are rare. Ninety-nine percent of the time markets are opened only through tough, hard sledding at the negotiating table.

Why, then, is this such a controversy? Because many Americans are not yet persuaded that open trade is beneficial to them. They have heard negative arguments from the left and the right, and they have been frightened by those arguments, even though most of them are demagogic. What an irony that is, at a time when U.S. exports have hit an all-time high and trade accounts for about 30 percent of America's economic growth. With unemployment below 5 percent and "Help Wanted" signs appearing everywhere, little credibility can be attached to the arguments of Ross Perot, Pat Buchanan, the labor unions, and others who argued vehemently a few years ago that we would hear a "sucking sound" of jobs leaving the United States.

The "sucking-sound" syndrome was primarily the product of the far right. The far left has contributed its own negativism, with labor unions insisting that worker-rights provisions be included in any trade agreement brought to Congress by the administration, and environmental groups insisting that environmental measures also be included. Because most other nations of the world have rejected such demands repeatedly, including them as a requirement would make it essentially impossible for the administration to negotiate anything. Regrettably, the voices on the far left and the far right have been much more vocal than those of us in the middle, so Congressional approval of fast-track authority is by no means assured. In the absence of fast track, the United States will be unable to engage in any significant negotiation, for other nations will have no desire to work out an agreement with us and then have it unravel when it is presented to the Congress for approval.[1]

A recent survey found that 60 percent of Americans believe that the U.S. market is too open, and 51 percent believe that multilateral corporations benefit more from international trade than do typical Americans (even though the shareholders of such firms are, of course, typical Americans). Only 37 percent believe that international trade contributes to economic growth (even though during the difficult economic times at the turn of the present decade, nearly all of our economic growth was attributable to international trade). That suggests that those of us who understand the benefits of open trade must do a far better job of communicating those benefits to the American public. There must be a myriad of ways in which we could carry out that task more effectively than in the past. The survey numbers just cited clearly illustrate the magnitude of that challenge.

Let us assume for now that Congress will eventually grant the executive branch fast-track negotiating authority as we approach the next century. What then should we do? What should our trade negotiating priorities be over the next few years?

My answer would be, first, let us finish what we have started. The Uruguay Round of General Agreement on Trade and Tariffs (GATT) negotiations was a major success, for the United States and for the world. That negotiation, which took almost eight years, had the most ambitious agenda of any trade negotiation in history. But it accomplished a lot, and we are now reaping the benefits of the market opportunities that came our way as a result of that effort. Our record exports in the 1990s are attributable—not wholly but in a significant degree—to the successes of the Uruguay Round and several bilateral negotiations of the late 1980s and early '90s.

Notwithstanding those successes, numerous "loose ends" remained at the conclusion of the Uruguay Round. That is not surprising, for one never solves with finality all the problems of the world, in trade or anything else. So let us go back to work on those loose ends, on which a lot of preliminary negotiating activity has already taken place. Rather than abandon those preparations, let us carry them forward to their final conclusion.

Among these issues would be services, where the first GATT disciplines were agreed to in the Uruguay Round. But that was just the beginning, and much remains to be done. For example, an agreement on financial services (extremely important to the United States because we have a major competitive advantage in that area) was nearly consummated in the Uruguay Round and now needs to be brought to fruition. The agreement also needs to be broadened to encompass other service sectors. And in some instances the Uruguay Round disciplines need to be extended and expanded, so that economic interchange in this growing segment of the world economy is far more free and open than it is today. The United States has an enormous amount to gain in such negotiations.

A second area is telecommunications, where we have already negotiated some agreements but the world is only beginning to evaluate the problems and opportunities of privatizing government monopolies and subjecting this industry to the disciplines of competition. That will be a learning process for years to come, and one in which the World Trade Organization (WTO) should play a major role.

A third area is government procurement, in which essentially all nations have followed discriminatory purchasing programs for years, if not decades. That is slow to change, and it needs the push of a multilateral negotiation to move the reform process forward.

Another area is standards, in which we already have an international code in the WTO and many standards-making bodies, both domestic and international. All of this has achieved some global harmonization, but not nearly enough. The contribution that could be made to efficiency and productivity in the private sector through a harmonization effort, and the benefits that could thereby be passed on to consumers throughout the world are of inestimable value. The potential savings, going into the next century, would be many billions of dollars.

Investment is another area in which only a beginning was made in the Uruguay Round. A major effort to negotiate fundamental rules in the investment area was carried out in 1997–98 in the Organization for Economic Cooperation and Development (OECD). A model agreement on investment will ultimately need to be brought to the World Trade Organization for adoption. It is hoped that all the major economies of the world will adopt it.

Finally, as an agriculturalist I must emphasize the importance of sustaining the agricultural trade-reform momentum that was generated in the Uruguay Round. Meaningful reforms were approved in that negotiation, for the first time in the half-century history of the GATT. But agricultural trade was the most distorted of all, so there is still plenty of reforming to do. Fortunately, an agreement to commence another tranche of agricultural negotiations in the WTO is already agreed to and scheduled for 1999.

One must also add that we still have some major loose ends in attempting to negotiate regional trade agreements. We have taken the lead in plans to establish a Western Hemisphere free-trade area in the early twenty-first century, a most laudable objective in light of the dramatic improvement in the performance of most Latin American economies. If that improvement continues, as we hope, it will provide impressive export opportunities for American business firms. But without negotiating authority, and without American leadership generally, the Western Hemisphere trade agreement will be only a dream in the next century, not a reality.

We also have under way what is called the Transatlantic Business Dialogue, involving representatives of government and the private sector from the United States and the nations of western Europe. I would like very much to see us move from a dialogue to a major trade negotiation in that context as the twenty-first century approaches. I have long been a proponent of a United States–European Union free-trade agreement, for I believe that offers more potential for trade expansion, and thereby greater potential for job creation in the United States (and in western Europe, for that matter), than any other regional negotiation we could undertake. For me that would be the highest priority non-WTO negotiation we could launch as the new century emerges.

Long-term Priorities

What I have covered thus far would constitute most of my short-term agenda, but we need to contemplate also what our long-term trade-policy priorities should be. In that regard we first need to get all the major players in the game. As of 1999, China, Taiwan, and several other significant economies are still outside the World Trade Organization. That means they are subject to none of the "rules of the game" of the WTO, and none of the disciplines for violating those rules. We can deal with troublesome trade conduct in those nations only on a bilateral basis, and that is not a very efficient or effective way of monitoring or influencing their trade conduct. We need to get all these major nations "under the tent," but only on terms acceptable to us and to the other WTO member nations. These may be among the most difficult negotiations we have ever attempted, but we need to get them done, and with the right result. That is a formidable task, but not an impossible one, and such an outcome will not only be in our long-term best interest but also in the best interests of the nations that are now on the outside looking in.

Another of our long-term priorities should be to expose violations, not only of the formal rules of the WTO, but also violations of the spirit of open trade. One of the major achievements of the Uruguay Round was to provide for us and the rest of the world a vastly improved dispute-settlement mechanism. We can now take trade-policy grievances to the WTO, obtain a decisive result, and achieve that result in a specified period of time. But just as a private individual cannot go to court every day of the week, neither can a nation take disputes to the WTO every day of the week. One must be selective, which means a lot of grievances go unpunished. What is the alternative? The alternative is to require nations to be transparent in their trade-policy decision-making process, exposing that process to public scrutiny, not only by their own citizens, but by the rest of the world as well. We are already transparent here in the United States; there is very little that our government does secretly, in any area, and we are assuredly transparent in trade policy. Unfortunately, that is not the case with many of our major trading partners, which means that we need to work on the transparency issue within the WTO.

I also believe the WTO should begin an effort to encompass competition policy, i.e., antitrust laws, within its twenty-first-century agenda. That was done successfully, although embryonically, with intellectual property, services, and investment in the Uruguay Round. So there is ample precedent for adding work in major new areas that have an impact on international commerce. Without question, predatory competition adversely affects trading activity and severely distorts the outcome. And without question, there is nothing approaching harmonization of antitrust laws throughout the world today. Developing serious activity in the competition-policy arena has its complications, for it brings ministers of justice into the picture for the first time. But finance ministers are there for the negotiations on financial services, agricultural ministers are there for ag negotiations, and other ministers are there from time to time as their specialties come to the fore in the negotiating process. And if one could develop sensible, harmonious rules of competition policy, it might be possible to reduce our present dependence on antidumping laws, which are a costly, cumbersome mechanism for dealing with troublesome pricing policies.

Finally, and perhaps most importantly, we need to alter the psychology of trade negotiations. For half a century, the GATT has based all its rounds of negotiations on "mutual concessions." That worked well in the early years, when mutual tariff concessions were exchanged and the outcome was a general reduction in tariff levels on thousands of products in many countries throughout the world. Mutual concessions work less well when nontariff measures are involved, for they are often difficult even to identify, let alone quantify. And they work less well in some of the new areas such as services and intellectual property, in which the negotiating objectives are far different from those of a traditional tariff exercise. Beyond that, the whole concept of mutual concessions implies that all nations are "giving up" something, and that has a negative connotation. The objective of a negotiation then becomes one of giving up less than other nations do. The reaction of an observing general public quite naturally becomes, "Why should we have to give up anything?" And in the United States, with its tradition of global generosity, the next comment is, "Our negotiators are going to give up more than anyone, so we will be better off if they do not negotiate at all." That, in fact, may well be one of the reasons why fast-track authority has been so controversial.

What we should do is put emphasis on what is to be gained as a result of a particular negotiation, rather than what is to be given up. And then we should credibly demonstrate, after a reasonable period of time, that those benefits were obtained. We have often simply taken those benefits for granted, and we have not done the fundamental, comprehensive economic research that is necessary to be persuasive in a democratic society. Trade is not a zero-sum game, and neither are trade negotiations. The implied outcome of mutual concessions is that for everything we gain, someone else loses, and for everything that country gains, someone else loses—probably us. Yet there is a great deal of "win, win" in any sound, sensible negotiation.

For example, I am fully persuaded that the North America Free Trade Agreement (NAFTA) is now providing just such an outcome for Canada, Mexico, and the United States. There will, of course, be some economic dislocation as NAFTA is fully implemented, and some people in all three countries will lose jobs. But in the aggregate, the probability is very high that surveys a decade from now will show that NAFTA was an economic winner for all three participating countries. Considerable evidence to that effect is already at hand.

Trade negotiations have had a splendid track record in the last half century; we just have not been sharing that record with the people who count—the consumers and voters of the world.

I have just outlined an ambitious long-term agenda for the U.S. government and for our trade-negotiating team. Nothing comes easy in trade negotiations but, as in most things, hard work pays off. If we get our priorities right and then execute them well, both bilateral and multilateral trade negotiations will have a positive impact of major proportions on the American economy as we conclude the twentieth century.

NOTE

1. "Fast Track Trade Negotiating Authority," Hearing Before the Subcommittee, General Farm Commodities, of the U.S. House Committee on Agriculture, 105th Cong., 1st sess., 23 September 1997, Serial No. 105–26 (Washington, D.C.: U.S. Government Printing Office, 1997).

Chapter 15

Trade Sanctions

Unilateral Economic Sanctions: A Foreign-Policy Tool Whose Time Has Passed

Archie W. Dunham

Mankind has experienced more change in the last fifty years than in any previous half century in history. The changes have been driven by the great wave of trade and investment that began after World War II. Communism's collapse in the early 1990s was the final breach of the dike. It allowed the principles of democracy to take root and opened markets around the world. Although pockets of resistance remain in some countries, the power of open markets, trade, and investment to improve people's lives is now recognized almost everywhere.

For most of the postwar period, the United States led the effort to encourage trade in goods, services, technology, investment capital, and ideas across international borders. But in the 1990s, U.S. policy has gone astray, relying heavily on unilateral economic sanctions to punish countries whose policies we find disagreeable. Too often, we have ignored the dissenting opinions of our traditional allies and trading partners and proceeded on our own at high cost and with little, if any, benefit.

I believe strongly that it is time for the United States to develop new approaches for the achievement of our foreign-policy goals. Our policy tool kit needs to be expanded. My credentials for making this case are based in part on personal experience. I am the chief executive of a large energy company that the Clinton administration asked to withdraw from a contract to develop two oil fields offshore Iran.

But unilateral economic sanctions affect more than just energy companies. They damage the interests of a whole host of internationally oriented businesses and agricultural firms, as well as millions of American workers who are employed by those firms. More broadly, sanctions are a cause for concern to all Americans who want the United States to remain a vital force in spreading democratic principles, free markets, and higher living standards throughout the world.

The United States' use of economic sanctions is not new. They have been a feature of U.S. policy throughout American history. In the nineteenth century, for example, President Abraham Lincoln sanctioned the states of the Confederacy. This encouraged the British to develop cotton industries in countries such as Egypt—and the American cotton industry still feels the competitive impact of this decision. During the twentieth century, sanctions targeting North Korea and Cuba have been in force for decades.

Although sanctions are not new, until just a few years ago they were used sparingly. But recently, the use of sanctions has been escalating. In the four years 1993–96, the U.S. government imposed sixty-one sanctions against thirty-five countries, severing the access of America's businesses and farmers to 42 percent of the world's population.[1] In 1997, twenty-six additional bills proposing unilateral economic sanctions were introduced in the U.S. Congress.

The tangle of restrictions has grown worse in the last few years because of increasing "extraterritorial" sanctions legislation, most notably the Iran-Libya Sanctions Act and the Helms-Burton Act, both passed in 1996. These laws require the United States to impose penalties on companies from other countries that—contrary to U.S. policy—do business with Iran, Libya, or Cuba. Our historical friends and trading partners—including Canada, Switzerland, and Indonesia, among many others—have expressed frustration at how casually the United States seems to dismiss their differing viewpoints, and how aggressively we pursue policies that isolate the United States from the countries we are targeting and from our historical allies.

At times, it appears that sanctions have become virtually the only tool in our foreign-policy kit. When I see a list of potential target countries, I am reminded of the old saying, "When your only tool is a hammer, every problem starts to look like a nail." And when I observe the ineffectiveness of America's recent sanctions policy, I believe we are hitting our thumbs more often than the nail. The time has come to move away from unilateral economic sanctions and find new ways to influence the behavior of nations that have policies we oppose. I say this for several reasons.

(1) Unilateral economic sanctions do not work.

History shows that even multilateral sanctions are effective only in the rare instances when they have a broad base of support. The antiapartheid measures imposed on South Africa in the 1980s by most members of the international community are generally regarded as having been successful. But even in this case, the measures were only one part of a very broad strategy of engagement.

In the early 1990s Iraq's widely condemned invasion of Kuwait led to a set of broadly supported sanctions against Iraq that succeeded in temporarily restraining Saddam Hussein. But the sanctions were not successful in averting war or in toppling Saddam's government.

When only one country imposes sanctions against another, the challenge is even greater. Two key conditions must apply if unilateral sanctions are to be effective: The sanctioner must be overwhelmingly dominant economically, and the economy of the targeted country must be heavily dependent on the sanctioner. These are extremely restrictive conditions that throughout history have seldom if ever prevailed—even when the sanctioner was the United States.

To be sure, during the first quarter century after World War II, the United States occupied a dominant political and economic position on the world stage. But even then its economic might was incapable of achieving many of its foreign-policy goals for targeted countries—Cuba, for example.

Today, the globalization of markets; the rapid movement of capital, technology, and information across borders; and robust economic growth in many countries of the world mean there are even more alternatives to American goods, services, technologies, and markets. In the twenty-first century these trends will accelerate, further limiting America's ability to use economic pressure unilaterally to force other countries to change their policies.

When, against all odds, the United States insists on going it alone with sanctions, the benefit is often measured only in emotional terms. If the U.S. government takes a strong stand on a matter of concern to the American people—such as an abuse of human rights in another country—it may make Americans "feel good" that something is being done, but often no substantive foreign-policy goal is achieved. And in some cases, unilateral sanctions make matters worse. All too often, targeted governments gain political support internally by thumbing their noses at the United States.

Tragically, unilateral economic sanctions not only do not work, they sometimes harm those we want most to help. In an attempt to promote democracy in Haiti in the early 1990s, the United States imposed an oil embargo and other tough sanctions against that country, hoping to pressure its repressive military government to resign. The sanctions didn't work, although a threat of invasion, coupled with high-level, last-ditch diplomacy, eventually did cause the government to yield. In the interim, however, the oil embargo made it impossible for poor Haitian farmers to get their crops to market, further depressing the country's fragile economy and adding to the misery of the Haitian people.

(2) Unilateral economic sanctions have enormous cost to the American economy.

According to the economists' law of comparative advantage, free-flowing international trade raises incomes, wages, and wealth for everyone. The other side of the coin is that when barriers to trade are imposed, wealth creation is reduced.

That has certainly been borne out by the United States' experience with economic sanctions. A study by the Institute for International Economics concluded that U.S. exports to twenty-six targeted countries may have been reduced by $15 billion to $19 billion in 1995 alone as a result of sanctions that were in place during that year. A loss of about 200,000 to 250,000 relatively high-wage jobs was associated with that reduction in exports.[2]

A look at the export history of specific industries confirms the negative impact of U.S. sanctions policy on America's exporters. For example, the long-standing U.S. ban on the sale of nuclear-power-generation equipment to China simply allowed France, Canada, and Russia to step in and meet the needs of that large, fast-growing market, in the process generating export sales estimated at $15 billion. Fortunately, the U.S. government's policy toward China now appears to be changing, sparking hope that the ban on the sale of nuclear equipment and other high-technology goods and services to China will be relaxed.

The damage from losing market position on such a large scale can be long lasting. The United States' imposition in1980 of a grain embargo on the Soviet Union to force it to withdraw from Afghanistan (a futile effort, ultimately) ended up costing U.S. grain farmers $2.3 billion in exports lost to grain suppliers from other countries. American agriculture has still not fully recovered its share of the former Soviet market. Years later our exports remain well below preembargo levels.

It is important to recognize that the U.S. economy is becoming more global every day. Annual exports have averaged more than $700 billion throughout the 1990s, and they are growing rapidly. Export-related jobs have climbed as well, growing four times faster than total employment. In 1997, more than twelve million Americans and their families depended on exports for their livelihood; by the year 2000 that is expected to grow to twenty million. So when U.S. sanctions policy squeezes export-related jobs out of existence, the cost to the American economy can be very high.

The high cost of sanctions to individual states should be recognized as well. In 1996, Oklahoma-based firms exported $380 million of goods and services to countries threatened by sanctions. At risk are about 5,900 export-related jobs. In other parts of the United States, even more is at stake. California exported $11.2 billion to targeted countries in 1996; about 175,000 jobs are at risk in that state.[3]

Sometimes the mere threat of sanctions can damage the national interest. Prospective purchasers of U.S. products and technologies come to regard American suppliers as unreliable and shy away from doing business with them. After threats by the U.S. Congress in 1997 to impose unilateral sanctions on Indonesia because of concerns about human-rights abuses in East Timor, Indonesia canceled a $200 million purchase of F-16 fighters from Lockheed Martin. Subsequently, aircraft manufacturers from Russia and the United Kingdom filled the order.

Making sure the door stays open to developing countries such as Indonesia—as well as other Asian nations, Nigeria, Colombia, and the countries of the Middle East—is especially important to my own company because those countries possess much of the world's petroleum reserves.

Open access is equally important to many other sectors of the U.S. economy. The ten largest national markets in the developing world are expected to double their share of international trade in the next decade. U.S. companies should not be denied the opportunity to win their share of that trade. Yet the United States has imposed or threatened sanctions against five of those ten countries. Closing off the United States from those markets would seriously damage prospects for our nation's business enterprises and the jobs they provide.

(3) Unilateral economic sanctions fail to achieve political and human-rights objectives, which erodes America's influence in the world.

The goals of economic sanctions are not at issue in the sanctions debate. Most Americans share the desire to stop terrorism, human-rights abuses, religious discrimination, drug trafficking, and weapons proliferation. The question is, "What is the best way to accomplish these laudable goals?"

Unilateral sanctions are not the solution. Besides being ineffective, they erode U.S. credibility and alienate our friends. The U.S. government's shift in the last few years toward imposition of extraterritorial sanctions has made matters worse. In particular, the Iran-Libya Sanctions Act and the Helms-Burton Act, directed at foreign companies and governments investing in Cuba, have been special sources of frustration and even anger for many of America's traditional allies and trading partners.

I believe the increased reliance of U.S. lawmakers on extraterritorial sanctions in recent years has inadvertently revealed the problem with this approach. Policy makers have recognized that America's refusal to deal with a target country will not keep suppliers from other countries from stepping in to meet the target country's needs. So our lawmakers launch a "preemptive strike" against potential sanction breakers, in an attempt to force their compliance. Such efforts are not only counterproductive, they also harm America's interests by demonstrating the weakness of our position and by offending our friends.

Sadly, America's record of international relations in the last few years includes numerous instances in which traditional allies have ignored America's requests to honor U.S. foreign-policy dictums. The rebuffs range from the admission of Myanmar to the Association of Southeast Asian Nations (ASEAN) in spite of U.S. objections, to the open defiance of the United States by France, Russia, Malaysia, and other countries in response to Washington's attempts to isolate Iran. Every such rebuff is a blow to America's prestige and global influence.

When U.S. sanctions do not work, it looks as though America has failed. And when America fails, we not only lose our ability to lead other countries, we also lose our ability to even influence them. The United States must avoid—to the extent permitted by our vital national interest—taking stands that our friends and allies are unlikely to support.

(4) Unilateral economic sanctions are too easy to put in place, but very hard to dislodge.

In the 1990s there has been a communications revolution that has increased public awareness of the trouble spots around the world—armed conflicts, human-rights abuses, environmental accidents, and the like. In a world where the Internet and CNN disseminate information instantly and more widely than ever before, it is convenient for politicians and other high-profile media figures, even movie stars, to grab onto issues and use them to promote their own agendas.

Too often, members of the U.S. Congress have viewed unilateral economic sanctions as a risk-free way to improve their standing with voters, by tapping into public concern about an important issue of the day. This is often triggered by a specific news event that causes public outcry—raising the emotional thermometer and prompting demands for action. A notable example of this occurred in 1996, when Congress passed the Helms-Burton Act, immediately after Cuban fighters shot down two unarmed civilian aircraft in Cuba's airspace. Compared with the unattractive options of doing nothing or sending in the marines, imposing sanctions offered a convenient, quick response that *looked* tough, even though the actual impact was nil.

In the past, economic sanctions were imposed primarily by Congress or the executive branch. But in the last few years, officials of state and local governments have jumped on the sanctions bandwagon. From 1995 to 1997, various governmental authorities outside Washington imposed or proposed at least forty-nine unilateral economic sanctions. These sanctions would negatively impact exports to at least eighteen countries, including Switzerland, Turkey, Egypt, Indonesia, and China.[4] The sanctioning authorities include states such as Texas, California, and Massachusetts and cities such as New York, Seattle, and Berkeley.

Regardless of the level of government that imposes sanctions, the problem is the same: The decisions to impose sanctions are seldom put under the microscope of critical review and analysis. There has been no meaningful debate of questions such as, "Does this truly advance our national interest?"; "Will it really achieve our foreign policy goal?"; "Is there a better way to accomplish our goal?" And unfortunately, once a sanction is imposed, there is usually no process for removing it—even when experience proves its futility.

(5) Unilateral economic sanctions create the issue of legislating international moral standards, which is itself problematic.

Proponents of sanctions assume two things—that "right" is on their side, and that sanctions constitute an ethically responsible reaction to unacceptable behavior outside our borders. Proponents of international sanctions assume that what is right in the United States applies with equal force internationally: "Unacceptable behavior gets punished . . . failure to punish is morally wrong . . . inaction signals consent."

These are flawed premises. Economic sanctions are scattershot. They do not pinpoint evildoers or the perpetrators of crimes. As I asserted earlier, economic sanctions are more likely to hurt innocent civilians. They usually allow the guilty to go free and sometimes even strengthen them. Thus when we impose sanctions, we can be accused of actually promoting the behavior we are trying to deter.

The United States is proud of its Judeo-Christian heritage. We see ourselves as a moral beacon—"a city on the hill," as Jonathan Winthrop, founder of the Massachusetts Bay Colony, described this country more than three centuries ago. Our desire is for other countries to follow our lead and emulate our example. That objective can be achieved only when the moral values we hold dear are embraced by others—not imposed on them. We cannot force people to become believers through sanctions. But we can convince them by example.

Americans have tolerated the proliferation of poorly conceived, badly designed, and ineffective sanctions for too long. The consequence of this neglect is a tangled mess of economic restrictions and boycotts that hamstring multinational companies, penalize their employees, and frustrate America's trading partners. America's use of unilateral sanctions in international politics must be modified or eliminated.

What should replace unilateral sanctions? I believe the answer must take into account several key principles surrounding the use of economic weapons in international politics.

The first principle is: In matters of international political relations—just as in interpersonal relations—carrots usually work better than sticks.

Whenever possible, we should provide incentives for policies we can support, rather than trying to punish countries for behavior we find objectionable. If these incentives take into account the mutual interests of the target country and the United States, we can achieve a "win-win" result.

In some cases, it may be necessary to take action against a country. But even then we need to choose options that are likely to be effective and give these measures time to work before escalating to the next level.

A second principle is: Engagement is more effective than isolation.

Sanctions isolate the United States from the target country and disrupt international trade. We should remember that it was not a military action that tore down the Berlin Wall and sounded the death knell for Communism in the early 1990s; it was the growth of international trade—not only in products and services, but also in ideas. Free-flowing trade remains a powerful tool for long-term economic and political change. It should be strengthened, not disrupted.

When sanctions shrink international investment by American companies, they also shrink the ability of American companies to advance human rights and democracy around the world. Sanctions prevent us from promoting free enterprise, building infrastructure, training workers, imparting our values, and raising standards of living.

The positive impact of Conoco's Polar Lights project, Russia's first western oil-field development, clearly demonstrates the good that U.S. investment can do. Improving the quality of life for local people often favorably influences government policy.[5]

If sanctions prevent American companies from investing, competitors from other countries simply take their place, as shown by the forced withdrawal of my own company from the development of Iran's Sirri fields in 1995. Within weeks, the French company Total took over Conoco's hard-won position, very quickly and smoothly. As a result, Iran is completing the massive Sirri project without any U.S. participation and without the moderating influence I believe Conoco's participation would have had on Iran's views of the United States, the American people, and our way of doing business.

Whenever such an event occurs, the United States loses its ability to promote social, economic, and political change in the target country, even as the American company loses a valuable commercial position.

A third principle is: America's options for promoting change in the behavior of rogue régimes are not limited to doing nothing, sending in the marines, or imposing sanctions.

A wide range of alternatives exists. Conoco is working hard, along with other concerned parties, to demonstrate that point. We are active participants in USA*Engage, a coalition of more than 650 small and large businesses, agriculture groups, and trade associations working to find alternatives to unilateral sanctions and to promote the benefits of U.S. engagement abroad. USA*Engage members represent all regions and all sectors of the U.S. economy.[6]

In another initiative, I serve on the steering committee of the Economic Sanctions Project, an undertaking of the Center for Strategic and International Studies. As with USA*Engage, the goal of this group is to define viable and constructive alternatives for promoting America's national interests without damaging our nation's global leadership position and commercial interests. Table 15.1 shows that a variety of foreign-policy options is available to the United States for influencing other countries. In addition to economic and military options, which too often have been the main focus of our attention, there are also diplomatic, political, and cultural options. All should be employed.

In using these foreign-policy tools, our choices are also broader than simply "use it" or "do not use it." We can apply the tools in various degrees of intensity across a spectrum ranging from "friendly persuasion" to "coercion." Thus, depending on the approach most likely to work for a given country, the tools can be used as "carrots" or as "sticks." For example:

- Visa policies can be liberalized to those we want to reward, or they can be restricted to targeted groups. In extreme cases we can completely suspend the granting of visas.
- State visits can be encouraged, postponed, or canceled.
- Exchanges of academics can be established or expanded. At the other extreme, they can be suspended.

Table 15.1

U.S. FOREIGN-POLICY TOOLS Examples of Available Options	
DIPLOMATIC	Visa policy Landing rights Ambassadorial representation
POLITICAL	Congressional resolutions State visits Sister-city agreements
CULTURAL	Scientific or academic exchanges Training and education in the United States Athletic competition Broadcast policy
ECONOMIC	Financial aid to target country Handling of target country's debt Investment policy Trade missions International financial institutions
MILITARY	Officer exchanges Cooperation with target country's military Neighbors Port visits Military action

- The United States can use its influence to encourage international financial institutions to extend credit to target countries, or it can urge that they be denied that favorable treatment.

- Overt military action, the final tool shown on the list, should obviously be avoided until all other options have been exhausted. When it is employed, it can range from limited local maneuvers to a larger show of force to an act of war.

My point is that the United States can and should develop a plan for influencing other countries in a systematic way. It should tailor its choice of foreign-policy options to each target country, matching the action to our policy goals. The options chosen for Myanmar, for example, would likely be very different from those for China.

In choosing options, we should take advantage of the ramp of escalating possibilities, applying no more pressure than is necessary. This will free the United States from its tendency to use a sledgehammer when a mild diplomatic rebuke would suffice. For some countries, the "lighter" application of foreign-policy tools can sometimes have a very powerful impact on their behavior, e.g., liberalization of landing rights (a "diplomatic" tool), debt rescheduling on favorable terms ("economic"), or the staging of athletic competitions ("cultural").

As a specific case in point, the symbolism and power of athletic competitions to build bridges between nations has been demonstrated recently in Iran–United States relations. For nearly two decades, Iran has been the country perhaps most hostile to the United States. And yet in late 1997 even the government of Iran, led by a new, popularly elected, moderate president, began to hint to the United States that it would like to engage Americans in dialogue and begin to improve relations between Washington and Tehran. Joint appearances by United States and Iranian wrestling teams—in both Iran and the United States—have beem featured prominently in the tentative moves by Tehran and Washington toward reconciliation.[7] We need to broaden and strengthen these and many other threads of engagement between the United States and Iran.

As the wrestling example demonstrates, all interested parties should be enlisted in the effort to enhance America's influence through engagement; it is seldom just the task of government. As we build bridges through sports, athletic teams of many kinds can and should be involved. In the establishment of academic exchanges, universities, research institutions, and appropriate companies should be called on.

A final principle: If in the final analysis the use of economic sanctions is judged to be the only feasible alternative, the sanctions should be carefully controlled.

Ideally, any sanction the United States imposes against a target country will have broad-based multilateral support. In a world of growing economic interdependence among nations, that may be a necessary condition for sanctions to be effective. If a multilateral coalition cannot be put together, however, and unilateral U.S. sanctions are judged to be necessary, the decision to impose sanctions should at least be revisited from time to time. We cannot afford to wind up the economic-sanctions clock and then just walk away.

Fortunately, public awareness of the insidious damage that unilateral economic sanctions inflict on our national interest is increasing. A growing chorus of concerned academics, think tanks, business leaders, and agriculture and business associations has been speaking out in favor of changing our government's sanctions policy. The results of these efforts in the recent past have been encouraging: fewer new unilateral sanctions passed by Congress, fewer new sanctions imposed at the state and local level, and a significant trend in newspaper editorials advocating a foreign policy of engagement rather than isolation.

Table 15.2

Which Best Serves America's National Interest?		
isolation	or	engagement
sanctions	or	many policies
"cure"	or	"prevention"
reactive	or	proactive
backlashes	or	reciprocity
blunt instrument	or	situation-specific tools
friction with allies	or	cooperation with allies
declining influence	or	increasing influence
restricted opportunities	or	more opportunities
a "bully" on the world stage	or	a leader on the world stage

Perhaps most important, late in 1997 some of the most respected members of the U.S. Congress—Congressmen Philip Crane and Lee Hamilton and Senator Richard Lugar—stepped forward to cosponsor sanctions-reform legislation. If the Hamilton-Crane-Lugar Sanctions Reform Act becomes law, it will finally bring common sense to the federal government's use of unilateral sanctions. It would require every sanction to meet several tests before being imposed:

- Sponsors will have to make a persuasive case that the sanction will actually be effective.

- Alternatives will have to be explicitly identified.

- Independent studies of costs and benefits will need to be conducted.

- There will be a two-year "sunset" provision on each new sanction, meaning it will expire if it is not renewed.

It is critically important to America's national interest that the Sanctions Reform Act be passed. Fortunately, the Clinton administration seems to support the principles embodied in the proposed legislation, which should enhance its chances for passage.

America's global leadership will face many challenges in the twenty-first century, including the challenge of responding effectively to the political misdeeds of other countries. The United States must improve its ability to modify such behavior in a nonconfrontational and effective manner. How can our nation effectively carry out this important leadership role? I believe Americans and their governmental leaders face a clear choice between two ways of thinking about our role in the world, as shown in table 15.2.

In my judgment, the choices are clear. The options on the right side of the ledger provide the best framework for developing U.S. economic policies capable of effectively serving the nation's foreign-policy goals.

Working within that framework, U.S. companies will help the nation achieve its goals for economic and foreign policy by doing what they do best—promoting trade, spreading investment, developing markets, imparting values, and creating jobs and opportunities. In fact, American business can be another tool in our nation's kit—a tool for positive change all over the world.

Pluses and Minuses in United States Foreign Policy

Luke R. Corbett

The subject of trade sanctions has a great deal of meaning for me as CEO of a global energy and global chemical company. It is not hard to find ourselves caught many times between both sides of some very difficult issues, but let me state at the outset that I believe that Congress and the executive branch need to exercise extreme caution in the use of unilateral economic sanctions.

Each time I think of traveling down roads fraught with obstacles and ignoring the signs that come up along the way, I am reminded of the story about the driver from the city on his way to do business in a country town. He comes to a crossroads and there is a detour sign posted on the road he needs to go down. He looks, and the road looks good as far as he can see so he ignores the sign, turns onto the road, and begins his journey. Three miles down he comes to a bridge that is out. He turns around, retraces the three miles back to the crossroads and the detour sign, and to his amazement, a note on the back of the sign he ignored said, "Welcome back, stupid." I use this only to illustrate that careful, thoughtful, and wise consideration should be afforded all intelligence and all signs before economic sanctions become the road we follow.

My stance and our company's position are really not a reflection of a lack of moral fiber or any reluctance to take a stand—far from it. Our attitude really is a direct result of our experience, and we believe it offers a balanced view of the far-reaching and perhaps unintended effects on American business of heavy-handed foreign-policy approaches.

Let me first clarify some of the principles that we embrace in Kerr-McGee's approach to international risk, and amplify our attitudes toward developing nations with vastly different cultures from our own.

First, we recognize the political necessity and common sense of marking some nations as off limits to American business. Iran, Iraq, Libya, and perhaps Myanmar fall into this group. Our government also includes the Sudan, Syria, and Cuba and only recently took Vietnam off the list. There are without a doubt other countries—North Korea, for instance—whose material resources hold no real attraction for the majority of American business in general, specifically energy companies such as Kerr-McGee. In cases such as these, we see little downside in the application of sanctions—provided there is a justifiable connection between cause and effect. In reality, all must recognize, however, that the application of sanctions, moral or otherwise, has had very little discernible effect on the politics of the nations involved. In fact, the United States provides the necessary "external evil" required by these governments to maintain themselves in power.

So as a statement of principle, economic sanctions may be justifiable, but as a means of effecting fundamental change in a reasonable period of time, in my opinion they are ineffective. History supports this observation. One study analyzed the cost and effectiveness of 110 cases of economic sanctions between 1915 and 1990 and found that only 34 percent achieved their goals. And to the extent that they are detrimental to the health of the average citizen within the targeted nation, they even make normalization of relations after the passing of a repressive régime more problematic, and the transformation to a free and democratic society that may follow fraught with difficulties. History even suggests that the potential successors often develop behavioral characteristics not too dissimilar to their predecessors in order to survive.

In the case of the fall of the Soviet Union, an issue involving sanctions regarding military materials and items deemed proprietary (such as computer parts), the transformation has been extremely agonizing. Even governmental organizations and former state-operated enterprises know no rational or fair means of operating their businesses. They simply lack training and experience. Witness the recent denial of due process afforded Exxon in Timan Pechora when local manipulation resulted in confiscation of an oil deal, long in the works. Would sanctions or censure affect the process? I do not believe so. The former Soviet Union nations appear unwilling or unable to do business following accepted Western standards and have repeatedly undermined legitimate business efforts. However, those corporations that can monetarily afford to endure soldier on, pursuing enormous opportunity that may come but is certainly a long way off.

I would add that the newly emergent democracies—in which the only organized businesses prior to democratization were criminal elements whose characteristics dominate the new business environment—will be censored by businesses themselves without our government's help.

At Kerr-McGee we spend a great deal of time assessing any host country's attitudes toward business—its willingness to strike a fair deal in which both sides will prosper. We are truly guests in their house and we must act accordingly.

These are not merely words at Kerr-McGee. As of 1998 we have operations in eight countries around the world: the United States, Australia, United Kingdom, Ireland, Indonesia, People's Republic of China, Thailand, and

Yemen. We are evaluating exploration potential in newly opened areas in South America. We have oil and gas production from the United States, United Kingdom, the People's Republic of China, and Indonesia, the latter two since 1995. We are not in the former Soviet Union, Africa, and many parts of South America, either because there have been signs that business cannot be run in a manner acceptable or legal in the United States or because the host country is not hospitable. It did not take an executive order by our government to cause us to arrive at that conclusion—it was common, ethical business sense.

We represent mature institutions possessing strategies to minimize risks to our shareholders and employees that balance the potential upside offered by a major discovery or major operation in any country. I believe that business can and will assess the need for appropriate sanctions. In all but the full-fledged rogue nations, we ask our government to allow us to vote with our feet.

Where things can and do get confused and U.S. business really needs to be consulted is along the border between political expediency and real necessity. For instance, each year we subject the People's Republic of China to a debate about most-favored-nation (MFN) status. This debate is always couched in terms of human-rights abuses. For those of us privileged to work in and with the PRC, we can only suggest that the debate be tempered with realism. Beijing is not Washington, D.C. It has the enormous responsibility of bringing 1.2 billion Chinese peacefully into the next millennium while simultaneously changing a culture that has been in place for many years. For those of us who travel to China regularly and conduct business there, we are well aware that things are not the same as in our home, but they are improving. China has averaged 10 percent real growth annually for two decades, and per capita income has reached about $2,750 in purchasing-power terms, which makes China "middle income" by World Bank standards. If China can sustain this rate of growth, national output will double in seven years and quadruple in fourteen years. This growth has some analysts projecting China's economy as the world's largest by 2020, and its people achieving parity with U.S. living standards by the middle of the twenty-first century.

Hong Kong appears to have been successfully integrated into China, at least at this time. From the PRC's perspective, so eventually will Taiwan. China believes it will set an example so compelling that the Taiwanese will vote to rejoin the mainland. That is the plan. It may happen in our lifetime; it may not. Life in China is no piece of cake—personal freedoms as we know them are nearly nonexistent, yet you can walk around Beijing at night with a lot less concern for safety than you might feel even in some modest-sized American cities. And do not think that sanctions will not hit hard in the United States if applied to China. The next time you pick up a Tickle Me Elmo or Beanie Baby or most reasonably priced textiles sold in this nation, check the label, understand the limits of what is being advocated, and have someone calculate the cost to the U.S. economy.

We also have no naïve view of China's ability to impact the whole of Southeast Asia. It is a major economic and major military power and should be viewed accordingly. Yet I believe that with China as a friend of the United States, we have a much greater opportunity for constructive engagement and influence than we would as a barrier to its integration into the world economic order. In short, I believe that it is in the best interest of the United States and the world to guide China toward normalization of trade and economic relationships. If any more obvious indicator of China's influence is needed, note the recent devaluation of the Southeast Asian currencies and the apparent stability of China's currency.

I also believe that we as a nation would do well to review the sixty-one-odd nations that in late 1997 we were sanctioning, blockading, or embargoing. What does the future of United States industry look like without Iranian, or perhaps Central Asian, oil ten or fifteen years from now? Or products from China? Or cooperative relationships with at least some Middle Eastern nations? I am concerned that with the exception of the true rogue nations, our approach is ineffective, haphazard, uneven, and lacks the necessary long view required to make it an act of diplomacy rather than a reflection of narrow partisan politics that seek short-term public favor. Foreign policy is about promoting this nation's interest—all of its interests.

Shareholders and employees expect me, as CEO of Kerr-McGee Corporation, to invest wisely in areas and projects that offer a balance between risk and reward. I have faith in our intelligence and technical capabilities to assess the business risk in any country. I do believe, however, that U.S. business should not have to deal with the added risk of sanctions imposed by Congress and the executive branch merely to vent anger or achieve short-term positions. I appreciate that sanctions offer members of Congress and the executive branch an attractive compromise between doing nothing and sending in the marines, but again I reiterate that foreign policy is about promoting this nation's interests—all of them! I also know that in some instances, sanctions will be the best way to do this. Today's Iraq comes to mind. But in many other situations, sanctions would do more harm than good.

We want to do the right thing as a corporation, and I know we want to as a nation. I believe American business is willing to spend a considerable portion of its energies to assure that an appropriate response is framed to international situations. I know our company is. I would hope that our government would include appropriate business intelligence before enacting sanctions. Our on-the-spot experience and our informed opinion are available to policy makers for the asking. I believe that such up-front input will result in more effective use of economic sanctions and, in the long term, will be better for government and business.

NOTES

1. Executive Summary, *Catalog of New U.S. Unilateral Economic Sanctions for Foreign Policy Purposes, 1993-96* (Washington, D.C.: National Association of Manufacturers, March 1997).

2. Donald V. Fites, "From Isolation to Engagement: The Case Against Unilateral Sanctions," CEO Series Issue No. 18 (Saint Louis: Center for the Study of American Business, Washington University, November 1997), p. 1.

3. "U.S. Economic Sanctions: Their Impact on Trade, Jobs, and Wages," working paper (Washington, D.C.: Institute for International Economics, April 1997).

4. Ibid.

5. Frank Kittredge, president, National Foreign Trade Council, quoted in a July 23, 1997, press release issued by USA*Engage, Washington, D.C. (available at *www.usaengage.org/news/970723pr.html*).

6. Conoco is the largest Western investor in the Russian petroleum sector. Polar Lights was the first joint venture between a Russian company and a Western company to develop a new Russian oil field, Ardalin Field, 1,000 miles north of Moscow. Ardalin went on stream in 1995. The Russian government and the oil industry regarded it as a model for how to design oil production in a sensitive arctic tundra environment inhabited by abundant wildlife. The project has won several environmental awards in Russia. Staffing the operation are 200 highly skilled workers, most of them Russian.

7. A good summary of the positive signals sent by Iran to the United States in late 1997 and early 1998 is given in "More Signs of Thaw in Icy U.S.-Iran Relations," *Washington Post*, 17 March 1998.

Chapter 16

Trade Liberalization

John S. Wolf

I am delighted to address a subject important to each of us: how to keep America competitive. Let me be clear from the start. I am not one of those people who believe we are a nation in decline, that we are on a slow track, or even the wrong track, or that we are getting our clocks cleaned in the global market. Quite the contrary. I believe we can still win in the big races. But we can, and must, run faster.

There are lots of impressive statistics about the early and mid-1990s economic performance. But even better, I have seen it myself. I have seen the productivity of American workers from Bath, Maine, to San Diego, California, and from Sioux Falls, South Dakota, to Saint Louis, Missouri. I have seen the high demand in foreign markets for American products ranging from jet aircraft and computer software to corn and soybeans. I have seen how American investments abroad support high-wage jobs here at home. The task that faces us now is to keep our front place as we look to the next century.

What does it take to do that? It takes a combination of deficit reduction to give us the right macro environment, education and training to keep our labor force on the cutting edge of technology, and trade liberalization so our companies and farmers can sell into foreign markets on an equal footing. I want to focus on the third item, trade liberalization.

What is the role of government in this? My view is that the federal government should work to create the right economic environment for business to flourish and workers to compete. As international trade has grown in both absolute and relative terms to the point where trade represents about one-fourth of our economy, it has begun to touch more people's lives than ever in our history. But it is not just breaking down barriers that matters; we also have a clear self-interest in seeing markets grow. Malaysia, where I was U.S. ambassador, grew at 8 percent plus for seven years; in 1996 it bought another $4 billion in Boeing aircraft! Does anyone think these two things are not connected?

In trade, we operate on three levels: multilaterally, regionally, and bilaterally. The aim is always the same, to open markets for our goods and services and to ensure that our companies are allowed to compete on an equal footing abroad. I will address only our multilateral and regional work.

Let me mention here that one of the tools we need to do our work is new trade authority so we can negotiate agreements that will be subject to congressional scrutiny, but not to congressional renegotiation. Every president has had such authority for the past twenty years. We need it to maintain our leadership role in worldwide, regional, and bilateral trade negotiations.

Trade Organizations

Where do we do this work? On the multilateral front, the World Trade Organization (WTO) is the main venue. Major negotiations will occur there. Negotiations on agriculture, services, financial services, and intellectual property rights are of particular importance to the United States; we are the global leader in these sectors. We have racked up some big successes since the Uruguay Round was finished. In 1996 we concluded the Information Technology Agreement (ITA), which freed up $500 billion in annual trade, and we completed the Agreement on Basic Telecommunications—another $500 billion. These are precisely the types of market-opening measures we need to keep the United States out in front.

Another venue we use to further our trade agenda is the Organization for Economic Cooperation and Development (OECD). In the OECD we have pursued a landmark accord, the Multilateral Agreement on Investment. The goal here is to ensure fair treatment for U.S. investors. In both this forum and the WTO, we engage actively in efforts to address bribery and corruption, competition policy, and transparency in government procurement. Can you imagine that some of our closest allies actually allow their companies to deduct bribes from their corporate taxes? We have worked hard in this hemisphere and in the OECD to win agreement to end such odious practices. We are also working in this hemisphere, at the WTO, and in the Asia-Pacific Economic Cooperation (APEC) to get greater transparency in areas such as government procurement.

In the Western Hemisphere, the Free Trade Area of the Americas (FTAA) will help reduce barriers and increase protection for U.S. business in the lucrative and rapidly growing Latin American and Caribbean region. This region's markets for U.S. goods exports in 1996 grew by more than 13 percent. That was more than twice the rate of the rest of the world. The next step in the FTAA process is to establish a comprehensive trade agreement and to solidify our position in the region as a leader.

The Asia-Pacific region, likewise, offers excellent opportunities for the United States. I would like to focus in somewhat greater detail on our involvement there, giving particular attention to the Asia-Pacific Economic Cooperation.

Asia-Pacific Economic Cooperation (APEC)

President Clinton's vision of a Pacific community forms the basis for our engagement in the region. U.S. economic policies for the Asia-Pacific region are aimed not just at business, but also at creating real opportunities to sell goods made in the United States by American workers and services provided by Americans.

We have made the APEC forum the cornerstone of our economic policy in the region. APEC's eighteen member economies had a combined gross domestic product of more than $13 trillion (U.S.) in 1995, approximately 55 percent of total world income and 46 percent of global trade. (Note: APEC membership now totals twenty-one with the addition in 1998 of Russia, Vietnam, and Peru.) U.S. trade with APEC members accounted for 65 percent of total U.S. trade in 1996, more than $920 billion. The APEC region has, until the 1997–98 crisis, contained the fastest-growing economies in the world, with a total population nearing three billion people. Within APEC, we estimate that reaching the goal of open markets would increase U.S. goods exports alone by 13 percent annually.

For the United States, APEC is not an end in itself, but a means to advance key objectives that incorporate our economic, political, and security interests. APEC anchors the United States in Asia. It reinforces multilateral and bilateral efforts to open markets. It numbers among its members China, Hong Kong, and Taiwan ("Chinese Taipei" in APEC speak). It provides high-level interaction with countries such as China, Japan, and the members of ASEAN. It can help build safe and efficient capital markets. APEC also assures that growth in Asia is environmentally sustainable. Finally, but definitely not least of all, APEC provides opportunities for U.S. business and U.S. products.

Although APEC has as a major goal free trade and investment in the region by 2010 to 2020, it is not a trade organization in the traditional sense—and that is good news for business. APEC does not produce mind-numbing treaties deliberated over endless years in smoke-filled back rooms. What we do in APEC is not hard to understand. It is the private sector that drives the region, and APEC strives to make it easier for business to do business. We seek tangible results. We work with our Asian trading partners to open markets for goods, services, and investment and then build those markets on the basis of level playing fields.

APEC's Recent History

I have been the U.S. ambassador to APEC for three years. After each Leaders meeting, I have been challenged to prove that APEC succeeded, that APEC is relevant, that as Fred Bergsten says, "the bicycle is still moving forward." It is important to remember, these meetings go beyond twenty-one leaders gathering to talk about APEC and the APEC work program. Leaders meet as leaders of over half of the world's population, and half its economic activity. Their instructions are our guidance for work not only in APEC, but in other multilateral forums and bilaterally as well.

One can look at the 1996 Leaders meeting at Subic Bay as a prime example of this. It was APEC Leaders that gave the Information Technology

Agreement the nudge it needed to build momentum for successful conclusion in the WTO. The result: liberalization of $500 billion in annual trade.

At Vancouver in November 1997 the APEC Leaders meeting was complicated because the 1997 Southeast Asian financial crisis had revealed itself as more than a regional crisis. Reverberations were affecting markets as far away as Latin America and Russia. To try to restore stability, Leaders endorsed the Manila Framework, which recognized that national efforts must come first and that where international help is needed for adjustment only the IMF has the resources and expertise required to set up credible readjustment programs.

Although the financial issue dominated at Vancouver, it was by no means the only issue. Leaders adopted the trade ministers' recommendations on a broad Early Voluntary Sectoral Liberalization (EVSL) package containing fifteen sectors, $1.5 trillion in traded goals and services. This was an important step towards APEC's goal of free and open trade. It was also an important signal to markets that despite the brewing financial troubles, Asia was still open for business.

The 1998 APEC Leaders meeting in Kuala Lumpur had quite a different tone from previous meetings. The financial crisis remained, and growth was off sharply in many of Asia's former "tigers." Financial disorder had spurred political upheavals and the social fabric was frayed all across Asia. The leaders made a sober, hardheaded assessment of the situation in the region. They acknowledged that even though progress had been achieved in the region, many challenges remained. Their main message, however, was of confidence that the region had the ability to restore sustainable economic growth.

The Kuala Lumpur message was overshadowed by a variety of news stories—one important one, admittedly, was concern about President Clinton's absence—because of events in Iraq. The meeting's atmospherics notwithstanding, when one looks carefully at the Leaders' Declaration, and as I review the Leaders' own discussions, I see that the Leaders embraced a credible strategy to restore sustainable growth, a strategy President Clinton previewed in a September 14, 1998, speech in New York.

APEC economies are charting a path forward—together—a path based on restoring growth in Asia, helping to strengthen the international financial architecture, and making economic governance more transparent and predictable. We have agreed to intensify efforts to address the plight of the most vulnerable people in this crisis and to help develop the institutions necessary to protect them in the future. We are continuing forward toward our goal of free and open trade and investment. We are creating new visions—and long-term work plans—to strengthen public-private partnerships. We will work in all these areas not only in APEC, but also in the WTO, the Group of Seven (G-7), and the OECD, through other multilateral organizations such as the World Bank, the Asian Development Bank, and the IMF, and bilaterally too.

There was forward movement on sectional liberalization. Notwithstanding Japan's obdurateness, we succeeded in gaining APEC endorsement to move EVSL into the WTO—our charted path since trade ministers first agreed on sectoral liberalization at their Montreal meeting in 1997. There will be considerable work that needs to be done in Geneva, and still within APEC, to transform the EVSL vision into a reality. But by agreeing to take the eight sectors intact to the WTO in Geneva, APEC continues to push the world system as it moves forward with the Information Technology Agreement of 1996.

Additionally, ministers pressed ahead in other sectors. Notably, this agreement launched an APEC auto dialogue—the first regional forum to address trade and investment issues in the auto sector.

APEC does have some homegrown successes too. APEC is well suited to make great strides in helping build markets and facilitate business. The past years have provided many examples. There are improvements in custom procedures. Via the mutual recognition agreement on telecommunications equipment, APEC has helped reduce duplicative testing procedures. APEC has also done work on improving air-express delivery procedures. These are things that make incremental differences to business. There are large-scale examples too. APEC worked hard in 1998 on electronic commerce to help prepare the region for the twenty-first century. There was also progress in energy infrastructure. Leaders welcomed the idea of an Asian natural-gas infrastructure. U.S. businesses are proceeding to develop a common approach to implementing this vision.

Conclusion

The fundamental test of all of APEC's accomplishments over the past years will come in the willingness of APEC economies to flesh out the details and implement the policies envisioned by the Leaders. However, a great deal of responsibility rests on the shoulders of the private sector. The private sector knows the specific issues that can make the biggest difference as we work to build a Pacific community. We in government need to be equipped with the specific ideas to overcome obstacles to business. We need continued engagement by the private sector to guide and prod us as we work to tear down those obstacles. With this kind of public-private partnership, we can get the job done—be it in APEC, the WTO, or elsewhere. That means not just in the corporate sector but also in the workforce and in one of our most competitive service industries—higher education. The skills that educational institutions instill in future workers and their managers are the key to America's success.

an aerospace business, Hexcel, in this country. We have had tremendous market-share gains. We have to maintain the ability to put deals together across borders because it brings higher valuations to our stocks. We do not want trade sanctions or any interference with the ability of American companies to merge with companies around the world.

I think what we are seeing now investmentwise is a lot of restructuring activity in Europe, and especially in countries which are somewhat stagnated, such as France, which has not done much in the last ten to fifteen years. All of a sudden it is emulating the American restructuring of the last ten years. That emulation is going to expand across southern Europe, and obviously into southeast Asia, as the impact of the currency crisis takes hold. For an investor in America, these are wonderful opportunities. The capital flows are easier. Custody of securities and hedging of currencies get much cheaper and easier. We find lots of opportunities. All this is based on confidence. We have to have confidence in the markets. That comes from confidence in our government, from seeing our government engage successfully in trade negotiations. This does not mean beating other countries over the head. Unbalanced and unfair negotiations will come home to roost in the future.

I was fortunate enough to give Henry Kissinger a lift to the University of Oklahoma conference. Henry, on the plane, talked about his worries that China is going to hit us hard five to ten years from now if we do not do the right things now in paving the way for future mutually beneficial trade relations. I said, "What do you mean, hit us hard? They are not going to invade us?" He replied, "No, but when they are ready to award a telecommunications deal or a big computer deal or a giant water-systems deal or whatever it is, they are going to pick a French company or United Kingdom company or a Russian company."

I was at a meeting in 1997 at which a senior administration official expressed worry about future U.S.-China relations. Yet when you listen to the Chinese ambassador to the United States and to Henry Kissinger's incredible perspective, I sense that we are not heading toward crisis and disaster, but we have the possibility of a greatly mutually beneficial economic relationship. I think this administration needs to do a lot more work with our large trading partners such as the Chinese. If so, American businessmen's confidence will continue to increase and we will continue to invest even more around the world.

W. DeVier Pierson

This book deals with subjects that are of greatest importance to this nation and, in turn, to the world. The recurring themes have been economics, politics, the rule of law, U.S. leadership, and peace and stability. Trade and investment implicate all of those issues.

When I dealt with trade matters thirty years ago, there was a raging debate as to which policies made economic sense. I think that debate is largely over. No one really supports the protectionism of the 1950s and early 1960s on purely economic grounds. One reason the economic debate should be over is simply a reflection of the economic world of the 1990s. In the information age, when customers have a global choice in buying their goods, it is imperative to be able to buy and sell on a global basis. There are very few natural trade barriers.

Ed Corr told about one company, Ditch Witch, in Perry, Oklahoma, a town of 5,000 persons, that now sells to 100 countries. That story is being repeated over and over in every state in the union. When business leaders such as Kerr-McGee's CEO Luke Corbett tell you that they do not want trade sanctions, that is another way of saying that we are better off when our industries are permitted to compete worldwide with others. After all, we have only 4 percent of the world's consumers in the United States, so it makes sense that our businesses have to reach out across the world.

That is the economic story, but there is also a political dimension. There is a raging debate in Washington, D.C., that goes deeper than simply short-term political advantage. It is no less than a fight for the heart and soul of both political parties. It is, as David Gergen states in Part VII, the issue of the advantaged versus the disadvantaged. There are people who are hurt in the short term by the opening up of trade. The Democrats, such as Dick Gephardt, and the Republicans, such as Pat Buchanan, focus on the concerns of these disadvantaged in their approach to trade initiatives. The fight over fast-track authority is really a symptom of a fight that is going to continue, certainly to the election of 2000 and probably far beyond that. It is an argument about the wisdom—or feasibility—of attaching environmental or labor standards as prerequisites to new trade agreements. In other words, it is a question of whether we can insist on other nations moving closer toward our values when we enter into commercial relationships with them. So although the economic case for free trade has been made, the political dispute will have a profound effect on legislation and governmental initiatives that seek to open world markets.

Labels are also important. Ambassador Clayton Yeutter was very perceptive in pointing out the problems of trade jargon. For example, the term *most favored nation* does not really mean that a country gets favored treatment. It simply means that a country is not being penalized in its trade with the United States and is entitled to receive the same trade treatment as other friendly nations. Recent legislation uses the term *normal trading relations* rather than *most favored nation*. There is also some effort to relabel *fast-track authority*. One of the latest suggested terms is *renewal of traditional trading authority*. In other words, "every president has had it, just give it back to him." The idea is that the authority is not new and is not particularly fast; it is just traditional presidential authority.

With regard to the rule of law, again, the United States is somewhat schizophrenic. It also depends in part on what term we use. When we talk about the rule of law, it is very comforting to Americans; we like it. But when we talk about loss of sovereignty, we do not like that at all. How we view organizations such as the World Trade Organization (WTO) is a prime example. The WTO is the most ambitious effort to date to regulate trade on a global basis. It is far more ambitious than the General Agreement on Trade and Tariffs (GATT)—our basic international regulator for the past fifty years. The World Trade Organization will encompass such diverse areas as agriculture and services as well as manufactured goods. We are going to have to understand when we take issues to the WTO that this is a dispute-resolution group. We are going to win some and we are going to lose some. Michael Price mentioned the Boeing–McDonnell-Douglas matter. In that case, the administration threatened the European Union (EU) by saying the United States government would go to the World Trade Organization with a complaint. So when the EU tried to block a merger between these two U.S. companies by the device of transportation barriers, the United States used an international organization to advantage.

We have to be able to play the game and we have to know that we are not going to win every time we approach the WTO. The dirty little secret is that participation in the WTO does, therefore, require a relinquishment of some "sovereignty." The simple truth is that if we trade globally, we are not going to be able to make all the decisions as to how that trade takes place. It does not mean that we give up our vital national interests. Every country has an escape hatch from the WTO, but it is very disruptive to assert. It is very important that the large nations, such as China and Russia, become WTO members just as soon as they can qualify. My old boss of many years ago, Lyndon Johnson, used to say of someone who was causing a lot of trouble that he would rather have him inside the tent looking out than outside the tent looking in. That is not exactly what he said; but that is the closest I can come to it publicly. What he was saying was that it is important to have people bound to play by the rules if you are going to have to deal with those people anyway. It is important to us as a nation. It is in our security interests that nations such as China and Russia are part of the international organizations that govern trade and commerce and are "bound by their rules."

Trade is a test of U.S. leadership, no question about it. In exercising this leadership we are also forced to look in new directions. We are accustomed to dealing with Europe. We are accustomed to dealing with Japan. But as Jim Hoagland stated in his description of Europe, it is in some ways struggling to stay relevant. And Japan is now a much higher-cost producer of goods, with significant economic problems and thus less competitive. Ambassador Jeane Kirkpatrick mentions the ten BEMs, the big emerging markets. Those markets have now about half of the population of the world; they are scattered in South America, in South Asia and, in the case of South Africa, in

Africa. These are countries that American businesses must look to if we are to remain competitive, if we are going to be where the action is.

There is not any question that if the United States falters in this test of leadership, there are plenty of others ready to pick up the slack. Ambassador Yeutter described the Brazilian initiative of MERCOSUR. MERCOSUR controls 220 million people. It has a GDP of a trillion dollars. And it is ready. When President Jacques Chirac of France went to Brazil, he told Brazilians that the interests of South America were more closely aligned with Europe than with the United States. That is obviously not true, but it does show how others are willing to come into the vacuum if we do not make the deals. Indeed, Chile has already made deals with Canada and Mexico while we are waiting on fast-track authority to expand NAFTA. The race goes to the swift.

Finally, there is the question of peace and stability. Experts on foreign relations stress that the competition of the future is going to be, in large measure, economic. We have heard that democratic countries with market economies are good neighbors, that they do not go to war, but that they do trade and they do invest. That is the wave of the future. The flip side of that equation is more ominous. A country that is starved for trade, starved for investment, and economically isolated from the world, such as North Korea, is a prime candidate for armed conflict. It is just common sense that nations are less likely to pick fights with their customers or their suppliers or their trading partners than with someone they do not understand and have no economic ties with. This being the case, one of the essential bonds that will hold the international order together is the capacity of this country and others to trade and invest with one another. In the architecture of our foreign policy for the twenty-first century, surely trade and investment are a vital pillar.

Max N. Berry

I am concerned that our Congress, which establishes trade policy by legislation after our presidents negotiate such, is about to reverse our country's long trend toward liberal trade. As we enter the twenty-first century a "trade pendulum" is swinging. History shows that the pendulum does not stay still. I fear it is now swinging toward protectionism. There is growing evidence of labor unions becoming more powerful after being weak for many years. Unions are stronger, and in 1997 they again won an important victory on fast-track authority. They have a growing political influence with Congress.

I worry about new congressmen elected during the 1990s. I have visited many of them on trade issues and on other matters, such as supporting the Kennedy Center in Washington, D.C. Many border on being protectionists and are against supporting the arts. Every White House since Hoover has been liberal on trade. In different ways they all, including the current Clinton administration, have sponsored aggressive, liberal trade policies. That has been good for America. Congress is not right now of a mind, in my opinion, to continue to follow this trend.

I repeatedly advised our United States Trade Representative (USTR) office in the spring of 1997 to bring out the fast-track bill for Congressional debate. I told them to draft it and put it on the table—not to wait until the fall, because that would be too late. USTR was sitting in glue on this matter and did not move in time. It did not listen to the advice of many people. USTR tried to appease everybody and ran out of time. They knew, in the final analysis, that they did not have the votes, and were smart enough to postpone it. If they had started earlier, a compromise bill might have been accomplished.

This unfortunately meant postponing the negotiations with Chile. The atmosphere could get worse during that postponement. The opposing side, the protectionists, now see an opportunity to win; that pendulum is swinging in their direction.

Criticism is mounting against fast-track trade with Mexico. An article—like many others in almost every news media—appeared in the September 15, 1997, *U.S. News and World Report* quoting figures that in 1993 the United States had a $1.7 billion favorable trade balance with Mexico, but that since NAFTA the balance is now $17 billion in the red.[1] The claim by the Gephardts and the Buchanans and other protectionists that DeVier Pierson mentioned accurately is that the United States has lost 420,000 jobs because of the NAFTA with Mexico. Unfortunately, people listen to those statements. The protectionists put it on radio, on television, in magazines, and in newspapers. Those figures are not true! According to a White House statement, the United States has gained thirty million jobs because of NAFTA. Interestingly, most of the U.S. economists who have been polled say neither side is right; neither side's numbers are correct.

Mexico is our second-largest trading partner after Canada, having recently passed Japan. Even so, Mexican-U.S. trade is less than 2 percent of our bilateral total trade. NAFTA is important. Mexico is our good neighbor to the south and we should hope she gets stronger. Liberal trade is the only policy to pursue. I have not met any industries that have complained about NAFTA. I have met a few agricultural groups that have valid complaints, but they are in the distinct minority, and they have been protected, with certain exceptions, within NAFTA. I have not seen a valid critique of the NAFTA agreement with Mexico. Yet I am telling you it is in trouble.

We do not need 535 people in Congress negotiating a trade treaty! That is the president's job. We do not need 535 people putting Christmas-tree ornaments on a trade bill. That would be a disaster! To get a meaningful and workable trade bill, we need fast track. The fact that fast track is in trouble reflects the legislative clumsiness of the Clinton White House in handling it, plus the growing tide of the Gephardts wanting to get into the White House, and the labor unions backing protectionism 100 percent.

We are in a worrisome time. In the 1930s, 2,200 economists told President Herbert Hoover not to sign the Hawley-Smoot protectionist trade bill. He nevertheless signed it. The unions said, "Keep out imports; save American jobs." That legislation was probably the biggest cause of our country's plunging into the Great Depression. It took World War II to get us out. It worries me to see these same symptoms today as I watch the swing of the pendulum back toward protectionism.

Dr. Clayton Yeutter is absolutely right that we need a new antidumping law to prevent imports from entering the United States at very unfair, below-market prices that undercut our own markets. We have an injury provision in U.S. law now, as does the World Trade Organization. If imports do not injure an American industry, the exporters and importers cannot be penalized. The problem with the U.S. antidumping law, however, is that some protectionist industries in America have found out that by filing a dumping complaint they can delay the process and achieve a big advantage. Each side hires lawyers. It takes a year at least to complete a case. In the meantime, the United States withholds customs appraisements on imports at the port of entry. No one knows what the merchandise is going to ultimately cost, whether it will have a penalty duty or not. The side filing the complaint tells the world it is going to win. Consequently, purchasers begin to shy away from buying imports. If you do not believe this, look at the annual complaints of the U.S. steel industry.

I have won several dumping cases in my practice. My clients lost much money in that year because of the high cost of these cases. The complaint itself is a nontariff barrier in disguise. The Department of Commerce is charged with initially judging dumping complaints on their merits. If they have merit, there is a full investigation in the International Trade Commission (ITC) to determine "injury." The Department of Commerce should do a much better job in scrutinizing complaints. It routinely allows many frivolous complaints to reach the International Trade Commission. That year's duration for cases causes unfair trade. Many complaints should be dismissed immediately as frivolous, but they are not. The USTR should urge Congress to stop this unintended nontariff barrier.

The most-favored-nation (MFN) trading clause is interesting. In 1962 at Georgetown University, I studied MFN and traced the clause back to a treaty between Portugal and Spain in 1648. That was the first MFN clause to my knowledge. We trade, in this country, on the basis of politics. That is a mistake! For instance, we made a mistake with the Jackson-Vanik Amendment in the 1970s. When we tried to tell the Russians that they would get better MFN trade if they let more Jewish immigrants immigrate, it backfired. The Russians were letting large numbers of Jews out before the Jackson-Vanik Amendment was passed. I was one of the few Jewish lobbyists in Washington lobbying against Jackson-Vanik. What happened? Congress passed it. The Russians then turned the faucet off, and there was not any meaningful immigration for many years.

I have strong reasons to believe in human rights, but other countries do not base their trade on politics or on human rights. I understand that human rights are a popular thing to promote in Washington. Many persons and groups get behind the issue emotionally. So do I. Nevertheless, I have to tell you that our industries—General Electric, IBM, Kerr-McGee, other U.S. companies—cannot easily trade in this world and compete with other sophisticated competitors of other countries if we follow such policies, which other countries do not follow. Governments of other countries help their companies compete against our industries. The U.S. government is not helping our companies when it demands human-rights improvements in countries before it extends MFN. We have to avoid linking political conditions to trade. It penalizes our own corporations, while foreign entities are doing business that our companies would otherwise capture.

Our government and embassies should have as one of their primary missions the promotion of trade and the protection of American businesses operating abroad. Much of the information a small U.S. business operating overseas wants to know should be available at our American embassies. The State Department has come a long way in providing such services to American businesspeople, but it still has much work to do to match other countries.

However, I believe help for American businessmen to operate abroad should also be provided by our education system. I hope the University of Oklahoma is one of those universities, via its International Programs Center, which can begin to be a better source of expertise and help for small businesspeople trading abroad. Some U.S. universities did it very well for the agriculture industry. Using extension agents, our agricultural universities taught farmers how to have better techniques in planting crops, harvesting, and marketing them throughout the world. We need to do the same for other business interests. We need specialists who can go out into the community to work with small businesspeople. There should be an "international business extension service" operating out of university programs such as that which exists at the University of Oklahoma.

N O T E

1. Matthew Miller, "Art of the Trade Deal: Beyond the Rhetoric of Fast Track, the Stakes are Huge," *U.S. News and World Report,* 15 September 1997, 41.

PART VI

The Environment and International Relations

Overview

Zev M. Trachtenberg

As the world enters the twenty-first century it is universally recognized that any discussion of international affairs must take substantial notice of the natural environment. Among the most serious challenges human beings face are those posed by environmental degradation, and the seriousness of these problems is due in no small part to their international character. The prospect of global climate change is paradigmatic in this respect. No one nation can reverse the apparent and alarming trends on its own; strong cooperation among nations is necessary. Part VI examines one of the leading proposals for coordinating international action to avert global warming.

By way of introduction, let us frame global climate change as an economic problem. The scientific evidence seems to show that many of the activities associated with an industrial economy—from manufacturing to driving cars—produce emissions that stimulate global warming. To redesign industrial processes and transportation systems to lower their emissions would be expensive. What then is the best way to encourage firms to spend the money required to lessen their environmental impact?

Perhaps the most obvious way is simply to force firms to make changes through direct regulation. But this "command-and-control" model is perhaps the least acceptable. Its opponents in the United States hold direct regulation to be extremely inefficient. The prospects for enforcing a global régime of direct environmental regulation seem massively more daunting, because sovereign states are generally unwilling to grant international institutions the power to effectively prevent noncompliance.

A second model involves the imposition of taxes on greenhouse gases. In economic terms, this method forces firms to "internalize" their "external" costs, giving them a financial incentive to reduce their emissions. But in the United States alone the current political climate makes the establishment of "carbon taxes" extremely unlikely. And again, it is unclear what international institution would have the authority to impose taxes on firms or individuals.

In chapter 18, Richard Sandor advocates a third model, which proposes the use of market mechanisms. This model is gaining increasing favor across the globe, in part because of Dr. Sandor's efforts as an adviser to the United Nations. Sandor argues that because the atmosphere is a "commons"—i.e., it is unowned—firms and individuals are free to use it as a sink for emissions from factories and cars. Global warming, in his view, is an example of the familiar "tragedy of the commons," by which unowned resources tend to be degraded through overuse. The solution Sandor offers is, in effect, to privatize the commons by establishing a property right in the atmosphere's ability to absorb waste. The instrument of that property right is a permit that gives its holder the right to emit a certain amount of greenhouse gas. If the holder, say a firm, needs to emit more, it must obtain an additional permit. That is where the market enters. Other firms will see the opportunity to sell their permits to the first firm, but only if they have managed to reduce their own emissions below their permitted levels. Thus, the prospect of selling unused permits gives firms the financial incentive to make the investments necessary to lessen their own environmental impacts.

Sandor explains some of the conceptual and practical difficulties that must be overcome to establish a market in unfamiliar commodities such as pollution permits. He reviews analogous situations in history to argue that not only is such a market possible, it would in fact be an extremely efficient solution to the problem of global climate change. However, market mechanisms are not without their critics. In response to Sandor, Professor Rajeev Gowda, in chapter 19, explores some criticisms that can be leveled against market-based solutions. In addition to practical and political obstacles to the creation of a global market in pollution permits, Dr. Gowda raises the ethical concern that although the market may offer tremendous efficiency, its operations may produce certain inequities because of unfair distributions of the benefits and burdens of industrial development.

In the wake of the 1997 Kyoto Conference, the effort to curb global climate change will increasingly involve market measures. Dr. Sandor's chapter presents a comprehensive, technical overview of the backgrounds and implications of the market-based approach to environmental protection.

Chapter 18

A Limited-scale Voluntary International Greenhouse-gas Emissions Trading Program as Part of the United States Environmental Policy in the Twenty-first Century

Richard L. Sandor

This paper has two basic goals: (1) to present a rationale for a limited-scale, voluntary international greenhouse-gas emissions trading program; and (2) to outline the steps necessary for its implementation. Alternative policy options such as emission taxes and the even less dynamic "command-and-control" regulatory régimes have well-known limitations. These approaches may not yield the desired emission reductions and they fail to exploit cost efficiencies. Another framework may help solve the climate-change problem, with the desirable trait of offering a dynamic flexibility that quite likely translates into cost-effectiveness: It is an international, market-based, emission-allowance trading régime. However, opponents to a primarily market-based solution offer two basic arguments to support their contention: (1) Such régimes are too complex to establish; and (2) they have had limited success. Both of these arguments are inaccurate. If we understand the evolutionary process, we can identify specific steps to be taken to establish a market. Furthermore, although well-designed environmental markets are few in number, the dramatic success of America's sulfur-dioxide allowance market in combating acid rain (coupled with other régimes mentioned below) strongly argues in favor of managing climate change by establishing a greenhouse-gas (GHG) emissions trading program.

This article has four sections. The first postulates and illustrates the existence of a seven-stage process of how markets evolve. The second section presents a brief history of the sulfur-dioxide allowance trading program. The next section rationalizes a limited-scale, voluntary international GHG emissions trading program because it likely will have a minimal impact on the economy. The final section draws on what we have learned from the seven stages of "market evolution" to outline a "clean dozen" implementation steps.

The Origin and Evolution of Markets—
A Seven-stage Process

Like their commodity, equity, and bond predecessors, environmental markets did not appear by spontaneous combustion. On the contrary, like any other good or service, they are responses to latent or overt demand. Their successful evolution requires the development of specific legal and institutional infrastructures. Once we readily understand the evolutionary processes, the specific steps necessary to implement a greenhouse-gas emissions trading program will become more obvious.

After studying the history of markets and after participating in the inventive process, let me postulate a simple seven-stage process that describes how markets evolve. Concisely stated, they are: (1) a structural economic change that creates the demand for capital; (2) the creation of uniform standards for a commodity or security; (3) the development of a legal instrument which provides evidence of ownership; (4) the development of informal spot markets (for immediate delivery) and forward markets (nonstandardized agreements for future delivery) in commodities and securities where "receipts" of ownership are traded; (5) the emergence of securities and commodities exchanges; (6) the creation of organized futures markets (standardized contracts for future delivery on organized exchanges) and options markets (rights, but not guarantees, for future delivery) in commodities and securities; and (7) the proliferation of OTC markets/deconstruction.

Importantly, the seven-stage process is not an unalterable course that markets must pass through sequentially; rather, it is an analytical construct which seems to fairly well describe the multiple forces which accrete over time and sometimes develop into standardized contracts at organized exchanges. As such, it does not purport to prove a causal connection but only to highlight a natural dialectic.

History is replete with market "evolutions" that can be analyzed by using the seven-stage heuristic. Let me illustrate this process with a selected example from each of three market sectors—equity capital, commodity, and fixed-income security. Because the examples touch on the highlights of the market process under our review, they are intended as nothing more than historical sketches.

(1) We consider how the equity-capital market evolved. When Christopher Columbus arrived in the New World, that "discovery" (from the European perspective) brought upon the world economy a fundamental structural change. Obviously, this age of discovery required financial capital. Initially, the instrument of the day used to deploy capital was a "partnership," often devoted to specific purposes. A financial restructuring of sorts occurred with the invention (and subsequent adoption) of the "limited-liability corporation."

The Dutch East India Company was a novel creation that would become the archetype of the modern corporation. It unquestionably provided a more highly evolved "standard" because its "evidence of ownership" was transferable equity shares. With the innovation of shares came the need to efficiently convey these financial rights. In response, the next level of market evolution surfaced as an organized marketplace: the Amsterdam Stock Exchange (as well as its regional exchange precedents). Spot trading then spawned the first documented examples of futures and options trading. In the seventeenth century, Joseph De La Varga wrote "Confusion de Confusiones," an essay that clearly articulates the Amsterdam Stock Exchange's development as well as provides insights into the institution's structure.

(2) We look at how the market evolution in America of trading agricultural commodities seems to fit our simple seven-stage process. In the nineteenth century, the United States simultaneously experienced population growth and westward expansion; this coupling embodied a fundamental structural change to the national and regional economies. The bulging population on the East Coast translated into the demand for new and additional food sources. The emerging agricultural sector in the Midwest would provide the supply, but capital was needed to finance the grain in storage that would be shipped to the East Coast. Unorganized trading was followed by the formation of the Chicago Board of Trade (CBOT), which codified grain standards. The warehouse receipt became the accepted evidence of ownership that facilitated both raising capital and transferring ownership. Spot trading in wheat evolved into forward trading. Organized futures trading began at the CBOT in 1865. Ultimately, options trading emerged.

(3) We see a more modern, yet still American, variant of the seven-stage evolution by examining the market in the 1970s for mortgage-backed securities, or what came to be called "collateralized mortgage obligations." Through two of its agencies—the Federal Housing Authority (FHA) and the Veterans Administration (VA), the federal government had guaranteed home mortgages, and in so doing started a process that would help transform formerly nonmarketable loans (which tended to stay with the lending institutions) into a standardized financial instrument. Throughout most of the 1960s, eastern financial institutions (e.g., savings and loans) furnished much of the capital to the booming housing market in California and other parts of the United States. Although the standardized FHA/VA mortgages assured capital flows to that sector, the market was still inefficient. This was so for two primary reasons: (1) Mortgages were sold individually or in small packages; and (2) the buyer had to have individual documentation for each loan. Although the government guarantee prevented an ultimate default risk, there was no guarantee of timely payment of principal and interest during the foreclosure period. As inflation increased in the United States during the "credit crunch" of 1966–69, demand for capital was further exacerbated, which promoted further standardization of mortgages.

With the formation of the Government National Mortgage Association (GNMA), the institutional infrastructure was in place to "bundle" small loans into a security collateralized by FHA/VA mortgages in which the U.S. government granted its full-faith-and-credit guarantee of the timely payment of interest and principal. This collateralized mortgage obligation provided an efficient ownership-receipt and conveyance vehicle. Soon thereafter, spot and forward-market trading emerged, primarily among Wall Street dealers and mortgage bankers. Although informal, these markets performed functions similar to an organized exchange. The evolution continued when the world's first interest-rate futures contract—the GNMA mortgage-backed contract—was born at the CBOT in 1975.

Environmental Markets

We are witnessing yet another variant of the seven-stage process with the emergence of a market in sulfur-dioxide emission allowances in the United States. A latent demand for this market in abating sulfur gases resulted from a significant increase in the burning of high-sulfur coal by electric utilities to satisfy the demand for electricity. Increased pollution in the form of sulfuric emissions accompanied the increased output of electricity. Generated in more densely populated areas, this power and pollution resulted in large increases in respiratory problems for affected populations. In addition, acidification damaged rivers, streams, and forests. Latent demand became effective demand as public concern about human health and environmental problems motivated legislators to pass the Clean Air Act Amendments of 1990.

This legislation set a national limit on sulfur-dioxide emissions that would be consistently lowered during a twenty-year period. Under a traditional command-and-control régime, coal-fired utilities would have had little choice but to purchase expensive pollution-control technologies to meet the lower emission targets. As its major innovation, the act provided for a market-based "cap-and-trade" system. This gave utilities the flexibility to reduce emissions directly or to purchase allowances from other utilities that were beneath their targeted cap because of having made extraordinary emission cuts. Utilities that were most efficient in reducing emissions were motivated to do so because they could profit by selling unused allowances. Utilities that did not reduce emissions bore the cost of purchasing allowances or faced stiff fines. All rules protecting local air quality remained in force.

In a single stroke, this legislation concomitantly performed three functions: (1) It standardized an environmental commodity (a legally authorized allowance to emit one ton of sulfur dioxide); (2) it produced the "evidence of ownership" necessary for financial instruments; and (3) it established the infrastructure to efficiently transfer title. Ultimately, an informal forward market emerged even before the act required compliance. Options followed. Organized exchanges entered when the CBOT competitively won the right to conduct the annual auctions of spot and forward allowances on behalf of the Environmental Protection Agency (EPA). The CBOT continues to provide this service pro bono.

It is instructive to see in what ways this program and others like it proved better than predicted, in that appropriate parallels may inform and may help motivate members of the international community to establish a pilot phase for a voluntary GHG emissions trading program. Prior to launch of the U.S. sulfur program, forecasts put compliance costs in the range of $300 to $900 per ton; some were as high as $1,500 per ton, with most centered on $400 to $600. (See Appendix A.) The first trades were executed in 1992 at about $300 per ton; in 1993 the price from the first EPA/CBOT auction was $131 per ton. In 1996 the auction price dropped to $66; in 1997 it bounced up to $107; in 1998 it hovered at $115. (See Appendix B.) Furthermore, Appendix C demonstrates that the total physical emissions came down ahead of schedule. Indeed, for the 1995–96 period, aggregate emissions were more than 34 percent below sanctioned levels. Perhaps *The Economist* put it most succinctly: "Overall, this [program] has cut sulphur emissions faster and more cheaply than anyone predicted."[1]

To summarize, market prices signal that the national current per-ton cost of lowering sulfur-dioxide emissions has been (and continues to be) a small fraction of the original projections. Moreover, total emissions have been appreciably less than mandated by the statutory caps. Responding to incentives, participants in this program have reduced emissions ahead of schedule and at a cost far lower than even the most optimistic forecasts. This major success has piqued the interests of both the environmental and business communities because it reflects the "win-win" possibility of emissions trading. Turning such possibility into probability includes a few conditions such as strictly limiting and precisely measuring pollution levels, as well as enabling industry to comply with the law using flexible and creative instruments.

Other less well known programs involving resource permitting and emissions trading have emerged in the United States and elsewhere, including the introduction of new schemes in such diverse places as Poland, New Zealand, and Chile. Moreover, trading was instrumental in helping to phase out lead from gasoline in the United States in an economically rational manner. Internationally, the Montreal Protocol allowed the use of market-based tools that have contributed to the successful effort to cut the production of ozone-depleting substances.

Another type of market tool is emission taxes. In the case of carbon taxes, "politically infeasible" probably best describes its status in a large number of countries. Besides, such emission taxes suffer from having an unpredictable quantitative effect on emissions. Although joint implementation is a movement in the right direction, it is understood to be a step on the path to a clearly defined emissions trading program.

If a GHG-trading program can bring cost-lowering effects similar to the U.S. sulfur-trading experience, it would move us from facing a potentially significant drag on our economies to one that is, for practical purposes, economically imperceptible. Our next section explores this possibility.

Extending the Market to Greenhouse Gases

Because the demand for energy services has increased steadily, it is far from surprising that the world has experienced a significant rise in consumption of fossil fuels. Scientists and policy makers continue to debate whether global warming is a natural phenomenon with cycles and oscillations driven in geological timescales or an anthropogenic event driven by the increase in fossil-fuel use associated with high levels of economic activity. Empirical data, including evidence from the Intergovernmental Panel on Climate Change (IPCC), continues to emerge that a human imprint may be introducing significant risk of serious economic and societal damage. At the same time, policy makers continue to debate alternative tools to restrict GHG emissions, such as command and control, carbon taxes, and market-based solutions.

In 1991, I began to articulate the preliminary market architecture that would support trading in GHG emission allowances. At that time, there was little support for the idea. Some people felt that it was premature and should not detract from efforts to introduce more conventional measures such as carbon taxes and new regulations, or from the newly launched effort to gather support for bilateral offset programs ("joint implementation"). However, in just a few years, the idea of using tradable permits to combat global warming appears to be gaining widespread acceptance. The paper that emerged from those early efforts represented a contribution to the "Rio process" and its search for workable mechanisms to deal with climate change. It was published in the first report of the United Nations Conference on Trade and Development (UNCTAD) research program.

With an agreement to reduce GHG emissions emerging from the 1997 Kyoto Conference, we must now prepare for the challenge of moving from the drawing boards to implementation. A wealth of lessons is available from the seven-stage process as well as from other examples of inventive activity ranging from aircraft to computers. Also pertinent is the evolutionary-development pattern observed for many international agreements such as the World Trade Organization and its GATT predecessors, and integration compacts such as the European Union and its antecedents. The dialectic can be stated: Most of the expansive, large-scale, multilateral institutions started as targeted, small-scale, plurilateral protocols.

Consequently, the lessons convince many of my colleagues and me that the best approach to the realization of a large-scale GHG-trading system is to begin with a no-frills, limited-scale, voluntary carbon-dioxide pilot program. National governments that participate voluntarily would agree to enforce a system in which their domestic emission sources can reach emission limits jointly by trading with sources in other participating countries. Because the protorégime seeks to be inclusive, nonmember governments can choose a more limited "opt in" by agreeing to monitor emissions and certify emission reductions for industries or individual firms that voluntarily choose to participate in the international pilot. Member governments need to institute provisions to add not only new members and unregulated gases but also to add uncovered emission sources and sinks. In this way, the market will be flexible and resilient enough to assure its structured evolution over time. In the emerging field of market-based instruments, a coalition of "leaders" is now being formed, consisting of leading governments, energy companies, insurance companies, and financial institutions. The first step is to agree to a plan that would operationalize the program.

A limited-scale GHG-trading program is an essential step on the path to a larger international trading system, so we must act now. But pioneers will be needed to face the challenge of innovation. It is in the interest of the major emission sources to assume the pioneering role. Indeed, pioneers have already been transacting in the inchoate carbon-trading market. Appendix D summarizes some of those transactions and describes a pending transaction in rain-forest protection carbon offsets that the Republic of Costa Rica offers.

The search for new, innovative mechanisms to finance the post-Rio sustainable development program (Agenda 21) has revealed the remarkable "double-dividend" capability of tradable emission permits. Initially, an international trading system can pay handsomely by achieving the emission-reduction target at minimum cost, by mobilizing private capital to protect the environment, and by providing strong incentives for technological innovation. As it expands from a plurilateral pilot to a multilateral institution, emissions trading has the potential to act as a powerful mechanism for transferring clean energy technologies and financial resources from the industrialized states to developing countries.

The economic benefits of driving down the cost of cutting GHG emissions are impressive. We have considered some simple cost scenarios for lowering total U.S. emissions to 10 percent below 1990 levels starting in the year 2000. Using the latest U.S. numbers, such a cut would require a reduction of 323 million metric tons carbon equivalent (mmtce) to go from the projected 2000 level of 1,757 mmtce to 10 percent below the 1990 level of 1,594 mmtce.

At a reduction cost of $100 per ton in U.S. dollars, the annual U.S. expenditures would total $32.3 billion. On the other hand, let us consider a cost of $20 per ton, a price in the range of many proposed offset transactions and a level which many analysts believe would generate very large emission-reduction quantities. If a market system succeeds in driving the cost down to $20 per ton, the annual U.S. cost would total $6.5 billion. This total figure is less than 0.09 percent of U.S. national income (1996 GDP), or 1.3 percent of the 1993 U.S. final energy bill ($493 billion). Similar numbers arise for Canada, but costs as a fraction of national income are far lower for Japan and the European Union. The bottom line is that the industrialized world can take very meaningful steps to bring down GHG emissions at a cost that is rather small, provided we use methods that help drive down compliance costs. (Appendix E presents additional compliance cost scenarios at the national and energy-unit levels.)

How Do We Get Started?
Lessons from the Seven-stage Process

To date, we have treated our atmosphere as a resource available to all, in unlimited quantities and at no charge. It is no wonder we have managed to fundamentally alter its chemical composition. To respectfully treat the atmosphere as the limited resource it truly represents, we must place limits on its consumption and institute a process for treating it responsibly. Nobody owns the atmosphere now, so nobody takes account. This observation about commonly held resources was recognized as early as ancient Greece, when Aristotle observed, "[W]hat is common to the greatest number has the least care bestowed upon it. Everyone thinks chiefly of his own, hardly at all of the common interest."[2]

Establishing and then enforcing legal ownership will help usher in an era of responsibility and care. The zero price now being charged for use of the atmosphere means there is no direct reward to those who might supply carbon abatement and sequestration services. Private capital is not being mobilized. In brief, the market is missing; it must be introduced.

The first step in developing the missing GHG market is to define the commodity. This requires an international agreement among market participants that caps total emissions and delineates the basis for the creation of the property right or commodity. Other key ingredients needed to implement the market include participants' baseline emission rates, initial allowance allocations, and protocols for monitoring emissions and calculating the benefits of emission avoidance or sequestration programs.

Drawing from the lessons from the introduction and evolution of new markets, let me list twelve steps to implementation, or what might be called the "clean dozen":

1. Clearly define the tradable commodity for greenhouse-gas emissions.
2. Establish a market oversight body.
3. Establish emission baselines.

4. Clearly specify allocation and monitoring procedures.
5. Establish uniform, nonsegmented allowances.
6. Launch an international allowance clearinghouse and registrar.
7. Employ existing exchange and trading systems.
8. Use allowance auctions to assist the market.
9. Develop standardized trade documentation.
10. Require cooperation among trade forums, including provisions for information sharing and mutual offset.
11. Use existing expertise to design bookkeeping and accounting systems.
12. Provide assistance to market forums in emerging economies.

Conclusion

Emissions trading is an environmental and economic winner. The seven-stage process enables us to describe a common dialectic of how markets evolve. With these insights, my colleagues and I (along with myriad other advocates of market-based environmentalism) have been building a market architecture for a GHG-allowance trading pilot program, and we are working diligently for its practical implementation. Such a régime has two favorable characteristics: (1) It can target emission levels directly (which carbon taxes cannot do); and (2) it is likely the most cost-effective option. Therefore, emissions trading must be near the top of the full menu of policy options needed to prevent the costly threat of climate change. Or, in the words of *The Economist:*

> So there is reason to think that global emissions trading might work. And if, in the end, it does not? Little harm would have been done. The risks are negligible, and the potential economic benefits very large.[3]

Given this "low-risk, high-reward" profile, we must act now to capitalize on the opportunity to take the vital first step to implement a voluntary trade régime with binding emission limits. Fundamentally, it is a step that provides sufficiently flexible incentives so that the private sector taps into unparalleled wealth of specialized knowledge and entrepeneurial creativity. Stated positively, we must "learn by doing."[4] Stated negatively, we must not follow the fallacious rhetoric of the status quo that offers a map down a road with no outlet: "Do not initiate a program until you learn all the drawbacks. And you cannot learn about the drawbacks until you initiate the program."

The world now needs to send a clear message that emissions trading offers a promising way forward. This is to say the world needs its leaders to lead. Innovative private entities and nongovernmental organizations, along with leading governments, possess unique sets of knowledge and skills. Only when these resources are brought to bear individually and collectively on the climate-change problem will the risk be appropriately managed. Although the awaiting reality of choosing climate-change policy instruments may appear daunting and insurmountable to some people, others see the unmet need as an exciting and promising challenge.

To conclude, an international GHG emissions trading program already has moved from a possibility to a probability. The time has come for the public and private leaders of the world community to take the next step of making it a reality.

Appendix A

Some Prominent Pre-1992 Price Forecasts for SO_2
Emission Allowances ("middle" price projections for Phase 1)

Resource Data International	$309
American Electric Power	392
Sierra Club	446
Electric Power Research Institute	688
Ohio Coal Office	785
United Mine Workers	981

Source: R.W. Hahn and C.A. May, "The Behavior of the Allowance Market: Theory and Evidence," *Electricity Journal* 7, no. 2 (March 1994).

Appendix B

SO$_2$ Allowance Prices

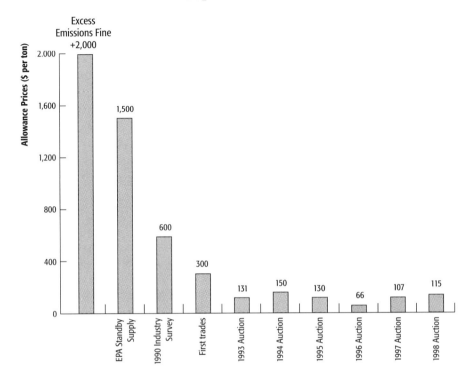

Appendix C

SO$_2$ Emissions 445 Phase I Affected Utility Units

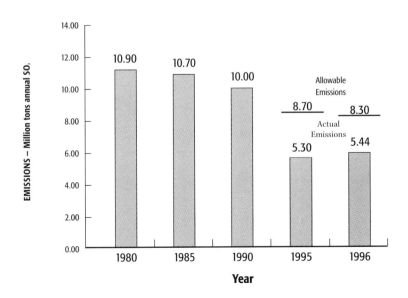

Appendix D

Examples of Recent and Pending
Transactions in the Inchoate Carbon Market

1. Niagara Mohawk and Arizona Public Service executed a swap of carbon offsets for sulfur-dioxide emission allowances, 1996.

2. A consortium involving Norwegian industry and the government of Norway purchased from the Republic of Costa Rica rain-forest-protection carbon offsets produced in Costa Rica's Private Forestry Project, 1996.

3. Environmental Financial Products Limited (formerly Centre Financial Products Limited) purchased from the Republic of Costa Rica rain-forest protection carbon offsets produced in Costa Rica's Private Forestry Project, 1997.

4. Ontario Hydro agreed in principle to buy carbon offsets from Southern California Edison that resulted from efficiency improvements at various power plants, 1997.

5. Tesco, a U.K.-based operator of retail gasoline stations, announced its intention to offer gasoline that is neutralized of carbon emissions, as a result of a tropical-forestry initiative in Uganda, 1998.

6. Japan-based Sumitomo announced a plan to help convert numerous coal-fired electric power plants in Russia to natural gas and to earn carbon offsets as part of the transaction, 1998.

7. Canada-based Suncor Energy announced a purchase of carbon offsets from Niagara Mohawk, 1998.

8. The government of Costa Rica is offering certified tradable offsets (CTOs). These arise from carbon sequestration in a new national park. CTOs are the first financial instrument that represents the monetization of environmental services produced by tropical rain forests.

Appendix E

Compliance Cost Scenarios at the National and Energy-Unit Levels

Annual cost to cut GHG emission 10 percent below 1990, from projected year 2000 levels, using tradable permits with assumed price of $20/metric ton carbon.

	Required Cut (mmtce)	Total Cost (in billion dollars)	Percentage of Year 2000 National Income (Nominal GDP)
USA	323	6.45	.072
E	68	1.35	.015
Japan	43	0.87	.014
Canada	27	0.54	.073
Total	**461**	**9.22**	**.037**

Note: Assumes allocation and compliance parameter analogous to the U.S. sulfur-dioxide allowance system. Projections of year 2000 emissions are based on latest available estimates for the United States (1,758 million metric tons carbon equivalent) and Canada (166 mmtce). Projections for Japan (340 mmtce) and EU (1,083 mmtce) are from FCCC projections. GDP projections assume 1 (current price) GDP grows 5 percent per year from 1993 through 2000.

Cost of Offsetting 25 percent of Carbon Emissions at a Carbon Mitigation Price of $20 per Metric Ton Carbon

	1 Gallon of Gasoline	1 Megawatt Hour U.S. Electricity
Carbon emissions	5.33 pounds	436 pounds
25% carbon offset	1.33 pounds	109 pounds
Cost to offset at $20/Mt	$0.012	$0.99
U.S. retail price	$1.25	$69.00
% price increase	1.0%	1.4%

NOTES

This article evolved from the presentation to the White House Conference on Climate Change, October 6, 1997. I wish to thank Michael J. Walsh for his very important contribution. Jim Perkaus provided valuable input, and Julie Sandor and Penya Sandor provided valuable assistance. Thanks to Marilyn Grace for help in preparing this presentation. Ellen Sandor, as always, provided the inspiration.

1. "Money to Burn," *Economist,* 6 December 1997, 86.

2. Aristotle, *Politics,* Book II, Clarendon Aristotle Series, Trevor J. Saunders, trans. (Oxford: Clarendon Press, 1996), chapter 3.

3. "Money to Burn," *Economist,* 6 December 1997, 86.

4. "Learning by doing" is the theme of an UNCTAD publication, *Legal Issues Presented by a Pilot International Greenhouse Gas Trading System (Among Countries with Binding Emission Targets under the UNFCCC),* by Richard B. Stewart, Jonathan B. Wiener, and Philippe Sands. The report was published by the United Nations Conference on Trade and Development, United Nations, New York and Geneva, 1996.

ADDITIONAL RESOURCES TO REFERENCE

1. R.W. Hahn and C.A. May, "The Behavior of the Allowance Market: Theory and Evidence," *The Electricity Journal,* vol. 7, no. 2, 28–37.

2. R.L. Sandor, "Implementation Issues: Market Architecture and the Tradeable Instrument," in *Combating Global Warming: Study on a Global System of Tradeable Carbon Emission Entitlements* (New York: United Nations Conference on Trade and Development, 1992).

3. R.L. Sandor, "Toward an International CO_2 Entitlement Spot and Futures Market," in R.F. Kosobud and J.M. Zimmerman, eds., *Market-Based Approaches to Environmental Policy: Regulatory Innovations to the Fore* (New York: Van Nostrand Reinhold, 1997).

4. R.L. Sandor, "Innovation by an Exchange: A Case Study of the Development of the Plywood Futures Contract," *The Journal of Law and Economics* (University of Chicago) 16, no. 1 (April 1973).

Chapter 19

The Environment:
Commentary and Discussion

Rajeev Gowda

In my environmental-policy class we have covered the problems of public goods and externalities. One of the central problems in that area is that of trying to match our environmental-protection goals with the profit-oriented incentives of the private sector. The traditional way in which governments have responded to these problems is the same that I have used to get my class to attend this lecture—using command-and-control techniques. What Dr. Richard Sandor's provocative ideas are telling us is that there are better ways to try to achieve these goals—methods which are much cheaper in terms of transaction costs. That is the fascinating aspect of this proposal. As he has pointed out, we already see positive results in the case of emissions trading in the context of sulfur dioxide.

Thus, ultimately, what Dr. Sandor is trying to tell us is that the green of ecological consciousness and the green of the dollar bill are the very same color. After all, it is truly inefficient to routinely squander the wealth of nature without considering the true opportunity cost of our actions. Sandor's proposals are innovative ways to mitigate such damages as society figures out how to fully value environmental protection.

One thing I find very attractive in Sandor's proposal is that it is pragmatic in orientation. It takes into account the fact that people are self-interested and corporations are profit oriented, and that both have short time horizons. It is important to work creatively within these constraints to improve environmental quality. In this regard, Sandor's work offers the same promise as other recent pragmatic ideas. These include: (a) life-cycle analysis, which attempts to minimize environmental externalities; (b) producer responsibility, which is expected to radically change product design and minimize waste; and (c) attempts to remove the hidden subsidies which promote inefficient behavior, for example, in the energy and transportation sectors.

In considering Sandor's proposals, three challenges come to mind. These are:

(1) The practical challenge of enforcement.

For schemes such as emissions trading and debt-for-forest swaps to work, enforcement is critical. Countries must monitor emissions. Protected forests must indeed stay protected. However, these will be difficult to enforce, especially because powerful local interests may work to diminish this protection.

Consider that although the worldwide ban on chlorofluorocarbons (CFCs) after the Montreal Protocol has been successful in slowing production, it has also led to a black market in CFCs.

(2) The political challenge of corporations working with nations.

The parties involved in these new arrangements are typically multinational corporations and sovereign nations. The memories of the colonial era are still strong in many developing countries and there is tremendous mistrust of multinational corporations. This mistrust can lead to public opposition and thus make emissions-trading programs unworkable.

This problem is part of a larger challenge for Western governments. If these governments support an emissions-trading treaty, developing nations may view such support as merely a ploy to secure a market advantage for Western corporations. Then people of developing nations may oppose emissions trading because their distrust of corporate greed overwhelms their support for environmental protection and its moral thrust. For example, in the case of marine-wildlife protection, Mexico is suing the United States in the World Trade Organization for its stringent controls on fishing. Mexico views these controls as unfair trade barriers aimed at protecting America's fishing industry.

(3) The ethical challenge of inequity.

One of the problems that arises when you have—to use Dr. Sandor's example—the Le Mans automobile races balanced with forest protection somewhere else is that an inequality in distribution of and access to economic opportunities results. One outcome of emissions-trading arrangements could be that developing countries with low levels of industrial pollution will see a deterioration in their overall environmental quality when multinationals locate factories there, even if the factories are state of the art in terms of pollution control.

In the case of forest protection, another problem is that it may result in barring local peoples such as indigenous tribes from living in or harvesting material from forests. These groups often have had a symbiotic relationship with the forest, and the change may be devastating to their very existence.

Both these results are fundamentally inequitable. Each worsens the living arrangements of people in the developing world while people in the West continue to maintain their gas-guzzling, high-taste lifestyles and pat themselves on the back that they are saving rain forests.

We have to pay attention to equity and values when we make such arrangements. Larry Summers, former chief economist of the World Bank, learned this lesson the hard way. He once floated the idea that an international market in hazardous wastes would be beneficial to developing countries because they could make money by disposing of these wastes cheaply. The furor that greeted Summers' remarks sent a clear message. Economic arrangements which do not take equity and distributional issues into consideration jeopardize their very legitimacy and are therefore rendered inefficient and ineffective. People are motivated not just by dollars but also by values and other higher-order goals.

I am confident that these challenges will be considered and addressed as Sandor's proposed emissions-trading arrangements are fine-tuned. I commend him for pursuing his mission of harnessing the tremendous creative potential and energies of the private sector toward the goal of a sustainable world.

Q: Dr. Sandor, with respect to trading-emission credits, I was wondering if you think the environmental-futures market would discourage big corporations—the ones that pollute the most and have the most money to buy the credits—from implementing technologically newer ways to reduce emissions and control pollution.

Richard L. Sandor

Well, if they were to buy emission credits, it would mean that somebody else can do the same amount of cleaning up of the global environment for less money. It is no different than the gains that come from any kind of trade. For example, New England Electric agreed on a voluntary basis in the mid-1990s to give physical and human capital to Borneo to teach people how to log for six or seven hardwoods in an acre of land rather than clear-cutting it all. They are teaching them how to do that, and that is much easier than New England Electric scrubbing, reducing, and developing the forest. It is maintaining and transferring intellectual capital to Borneo that allows people to log better and not to clear-cut an acre to get at six trees. New England Electric says, "Look, that is much cheaper. It will cost me X dollars, and at a cost of 10 percent of X, I can do it in Borneo while reducing the world's carbon emissions."

Q: I want to question the whole idea of providing incentives for industries not to pollute. We do not provide incentives for industries not to beat their workers. We do not provide incentives for them not to loot the surrounding communities. Why not take an approach like the Netherlands of setting the standard of allowable pollution limits and allow each individual corporation to use its ingenuity to provide the most efficient way to cut pollution?

Richard L. Sandor

The SO_2 program does indeed set caps and you can have voluntary baseline standards. Detroit Edison and British Petroleum do it. You can get a pilot program. Ultimately, the fear of a cap and the reduction of emissions are not going to cause that much strain in the economy. As a first step we have to figure out how bad a problem it is. A voluntary pilot program is going to create price transparency and, I think, alleviate a lot of people's concerns. Start with the levels very high. Make as much of it voluntary as possible. Let the market tell you how bad a problem we have. That will be ultimately a point of a program and the caps and emissions.

I might say that in the SO_2 program there are 400 sources of SO_2 emissions. They were emitting, in the late 1980s, about 11 million tons of sulfur dioxide. There is a very, very high level. They were mandated to cut their emissions to 8.7—from 11 to just under 9. And in 1997 they were at 5.3. They are 40 percent below the mandated emission levels. Why? Because it has been cheap to do it. I am suggesting that the same kind of clarity will be brought to bear if we dare to see how cheap it is to stop global warming. We have to have industry involved, and we have to give it the flexibility to comply and to show that it can steward the environment. It will not work to simply mandate very low levels of tolerance, causing immediate economic dislocation.

The markets can help us. We saw that with water rights in New Mexico. Water often does not go to its most appropriate use. When New Mexico allowed water to be traded, Intel all of a sudden built a $5 billion chip factory outside Albuquerque. It bought up water rights. That was the highest and best use. It created employment and economic growth. It was clean. Instead of water rights being used to irrigate marginal land, they were used to manufacture semiconductors. So markets allow us to use resources more efficiently. If you did not have tradable water rights in New Mexico, you would not have the finest chip factory in the world there. You cannot just mandate inflexible environmental-protection behavior.

Q: You gave the example of a power company in New England that is paying money in Borneo to help reduce carbon emissions, which helps the whole system. However, what about in that local area of New England? That company has not done anything for New England because it takes a long time for the air quality in Borneo to transpose to New England. What about the local people involved that are being affected by that local polluter?

Richard L. Sandor

The emission of a greenhouse gas, be it methane or carbon, is a global problem, and improvements in Borneo help the worldwide problem. For local problems, local markets are springing up, e.g., for SO_2 in Los Angeles, in Ohio, and in the Northeast. A quote from the treasurer of Mobil Oil shows how he trades emission credits as part and parcel of doing business. Only six or seven years after the SO_2 program was started, in 1997, Mobil routinely traded in emission credits to meet local, regional, or international standards. We have come a long way. The local problem can be solved with local markets, and localities such as Los Angeles are doing this.

Q: Do you think groups, corporations, and nations will choose to use the market to work on the global environmental problems to the neglect of other social problems of the world?

Richard L. Sandor

I think family and community are critical. I do not think they should be separated. Why I am concerned about global warming is the irreversibility of it. I think you are supposed to buy health insurance when you are healthy. The planet is still healthy. If the price tag is cheap now, let us fix it before it becomes too costly. My concern is you get to an irreversibility— palm trees are growing across Lake Michigan, there is no Hawaii, half of Holland is gone, and there have been enormous climate changes. This is a big planet. You cannot just turn the air-conditioning on and off. I do not think what I am proposing has such a big price tag. I think it is cheap insurance, and I think it can be done voluntarily with the cooperation of industry. What I am saying is that protecting the environment can be undertaken without distracting ourselves from social problems such as drugs, families, and education.

Q: I have a few concerns about emissions permits. The first one is that although they may reduce the overall pollutants in the air over a vast area, they contribute to concentrated pollution pockets. For example, some companies in the northeastern states sold emissions permits to the companies in the Midwest, and pollution in Midwest regions increased.

Richard L. Sandor

Ohioans passed the Tall Stacks Law, intended to stop pollutants. In response, the utilities built tall stacks, and winds carried the smoke into New York. There was compliance locally but New York got the problem. We have to combine local and federal standards. None of these programs is perfect, but as George Patton said, "A good plan violently executed now is better than a perfect plan later."

Q: I was wondering how exactly would a market form for something like the spotted owl?

Richard L. Sandor

In an interdisciplinary course we did at Columbia with lawyers, MBAs, and biologists, one of the teams developed a spotted-owl futures contract and a spotted-owl option contract. They priced them, developed computerized pricing of the contracts, and basically set up a public trust. It is this kind of thing that the Nature Conservancy is promoting. It buys wetlands at a low price and sells them at a high price, thus ensuring a more efficient and less wasteful use of those lands.

Q: What do people who are opposed to your program say, and how do you respond to them?

Richard L. Sandor

It depends on how they articulate their opposition. In 1997 we held a policy forum in Chicago and were quite privileged to have Ronald H. Coase, who wrote an article called "The Problem of Social Cost,"[1] which won him the Nobel Prize in economics. He was eighty-seven years old, a wonderful man, and gave the opening speech. Fifteen countries were represented. We felt the best way to deal with the opposition of Greenpeace was to give representatives a spot on the program and opportunity for debate. Continual open dialogue is how to deal with "the opposition." So education is the answer.

Rajeev Gowda

Q: My question really focuses on the values issue. We are commodifying things that we value primarily for moral reasons. When we talk about commodifying the spotted owl, is that the first step toward commodifying human life? In cost-benefit analysis, how much is a life worth? Are we going in that direction?

Richard L. Sandor

Yes, we are, but I don't have a problem with it. I do not think the commoditization of the pharmaceutical industry—patent protection and market incentives—has had anything but positive results. Pharmaceutical R&D tends to solve a lot of our medical problems. The delivery system is not so good, but I blame that more on market failure. I think it is good to "incentivize" people to develop cures for disease by giving them patent protection.

Zev M. Trachtenberg

If I can just follow up on Rajeev Gowda's question, I think there are some things in the world that we just think ought not be commodities and ought not be subject to a market régime. It is true that we have long thought of what are known as public goods—such as the air and the water—as being inappropriate for a market régime or a commodity régime. We all know this line from the famous poem attributed to Native American Chief Seattle—"How can you sell the air?"[2] That is not a technological question. The question really is, "Ought we to sell the air?" Maybe the best way to lower sulfur-dioxide emissions and take care of global warming is to commodify or to impose a commodity régime on these previously free goods. But the question remains: "Are there certain things which ought not be a commodity?"

Richard L. Sandor

The answer is unambiguously no. We have to separate two issues. The first issue is, how do you make the pie bigger? If you are sitting in your kitchen, how do you get the largest apple pie from seven apples? The second question is, how thin do you cut the slices for everybody at the party? Environmentalists confuse the second issue with the first issue. The first thing to do is to address the fundamental problem, to separate it from issues of distribution and equity. Markets can help us use air and water in the best way.

If you want social issues addressed, address them outside the marketplace. We have learned that government programs—whether food stamps or agricultural subsidies—distort prices and get you neither equity nor efficiency. Leave the actors in the economic system to do resource allocation. During the Korean War we decided to subsidize alpaca so that our soldiers would have warm coats. The alpaca subsidies of 1952 were taken off the books in 1995!

I would rather separate the pie-making from the division of the slices of a pie, and I would leave it to businessmen to optimize the pie. It is not that I am unconcerned about equity. I just do not want to design a bad machine that is equitable. I would rather design a good machine, maximize the output, and then worry about the distribution.

NOTES

1. Ronald N. Coase, "The Problem of Social Cost," *Journal of Law and Economics* 3, no. 1 (University of Chicago Law School, 1960).

2. *How Can One Sell the Air: Chief Seattle's Vision* (Summertown, Tennessee: Book Publishing Co., 1992).

PART VII

**The
Media
and
International
Relations
and
Foreign
Policy**

Overview

David Dary

The mass media and their influence on foreign policy have been subject to much discussion in recent decades. One group of commentators, including many from the media, has criticized television, radio, newspapers, and magazines for placing foreign-policy decisions under too much scrutiny, for distorting the news, for presenting emotional, dramatic depictions that do not put events in proper historical context, and for setting the foreign-policy agenda and rushing government leaders to imprudent, ill-thought-out actions. Another set of critics has seen the media as overly controlled and managed by the government, which they say can too easily and quickly use the media to put a "government spin" on events and thereby manipulate public opinion to support the ruling elite's foreign policies. In both cases the media have been seen as not fairly portraying American foreign policy and as preventing the true will and wisdom of the people from being exercised.

Interestingly, the mounting criticism of the post–cold war period has become not so much that the media distort news and the carrying out of a foreign policy truly reflecting the will of the American people. Rather, the focus has shifted to a concern that the media no longer give adequate coverage to foreign affairs and thereby bear a major responsibility for Americans' lack of knowledge about and interest in international relations. David Gergen, adviser to presidents and editor of *U.S. News and World Report,* booms out this thesis in chapter 20, and Lee Cullum of the *Dallas Morning News,* Lois Romano of the *Washington Post,* and I echo it in chapter 21.

The Media and International Relations and Foreign Policy

David R. Gergen

We are living in a time of paradox. Some fifty years ago Henry Luce called this the "American century," but it is only now that America has emerged as the undisputed leader of the world. Our ideas are transcendent around the globe. That is, the ideas that gave birth to this country in 1776 and are embraced in our Declaration of Independence are now accepted in most countries. For the first time in history one half of all the world's population lives in democratic countries. The writings of the author of the Declaration of Independence, Thomas Jefferson, are now held aloft from Prague to Beijing. I learned just recently that of all our presidents, Thomas Jefferson is the one now most cited in cyberspace. Jefferson is suffering at the hands of historians while his ideas are making a serious comeback around the world.

Our military, as Sam Nunn described, is the best-equipped, best-prepared fighting force in world history. We represent only 4 percent of the world's population but produce 21 percent of its gross product. More importantly, we have become the home of the revolutions that are now changing and transforming the world—the revolutions in telecommunications and in biotechnology. These are American products. The United States is on the cutting edge in most of the critical areas of change.

America is changing the world's culture. Some of our friends overseas do not like that. Particularly in France there is not much they do like about America. They would like to keep our culture out, but in most parts of the world young people are enchanted by it. Books written in America now have a 32 percent share of the world market. Music recorded in America occupies 60 percent of the world market, and prepackaged software now dominates 75 percent of the world market. This is from a country that has 4 percent of the world's population. We are deeply embedded in the world and we are a leader of the world.

In a related vein, technology obviously is bringing the rest of the world much closer to our doorstep—really to our fingertips—than ever before. When cables were first laid for international telephone calls it cost more than $200 a minute to call overseas. In 1998 you could call from Oklahoma City to London for $1.09 a minute, and you could call from Oklahoma City to Tokyo for $1.45 a minute. That is a remarkable change. When Abraham Lincoln was assassinated it took seven days for word of his death to reach London. When Ronald Reagan was shot in 1981, a British correspondent sitting in Washington learned of it from his editor in London through a telephone call. The editor was watching the event live on television. That is how much closer satellites, E-mail, faxes, and phone calls make us. The world is truly at our fingertips. It is right here.

Meanwhile, American corporations are rushing to embrace the rest of the world. Responding to global economic pressures, especially from Japan (and I think the Japanese threat was good for us in the end), made us much more competitive. American companies have reinvented themselves during this past decade and a half, and once again, "Made in America" is a label of which we can all be proud. Since 1993, the United States has increased its exports by 40 percent and it is once again the world's largest exporter. By the year 2000, we are likely to be selling $1 trillion a year in goods and services overseas. Those exports support sixteen million jobs here at home, jobs that pay well above the national average. All together, experts say, 32 percent of our economy is now tied to trade and investment overseas. That share is certain to grow in the years ahead. We still need to knock down the barriers. The president does need fast-track authority to negotiate new trade agreements. There is no doubt that the U.S. economy is inextricably entwined with the rest of the world, and the best CEOs all know that.

To their great credit, just as business is embracing the rest of the world, American universities are also embracing the world far more than they have in the past. There is no better example than the University of Oklahoma, where the president, the regents, and others are so committed to the program of "internationalization." But it is also happening elsewhere. I teach part time at Duke University. At Duke, 35 percent of the students now study abroad sometime during their four years at the Durham campus. At Stanford, it is 40 percent. In the summer of 1997, Neil Rudenstein of Harvard went to Europe where there were thirty-five Harvard clubs, to give a major address on the internationalization of Harvard. The Yale board is engrossed in the internationalization of that university. So universities are moving in this direction, but none more than in Oklahoma. Clearly, the internationalization of great universities such as the University of Oklahoma not only strengthens the education of young people, but it also makes good economic sense.

A high degree of synergy comes from the international training of young people and the creation of jobs back home. In 1996, the *Wall Street Journal* ran an intriguing piece on Utah.[1] It is a landlocked state hundreds of miles from the nearest seaport. Utah, notwithstanding, had the second-fastest growth in jobs of the fifty states of the union, and its growth was directly tied to an explosion in international trade from companies located in Utah. What was the secret behind that? That is the fascinating point. The success of those Utah companies in penetrating overseas markets grew directly out of the Mormon tradition of sending young people overseas as missionaries. More than 41,000 young Mormons now serve in 111 countries around the world. They bring home not only a sense of religious accomplishment but also a much keener sense and understanding of the world itself, and an embrace of the world. Incredibly, no fewer than 30 percent of adults who live in Utah reportedly speak a second language. Because they see the world as a friendly, inviting place of opportunity, they have grown as a state. They have developed companies that are taking off internationally.

What we see then is an America that is preeminent. American technology is helping to bring the world to our doorsteps. American corporations are rushing out to compete in the global economy. And increasingly, American universities are embracing the world—a world that is rich with opportunity. This is a time when we have a chance to change the world in ways that we want for the next generation.

The paradox of which I spoke in the first sentence of this chapter should now be obvious. At the very time we are integrating with the rest of the world on so many other fronts, our political culture is turning inward in both politics and the press. CEOs and university students may be heading overseas, but politicians and reporters are coming home. It is peculiar, it is contrary and, in the long run, it could be very dangerous.

Let us examine the evidence. With the collapse of Communism some change in orientation in our national politics was inevitable. If nothing else, new people came into political office with new concerns. Since the fall of the Berlin Wall there has been a huge turnover in both the U.S. House and Senate. Sixty-two percent of House members in 1998 were elected for the first time after the collapse of the Berlin Wall, as were 40 percent of the United States senators. No one foresaw how radically different their political perspectives would be.

During the cold war, for example, senators and congressmen regularly traveled overseas during their breaks. Responsible senators such as Sam Nunn, David Boren, and Dick Lugar, along with Speaker Tom Foley, came to know Helmut Kohl as well as any U.S. president did. The men and women who went overseas from the House and Senate not only brought back an intimate knowledge of the world itself, but they also provided a sense of continuity to other nations as the White House changed hands with great frequency. In recent years, however, there has been a precipitous decline in overseas travel by members of Congress. In fact, we have hit the lowest levels since the end of the cold war.

It is extremely difficult now to persuade members of Congress to go to China, Japan, or Europe. In 1995, 200 members of the German parliament came to Washington for talks. Not one member of the U.S. Congress went to Bonn—not one. That is extraordinary. A growing number of people in the House and Senate do not have an overseas orientation. One-third of the members of the current House and Senate do not own passports.

We are fortunate that at the top of the party ranks, the men and women who are leaders in both parties remain internationalists. Newt Gingrich was an internationalist. Trent Lott is an internationalist, and so was Bob Dole. That same thing is true at the top of the Democratic ranks. But when you go down into the ranks to the younger membership it is different. It is a very inward-looking group. Out of that generation will come the future leaders, and they are not at all oriented toward the international side. Larry Eagleburger, who served with distinction in several administrations, especially under Republicans—he was secretary of state right at the end of the Bush administration—put it well regarding the Congressional class of 1994, a class that he admired in many other respects because they were mainly Republicans. He said it is not that they are isolationists; they just do not give a damn about international affairs. I am afraid the same thing may be said about a lot of Democrats as well.

This is not a phenomenon limited to the congressional branch. During the 1996 presidential campaign debates Jim Lehrer tried in vain to get the candidates to focus on foreign-policy questions. They kept veering back to national passions. In my service in prior administrations, 65 percent of a president's time typically was devoted to foreign affairs, the rest to domestic affairs. That ratio has now been reversed, perhaps for a long time to come. We see then, on one hand, that politics is turning inward.

We see much the same in the media, despite the fact that we are prone to think the press has cameras everywhere, especially CNN. Not long after I joined the Clinton administration, the president had evidence that the Iraqis had decided to try to assassinate former President George Bush on a visit he made to Kuwait. President Clinton vowed that if that evidence were substantiated he would retaliate. So when the evidence was in hand, he determined to conduct a military strike. After consideration with the Joint Chiefs of Staff and others, he decided to launch missiles from ships in the Persian Gulf to strike the Iraqi intelligence headquarters, just southwest of Baghdad. The missiles were to be launched at 4:00 A.M. eastern standard time (EST) and scheduled to hit the target at 6:00 A.M. We did not have intelligence satellites that would see the impact. We therefore planned to turn on CNN to see evidence that they had hit. The president intended to go on national television at 7:00 A.M. EST to explain to the country what had happened. The missiles were fired. At 6:00 A.M. we turned on the TV to watch CNN and there was no report. At 6:15 there was no report, and at 6:45 there still was no report from CNN.

President Clinton called me and said, "What's going on? Did we hit those sites or not? I cannot go on national television until I know if we hit the targets." I replied, "We have to wait a little while to confirm." About fifteen minutes later the president was getting agitated. He asked me, "Is there anything you can do to find out?" I said, "Let me call Tom Johnson. He is the president of CNN News. He is someone I have known for a long time. I will find out from him if they have any reports." I called Tom Johnson, and he said, "You know, we have pulled our reporters out of Baghdad. We do not have any in there." I asked, "Where are your closest reporters?" He said, "They are in Beirut. However, they are on their way to Baghdad because we sensed there may be trouble brewing." I asked, "When will they get there?" "Tomorrow night," he responded. I said, "Wow, we have a real problem! Can I take you into my confidence?" I explained what was going on. He said, "You know, it does occur to me that we did receive a call at our bureau at Baghdad, where we have an Iraqi national working, saying there had been big explosions outside of the city." I said, "Bang! That's it!" I told the president, "I think we have confirmation." He said, "Call the networks," and he went on national television. Just before, Tony Lake, who was national security adviser, said, "Tell the president we are relatively sure we hit the target."

Let me tell you what is happening in television, what is happening in print. Their reporters are coming home. A study coming out of the Kennedy School of Journalism shows a dramatic drop in coverage of international affairs by ABC, CBS, and NBC. During the 1970s, they devoted 35 percent of all their stories to foreign affairs. In 1997 they were down to 23 percent, and the amount of time they spent on international affairs had dropped from 40 percent in the 1970s to 13 percent today. Only 13 percent of the time was devoted to international affairs! The truth is that international news is mostly a blip on the screen these days.

We see the same trend in print. I am associated with *U.S. News and World Report,* and I must tell you it has been distressing for me. *Time, Newsweek,* and *U.S. News* have had less than a dozen covers on international affairs during the past year and a half. This is fewer than 5 percent of the covers. With a few exceptions—the *New York Times,* the *Wall Street Journal,* and the *Washington Post*—our newspapers are not doing much better. According to one study, regional newspapers are carrying even fewer words on international stories than is television, a visual medium. During the 1997 foreign-policy conference at the University of Oklahoma, the morning after Dr. Henry Kissinger spoke, the lead article was, "Oklahoma University to Profit from the Rolling Stones Concert."

There is a growing disengagement from international affairs by the press, just as in politics. Some people say the Internet will make up the difference. The Internet is making great inroads. On September 2, 1997, a typical day, 1.2 million Americans went to the movies and 10.9 million Americans tuned into *Home Improvement.* More than 12 million tuned into AOL! AOL is making a big change. But I do not think we can count on the Internet to fill the growing gap on international news. The people who are making the most money on the Internet these days are the pornographers. The Internet is not a great source of news for most Americans.

There is disengagement taking place in American political culture at the same time there is engagement in many universities, corporations, and nongovernmental organizations. What does this all mean? I think it brings some dangers with it, but that it is not all bad. There was some needed reorientation toward the domestic side after the cold war ended. CBS had a special on Mike Wallace in which he told how excited he used to be when he boarded an airplane to fly off to some place such as Lebanon. Now, he sighed, he gets on airplanes to go to places such as Tulsa. It is a good thing to go to Tulsa. All of us as journalists need to spend more time in American cities. There was a time when American journalists were more familiar with the streets of London than those of Los Angeles. It is time we understood what is going on in our own country and pay attention to it, but the pendulum has gone too far. We are learning more about our own country at the expense of knowing what is going on internationally.

Many people worry that there is a CNN effect that is driving us hither and thither in foreign policy, e.g., when it turned its cameras on Somalia. This does happen occasionally, but I do not think that is our major media problem. If anything, the growing indifference in the political culture has given policy makers a more permissive atmosphere in which to make decisions. Most people just yawned when we sent our troops into Bosnia. It was fine as long as we did not have to pay too much money and as long as no blood was spilled. Presidents can now more easily send troops overseas. We had American troops in more than 100 countries in 1997. Nobody talks about it.

There are several dangers. First of all, as the political culture becomes indifferent to international affairs there is a serious danger that we will experience—and I believe we are experiencing—a decline in the quality of people who serve in government, especially in our diplomatic corps. At the Kennedy School of Government less than half the graduates now go into government. Most of them are going off to high-salaried private-sector jobs. Some are interested in the entertainment business. Some are interested in the nonprofit world, but they are not going into government. Just before he died, former Secretary of Defense Les Aspin told a group of us at dinner that the big change he had seen at the Pentagon from the time he was first there in the 1960s was that in Pentagon planning sessions at that time the military officers sat quietly while civilian strategists ran the meetings. Civilians were the conceptualizers who had thought about the world at large and knew where they wanted to go with it. In the 1990s the civilians sit quietly because they do not know much about the world, and the military people do the talking. They go to graduate school. They read books. They think about the world and have a much clearer conceptual sense of what the world might be like. It is important that we keep our civilian side of the government—the State Department and the Defense Department and other agencies—as intellectually engaged and strong as the military. We select and train our military well, but we are not doing what is needed to recruit our best people to serve in civilian foreign-affairs agencies and diplomatic posts.

There is, second, the danger of the growing gap between the elite and the rest of the country. We have all been made familiar with the growing income gap between the wealthy and those in the middle class whose wages are dropping or stagnant. There is also an increasing gap between those who are information rich and those who are information poor. People who graduate from distinguished universities are becoming a privileged group within our society, while the rest of the society is dropping behind. Those who are privileged, those who have "information wealth," are internationalists. They are committed to American leadership in world affairs. They are committed to America taking a strong, active, and creative role in the world. But those who are information poor increasingly regard the rest of the world as threatening. They feel that globalization is menacing and spells trouble for them.

In the current trade debate, the Hispanic congressmen who voted for NAFTA in 1993 have turned against NAFTA because they feel their constituents are getting hurt by trade. Opinion polls show that those who are sour about trade tend to come out of unions, to be Hispanics, or to be African-Americans. They tend to be people who are not engaged in or enjoying the fruits of the new international environment. They are turning inward, and they oppose internationalism. Increasingly, there is an elite that is small and internationalist, while the rest of the country is turning inward. The passions of our politics are focused on home.

In politics, it is so easy to pander, to look at the polls and say, "Wow, look how the public has turned against trade! Let's forget it." Politics is increasingly driven by domestic interests, by domestic concerns, and by domestic special-interest groups. Believe me, our policies toward Cuba would be quite different were it not for the voting groups in Florida and New Jersey. Our policies toward Haiti and our intervention in Haiti were heavily driven by American politics. We have treated Turkey shabbily as a nation primarily because of the pressures of the Greek-American community. In one area after another, domestic pressures, especially from people who are not enjoying the benefits of the world, are driving our foreign policy.

There is a lack of support for sustained American leadership overseas. When the political culture turns inward there is declining support for American efforts overseas. From 1985 to 1995 we cut the budget to the State Department and other international activities outside the Defense Department and the CIA by 50 percent in real terms. We are closing embassies and consulates and bringing diplomats home. These budget cuts make it more difficult to be active overseas. America is dragging its feet in one international forum after another, whether it be on land mines, chemical weapons, population control, financial help for poor nations, women's rights, or shoring up the World Trade Organization.

This is not the American leadership that we have been accustomed to in the past. After the Second World War we took the lead in one area after another. We had the finest generation of leadership the country had known since 1789. The U.S. government took the lead in forming international organizations, committing America, and changing the world to make it safer for America—which it did. Now, we are pulling back. We need to address this issue, to take hold of it. We need, first and foremost, leadership from the top. We have seen at the University of Oklahoma how one person can galvanize and inspire everybody and get people to work together. Effective leadership at the top is needed to articulate America's interests and to talk about the opportunities we have.

I cannot remember a prime-time speech on television about international affairs by a president of the United States since the Persian Gulf War. We went from 1992 to 1997 without a prime-time address about what we should be doing overseas. Our Congress has to reengage. We in the press are paying too much attention to the bottom line. We are pandering, frankly, to what we think the audience wants to hear. We take polls to see what the audience wants to read about, and because the public does not want to read about international affairs, we do not cover them. We need to get back to the notion that we owe people what they need to hear. We need to address the problems in this country, such as the growing inequality between those of us who are privileged and those who are not. We will not stay together as a family, as a nation, unless we address this issue.

Finally, we need to understand that we have a window of opportunity. We live at a time of enormous promise. Our generation—those of us who now have this opportunity to shape world affairs—should work with the younger generation that will reap the benefits. We should work together to create a world in which families can grow up not with the image of the mushroom-shaped cloud but with a sense that the world is a friendly place, a place to explore. We need to recognize that the world is rich in other cultures that we need to understand and learn from, and that our ideas are something we can take to others to help them. America is not only the indispensable nation for solving problems, it is also indispensable for creating a world in which all people can enjoy the benefits of freedom and the values enunciated by Thomas Jefferson.

NOTE

1. Bernard Wysocki Jr., "Utah's Economy Goes Global, Thanks in Part to Role of Missionaries: Mormons' Overseas Stints Yield Linguistic Skills and Network of Contacts," *Wall Street Journal,* vol. 100, no. 45, p. 1.

Chapter 21

The Media and International Relations: Commentary and Discussion

Lee Cullum

Iapplaud everything David Gergen has said in chapter 20. On the matter of members of Congress, I am afraid that Washington has become a big political funding office and people there are so busy raising money that they have to stay at home. You may think they are raising money abroad, but in fact, the funding sources are here, so this is where they spend their time. It is a subject of serious concern. I would certainly like to see some campaign-finance reform so our members of Congress could give thought to other things

Of course, when I think about foreign news and foreign correspondents, I naturally think of coverage of wars. There is great confusion among the American people about the uses of military power. There is nothing new in this. Think back to the nineteenth century and a man named Artemus Ward. (That was a pseudonym for a humorist of the day.) He had this to say about the military: "I have already given one cousin to the war, and I stand ready to sacrifice my wife's brother."[1] The question is, will there be enough brothers-in-law to go around to protect this new world order that we used to talk so much about?

Wars have become very difficult for journalists to cover. The Persian Gulf War was not easy. The government did its best to manage the flow of news. But it was nothing compared to the Bosnian War. I have read reports that the belligerents were very concerned about their image. The Bosnian Serbs were terrified that they would get an image as brutal, and that might affect United Nations sanctions that they hoped would be lifted (they finally were lifted after the Dayton Accords). The Muslims were concerned that they were going to lose their image as a victim. They had to be victims to maintain support in the United States. The media were in Bosnia with their most sophisticated equipment, but producers could not get the shots they wanted. Some were guilty of setting up their own shots. They would say to a soldier, "Would you please fire the gun over there?" This is unethical, but I think it was done.

The press in Moscow covered the war in Chechnya very well and often under considerable duress. I read a story of an anchorwoman working for a television station who read a script one day, obviously approved by some authority, in which she said that the road to Grozny had been cleared and the way was open for the arrival of Russian humanitarian aid. The video picture on the screen at the time the script was read showed those same streets strewed with the bodies of Russian soldiers and a tank roaring through bearing the green flag of the Chechyna secessionists. That was the true story. They were very clever in getting it out. As a consequence, and for other reasons, it is very dangerous to be a journalist in Moscow. One of the most popular broadcast newsmen was gunned down gangland style.

Indeed, journalism is dangerous in much of the world. I understand that in Colombia seventy journalists have been killed in the last ten years. In Argentina there was a report that there have been 800 attacks on journalists in recent years. The government has investigated only ninety of those, and there has not been one arrest, not one indictment. The Menem régime was very hostile to the press and was constantly seeking legislation to make the laws of libel even worse, even more difficult, so that nothing could be done. I am afraid the time is going to come when we are not going to have news from some parts of the world because it is too dangerous. Algeria is one of those places. In this country, however, we still have access to good reporting, but our own news organizations increasingly refuse to spend money for foreign coverage. Nonetheless, we certainly still do have access to international news, if we would only use it.

I especially want to second what David Gergen said about the dearth of foreign coverage in most of our papers. This is not true of Lois Romano's paper. The *Washington Post* does a great job. The *New York Times* does a great job. I would like to stand up for my paper, the *Dallas Morning News*. I think we do a very responsible job. But as you know, on evening television news, on local news, it is murder and mayhem. That is all you get.

We have a growing cadre of people in this country who are working in foreign markets. They are businesspeople. They are professional people. These people are very interested in global markets. I have heard some of them say they feel they have more in common with their counterparts around the world than with some of their fellow citizens. That is not altogether healthy, but it is the case. They want news of those international colleagues. They want news of those countries. These Americans would be good for advertisers. That is not the reason to run a news story, but I know publishers do occasionally think of advertisers. The advertisers are missing the boat. They are losing this group to the Internet, even though Gergen is right; the Internet cannot fill the gap.

And finally, the broad general public that looks first to television has no way of knowing that the outside world exists. Except for the *News Hour with Jim Lehrer* and a few other shows, most TV newscasts are breeding isolationism. The day will come when the stories they refuse to cover will fester into crises that demand coverage and compel the expenditure of dollars they are loath to send abroad. It is a case of neglect. It is cause for considerable alarm.

David Dary

I want to comment on what David Gergen said, and also on what Lee Cullum mentioned about television news not covering foreign news. I can remember the time when national news media did cover foreign news extensively, when television, radio, and newspapers had bureaus in cities across the world. That is not the case today with broadcasting.

There was a time before cable arrived when we would turn on our television sets and there were only three or four channels to watch. We had three network news operations—CBS, NBC, and ABC. They were pretty good. We would watch Walter Cronkite, Huntley and Brinkley, and others, and get a feel for what was going on in the world. Today, this is not the case. Cable has brought countless numbers of channels to watch. The audiences that were once divided among the three over-the-air networks are now spread over many channels. No single channel dominates today.

What does this mean? Very simply, ABC, NBC, and CBS no longer have the number of viewers they once had. Because advertising rates are based on the number of viewers, they cannot generate as much advertising income as before. The three major networks have cut back, and the easiest operational area to cut is news. As a result, all three networks have cut their news staffs and foreign coverage in recent years. Few of the networks have bureaus around the world. CNN is an exception, and a couple of other networks still have major bureaus, but they are now more regional in nature—one in London to cover all of Europe, for instance. With less money to spend, the networks try to cover easy news.

What is easy news? It is news that does not cost much to cover, and it is often soft news. It is where the cameras are already set up. I like to think of Washington as an easy place to cover news. For some time, Washington politicians have realized this. They take full advantage of the situation by staging easy-to-cover events. And because of television, far too many Americans now view politicians as television personalities, much like actors in seamy dramas and in movies. It is not surprising that the public seems to tolerate the misadventures of Washington politicians. Then, too, the images portrayed on television have in many instances become, I believe, more important than the substance or lack of substance of what is being said.

But the media are not solely to blame. Why should Americans pay more attention to foreign policy and world affairs when many of them have not been taught their importance? I believe public education, especially in high schools, needs to do a better job of teaching world affairs and teaching our young people what their responsibilities are as citizens. I remember a course in high school called civics. It taught me my responsibilities as a citizen. I still remember those responsibilities. On September 15, 1997, the National Constitution Center, which Congress created in 1988 to increase awareness of the U.S. Constitution, released the results of a survey. The survey indicates that one in two Americans does not know how many U.S. senators there are in Washington. That survey also indicated that only two in five Americans know that there are three branches of government—let alone what they are.[2] The poor voter turnout in national elections raises the question, "Do we really qualify to be a democracy?" One solution is to challenge students more to be critical thinkers. Education today seems to focus more on how to make money and to fill the stomach than on how to fill the mind.

There is another group that bears some responsibility for the problem. Article II of the Constitution says very simply, "The President is responsible for making foreign policy." How many Americans understand what foreign policy is, and how it is established, and why it is important? As a journalist, I believe government also needs to be a little more responsible. Government needs to explain, in simple and honest terms, why things that happen in Russia or China or North Korea or the Middle East are important to America and Americans. In the eyes of too many Americans there is a lack of credibility in what comes out of Washington. Because credibility exists only in a climate of trust, the problem is obvious.

I believe all three of these—the media, education, and government—have a lot of freedom, but they also have the freedom to be responsible. I hope that by the twenty-first century they will be more responsible, but I am not going to hold my breath and would not advise you to hold yours.

Lois Romano

I am happy to report that the *Washington Post* is not coming home. We are not pulling up roots on our foreign coverage. To the contrary, we are adding overseas bureaus, adding staff, and adding resources. We are trying, as many other news organizations are, to redefine our foreign coverage in response to the new world order.

With the end of the cold war, the news media in this country—both print and broadcast—have been confronted with the need for dramatic change and innovation to keep up with this new world order and global economy. The paradox of foreign coverage has been that although the major media have spent enormous resources on overseas bureaus, during the cold war the story was driven by Washington. The president and, to a certain degree, the secretary of state, decided what was important—and that is what the media covered.

For decades, this meant foreign-affairs coverage was dominated almost exclusively by the East-West conflict, the threat of Communism and how this could affect us as Americans. Major news outlets were not simply required to report on major developments in other countries just because they were intrinsically interesting or significant. All major events were placed in the context of the global environment in which America lived—and that was

Soviet-American relations. As Garrick Utley wrote in *Foreign Affairs* in 1997, "as long as nuclear weapons were aimed at American communities, the question of personal security took an international dimension."[3]

The passing of the cold war is forcing news organizations to reexamine their foreign coverage. News organizations must greatly expand their coverage if they want to truly capture the world in which we live. They must cover politics and culture in regions and nations as if they were local stories, as well as the issues that could affect our lives. These issues include economics, drugs, immigration, terrorism, and the environment.

Ambassador Jeane Kirkpatrick and I discussed this topic. She made the observation that she thought print foreign-news coverage was greatly reduced, and I observed that I thought I had been reading more of it. I realized that, in a sense, we were both right. The stories that she would naturally be interested in—hard news, policy-driven stories—have been fewer in number. The stories that I would notice, as a longtime feature writer, have been in greater abundance. I have been reading much more about the culture of Japan, about Russians standing in picket lines for the first time, about the personality of the British prime minister. One of the goals we must have as journalists, if we are to continue to cover foreign news, is to explore this type of diversity of coverage.

But news organizations first must determine whether such an investment of resources can be justified—that is, whether readers and viewers really *want* expanded and sophisticated foreign coverage. Indeed, other than CNN—which has truly positioned itself for the twenty-first century—television foreign coverage is not only failing to meet this new challenge, but coverage is also dramatically declining. The other major networks seem to have already made their choice, closing bureaus and reducing their coverage in the past decade. Most major print outlets have made a similar financial decision to close bureaus around the globe.

I am delighted to report that among the exceptions have been the *Washington Post,* the *New York Times,* and the *Los Angeles Times.* We at the *Post* made the decision to try to tackle this new world order by shifting resources, adding jobs, and even adding bureaus. The world is getting smaller—we are a global economy. The *Post* takes the position that people genuinely care about what is happening in various countries, both politically and culturally. To this end, we have taken the unusual step of creating a reporting job on the foreign desk covering the international drug trade from Washington. We have also opened a new bureau in Africa as part of our efforts to examine how Third World nations are coping with the new global economy and political landscape. All news organizations must try to understand the challenges of the changing world and adjust—or they will simply be left behind.

David R. Gergen

I think the question of educating the American people on foreign policy is very much related to what we might call the elite of the country—people who are in positions of influence and power. I think the elite ought to be very open. We ought to encourage more people to join it and it ought to be extremely tolerant. I think the elite in this country is too condescending to the rest of society and that people in positions of authority too often lose their nerve. They are not willing to stand up and say things that go against the contemporary grain, or to concede the floor to others with very different views.

If we let radio talk shows drive foreign policy, we are crazy. That is no way to run a country. There are some very interesting voices on talk shows and it is great that people participate, but there are not many who call to take a contrary position. The radio talk shows normally are off to the right or to the left, at the extremes of our politics. They seldom represent a moderate, modulated view.

I think the people starting at the top—beginning with the president of the United States and including others of our society's leaders—must be willing to have their voices heard too, even though their views may not be popular. Over time, with a concerted effort, public opinion can be changed, because public views are often mushy and not deeply held. On the question of NAFTA, for example, the administration started late in its efforts to secure congressional approval, but a lot of people made a concerted effort. They included not just the president and vice president going up against Ross Perot, but also the business community, editorial writers, and other people who believe in free trade. We were able to change public opinion over time. The public swung around and said, "We are for NAFTA." The proposal passed. Now, opinion against NAFTA has resurged.

One of the things happening in our elite universities is that some of the traditionalists who believe in Western culture have lost their nerve. I think it is extremely important to study other cultures. Multiculturalism has a lot to offer and it ought to be part of our education, but we want our children to understand the culture that has been at the basis of so much of what we believe. At some of the major universities people are walking away from the values on which our country was founded. We cannot afford to do that.

Lee Cullum

I would like to pick up on what David Gergen was saying about higher education. We are going to have to look seriously at the study of history on our university campuses. I am afraid educators have become obsessed with teaching computers and little else. I met a young woman who conducts tours at the White House. She related that after the Republican sweep of Congress in 1994, she took some of the new members of Congress through. They had no idea who Dolley Madison and Abigail Adams were, scant notion of Lyndon Johnson's Great Society, and knew less about the New Deal of Franklin Roosevelt. They believed, she said, that history began with Ronald Reagan. These were Republicans, but Democrats were just as bad. They go back to John F. Kennedy, but no farther. So of course they do not know about Yorktown or the North African campaign. If they had that kind of knowledge, it would enable them to have greater perspective about current events.

Bill Nations

I am the mayor of Norman, Oklahoma. I think Oklahoma, generally, would be perceived in America as being a relatively provincial state. As mayor, I come with a little different perspective, kind of a bottom-up as opposed to a top-down perspective. The city of Norman, under the leadership of Ambassador Edwin Corr and his wife, has established the first three sister-city relationships in its history, which is indicative of growing internationalism at the local level.

I want to ask if the decentralization of the delivery of services from federal government to state and local governments is regarded as a turning in. And if it is a turning in, does that contribute to this deemphasis of internationalization? State and local governments are asked to do more and more. Does that contribute to the lessened attention to international matters at the national level? Also, does it mean that state and local governments need to pick up the ball and become more international in their nature?

Lois Romano

I do not think decentralization of government is the cause for people just losing interest in foreign affairs. I think the movement away from international affairs has much more to do with our not finding ways to make it interesting for them. The tension is gone. The threat of Communism is gone. The threat to our personal security is gone. If we want to get people more interested, we have to find ways at the university level, in the media, and at every different level to bring people back to the importance of the subject.

David R. Gergen

South Carolina is a state that very much believes in decentralization. Conservatism is very strong there. People do not want Washington to tell them what to do. South Carolina has committed itself to education and has lifted achievement scores in its high schools tremendously. And although its citizens believe in decentralization, they have also reached out to the international community. They have enticed all sorts of international investors. The Greenville/Spartanburg area has been transformed. South Carolinians, while believing in decentralization, have internationalized their state. Rosabeth Moss Kanter from the Harvard Business School has a new book out on this phenomenon of centers which grow up in various states to become international in their orientation. They suddenly just get this economic drive, and it improves the lives of everybody in the area. Local control and local decentralized institutions are maintained while living standards are raised by linking into the global economy.

David L. Boren

That is a very interesting point. As we are seeing in Norman with our sister-city relationships and particularly in the relationships of local companies that have gone international, very often Washington is bypassed. More and more there are links between localities—states, cities, counties—with the rest of the world. We are engaging in international relationships in a very new way.

NOTES

1. John Pullen, *Comic Relief: The Life and Laughter of Artemus Ward* (Hamden, Connecticut: Archon Books, 1983).

2. Survey of National Constitution Center, 15 September 1997.

3. Garrick Utley, "The Shrinking of Foreign News: From Broadcast to Narrowcast," *Foreign Affair* 76, no. 2 (March-April 1997): 2.

PART VIII

An American Foreign Policy for the Twenty-first Century

Overview

David L. Boren

Ialready have made remarks in chapter 1 that could be considered an overview to Part VIII, the heart of this book, in that it is where authorities outline what they think the United States' new strategy or paradigm should be for the conduct of foreign policy in the twenty-first century. We address this question more conclusively in our final chapter, 29. We present here a remarkable group of proven, experienced, recognized masters of geopolitics, both as practitioners and scholars: former Secretary of State Henry A. Kissinger in chapter 22, former National Security Adviser Zbigniew Brzezinski in chapter 23, Ambassador Jeane Kirkpatrick in chapter 24, Ambassador David Abshire in chapter 25, and Ambassador George McGhee in chapter 26.

These contributors to Part VIII have served in the top positions of our nation's foreign-policy machinery in the past half century and are recognized not only for their broad and deep knowledge, analytical skill, and strategic acumen, but also for having been the intellectual authors and implementers of some of our nation's boldest and most innovative foreign policies and actions. Let us read now what they offer to guide us out of the fog in our approach to and conduct of foreign policy in the new era we have entered.

Chapter 22

The Architecture of an American Foreign Policy for the Twenty-first Century

Henry A. Kissinger

We Americans have had a very unique history. We are the only major country in the world whose origin can be precisely dated. My son wrote a school play once about the Declaration of Independence that ended with this line—he was only ten, so you have to forgive him—delivered by one of the founders of the country: "We better stop now, it's the July 4th weekend." We are the only country whose history can be precisely dated. We are the only country, the only major country, populated almost entirely by immigrants—by immigrants who turned their backs on their mother countries and believed that they were creating here a new set of institutions dedicated to liberty, and believing that this had universal applicability to all of mankind. We are the only country, the only major country, that has never had a powerful neighbor. So for the overwhelming part of our history, we believed that we could engage ourselves—or not engage—in foreign policy at our choice.

When we involved ourselves, it was against what we perceived to be overwhelming dangers. And we thought we could withdraw into isolation again when the danger had been dealt with. Unique among the countries in the world, we believed that the key to permanent peace was to transform all the other countries in our image. World War I was a traditional European war, more costly than its predecessors but about familiar crises. When we appeared on that scene, we announced that the transformation of government was the key to peace, and that spreading democracy and the principle of self-determination was the way to bring about universal reconciliation—a thought that had never been put forward by any other society and which we then refused to undertake after we had established its principle.

After World War II, we again became involved in world affairs but in a very particular set of circumstances. First we had an atomic monopoly. Then we had a huge superiority. For a long time, we produced nearly 50 percent of the world's gross national product. In those conditions, foreign policy was a challenge to the allocation of resources, not to strategic design. Any problem we recognized as a problem we could overwhelm with resources. And we presented every challenge—all the great initiatives of the postwar period—

as terminal enterprises which, once completed, would solve the problem.

I have discussed the history because we now find ourselves in an entirely different environment. We no longer have an atomic monopoly. Russia still has a large arsenal, although not as threatening as it was in the Communist period. But nuclear weapons are beginning to spread around the world, creating a substantially new set of challenges that all the countries that have the capacity to produce nuclear weapons really must share in together. Second, we still are the most significant economic power. But we now produce 20 to 22 percent of the world's gross national product. Our resources are not enough for all the conceivable challenges. Indeed, theoretically, if all the resources of the rest of the world were marshaled by some hostile country, we would be outmatched. Therefore, for the first time in our history, we face a realistic challenge to the balance of power, and we now have a national interest to prevent this marshaling from happening.

We also live in circumstances for which there is no historical precedent. Never before has every part of the world participated simultaneously in international affairs. Either they lived in ignorance of one another—in the same sense that, in the sixteenth century, China and Europe in effect lived in different worlds—or they had no significant capacity to interact with one another. In the eighteenth and nineteenth centuries, indeed, until the middle of the twentieth century, Europe and then the North Atlantic dominated world history. Today, every part of the world participates in international affairs. Major powers are developing in different regions, and this presents us with new challenges. (1) How does one define a major power under present conditions? (2) How do we manage their interaction? (3) For the first time in history, events can be observed as they occur. Communications straddle the globe in real time. (4) The world is linked integrally, not only by communications, but also by economics. A few years ago, an obscure bank clerk in Singapore brought down one of the oldest banks in England and nearly sparked an international financial crisis. Indeed, for any student of economic affairs, there are two nightmares. One problem is that the systems break down because of different conceptions by different parts of the system. But it is even worse that everybody comes to the same conclusion simultaneously and rushes to the same side of the boat and capsizes it. That is an even greater danger. How, under those conditions, can one deal with the automaticity of the systems we have developed?

This globalization of parts of international relations is accompanied by the fact that political loyalties are in no way globalized. Political localities are national and, in some regions, ethnic. Moreover, political processes that place an enormous emphasis on the immediate marshal those loyalties.

When I started out as adviser to political figures, they used to ask me what they should think. Today, political figures ask experts what they should say. It is a totally different approach, and it is compounded by the revolution in information that is taking place as we shift from learning from books to learning from pictures via computers and television. Book knowledge requires concepts. Picture knowledge is based on impressions. Computer knowledge produces an extraordinary accumulation of facts, unheard-of and unimaginable in any previous period, but it does not necessarily help you to understand the significance of these facts or, even less, the trends on which, finally, political judgment depends. The nineteenth-century German statesman Otto von Bismarck, who was considered to be a principal architect of what is called realpolitik—a policy based on the balance of power—nevertheless said the best a statesman can do is to listen carefully to the footsteps of God through history, to get hold of the hem of his cloak, and to walk with him a few steps of the way. No modern politician that I know can even begin to think in this manner. Therefore, it has become very hard for modern politicians to deal with the multiplicity of challenges that our nation faces.

Our experience has been an idealistic one. There is no other nation that has ever undertaken so many great projects on an essentially altruistic basis. When I was a young professor, I had an appointment with President Harry Truman. Quite awed, I asked him what he had done of which he was the most proud. He said, "I am most proud of the fact that we completely defeated our enemies in the war and then brought them back to the community of nations as our equals. I would like to think that only Americans would have done that." I think he was right. That was our historic experience and our historic achievement.

Today, we live in a more complex world. We do not have a clear-cut enemy. We do not confront an overwhelming military challenge. We do not confront an overwhelming ideological challenge. The question we have to answer is, what are we trying to do and why? And we do that under extremely difficult circumstances. I served in government during the tragic period of the Vietnam War, in which America had engaged itself in a distant enterprise for what I believe had been the noblest of motives. But we did not understand the limitations of our reach. We applied our principles to regions we had never studied and on the basis of the belief that they had universal applicability. Having thus launched ourselves on the basis of universal principles, those of us who wanted to extricate on the basis of the practicality of the situation were assaulted by those who wanted to turn it into a great moral issue on the failings of America—which is what the protest movement was really about and where I parted company. So Vietnam was the watershed.

But now we find ourselves in this situation: There are many who believe that all we need to do is to restore the pristine innocence of our early period, when two great oceans protected us. Economics was not yet global then, and we could choose our involvements. Therefore, our political parties are now very split. In my day, difficult as it was, there was a coherent administration which could appeal to the opposition and usually achieve a great deal of support—whether the administration was Democratic or Republican. Today, every party is split into a radical and an extreme conservative wing. Neither administration nor opposition has found a clear foothold. Each is looking for some issue to turn foreign policy into an aspect of domestic politics, which is a long-term disaster.

What we must do is try to reestablish some national consensus. We must not be embarrassed to ask what our national interest is. Without it, we have no yardsticks. Of course, our national interest includes the preservation of not just our well-being, but also of our values. All of life, including foreign policy, involves a balancing of various considerations, and it is important to have some convictions about one's society and its role in the world. The president and the secretary of state get to deal with the 50.1 against the 49.9 cases, on the basis of assessments that they cannot prove at the time they make them. Therefore, it depends, in an ultimate sense, on convictions. Also, as a statesman, you must achieve your goal in stages. You cannot reach it in one jump. Every step is imperfect in relation to the absolute value. That is the dilemma. And that is what we now face. It becomes more complicated when we consider that in different parts of the world we face different issues.

With respect to Europe and the Western Hemisphere, we are dealing with countries with comparable histories, similar values, countries which do not look at one another as strategic opponents. In these regions, we can practice the methods we are most familiar with, and I strongly feel that we have neglected building on the cohesion of the Western Hemisphere and the North Atlantic area.

In relation to Russia, we deal with a more complex case—a country of continental size with a quite different background. One component is Communist, historically imperialist, whose identity has been tied up with expansion. One of the disputes in American policy with respect to Russia is that some people believe our challenge must be to bring about democracy in Russia. I would certainly like to see that happen. I also believe that historically the Russians' tragedy has been that they have not been able to find security in their own development. Therefore, it means convincing Russian leaders that if Singapore, Japan, Austria, and almost every country in the world could grow and develop without expansion, it is absolutely a possibility for a country with ten time zones. And we have to understand how to conduct these policies simultaneously.

Therefore, I would now like to focus on China. The Clinton administration was my second choice in the 1996 election, but I strongly support the initiative it took with respect to China.

China's historic experience is quite different from ours. The Chinese have five thousand years of recorded history, whose beginning is lost in the mists of time. They believe that they have gotten through 4,800 years of this history without significant advice about their domestic structure from the

United States, so it is not taken for granted that we are necessarily competent to teach them. Second, there is a different historical perspective. If I asked one of you when something happened in American history, you would give me a date. If I asked the Chinese ambassador when something happened in Chinese history, he would give me a dynasty. There have been fourteen dynasties—ten of which have had a longer history than the entire history of the United States so far. When my friend the Chinese ambassador tells me when something happened, with luck I am within 200 years of what I want to know. When you travel in China, you rarely come to a province that is not larger than the largest European country in terms of population. In other words, you are dealing with a country with a different rhythm and a different experience. China's experience with its neighbors has been that they have been generally threatening. So China does not live in a world which it believes to be inherently harmonious, as we do ours.

I had the privilege of visiting China for the first time in 1971. The transformation from those days is unbelievable. If anyone had described to me as late as 1979 the difference in just the physical appearance of cities and in the style of life of the population, I would not have believed it possible. So whatever one says about China, the quality of life of its population has greatly improved. Without any doubt, things have occurred in China that none of us would have recommended or approved. Without any question, there are differences in perception between China and the United States. The question is whether the most populous country in the world and the most technologically advanced country in the world have a basis for cooperation. Now it has almost become part of our political process to argue that China is our next enemy—that it is growing at the rate of 10 percent a year, that sooner or later it will take us on and we should anticipate this, and that American pressure must alter China's domestic institutions.

I think it is important to get this into some perspective. The Chinese gross national product (GNP) is 10 percent of the American GNP. Even when it grows at a rate of 10 percent, this would still not match the 2.5 percent at which we grow. Even if you do it at compound interest, somebody has figured out that it would take thirty-four years for China to reach the present American GNP, at which point the per capita would still be much lower. Second, the Chinese military budget is about 22 percent of the Japanese military budget and about 5 to 10 percent of ours. China is not a military threat for the next decades. Without any question, however, China will develop and become politically and economically more influential.

In Asia, however, the situation of China, as compared historically to that of the Soviet Union or Germany, is quite different. The last two countries were surrounded by weak states. China is surrounded by strong states—Japan, Russia, India—and by medium-sized states such as Korea and Vietnam. The normal perception of Chinese leaders is directed not at opposition to us, but at fear of their historic opponent. Therefore, I believe that the visit of Jiang Zemin to Washington was of fundamental importance.

President Richard Nixon and to some extent I, as his associate, have been given credit for creating an opening to China. That is actually not fully deserved, because the opening would have happened anyway. We did it perhaps a little more elegantly, a little faster, but it was dictated by reality, and the Chinese wanted it very much, too. What we did do—for which, in my view, we do deserve credit—is that we managed to distinguish the essential from the peripheral. When you read accounts of that period, it is said that Nixon and I carried these things directly into the White House and away from the established institutions. That is not actually true.

The established institutions began the dialogue in Warsaw, where the Chinese first intimated that they wanted us to come to Beijing. The U.S. State Department thereupon prepared three huge loose-leaf notebooks of what we should discuss—arms control, claims and assets, communications, immunities, and visa requirements. And it had another big book on whom we should brief about all this. Nixon said, "They are going to kill this baby before it's born." That is when it wandered into the White House.

What was important was that we talked to the Chinese leaders about the structure of the international order as we understood it. And they talked to us in an extraordinary way. Part of the reason was luck. There had been no previous contact, so we had no commerce and such to talk about, just important things. This was the foundation of a relationship that worked quite well for nearly twenty years. Even the issue of Taiwan was handled in such a manner that a territory which had been historically a province of China was nevertheless not permitted to be an obstacle to an improvement of our political relations.

This is being challenged today. In Asia, we are dealing with a whole set of nations in the process of rapid transformation. Japan is surely moving in a more nationalist direction as the single threat of the Soviet Union has disappeared. Japan is bound to look at Korea and at other neighboring regions from a somewhat different perspective than we do. India is moving into great power status. Southeast Asia is growing. All these nations think of one another, to some extent, as possible strategic opponents. In these conditions, why should the United States anoint one of these countries as our permanent enemy? There is absolutely no question that if any nation—China, Japan, India, any nation in Asia—sought the domination of all of Asia, the United States would oppose it. With all my love for China, if China were to do this, I would urge opposing it. But this is not the situation today. It need not be the situation in any foreseeable future. It must not be the situation without careful attempt by both sides to analyze how the world should evolve. I hope we can distinguish the important from the peripheral and start a dialogue which will be of tremendous importance for the peace of the world.

We have many other problems. We have Bosnia. We have many other troublesome regions. But I wanted to give you a conceptual overview of the challenges we face as a nation. I have a Chinese friend, former prime minister of Singapore Lee Kwan Yew, who claims that there exists a Chinese proverb. (I say he *claims* because I sometimes suspect that our Chinese friends invent these proverbs as they go along to intimidate us poor Westerners. When I told this Lee Kwan Yew story to a Chinese friend in Beijing, he said to me, "Next time Lee Kwan Yew tells you a Chinese proverb, say to him the following: 'There is an old Chinese proverb that says Lee Kwan Yew invents Chinese proverbs.'") Allegedly, the proverb goes like this: "When there is turmoil under the heavens, little problems are dealt with as if they were big problems, and big problems aren't dealt with at all. When there is order under the heavens, big problems are reduced to little problems and little problems will not disturb us." That is our big challenge. For we are still the nation on which, globally, more depends than on any other. And the challenge we face is whether we can distinguish the little problems from the big problems, and whether we can unite in dealing with them.

Q: Dr. Kissinger, I just had the opportunity to return from a seminar in Israel at which we studied the peace process there. What role should we take? Should we take a greater role in our mission there? I want to know your perspective on that.

Henry A. Kissinger

Should the United States be more active in the peace process? Let me make a few general observations. Whether we are more active in the peace process or not depends on what we are trying to accomplish. It requires us to understand the fundamental issues in the Middle East. My view, which is now very truncated, is this: First of all, the Arab-Israeli issue is not the only issue in the Middle East. It is not even the most important issue. The most important issue is the relationship between fundamentalism and secular moderate régimes in the Islamic world.

Second is the stability of the Gulf, at a time when we are based in one country, Saudi Arabia, opposing the two overwhelming countries in the area, and at a time when our relations with Turkey have not received the attention they deserve. Those are the two issues I would put even before the Arab-Israeli issue.

On the Arab-Israeli issue, I think I was at least one of the inventors of this step-by-step approach, based on the fear twenty years ago that any attempt to make a comprehensive solution was bound to blow up the whole region at a time when we were facing an energy crisis, Soviet opposition, and no real preparation in the Arab world. The step-by-step approach has been very successful for twenty years. Obviously, the more steps you take the fewer steps are left. I believe at this point it is senseless when talking about the West Bank to continue this approach. The whole area of the West Bank is fifty miles from Jordan to the sea. How thin can you slice the salami, and what progress do you make by debating whether the Israelis should give up 8 percent of the territory, 10 percent of the territory in the next slice, after which the Israelis know there will be another slice? Therefore, I believe there is only one negotiation now that we should be doing, which is to determine what the final borders are. Israel has not yet ever been willing to accept the Palestinian state, but the whole rest of the world treats Yasser Arafat as if he were the head of a Palestinian unit. I believe that if we want to make a contribution, we should stop the outflow process and move to a final negotiation and exert our influence in that direction.

Q: Would you define what you consider the United States' moral and political obligations in Bosnia and the former Yugoslavia republic?

Henry A. Kissinger

Once at a briefing with a military commander, I asked him a question, and he said, "I am so glad you asked that question; may I have the first slide, please?" Again, let me give you a truncated answer. First of all, what is Bosnia? Bosnia is an administrative subdivision of the former Yugoslavia. In 1992, during the Bush administration, the mistake was made to recognize Bosnia as an independent state. This made sense when the issues were Croatia and Slovenia, which are more or less ethnically homogeneous. But Bosnia is composed of Croats, Serbs, and Muslims whose hatreds have broken up Yugoslavia, and I do not understand why anyone ever thought they would live together peacefully in Bosnia.

We, as Americans, treat the Bosnian conflict as a political issue. In reality, it is a religious issue. These three groups not only hate one another in the abstract, but they also have existed in opposition to one another. The Serbs have existed to fight Islam and preserve the Orthodox faith. The Croats have existed for the same reason, but also to resist the Serb Orthodox, and both of them consider the Muslims, who are ethnically of the same group, as turncoats. Therefore, the problem that we face in Bosnia is this: We did a useful thing in ending the war for humanitarian reasons. Terrible things were committed in the name of ethnic cleansing. Now, the three regions are more or less ethnically homogeneous. I have great difficulty in understanding why we want to meld them together or why we should insist that those three groups must live together. I am very opposed to risking American lives to bring about a shotgun wedding of these three groups. I believe that the principle of self-determination ought to be applied to them if they choose to live together, of course.

But I am afraid we are sliding into a situation in which our objectives are not backed by resources and in which our public will not support what will be needed to achieve the objective—a classic Vietnam syndrome. For all these reasons, I believe we have some humanitarian concern in preserving the existing dividing lines. I would be willing to see that happening for a while, and maybe it should be done by volunteers rather than by people who are assigned to it. I am extremely uneasy about the incompatibility between the military provisions of the Dayton Accords, which separate the three groups, and the political provisions, which will try to unify them.

Incidentally, I was in favor of intervening in 1991 when the ethnic cleansing started, so I am not supporting ethnic cleansing. But now that it has been done, to say that refugees must go back means that civil war has to start all over again. During the 1997 elections people could vote by absentee ballot in regions from which they were expelled. The weird aspect of that is that, for example, in the Krajina—a part that Croatia took away from the Serbs and where no Serbs were living—several towns had a Serb majority on the voting rolls although no Serbs were actually living there. I would strongly urge that we get our policies, our objectives, our means, and our declaratory policy in line with one another. I give the administration great credit for having brought the war to an end. I supported that. Right now, what is happening is neglect rather than a settled policy. I do not believe that Bosnia justifies the use of American military power at the cost of significant American casualties.

Q: At the risk of being philosophical, I am curious to know whether you believe that in the post–cold war era it is possible for human rights and freedoms that we in America hold so dear to exist in a Communist state?

Henry A. Kissinger

I believe that in Communist states the definition of human rights is quite different from our definition of human rights. I also do not think that China is a Communist state of the same kind that we have known in the Soviet Union and eastern Europe. On the economic level and on the day-to-day living level, the condition of the Chinese people has enormously improved in the twenty years that I have been going there. On the level of political organization, I have different preferences on how to organize the state. At the same time, my point is, to what degree should we make that the principal objective of American policy, and do we understand it well enough? It seems to me inevitable that as China becomes a modern industrial state, a certain degree of constitutionalism will develop, because you need predictable legal forms to run a complicated society. We, therefore, should have some understanding of the process as it evolves. My views are not based on an approval of everything that takes place in China. They are based on the importance of China and the United States cooperating to promote stability in Asia and in the world.

Q: Dr. Kissinger, what do you think our foreign policy should be concerning Latin America, and especially the certification of countries such as Mexico and Colombia on areas such as human rights and cooperation against narcotics trafficking?

Henry A. Kissinger

One difference I have with many of our foreign policies is this: They would like to apply our human-rights values in regions where they are being rejected. I would like to apply them in regions where they have been accepted and thereby try to create a more coherent structure in the Western Hemisphere and in the North Atlantic area. There, we do not have to intervene in the domestic structures fundamentally, and we can build on what exists and try to create, through performance, a demonstration of what democracies can achieve when working together. I, therefore, have strongly favored the administration's proposal of a free-trade area for the Western Hemisphere, and I would like to see a North Atlantic free-trade area. On the other hand, like many other things, the proposal has never been followed up by any concrete policies, and right now it is languishing because the fast-track authority, without which it cannot be implemented, is before Congress. It depends on whether fast-track authority can be granted and that it can in fact be used.

When you talk about Colombia and Mexico, you undoubtedly are referring to the drug problem. It is a nightmarish problem. Nobody has come up with a brilliant solution to it because what happens in these societies in which drugs become so prominent is that the drug dealers have much greater resources than the state, and they can pay off the police and the military forces. I have not had many conversations with Colombians, but in Mexico they tend to speak of the disappearing truck. That is, the United States can follow a truck filled with drugs all the way through Mexico and as soon as it crosses the border into Juárez it disappears, which implies that there must be a little corruption on our side as well. I think drugs are a problem, not just of production but also of consumption. We have put a lot of effort on production. I have no brilliant ideas about what to do. I am in favor of the toughest measures, and ideally one should create some sort of Western Hemisphere military force that can attack these drug-producing areas, because the countries of concern usually do not have the military strength. But in the immediate future, I do not see that as a possibility. Ideally, if one could get the major countries of Latin America to cooperate on this so that it is no longer a primarily national American effort, that seems to me to be one way of dealing with the issue.

Chapter 23

A Geostrategy for Eurasia

Zbigniew Brzezinski

Seventy-five years ago the United States was a self-isolated Western Hemispheric power, sporadically involved in the affairs of Europe and Asia. World War II and the ensuing cold war compelled the United States to develop a sustained commitment to Western Europe and the Far East. America's emergence as the sole global superpower now makes an integrated and comprehensive strategy for Eurasia imperative.

Eurasia is home to most of the world's politically assertive and dynamic states. All the historical pretenders to global power originated in Eurasia. The world's most populous aspirants to regional hegemony, China and India, are in Eurasia, as are all the potential political or economic challengers to American primacy. After the United States, the next six largest economies and military spenders are there, as are all but one of the world's overt nuclear powers and all but one of the covert ones. Eurasia accounts for 75 percent of the world's population, 60 percent of its GNP, and 75 percent of its energy resources. Collectively, Eurasia's potential power overshadows even America's.

Eurasia is the world's axial super-continent. A power that dominated Eurasia would exercise decisive influence over two of the world's three most economically productive regions, Western Europe and East Asia. A glance at the map also suggests that a country dominant in Eurasia would almost automatically control the Middle East and Africa. With Eurasia now serving as the decisive geopolitical chessboard, it no longer suffices to fashion one policy for Europe and another for Asia. What happens with the distribution of power on the Eurasian landmass will be of decisive importance to America's global primacy and historical legacy.

A sustainable strategy for Eurasia must distinguish among the more immediate short-run perspective of the next five years or so, the medium term of twenty or so years, and the long run beyond that. Moreover, these phases must be viewed not as watertight compartments but as part of a continuum. In the short run, the United States should consolidate and perpetuate the prevailing geopolitical pluralism on the map of Eurasia. This strategy will put a premium on political maneuvering and diplomatic manipulation, preventing the emergence of a hostile coalition that could challenge America's primacy, not to mention the remote possibility of any one state seeking to do so. By the medium term, the foregoing should lead to the emergence of strategically compatible partners which, prompted by

American leadership, might shape a more cooperative trans-Eurasian security system. In the long run, the foregoing could become the global core of genuinely shared political responsibility.

In the western periphery of Eurasia, the key players will continue to be France and Germany, and America's central goal should be to continue to expand the democratic European bridgehead. In the Far East, China is likely to be increasingly pivotal, and the United States will not have a Eurasian strategy unless a Sino-American political consensus is nurtured. In Eurasia's center, the area between an enlarging Europe and a regionally rising China will remain a political black hole until Russia firmly redefines itself as a post-imperial state. Meanwhile, to the south of Russia, Central Asia threatens to become a caldron of ethnic conflicts and great-power rivalries.

The Indispensable Power

America's status as the world's premier power is unlikely to be contested by any single challenger for more than a generation. No state is likely to match the United States in the four key dimensions of power—military, economic, technological, and cultural—that confer global political clout. Short of American abdication, the only real alternative to American leadership is international anarchy. President Clinton is correct when he says, "America has become the world's indispensable nation."

America's global stewardship will be tested by tension, turbulence, and periodic conflict. In Europe, there are signs that the momentum for integration and enlargement is waning and that nationalism may reawaken. Large-scale unemployment persists even in the most successful European states, breeding xenophobic reactions that could cause French or German politics to lurch toward extremism. Europe's aspirations for unity will be met only if Europe is encouraged, and occasionally prodded, by the United States.

Russia's future is less certain and the prospects for its positive evolution more tenuous. America must therefore shape a political context that is congenial to Russia's assimilation into a larger framework of European cooperation, while fostering the independence of its newly sovereign neighbors. Yet the viability of, say, Ukraine or Uzbekistan will remain uncertain, especially if America fails to support their efforts at national consolidation.

The chances of a grand accommodation with China could also be threatened by a crisis over Taiwan, internal Chinese political dynamics, or simply a downward spiral in Sino-American relations. Sino-American hostility could strain the United States' relationship with Japan, perhaps causing disruption in Japan itself. Asian stability would then be at risk, and these events could even affect the posture and cohesion of a country like India, which is critical to stability in South Asia.

In a volatile Eurasia, the immediate task is to ensure that no state or combination of states gains the ability to expel the United States or even diminish its decisive role. However, the promotion of a stable transcontinental balance should not be viewed as an end in itself, only as a means toward shaping genuine strategic partnerships in the key regions of Eurasia. A benign American hegemony must still discourage others from posing a challenge, not only by making its costs too high, but also by respecting the legitimate interests of Eurasia's regional aspirants.

More specifically, the medium-term goal requires forming genuine partnerships with a more united and politically defined Europe, a regionally preeminent China, a post-imperial and Europe-oriented Russia, and a democratic India. But it will be success or failure in forging broader strategic relationships with Europe and China that shapes Russia's future role and determines Eurasia's central power equation.

The Democratic Bridgehead

Europe is America's essential geopolitical bridgehead in Eurasia. America's stake in democratic Europe is enormous. Unlike America's links with Japan, NATO entrenches American political influence and military power on the Eurasian mainland. With the allied European nations still highly dependent on U.S. protection, any expansion of Europe's political scope is automatically an expansion of U.S. influence. Conversely, the United States' ability to project influence and power in Eurasia relies on close transatlantic ties.

A wider Europe and an enlarged NATO will serve the short-term and longer-term interests of U.S. policy. A larger Europe will expand the range of American influence without simultaneously creating a Europe so politically integrated that it could challenge the United States on matters of geopolitical importance, particularly in the Middle East. A politically defined Europe is also essential to Russia's assimilation into a system of global cooperation.

America cannot create a more united Europe on its own—that is a task for the Europeans, especially the French and the Germans. But America can obstruct the emergence of a more united Europe, and that could prove calamitous for Eurasian stability and America's interests. Unless Europe becomes more united, it is likely to become more disunited again. Washington must work closely with Germany and France in building a Europe that is politically viable, remains linked to the United States, and widens the scope of the democratic international system. Choosing between France and Germany is not the issue. Without both these nations, there will be no Europe, and without Europe there will never be a cooperative trans-Eurasian system.

In practical terms, all this will eventually require America's accommodation to a shared leadership in NATO, greater acceptance of France's concerns over a European role in Africa and the Middle East, and continued support for the European Union's eastward expansion even as the EU becomes politically and economically more assertive. A transatlantic free trade agreement, already advocated by a number of Western leaders, could mitigate the risk of a growing economic rivalry between the EU and the United States. The EU's progressive success in burying centuries-old European antagonisms would be well worth a gradual diminution in America's role as Europe's arbitrator.

Enlargement of NATO and the EU would also reinvigorate Europe's wavering sense of a larger vocation while consolidating, to the benefit of both America and Europe, the democratic gains won through the successful end of the cold war. At stake in this effort is nothing less than America's long-range relationship with Europe. A new Europe is still taking shape, and if that Europe is to remain part of the "Euro-Atlantic" space, the expansion of NATO is essential.

Accordingly, enlargement of NATO and EU should move forward in deliberate stages. Assuming a sustained American and Western European commitment, here is a speculative but realistic timetable for these stages: By 1999, the first three Central European members will have been admitted into NATO, although their inclusion in the EU will probably not take place before 2002 or 2003. By 2003, the EU is likely to have initiated accession talks with all three Baltic republics, and NATO will likewise have moved forward on their membership as well as that of Romania and Bulgaria, with their accession likely to be completed before 2005; between 2005 and 2010, Ukraine, provided it has made significant domestic reforms and has become identified as a Central European country, should also be ready for initial negotiations with the EU and NATO.

Failure to widen NATO, now that the commitment has been made, would shatter the concept of an expanding Europe and demoralize the Central Europeans. Worse, it could re-ignite dormant Russian political aspirations in Central Europe. Moreover, it is far from evident that the Russian political elite shares the European desire for a strong American political and military presence in Europe. Accordingly, while fostering a cooperative relationship with Russia is desirable, it is important for America to send a clear message about its global priorities. If a choice must be made between a larger Europe-Atlantic system and a better relationship with Russia, the former must rank higher.

Russia's Historic Task

New Russian ties with NATO and the EU, formalized by the Joint NATO–Russia Council, may encourage Russia to make its long-delayed post-imperial decision in favor of Europe. Formal membership in the Group of Seven (G-7) and upgrading the policymaking machinery of the Organization for Security and Cooperation in Europe—within which a special security committee composed of America, Russia, and several key European countries could be established—should encourage constructive Russian engagement in European political and military cooperation. Coupled with ongoing Western financial assistance and infrastructure investment, especially in communication networks, these steps could bring Russia significantly closer to Europe.

But Russia's longer-term role in Eurasia will depend largely on its self-definition. Although Europe and China have increased their regional influence, Russia still remains in charge of the world's largest piece of real estate, spanning ten time zones and dwarfing the United States, China, or an enlarged Europe. Territorial deprivation is not Russia's central problem. Rather, Russia must face the fact that Europe and China are already economically more powerful and that Russia is falling behind China on the road to social modernization.

In these circumstances, Russia's first priority should be to modernize itself rather than to engage in a futile effort to regain its status as a global power. Given the country's size and diversity, a decentralized political system and free-market economics would be most likely to unleash the creative potential of the Russian people and Russia's vast natural resources. A loosely confederated Russia—composed of a European Russia, a Siberian Republic, and a Far Eastern Republic—would also find it easier to cultivate closer economic relations with its neighbors. Each of the confederated entities would be able to tap its local creative potential, stifled for centuries by Moscow's heavy bureaucratic hand. In turn, a decentralized Russia would be less susceptible to imperial mobilization.

Russia is more likely to make a break with its imperial past if the newly independent post-Soviet states are vital and stable. Their vitality will temper any residual Russian imperial temptations. Political and economic support for the new states must be an integral part of a broader strategy for integrating Russia into a cooperative transcontinental system. A sovereign Ukraine is a critically important component of such a policy, as is support for such strategically pivotal states as Azerbaijan and Uzbekistan.

Large-scale international investment in an increasingly accessible Central Asia would not only consolidate the independence of the new countries, but also benefit a post-imperial and democratic Russia. Tapping the region's resources would increase prosperity and prompt a greater sense of stability, reducing the risk of Balkan-type conflicts. Regional development would also radiate to the adjoining Russian provinces, which tend to be economically underdeveloped. The region's new leaders would gradually become less fearful of the political consequences of close economic relations with Russia. A non-imperial Russia could then be accepted as the region's major economic partner, although no longer its imperial ruler.

Eurasia's Volatile South

To promote a stable southern Caucasus and Central Asia, America must be careful not to alienate Turkey, while exploring whether an improvement in U.S.-Iranian relations is feasible. If Turkey feels like a European outcast, it will become more Islamic and less likely to cooperate with the West in integrating Central Asia into the world community. America should use its influence in Europe to encourage Turkey's eventual admission to the EU, and make a point of treating Turkey as a European state, provided internal Turkish politics do not take a dramatically Islamist turn. Regular consultations with Ankara regarding the future of the Caspian Sea Basin and Central Asia would foster Turkey's sense of strategic partnership with the United States. America should also support Turkish aspirations to have a pipeline from Baku, Azerbaijan, to Ceyhan on its own Mediterranean coast serve as a major outlet for the Caspian Sea Basin energy reserves.

In addition, it is not in America's interest to perpetuate U.S.-Iranian hostility. Any eventual reconciliation should be based on both countries' recognition of their mutual strategic interest in stabilizing Iran's volatile regional environment. A strong, even religiously motivated—but not fanatically anti-Western—Iran is still in the U.S. interest. American long-range interests in Eurasia would be better served by abandoning existing U.S. objections to closer Turkish-Iranian economic cooperation, especially in the construction of new pipelines from Azerbaijan and Turkmenistan. In fact, American financial participation in such projects would be to America's benefit.

Although currently a passive player, India has an important role in the Eurasian scene. Without the political support it received from the Soviet Union, India is contained geopolitically by Chinese-Pakistani cooperation. The survival of Indian democracy is in itself important, in that it refutes better than volumes of academic debate the notion that human rights and democracy are exclusively Western. India proves that antidemocratic "Asian values," propagated by spokesmen from Singapore to China, are simply antidemocratic and not necessarily Asian. India's failure would be a blow to democracy's prospects in Asia and would remove a power that contributes to Asia's balance, especially given China's rise. India should be engaged in discussions pertaining to regional stability, not to mention the promotion of more bilateral connections between the American and Indian defense communities.

China as the Eastern Anchor

There will be no stable equilibrium of power in Eurasia without a deepening strategic understanding between America and China and a clearer definition of Japan's emerging role. That poses two dilemmas for America: determining the practical definition and acceptable scope of China's emergence as the dominant regional power and managing Japan's restlessness over its de facto status as an American protectorate. Eschewing excessive fears of China's rising power and Japan's economic ascension should infuse realism into a policy that must be based on careful strategic calculus. Its goals should be to divert Chinese power into constructive regional accommodation and to channel Japanese energy into wider international partnerships.

Engaging Beijing in a serious strategic dialogue is the first step in stimulating its interest in an accommodation with America that reflects the two countries' shared concerns in northeast Asia and Central Asia. It also behooves Washington to eliminate any uncertainty regarding its commitment to the one-China policy, lest the Taiwan issue fester, especially after China's digestion of Hong Kong. Likewise, it is in China's interest to demonstrate that even a Greater China can safeguard diversity in its internal political arrangements.

To make progress, the Sino-American strategic discourse should be sustained and serious. Through such communication, even contentious issues like Taiwan and human rights can be addressed persuasively. The Chinese need to be told that China's internal liberalization is not a purely domestic affair, since only a democratizing and prosperous China has any chance of peacefully enticing Taiwan. Any attempt at forcible reunification would jeopardize Sino-American relations and hobble China's ability to attract foreign investment. China's aspiration to regional pre-eminence and global status would be diminished.

Although China is emerging as a regionally dominant power, it is not likely to become a global one for a long time. The conventional wisdom that China will be the next global power is breeding paranoia outside China while fostering megalomania in China. It is far from certain that China's explosive growth rates can be maintained for the next two decades. In fact, continued long-term growth at the current rates would require an unusually felicitous mix of national leadership, political tranquillity, social discipline, high savings, massive inflows of foreign investment, and regional stability. A prolonged combination of all of these factors is unlikely.

Even if China avoids serious political disruptions and sustains its economic growth for a quarter of a century—both rather big ifs—China would still be a relatively poor country. A tripling of the GDP would leave China below most nations in per capita income, and a significant portion of its people would remain poor. Its standing in access to telephones, cars, and computers, let alone consumer goods, would be very low.

In two decades China may qualify as a global military power, since its economy and growth should enable its rulers to divert a significant portion of the country's GDP to modernize the armed forces, including a further buildup of its strategic nuclear arsenal. However, if that effort is excessive, it could have the same negative effect on China's long-term economic growth as the arms race had on the Soviet economy. A large-scale Chinese buildup would also precipitate a countervailing Japanese response. In any case, outside of its nuclear forces, China will not be able to project its military power beyond its region for some time.

A Greater China becoming a regionally dominant power is another matter. A de facto sphere of Chinese regional influence is likely to be part of Eurasia's future. Such a sphere of influence should not be confused with a zone of exclusive political domination, like the Soviet Union had in Eastern Europe. It is more likely to be an area in which weaker states pay special deference to the interests, views, and anticipated reactions of the regionally dominant power. In brief, a Chinese sphere of influence can be defined as one in which the first question in the various capitals is, "What is Beijing's view on this?"

A Greater China is likely to receive political support from its wealthy diaspora in Singapore, Bangkok, Kuala Lumpur, Manila, and Jakarta, not to mention Taiwan and Hong Kong. According to *Yazhou Zhoukan* (*Asiaweek*), the aggregate assets of the 500 leading Chinese-owned companies in Southeast Asia total about $540 billion. The Southeast Asian countries already find it prudent to defer at times to China's political sensitivities and economic interests. A China that becomes a true political and economic power might also project more overt influence into the Russian Far East while sponsoring Korea's unification.

Greater China's geopolitical influence is not necessarily incompatible with America's strategic interest in a stable, pluralistic Eurasia. For example, China's growing interest in Central Asia constrains Russia's ability to achieve a political reintegration of the region under Moscow's control. In this connection and in regard to the Persian Gulf, China's growing energy needs mean it has a common interest with America in maintaining free access to, and political stability in, the oil-producing regions. Similarly, China's support for Pakistan restrains India's ambitions to subordinate that country, while offsetting India's inclination to cooperate with Russia in regard to Afghanistan and Central Asia. Chinese and Japanese involvement in the development of Eastern Siberia can also enhance regional stability.

The bottom line is that America and China need each other in Eurasia. Greater China should consider America a natural ally for historical as well as political reasons. Unlike Japan or Russia, the United States has never had any territorial designs on China; compared to Great Britain it has never humiliated China. Moreover, without a viable strategic relationship with America, China is not likely to continue to attract the enormous foreign investment necessary for regional pre-eminence.

Similarly, without a Sino-American strategic accommodation as the eastern anchor of America's involvement in Eurasia, America will lack a geostrategy for mainland Asia, which will deprive America of a geostrategy for Eurasia as well. For America, China's regional power, co-opted into a wider framework of international cooperation, can become an important strategic asset—equal to Europe, more weighty than Japan—in assuring Eurasia's stability. To recognize this fact, China could be invited to the G-7's annual summit, especially since an invitation was recently extended to Russia.

Refocusing Japan's Role

Since a democratic bridgehead on Eurasia's eastern mainland will not soon emerge, it is all the more important that America's effort to nurture a strategic relationship with China be based on acknowledgment that a democratic and economically successful Japan is America's global partner but not an offshore Asian ally against China. Only on that basis can a three-way accommodation—one that involves America's global power, China's regional pre-eminence, and Japan's international leadership—be constructed. Such an accommodation would be threatened by any significant expansion of American-Japanese military cooperation. Japan should not be America's unsinkable aircraft carrier in the Far East, nor should it be America's principal Asian military partner. Efforts to promote these Japanese roles would cut America off from the Asian mainland, vitiate the prospects for reaching a strategic consensus with China, and frustrate America's ability to consolidate stability in Eurasia.

Japan does not have a major political role to play in Asia, given the regional aversion it continues to evoke because of its behavior before and during World War II. Japan has not sought the kind of reconciliation with China and Korea that Germany sought with France and is seeking with Poland. Like insular Britain in the case of Europe, Japan is politically irrelevant to the Asian mainland. However, Tokyo can carve out a globally influential role by cooperating closely with the United States on the new agenda of global concerns pertaining to development and peacekeeping while avoiding any counterproductive efforts to become an Asian regional power. American statesmanship should steer Japan in that direction.

In the meantime, a true Japanese-Korean reconciliation would contribute significantly to a stable setting for Korea's eventual reunification, mitigating the international complications that could ensue from the end of the country's division. The United States should promote this cooperation. Many specific steps, ranging from joint university programs to combined military formations, that were taken to advance the German-French reconciliation, and later between Germany and Poland, could be adapted to this case. A comprehensive and regionally stabilizing Japanese-Korean partnership might in turn facilitate a continuing American presence in the Far East after Korea's unification.

It goes without saying that a close political relationship with Japan is in America's global interest. But whether Japan is to be America's vassal, rival, or partner depends on the ability of Americans and Japanese to define common international goals and to separate the U.S. strategic mission in the Far East from Japanese aspirations for a global role. For Japan, in spite of the domestic debates about foreign policy, the relationship with America remains the beacon for its international sense of direction. A disoriented Japan, whether lurching toward rearmament or a separate accommodation with China, would spell the end of the American role in the Asia-Pacific region, foreclosing the emergence of a stable triangular arrangement for America, Japan, and China.

A disoriented Japan would be like a beached whale, thrashing helplessly but dangerously. If it is to turn its face to the world beyond Asia, Japan must be given a meaningful incentive and a special status so that its own national interest is served. Unlike China, which can seek global power by first becoming a regional power, Japan can gain global influence only if it first eschews the quest for regional power.

That makes it all the more important for Japan to feel it is America's special partner in a global vocation that is as politically satisfying as it is economically beneficial. To that end, the United States should consider the adoption of an American-Japanese free trade agreement, creating a common American-Japanese economic space. Such a step formalizing the growing link between the two economies would provide a solid underpinning for America's continued presence in the Far East and for Japan's constructive global engagement.

Transcontinental Security

In the long term, Eurasia's stability would be enhanced by the emergence, perhaps early in the next century, of a trans-Eurasian security system. Such a transcontinental arrangement might involve an expanded NATO, linked by cooperative security agreements with Russia, China, and Japan. But to get there, Americans and Japanese must first set in motion a triangular political-security dialogue that engages China. Such three-way American-Japanese-Chinese talks could eventually involve more Asian participants and later lead to a dialogue with the Organization for Security and Cooperation in Europe. That could eventually pave the way for a series of conferences by European and Asian states on security issues. A transcontinental security system would thus begin to take shape.

Defining the substance and institutionalizing the form of a trans-Eurasian security system could become the major architectural initiative of the next century. The core of the new transcontinental security framework could be a standing committee composed of the major Eurasian powers, with America, Europe, China, Japan, a confederated Russia, and India collectively addressing critical issues for Eurasia's stability. The emergence of such a transcontinental system could gradually relieve America of some of its burdens, while perpetuating beyond a generation its decisive role as Eurasia's arbitrator. Geostrategic success in that venture would be a fitting legacy to America's role as the first and only global superpower.

NOTE

Reprinted by permission of *Foreign Affairs*, vol. 76, no. 5 (October 1997), copyright © 1997 by the Council on Foreign Relations, Inc.

Chapter 24

United States Relations with Nations Emerging as World Leaders

Jeane J. Kirkpatrick

We are at a time when we must rethink much concerning America's role in the world and which policies are appropriate to our problems, our prospects, and the dangers that confront us in this post–cold war world. For nearly half a century the cold war was the focus of American foreign policy and defense policy and a focus of concern for Congress. The cold war shaped our economic and security policy, and it affected our military and industrial policy. It ended very suddenly, unexpectedly, quickly, and peacefully. When it ended, many of the assumptions about American foreign policy lost their relevance. But it did not end all of them, because the cold war was never the whole focus of our foreign policy. The United States was always concerned with other issues.

But now, a sense of uncertainty pervades much of our reflection on the world. Few persons are dogmatic today about what will happen next year, much less five or ten years from now. "Everything must be rethought," Edouard Balladur remarked as the cold war ended. We were—and are—confronted with new phenomena, new processes, and new questions. The first challenge has been simply to be clear about what has actually happened. The most important development, I believe, is the democratization of what was called the Soviet Union. That great realist Richard Nixon explained why this is the most important issue to a group of Washington foreign-policy wonks on his return from his last trip to Moscow. That report began and ended with Nixon's observation that he hoped Americans would understand that even with the end of the cold war, Russia remained the most important country in the world for the United States, if for no other reason than that it alone had the capacity to destroy us in a matter of a half an hour or so. That remained a simple, hard fact.

Russia still has in its arsenals many thousands of powerful, accurate intercontinental ballistic missiles. For this reason alone Americans have a very special interest in the democratic evolution of Russia. It remains the country that matters most to the peace of Europe, the United States, the Middle East, and the world.

I was asked to address the topic of emerging nations and U.S. foreign policy. Russia is not an emerging nation as those are usually considered. It is a historic European power. But it is an emerging democracy and its evolution has permitted the emergence of more than a dozen other new "emerging" democracies in central and eastern Europe.

Not only is Russia an emerging democracy, but a democratic Russia is hugely important to us. So also is the spread of democracy in central and eastern Europe especially important. Of course the spread of democracy in South and Central America, in Asia, and in Africa is important to us, as are the inroads democratic and constitutional government have made in the Middle East. Why?

Because democracies require the rule of law and do not undertake aggressive wars against their democratic neighbors. Democracies can be ferocious in defending against undemocratic aggressors—such, for example, as Hitler's Germany or the Soviet Union—but they do not commit aggression against their democratic neighbors. That makes democracies good neighbors and peaceful trading partners; it makes democracies good citizens of a peaceful world. That is only one reason we should give top priority in foreign affairs to reinforcing, strengthening, and preserving constitutional democratic governments, especially when there are new democracies taking shape right now that are fragile and young. We need to be alert to opportunities to help.

The trend to democracy has been especially strong in this hemisphere, in South and Central America and the Caribbean, where only Cuba remains a clear-cut dictatorship and Fidel Castro the only clear traditional strongman.

Most new Latin American democratic governments have emerged in the last two decades and in countries such as Argentina and Chile, which had prior experience with democracy, followed by an interlude of dictatorships, perhaps precipitated by an externally sponsored guerrilla movement or *golpe de estado.* The disappearance of the externally sponsored movements in the Southern Cone seems to have left the field open for democracy.

Today corruption has replaced guerrilla movements as the principal threat to democratic governance.

Another important process already under way at the end of the cold war was the reorganization and unification of Europe. Nobody quite knows when the European Union will be fully realized, but we know a United States of Europe would make a good partner in building a more open, peaceful, and democratic world, assuming, of course, that it were open rather than protectionist, inclusive rather than exclusive.

The integration of Europe, important to the world as it is, is a process over which we have little or no influence and in which we play no important role, despite the fact that Europe's evolution will affect us profoundly. We must face the fact that we cannot influence the evolution of these institutions as we might like, and accept the fact that others may not call on us, however qualified we may think we are, to help them resolve their problems.

Several "globalizing trends" are under way. Communications are still spreading, creating possibilities for global communications networks.

Another important trend at the end of the cold war was the rapid economic development of Asia, especially the economic and military growth of China, as well as the tigers of Southeast Asia and Korea. The "Asian model," to which the United States is linked by trade, features rapid growth, hard work, and a Confucian ethic with a high level of productivity to produce rising living standards and a new openness. Examples are found in virtually all the Asian countries, including China. This brings us back to democratization.

The successful development of industrial capitalism in Asia encourages the development of democracy, as can be seen in numerous Asian countries. The Chinese politburo still exercises pervasive control over the Chinese people, and the president of Malaysia has argued that democracy is not "Asian," but I see evidence to the contrary.

A certain level of individual freedom is encouraged by the development of industrial capitalism. Deng Xiaoping, for example, decided in the late 1980s to permit the Chinese to decide for themselves where and for whom they would work. I note that those are very basic decisions to leave to an individual. It should be remembered that these were among the first decisions permitted to individuals in Great Britain at the outset of industrialization and urbanization and the emergence of democratic capitalism in that country. Deng's decision to "open" China to this (limited) individual decision making has meant increasing individual freedom and entrepreneurship.

The rule of law is encouraged by an expanding democratic capitalism, and the rule of law is one of the major components and prerequisites of political democracy. Strengthening the rule of law leads to an openness of the kind necessary for investment and export, and encourages the growth of democratic capitalism.

Deng Xiaoping took the early steps toward opening China when he permitted Americans, Europeans, Japanese, and Taiwanese to invest in China, visit China, and trade with China, and when he permitted Chinese to travel to Europe, to northern Asia, and to the United States. He encouraged the opening of China when he allowed Chinese students to study at European and American universities. Many American universities have had Chinese students in their classes in recent years. This kind of openness strengthens trends to development and to more openness, and ultimately, perhaps, to democratization. The process is under way in other areas of the world besides China. Michael Novak noted that the culture of democratic capitalism seems to be a requirement of economic success in the contemporary world, and that it is not present in traditional societies.[1] Entrepreneurial skills, autonomy, and individual decision making are also characteristics of modern industrial development.

It is interesting that the newest developments in technology emphasize, invite, and require a high degree of individualism. Achievement and success in high technology require a substantial degree of individual autonomy and freedom. And autonomy and freedom encourage the development of democratic institutions.

I expect that the Asian countries that will develop most quickly in the next decade will be those whose populations already have acquired some of the personal and cultural qualities associated with modernity and democratic capitalism.

Jeffrey Garten's book *The Big Ten* identifies ten emerging countries already important because of their growing markets. All are examples of societies that are developing democratic capitalism, individualism, and freedom. Mexico, Brazil, Argentina, South Africa, Turkey, Poland, South Korea, China, Indonesia, and India are his big ten.[2]

They are already major markets which are growing despite their financial problems. They are also interesting examples of political development. Almost all these régimes have made significant progress toward democratic government and free-market economics in the last decade. Argentina, Mexico, and Brazil have made important strides toward the development of democratic capitalism in the last two decades. Argentina is a major success. South Africa has made major progress toward developing a genuinely democratic government. In Turkey there have been important developments to democracy in the last decade.

These societies have managed to establish some democratic institutions. The challenge now is to see if they can keep them. The challenge to us is to find ways to be helpful. Poland is an interesting example of a former Soviet satellite whose new economic and political institutions have struck roots. South Korea is another important new democracy in which democratic political institutions are being consolidated and economic freedom is growing. Indonesia is apparently headed in the same direction. It has established some necessary institutions, but it still has a ways to go. India is the longest-lived democracy of this group and it continues to make significant, if uneven, progress on economic growth and more inclusive social institutions. The United States is deeply involved in all these.

Among the most important economic and political developments of the post–cold war world is that governments are becoming less important while individuals are becoming more important. Both market economies and democratic governments reinforce the role of individuals and thereby enhance the prospects for continued development in these directions. Thus, the people of countries that have not yet achieved a market economy, a rule of law, and a free society and do not yet have government by consent will enjoy the benefits of freedom and economic prosperity. This will come about through trade, travel, communications, and working in modern industries, with luck and help from international institutions and other countries.

One of the great lessons of the last twenty years has been the failure of command economies—socialism and collectivism—and the success of free markets. A market economy that relies on the skills, imagination, energies, and choices of individuals and that permits individuals to profit from their work speeds development. It stands in sharp contrast to an economy run by a few men at the top who control everything. Naturally, an economy that reflects the creativity and energy of all the people in the society will do better than an economy that is managed from the top by just a few people, who are as fallible as we all are. It is no secret why market economies work so much better than command economies, which stifle creativity rather than encourage it.

And as an understanding of that message spreads over the world—and it is spreading—there will be further movement toward democratic capitalism.

Not all the important processes under way at the end of the cold war were positive. One was the spread of weapons of mass destruction. Events in Russia and elsewhere in the Soviet Union at the end of the cold war dramatically speeded up the spread of nuclear, chemical, and bacteriological weapons and the technology to deliver them. Today this is our principal security problem. Nuclear proliferation, the proliferation of other weapons of mass destruction, and the spread of Islamic extremism all came as surprises. The nuclear powers had come to believe that through the non-proliferation treaty, the International Atomic Energy Agency, and other controls, they could prevent the spread of the most deadly weapons and of missile technology as well. They were wrong. They also failed to anticipate the spread of weapons of mass destruction, and they failed to anticipate the spread of a virulently anti-Western, antimodern, antidemocratic, and very hostile movement. The spread of Islamic extremism to Algeria, where bloody assaults are carried out against civilian targets, and to Turkey, which is a very important country for the United States and Europe, makes it harder to develop and preserve a stable democratic government and a growing economy.

Obviously, not all countries are moving toward freedom. The contagion of Islamic extremism instills fear in Africa, Asia, and the Middle East. There remain some repressive and reactionary dictatorships and some other outlaw states. North Korea is an example. One of the places in the world where there is the greatest danger that an actual war might break out is on the Korean Peninsula. I have been in South Korea several times in the recent past and have come to understand more vividly that the North Korean régime is fanatical and dangerous. It is an economy run by a tyranny, starving its own people and bloating its military establishment. North Korea continues to enlarge its military establishment even though it already has one of the largest armies in the world—made up of soldiers who are not adequately fed. North Korea is a stark example of the failure of command socialism.

Libya and Syria are also examples of outlaw states that operate outside normal rules of international law and codes of morality. Iran and Iraq, too, are dictatorships dangerous for all in their region. All these states are explicitly antimodern, anti-Western, antidemocratic, and anti-American. All are dangerous because they are engaged in serious efforts to acquire weapons of mass destruction. And even if they cannot develop those weapons, they can buy them. Unfortunately, there are more weapons of mass destruction on the international market today. There has been little progress toward greater freedom, law, or prosperity in these outlaw states, and not nearly enough progress in stopping the leakage of weapons to them.

So the world is not wholly safe and it is not devoid of problems, but as compared with the cold-war period, our government can focus on trade, travel, and educational and cultural exchanges and less on security. The American society, economy, and culture are well suited for the world in which we live. Americans are well suited to our times. We are the strongest country in the world, the richest country in the world. We have the largest economy in the world. And we are still entrepreneurs. We still have enthusiasm and zest for development, progress, and prudent risk. I believe our future will be even more brilliant than our past, and that an even larger number of the world's people should share in the great rewards of freedom and effort.

Q: Ambassador, how well do you think the thesis enunciated in your essay *Dictatorships and Double Standards*[3] stands up two decades and some thirty new democracies later?

Jeane J. Kirkpatrick

Many Russians, most central Europeans, eastern Europeans, and Central and South Americans have told me that they found useful the distinction between authoritarian and totalitarian states, which was the most controversial aspect of that famous article, and they believe that the transition from totalitarian states into authoritarian states into democracies has validated it. Sheryl WuDunn of the *New York Times* emphasized the utility of this distinction for China in *China Wakes,*[4] the book she coauthored with her husband, Nicholas Kristof.

Q: How do you reconcile working with China, offering it most-favored-nation status, and the United States' moral obligation to human rights?

Jeane J. Kirkpatrick

I do not know that I am an advocate of constructive engagement; I am just an advocate of extending MFN to China. I believe the United States government has a moral obligation to stand clearly for the rule of law and respect for human rights. But we do not control the world. In many circumstances we can only say what we are for. I, for example, have been a strong advocate of better treatment of Tibetans. I have protested the Chinese government's treatment of Tibet. I have testified every year for years on this subject—ever since there have been hearings in the Congress on violations of Tibetan human rights by the government of China. I deplore it. And it is not only Tibetans whose rights are violated but also the rights of Buddhists, Christians, and adherents of other religions throughout China. However, I do not think that cutting ourselves off from the Chinese, having no trade or relations with them, no student exchanges with them, and no business exchanges or investment, would advance the cause of human rights in China. I think it would have the reverse effect. I believe we want an open China. And I support policies that will promote an open China.

Q: Peru, Brazil, and Mexico have in common with the United States the fact that democratic capitalism has worked very much against the interest of Native Americans. Indigenous populations have been displaced and marginalized. Do you have any suggestions on how this can be rectified and avoided in the future?

Jeane J. Kirkpatrick

Native Americans in Peru constitute a very large portion of that highly pluralistic society. I am sure you know that. And I believe that as the Peruvian government is democratizing, Peruvian society will be democratized. Peru is a long way from being an ideal democracy. It is in the early stages of democratic development, and I believe that the amelioration of human rights for Peruvian citizens and for Brazilian and Mexican citizens as well will come with further democratization. It is just that simple.

Q: What do you see as the role of the United Nations in this post–cold war era that we have entered?

Jeane J. Kirkpatrick

Well, needless to say, I have thought a lot about that. I believe that the United States should participate fully in the United Nations, but I think one of the ways we should participate fully is by helping to distinguish between those tasks that the UN can effectively accomplish and those that it cannot effectively accomplish. Not every institution is equally good for everything. I think the UN is an indispensable arena for deliberation, for listening to the representatives of all the countries in the world, for debating their responses and their problems. I think is enormously useful. I think the UN can promote the best kinds of trade and exchange programs—I do not mean trade for profit but trade of ideas and culture.

I think, generally speaking, that the UN is not very effective, however, in operations, and it is least effective in operations that require the highest levels of technology and intercultural coordination. I think the UN is least effective in trying to fight wars, and it should not attempt to do so. One of the unfortunate things that occurred under Secretary-General Boutros Boutros-Ghali, in my judgment, was that he so blurred the concept of peace-keeping that it came to mean everything, including real war. I think the UN has been effective at traditional peacekeeping, classical peacekeeping, which is not fighting wars but separating combatants once an agreement has been reached. Traditional peacekeeping was not carried out under chapter 7 of the UN Charter, which authorizes the use of force; it was carried out under chapter 6, which involves a different kind of international cooperation. I think it is a mistake to attempt to mobilize fighting forces through the United Nations where you have, as in Somalia, or as initially in Bosnia, troops from twenty-eight nations, speaking languages which are mutually incomprehensible, trying to implement tactics which cannot be integrated.

There are other things the UN can do very well. I think, for example, the UN high commissioner on refugees does an indispensable job in providing shelter, food, and sustenance for refugees who would otherwise perish. So I think we need to distinguish between what is likely to work and what is not likely to work.

Q: If, as you say, Mexico could slide from the path of democratic capitalism, what do you think would be the causes of this?

Jeane J. Kirkpatrick

The causes of it? I think Mexico has a way to go in democratization. The list of emerging countries I mentioned was Jeffrey Garten's, but I found that it had merit and was interesting. I think that Mexico is engaged in industrial development. Right now, it seems to be engaged as well in increasing inclusiveness in its political system. There has been a lot of resistance to that, as we all know, but there are also increasing pressures for greater inclusiveness. NAFTA, for example, mobilizes people and provides them with new opportunities, new hope, and new encouragement for a broader participation in society. NAFTA is likely to encourage democratization in Mexico.

Q: Could you give implications for American policy and perhaps a short evaluation of our inolvement in Bosnia?

Jeane J. Kirkpatrick

Bosnia is as an example of what can go wrong in this time of very rapid political change, even in the heart of Europe. I have followed the Bosnian conflict's evolution and the West's response closely. It is obviously a tragic situation and continues to be dangerous. I believe its causes are the traditional causes of war. I know many people think ethnic conflict caused the Bosnian war, but ethnic differences do not necessarily cause war. The desire of the Slovaks to separate from the Czech Republic did not lead to war. It led to a referendum, a peaceful settlement and, ultimately, to separation.

I think the conflict in former Yugoslavia was a consequence of the quick resort to force by the leadership of Serbia, namely Slobodan Milosevic, president of Serbia, and of his determined effort to maintain control over former Yugoslavia. At the very beginning of that conflict, Milosevic refused to permit a Croatian—the nationality whose turn it was to become president of Yugoslavia—to become head of the executive council and president of the national government. This was the first heavy-handed denial of what had been a traditional right to the states that made up Yugoslavia. Then you see Milosevic's withdrawal of the statute of autonomy for Kosovo and for the ethnic Albanians who are Muslims. Then you see him sending troops into Slovenia and Croatia after they held referenda in which their citizens declared in favor of independence. After declaring independence, the Yugoslav National Army, largely Serbian troops under the leadership of Milosevic, attacked Slovenia and Croatia. I think we see in the Yugoslav situation a classical, heavy-handed popular dictator in Milosevic, and an even worse dictator in Radovan Karadzic in the Republic of Srpska. I believe there is no place for them in contemporary Europe or in the contemporary world, for that matter. I believe the problems will begin to be solved when they have stepped down and been replaced by leaders willing to govern by democratic rules.

NOTES

1. Michael Novak, *The Spirit of Democratic Capitalism* (New York: American Enterprise Institute; and Simon & Schuster, 1982).

2. Jeffrey Garten, *The Big Ten: The Big Emerging Markets and How They Will Change Our Lives* (New York: Basic Books/ HarperCollins Publishers, 1998).

3. Jeane J. Kirkpatrick, *Dictatorships and Double Standards: Rationalism and Reason in Politics* (New York: Simon & Schuster, 1982).

4. Nicholas Kristof and Sheryl WuDunn, *China Wakes: The Struggle for the Soul of a Rising Power* (New York: Vintage Books, 1995).

Chapter 25

United States Global Policy: Toward an Agile Strategy

David M. Abshire

The end of the cold war poses immense challenges to United States global leadership. In this new strategic landscape, the simple, straightforward foreign and defense policies of the cold-war years no longer apply. The United States needs a new, adaptable, more classical approach for the post–cold war era, a strategy that remains faithful to fundamental U.S. national interests while offering innovation, greater freedom of action, and a new sense of priorities.

So far, few signs of such a strategy have emerged. From vague discussions of a "new world order"—quickly disowned by the administration using the term—to hopeful thoughts of democratic "enlargement," the United States has not enunciated a truly coherent strategic framework for the post–cold war era. Its absence can be felt powerfully in places such as Korea, Bosnia, Haiti, and Iraq, where debates on foreign-policy priorities have taken place in an almost eerie vacuum of larger thinking about the U.S. role in the world and the strategies required to serve it.

I believe the new U.S. approach should be characterized by agility—an agile strategy for the creative use of power and the achievement of peace. The dictionary defines *agile* with such terms as "mentally and physically nimble; quick; brisk; deft." This is what an agile strategy demands: in American thinking and action, a new flexibility and nimbleness; the ability to move quickly to take advantage of new opportunities or to head off rapidly emerging dangers; and, guiding it all, a keen long-range vision. I hasten to add that by *agility* I do not mean a flexible abandonment of core U.S. national interests and values; I mean only a less rigid and more forward-looking means of securing and sustaining them. The United States, as the leader of alliances and the chief member of other international institutions, must have consistent strategic direction, but it must also be capable of responding to new circumstances and sudden events.

In this essay, I define this new strategy and its basic elements. I discuss how it applies to key regions. I note what a strategy of agility says about key U.S. policy decisions such as criteria for intervention and international economic policy, and what it says about military-force structure and economic power, including the new and rather overwhelming financial dimensions. And I examine what kind of world this strategy aims in the long run to create—a world of greater stability, prosperity, justice, and peace, encouraged, underwritten, and enforced by the community of nations, and led by a powerful and more agile United States. It is now clear that if such a world is indeed possible, only the United States is capable of leading its creation.

A New World

To other countries it might not appear that the United States would have difficulty in dealing with the end of the cold war. After all, this historic shift represents a decisive victory for America, its allies, and their values. The United States is now the single greatest power in the community of nations, and it therefore seemingly ought to be able to act with even greater authority than it could during the cold war.

And yet, as the crises and national debates on Somalia, Bosnia, Iraq, and fast-track authority suggest, U.S. leaders and the American public have found the present era baffling. They appear unwilling to join in building President George Bush's so-called new world order, and instead seem bent on fostering new world disorder. Congress and the presidency, under both Bush and Bill Clinton, have frequently been divided, and Abraham Lincoln's warning that a house divided against itself cannot stand applies even more to foreign policy than to domestic policy. Partly as a result of these divisions, U.S. actions sometimes appear random and confused. The United States seems unsteady, unsure of its role, its interests, and the kind of world it wants to help create.

The reason is not hard to find. The cold war, for all its complexity and danger, posed a relatively straightforward threat—a linear division between East and West—to Western allied interests. The Soviet Union and its geopolitical allies endangered the security of western Europe, the Middle East, and Northeast Asia. Moscow's threat and America's response created a bipolar situation—two superpowers frozen in confrontation, with much of the world divided between their competing alliances.

U.S. leaders had little difficulty locating a foreign-policy doctrine for such an environment. Their obvious response was containment—the effort to deter the Soviet threat and contain the growth of the Soviet empire, with the hope that eventually the inefficient Soviet bureaucracy would collapse upon itself. Bretton Woods, the Marshall Plan, the North Atlantic Treaty Organization (NATO), other alliances, and global foreign aid were all part of this doctrine. Although fierce debates raged over the scope and nature of containment—whether, for example it demanded American intervention in Vietnam—very few Americans questioned its basic premises, because they perceived the Soviets as a clear and present danger.

Today we see a dramatic reversal of these trends, a shift to a far more complex, multipolar, interdependent world order operating under the novel influence of the information, business, and financial revolutions. This new strategic landscape is not rigid and linear but highly fluid and unpredictable. In most cases, threats in this era are diffuse and unclear. There is no equivalent of the Soviet Union, which posed a large and obvious danger to the world community. Thus it is harder to martial a consensus on smaller threats that do emerge.

At the same time, the range of "security" issues that confronts the U.S. government has expanded. Environmental and new economic issues have joined trade as top national priorities. The cold war's simple focus on military and defense issues is a thing of the past. Today, for example, the American public, many members of Congress, and even some top executive-branch officials might have a hard time answering the questions of which constitutes a greater security threat to the United States—the trade deficit with Japan, the Southeast Asian meltdown, or North Korean nuclear proliferation. Indeed, if one were to name the single biggest new player in world affairs since the collapse of the Soviet Union, it would have to be the awesome power of global financial markets—markets that are now largely beyond the control of central bankers and governments, and that almost brought down Mexico and may have reversed their own Asian miracle. This expanded definition of security is another factor that intensifies the complications of the present era. The fact that Treasury Secretary Robert Rubin brought Defense Secretary William Cohen with him to testify before Congress in the wake of the South Korean financial collapse well illustrates the new inclusion of global financial markets in discussions of security. More than ever, markets constrain and influence the range of options from which world leaders can choose when making decisions.

This evolving definition of security is in part a product of the information age—the increasing importance of information in all aspects of society. The implications of the information age for global politics are still poorly understood, but it is clear that they mean greater complexity, greater confusion, a renewed focus on nonmilitary issues, and a closer study of the interactions of military and nonmilitary dimensions of our world.

In addition to the quickly developing challenges posed by the new world order, many dangers are of a long-term, rather than short-term, nature. They do not develop all at once, but gradually, over time. The slow spread of nuclear, chemical, and biological weapons, the gradual deterioration of the environment, and the inexorable growth of world population pose long-term threats. And apart from some military confrontations, such as those between the two Koreas and between Iraq and Kuwait, few current dangers have the character of direct military threats by an aggressor. Most, indeed all, conflicts the United States has confronted since the end of the anomalous Gulf War arise more indirectly through such phenomena as ethnic hostility, resource depletion, or proliferation. Quite clearly, proliferation of chemical, biological, and nuclear weapons is potentially one of the greatest threats to the United States and its allies as we move into the twenty-first century.

The single most fundamental aspect of the current strategic environment is this: The United States and indeed all of the major powers have entered a strategic interregnum. At the end of an era, when the major foreign-policy doctrines of the cold war have not yet been replaced, this is not surprising. Massive changes are under way in world politics, and it is not yet certain where they will lead—to a new hostility and balance-of-power politics among the great powers, to a renewed East-West competition, to a more peaceful and stable concert of powers, or to some other outcome.

At such a time, it would be wrong to adopt a rigid strategic doctrine. Such a doctrinal strategy is appropriate when the threat is clear and singular, not diffused and diverse, when the U.S. purpose is obvious and well understood, not vague and controversial. It took several years for containment to emerge as the dominant U.S. approach to the cold war. Historically, strategic interregnums tend to last for five to fifteen years. But the United States—the only remaining superpower for the moment—faced with a disorderly and unpredictable world does not have that kind of time to get its strategic house in order. The end of the established order of the cold war actually increased the requirement for a constructive and balancing U.S. role in the world. U.S. leaders today need a bridging strategy—one that keeps the U.S. leadership on course during this immensely turbulent time while recognizing that the fundamental contours of this era remain to be set.

An Agile Strategy

Taken together, these various aspects of the post–cold war era make it enormously difficult for the United States or any other nation to deal with the new kind of security threats it faces. A single-minded, linear strategy such as containment is no longer appropriate. America needs an approach to the world that is consistent with its tradition of leadership and protects and advances its vital national interests, but that also builds for U.S. leaders unprecedented freedom of action and innovation in meeting the challenges of the new era. A strategy of agility meets these criteria.

It would be a mistake for U.S. decision makers to lock themselves into a fixed architecture or doctrine that would rule out certain outcomes. We are dealing with a highly contingent world. Certainly, beyond the turn of the century, the newly emerging superpower will be China, but a new doctrine of containment aimed at China would have the effect of encouraging the very tensions and hostilities that the United States wants to avoid. At the same time, a new U.S. global strategy that assumes the end of great-power conflict and focuses on peacekeeping in ethnic conflicts and humanitarian rescue alone—the strategy in favor in much of Washington at the beginning of the Clinton presidency —would be equally dangerous. If the United States does not have the kind of military power at the turn of the century to deal with and influence situations that would upset the great-power balance, it will have created the climate for great-power conflict.

In the history of military strategy, there have generally been two approaches. One approach consisted of deception, maneuver, and mobility, often adopted by military geniuses who had to win with inferior resources. The other was a strategy of attrition—more frontal and direct, intended to wear down an opponent through direct pressures. The first obtains a multiplier effect by upsetting the opponent. The second tries to wear him down in a more costly way on the broad front. World War I was generally a war of attrition. Vietnam was also such a war, but in a different way—attrition in guerrilla warfare through the infamous kill ratios of Secretary of Defense Robert McNamara. The cold war basically also amounted to a war of attrition—in military preparedness, economic vitality, and popular will. Ironically, it was President Ronald Reagan's oft-maligned "Star Wars" strategy (the Strategic Defense Initiative), along with the high-technology conventional innovations of the Carter and Reagan Defense Departments, that reintroduced strategic agility into the cold-war standoff. Moscow could no longer compete technologically. This maneuver was brilliant and decisive, regardless of whether Reagan's strategic defense was fully workable as he conceived it.

What the United States needs today is a grand strategy based on the classical principles of maneuver rather than the recent American tradition of attrition warfare. It needs an agile strategy that provides freedom of action and comparative advantages in areas where U.S. technology provides multiplier effects. U.S. foreign policy should be such that we do not squander our military and its precious (and declining) resources in attrition situations devoid of agility.

What do I mean by a "strategy of agility"? In the broadest sense, I have in mind a strategy that would do what any foreign policy should—define the truly vital U.S. national interests and use those as the enduring anchors of its approach. Most Americans agree that these interests exist in Europe, including in some eastern European countries now seeking entrance into NATO; in Northeast Asia; and in the Middle East. In other words, the strategy would first lay out those areas in which it will not be flexible, where the American commitment to allies remains steadfast even after the cold war. The United States should be agile in promoting those interests, but inflexible in abandoning them. This allows the agile strategy to become anchored.

I have in mind, too, a strategy that would return to classical formulations of the proper uses of power to influence the behavior of U.S. opponents and, indeed, allies. A sound strategy is proactive, not reactive, and it seeks to be anticipatory and create the desired strategic environment. The perfect victory in most classical military treatises, from Sun Tzu to Clausewitz, was to win without fighting. This involves, however, changing the opponent's will in advance by demonstrating the will to fight as well as the potential capability to win. This fundamental seems to have been ignored in the post–cold war debate over policy, a debate that has too often misdiagnosed the issue of when and when not to use force. Such a narrow focus guarantees a reactive policy.

The United States brilliantly fought and won the Gulf War, but how much better it would have been to have deterred it! For forty-two years, NATO deterred the Kremlin without firing a shot. It achieved Sun Tzu's perfect victory by the strength of its cohesion despite the Kremlin's attempts to divide the alliance. In the process, NATO used power and not force. Hitler faced no such united alliance of democracies in developing his power to World War II, nor did Slobodan Milosevic in the former Yugoslavia until late in the game.

Yale historian Donald Kagan, in his book *On the Origins of War and the Preservation of Peace,* argues that "peace does not keep itself." A nation wishing to preserve peace must not only maintain strength sufficient to make its deterrent power credible, but also must "act realistically while there is time," as opposed to avoiding the burden "until there is no choice but war." Power and influence are proactive; force is inherently reactive, coming into play when peace is lost because of failure to use power effectively.

Beyond the protection of a few unwavering interests through the effective use of power, a strategy of agility would maximize U.S. freedom of action and the success of U.S. foreign policy in several ways. First and most important, as I have suggested, a strategy of agility would be proactive and creative, not reactive. This means, first of all, cultivating a long-range vision in the government—studying trends, anticipating contingencies, and using the long-range analysis offices in the various departments to do their intended jobs. Without a long-range vision, the United States could wind up reacting to events, as it has been doing since the end of the cold war, rather than shaping them. A long-range vision is essential to deal with long-range challenges. But being proactive also means thinking in the long term about U.S. *capabilities* as well. Even if Washington understands future threats perfectly, that understanding will not count for much if it does not have the capability in its military-force structure to exercise power.

Second, a strategy of agility recognizes the need to strengthen the domestic roots of national power. In the long run, it is domestic strength that will determine whether the United States can implement a strategy of agility—and whether it is prepared for whatever new era, be it primarily competitive or cooperative, that emerges from the strategic interregnum. One element of domestic strength is a strong defense policy driven by investment in military needs and not in the domestic political requirements of congressional constituents. Another critical part of the revitalization of American strength is eliminating fiscal deficits and increasing investments and savings. Otherwise, beyond the turn of the century, America will encounter a new period of international and national financial vulnerability. Another element of national power is the enormous potential and influence represented by twenty-first-century technologies in areas ranging from telecommunications to medicine to military weaponry. Such technological mastery is especially critical given the emerging so-called revolution in military affairs, which will offer profound military advantages to those countries best able to harness the information age for defense purposes.

Third, and finally, a strategy of agility would limit U.S. actions in the service of nonvital interests by laying out clear criteria for intervention. The United States cannot adopt all the world's problems as its own. It must choose its fights and missions carefully, determining where the U.S. role would make the greatest contribution. Otherwise, the American public reaction to debacles such as Somalia will undermine the political foundations of U.S. foreign policy.

Thus, the elements of a strategy of agility involve:

- a recognition of the complex, nonlinear challenges of the post–cold war era
- a clear definition of vital national interests—the anchors of strategy
- a long-term vision
- national strength
- the application of key elements of U.S. power to carefully chosen commitments and interventions
- a commitment to get the U.S. financial house in order to ensure freedom of action

In more specific terms, I see the application of agile strategy as having eight distinct elements: proper use of power; defining national interests; setting clear criteria for intervention; safeguarding European anchors; preserving a Middle East balance of power; maintaining a U.S. balancing role in the Pacific; developing a defense investment strategy that capitalizes on the technology revolution and counters the threat of ballistic missiles; and promoting leadership, character, and education.

An agile strategy would assume that the purposes of U.S. foreign policy are straightforward, in the short term, to promote U.S. interests and respond to threats to them, and in the long term, to create a world in which U.S. interests thrive. The long-term goal reflects the idealistic elements of U.S. foreign policy, such as promotion of democracy and free trade. Foreign policy should recognize that the balance between the two—between short-term, pragmatic, realistic concerns and longer-range, more idealistic hopes—is an important and difficult one to strike, and that such a balance is especially important during a strategic interregnum.

Some in Washington today refuse to recognize the distinction between short-term realism and long-term idealism, regularly employing crusading language about democracy and even advocating massive interventions to force democracy where it is not ready to bloom. An agile strategy would make this distinction and would more seriously prioritize U.S. foreign-policy actions. In this strategic interregnum, the United States should not take short-term actions that foreclose long-term aspirations for a more peaceful and democratic world, nor should it expend precious resources on attempts to make those long-term aspirations a reality in the short term.

An Agile Strategy in Context

An agile strategy would draw insights from all the major schools of thought of international relations. It would treat the theories not as self-contained, mutually exclusive explanations of world affairs, but as a rich menu of thinking that as a whole can inform U.S. foreign policy.

The insights from realism would offer the foundation of assumptions for an agile strategy. World politics remains a modified form of anarchy in which power and influence are at stake. Therefore, conflicting national interests are a permanent and inevitable aspect of international relations. This does not mean that war among the great powers is unavoidable; it does not mean that the rule of law cannot be established in specific areas; it does not mean that states (or people) are necessarily more inclined toward competition than cooperation. What it does mean is that military conflict—subnational, regional, or global—cannot be ruled out for the foreseeable future, and that economic competition among the world's major powers will remain a permanent feature of world affairs. An agile strategy must therefore provide the United States with the ability to operate in a world where military conflict is always possible and economic competition is inevitable. The economic competition, however, becomes more constructive rather than destructive the more markets are mutually open, and not mercantilistic, thus providing a "win-win" situation.

Realism also suggests that balances of power tend to preserve peace, and imbalances of power invite conflict. In the nuclear age, the relationship between power imbalances and war may not be as simple as it once was, but it would be a mistake to assume that the relationship has disappeared altogether. The insights of realism therefore call for an agile strategy that works to preserve balances of power in the key regions of the world.

Finally, realism offers a cautionary note about foreign commitments. It enjoins national leaders to keep their ends and means in balance and to avoid global crusades, which almost always prove self-defeating—for example, rapid worldwide democratization, or unquestioning anticommunism in every corner. Thus, an agile strategy must recognize the limits to American power and must outline goals for foreign policy that operate within those limits. This, again, requires taking seriously the distinction between short-term and long-term aims: Long-run strategy can be more idealistic and can seek gradual transformation of world politics, but in the short term, pragmatism and prioritization must reign supreme.

An agile strategy, however, does not stop with realism. It makes use of the idealistic and institutional schools of international-relations thought that have grown in the last thirty years. This is especially true of the central tenet of idealism, the notion that ideas count in international relations. America's democratic system and ideals exercise a critical influence on its foreign policy—the making of that policy, its appeal, and its effectiveness—just as Japan's unique interpretation of capitalism and China's central Communist rule influence those countries' relationships with other states. Whether or not we believe, as Francis Fukuyama has argued, that world history has become a relatively unilinear trend toward free markets and democratic systems, it is clear that the democratic ideal has at least temporarily infected a much larger percentage of the world's population. It is just as clear that this carries substantial implications, largely positive, for U.S. national interests.

Apart from (and to some degree in contrast to) democracy and free markets, the category of ideas and identities to be found under the broad heading of culture also has powerful implications for world politics. Here the starkest model has been proposed by Samuel Huntington, who sees a coming "clash of civilizations" produced by cultural differences in political and economic matters. And here again, whether or not one agrees fully with Huntington's thesis, one cannot deny that cultural habits, identities, and biases exercise an effect in international relations—an effect that cannot be captured by looking at all actors as equivalent "black boxes" whose political structure, economic organization, and cultural norms are irrelevant to their behavior in the global community. In an information age, it could be true that the relationship of ideas to policy is closer than it has ever been.

In addition to the insights of idealism, an agile strategy must recognize that in many new areas, serious emergent problems and challenges must be addressed and hopefully solved on a cooperative transnational basis and with proper recognition of interdependence. This is not a modification of realism in favor of some sort of one-world idealism. Rather, it is the supremely realistic view that the perils as well as the promises of a range of global trends with revolutionary implications can be handled only transnationally, which means through U.S. leadership. These revolutionary trends include changes in demography, telecommunications, and world financial markets, and the increasing salience of international organized crime. Nongovernmental actors become more important than ever. Hence, ideas and even ideals count, and the various instruments of public diplomacy as well as private organizations remain important in propagating such ideas in the post–cold war world.

Finally, an agile strategy—which calls for continued strong U.S. engagement in world affairs—rejects isolationism and, ultimately, protectionism in the strongest terms. Historical U.S. recourse to isolationism helped to bring on world wars that demanded a massive and costly U.S. response. But the recurring theme of isolationism in the history of U.S. foreign policy does carry an important lesson: It reinforces the need, recognized in realism, to set clear and defensible priorities in foreign policy. Poll after poll has demonstrated conclusively that the American people, accustomed to world involvement by half a century of global leadership, are not isolationist. But they do expect their public officials to distinguish between what is critical to U.S. security and what is merely important, and they demand that their national leaders commit U.S. blood and treasure only in the former cases. Above all, our strategy must be agile and and we must not be bogged down around the world where we lose the initiative and have no exit strategy. In Bosnia, for instance, we were right to make the original commitment of ground troops. However, we should have used the following year to convince our European allies that they should lead the subsequent peacekeeping on the ground, while the United States provided vital logistical, air, and naval support. It was in our failure to do this that we lost our agility.

In terms of the core foreign-policy issues confronting the United States—such as promotion of democracy, nonproliferation of weapons, and stabilization of world financial markets—an agile strategy could suggest that although all remain important U.S. interests, the United States should avoid absolutist, crusading policies that violate the spirit of pragmatism and limits that lies at the strategy's core.

The agile strategy's appreciation of the role of ideas in world politics, for example, would suggest strong support for the goal of democracy and market economies. Yet the transitions of the former Communist countries offer a very strong lesson—the importance of ethical behavior, sound business practices, and the rule of law in the correct functioning of market economies. In their absence, the agile strategy's philosophy of limits would establish strict bounds to this support. Instead, it would advocate defending democracy in established U.S. allies such as South Korea and Japan and helping those countries that choose to become democratic to make the transition, but not attempting to enforce democratic norms on any country. Thus, an agile strategy would support continued U.S. security pledges to traditional allies; it would support strong transitional aid to new democracies of eastern and central Europe; it would support institutions designed to spread the word of democracy such as the Voice of America, Radio Liberty, Radio Free Europe, and Radio Free Asia. Indeed, failure to mount extensive broadcasting at Iraq is a great oversight in our policy. Furthermore, an agile strategy would not support the attempted imposition of democracy through policies such as peacemaking interventions (as compared to peacekeeping) in Somalia or Haiti, or denial of most-favored-nation status to China. Again, the agile strategy is making a distinction between short- and long-term strategies, being realistic and limited in the short-term steps taken to promote long-term goals.

The agile strategy's perspective on the issues of ethnic war and nonproliferation is similar. Responding to both these threats is a very long term proposition. Although both dominate the U.S. national-security agenda today, it is important to keep in mind—and the foundation of realism that undergirds the agile strategy urges us to remember—that they could slip to a less prominent status if major tensions emerged once again among the great powers. In both cases, therefore, it is important not to overreact; not to confuse peripheral interests with core ones; not to initiate new crusades or absolute foreign-policy doctrines; and most of all not to undermine long-term U.S. foreign-policy options or defense preparedness in the service of short-term interests. An agile strategy would therefore be hesitant about a major U.S. military commitment to the Balkans that is not clearly disciplined and circumscribed.

This sounds much like common sense. But these issues become far more difficult and complex when the short term crosses the long term, and that occurs over the issue of precedent. Advocates of strong responses in places such as the Balkans and North Korea ask a troubling question: By not responding to Serbian aggression or North Korean proliferation, does the world community undermine its efforts to establish reasonably clear norms of behavior? Those who favor strong U.S. actions in the Balkans and Iraq do so not because they refuse to consider the long term, but precisely because they consider it. Having done so, they conclude that the world community must act strongly to establish international rules of the road, to set precedents that will be followed in both the short and long terms. Hence the forthright world reaction to Iraq's 1990 invasion of Kuwait—a crystal-clear signal that such overt aggression would not be tolerated, a signal hopefully not lost on other would-be hegemons.

There is no magic answer to this dilemma of time frames. It demands a careful assessment of the precedent-setting importance of each case, and the risks of a less than absolute means of resolving the issue. In Korea, for example, the precedent the world has set seems just barely acceptable: Overt proliferation in contravention of Nuclear Nonproliferation Treaty commitments will not be tolerated, but proliferators may receive some benefits for surrendering their nuclear programs. Provided the admittedly flawed Agreed Framework is fully implemented, this compromise—the best of several bad alternatives—respects the short-term imperatives of nonproliferation without sacrificing it to long-term interests such as U.S. relations with China, Japan, and South Korea and the sustainability of the U.S. defense program. It therefore represents an example of how an agile strategy would work.

Applying the Agile Strategy:
Asia, Europe, and the Middle East

An agile strategy has specific implications for U.S. strategy in each of the three cornerstone regions for U.S. foreign policy—Asia, Europe, and the Middle East.

In Asia an agile strategy would contend that Washington must be clear about where its truly vital national interests lie—declaring where it will not be flexible or selective, and where it is determined to respond to aggression with an absolute commitment so publicly acclaimed as to add to deterrence. It was, after all, American uncertainty that encouraged Kim Jong-Il to believe that he could attack South Korea in 1950; the United States must not make the same mistake again. In Asia the list of vital U.S. interests includes the security of Japan and South Korea and the peaceful resolution of the disputes over the Taiwan Strait and the Spratly Islands. To defend these interests Washington must state unequivocally that Northeast Asia remains an area of vital U.S. national interest, that a firm U.S. commitment to the region will remain an anchor of the agile strategy.

Perhaps most important, defending U.S. national interests in Northeast Asia increasingly means encouraging respect for global norms on the part of China. China is the single most important emerging power in the world today. In twenty years its combination of economic prowess, military strength, and sheer size may have no equivalent in the world, yet China's future is by no means determined. It could adopt either hostile or accommodating attitudes toward regional disputes over Taiwan and the Spratly Islands, and it could suffer from the financial difficulties that have swept through the rest of Asia. The United States and its allies will play an important role in shaping China's behavior as it matures and emerges as a truly dominant regional power.

A second aspect of an agile strategy, being proactive, demands a long-term view of U.S. and allied interests and efforts to address threats that arise only gradually. In Asia, one can detect several of these creeping dangers. The most obvious is nuclear proliferation, already well under way in North Korea and South Asia. A second relates to possible conflicts over resources or a regional environmental catastrophe produced by rapid, unregulated economic growth in China, Southeast Asia and, eventually, the Russian Far East. A third is outbreaks of ethnic hostility, not only in places where conflict is already endemic but also among the major powers throughout the Asia-Pacific region. A fourth, given the economic turmoil spreading throughout Asia, is the delegitimization of some Asian governments, followed by internal revolt. A more proactive U.S. strategy in Asia would take steps to combat each of these growing threats.

An agile strategy would also have important things to say about U.S. policy toward Europe and the NATO alliance. Most important, an agile strategy reemphasizes the importance of the NATO alliance structure—to keep the United States anchored in Europe and to promote multilateral solutions to regional problems. Some observers have already written the alliance's obituary, claiming that without the galvanizing threat from Moscow, it has no purpose, despite its resolve in Bosnia.

Writers who make such a claim do not understand history. NATO was a political alliance before it was a military pact; it had a reason for being in the context of western Europe's striving for peace even before there was a Soviet threat. NATO's magic had always been institutional—providing a structured, disciplined organization and a set of established procedures and routines through which European disputes could be controlled and from which a more unified transatlantic voice could emerge.

It is important to recall the magnitude of what this coordinating mechanism has already achieved in Europe. From prehistory through 1945, Europe—from England across to Russia—was among the world's most conflict-prone regions. Western Europe was the cradle of two devastating world wars, and it formed the tense dividing line between East and West during the cold war. Now war is alien to the European mind-set, and the continent has moved boldly toward the deepest economic and political integration of any region in the world.

In this context, it becomes obvious that NATO enlargement must be disciplined by the more fundamental issue of keeping NATO's institutional and procedural routines vibrant and effective. NATO is appropriately offering membership in the North Atlantic Council to Poland, Hungary, and the Czech Republic. These nations are part of Europe and deserve membership in the alliance that defines Europe. From a more pragmatic standpoint, extending NATO's political umbrella to those countries will help extend stability to eastern Europe, making the region less prone to Russian expansion; otherwise, a zone of instability and uncertainty will be left on Europe's doorstep, an area that has played a major role in generating wars throughout history. The desire for NATO membership on the part of these countries played a major role in encouraging them to avoid the sort of ethnic warfare that has broken out in the Balkans and Central Africa.

At the same time, however, keeping the alliance open-ended will end up in dilution of the alliance. Nineteen or maybe twenty-two members around the table might obtain unanimity, but can twenty-five or thirty? Any one member can block a decision. The end game of NATO enlargement must be thought through with a long-term perspective. Keeping the process open-ended is a sure way of destroying the agility of this anchor. Secretary of State Madeline Albright has urged the alliance to consider the spread of nuclear, biological, and chemical weapons as the new "unifying threat" that would galvanize all member states together. However, even as currently configured, NATO has lost the agility to deal with such a threat, as evidenced by its inability to keep itself in step against Iraq in early 1998. Clearly, it is not disciplined enough as it is.

NATO is an alliance of Europe, not Eurasia. Other institutions can spread their reach from the Atlantic to the Urals, but to maintain its purpose and cohesion, NATO should remain an alliance of the West. An agile strategy demands that U.S. planners think creatively and proactively and recognize the danger of a rapid and unlimited expansion of NATO which would risk ruling out future options for East-West cooperation by symbolically branding Russia an adversary before it has decided to become one. This then will inevitably lead to concessions to Russia bearing on the decision-making process of the alliance. Again, the 1998 Iraqi crisis is telling. Russian Foreign Minister Yevgeny Primakov actively worked against U.S. leadership, demonstrating how geopolitical interests can still divide Russia and the West, despite the fall of Communism. A separate treaty of nonaggression and friendship has been negotiated between Russia and the alliance. Russia can participate in Partnership for Peace and in Western peacekeeping missions (as it is doing in Bosnia), and the West should redouble its efforts to assist the Russian transition to democracy and free markets. But we should be left under no illusions about future NATO membership for Russia.

The Middle East is the easiest of the three core regions to discuss, because the three U.S. regional priorities there fall squarely in the purview of an agile strategy: containment of regional aggression; a security commitment to Israel; and strong support for the peace process.

During the present strategic interregnum, military threats posed by regional aggressors are perhaps the defining security challenges of the era. The Middle East boasts two such hegemons—Iraq and Iran—and two other military states, Libya and (to a lesser extent) Syria. Deterrence of military aggression, terrorism, and proliferation by these actors should remain a cornerstone of U.S. regional policy, and increasingly this means close U.S. partnership with moderate Arab states such as Egypt, Saudi Arabia, and Kuwait.

A natural outgrowth of this policy is a continuing U.S. security commitment to Israel. Such a commitment rests on more than three decades of close U.S.-Israeli partnership. As free-market democracies, the countries have a natural affinity. And now, more than ever, the U.S. alliance is a critical element in the peace process, helping to set Israeli minds at ease about their security as they make compromises for the sake of peace. But at the same time, Israeli Prime Minister Benjamin Netanyahu's efforts to break Yitzhak Rabin's momentum had serious repercussions for the Middle East and helped to destroy the Gulf War coalition that President Bush put together.

The nimbleness demanded by agile strategy will be most evident in these rapidly shifting contours of the peace process. It is in the peace process itself that all the elements of agile strategy—and all the hopes for the region—come together like spokes on a wheel. The peace process is the apex of short- and long-term policy—the justification for short-term support and the route by which long-term progress toward U.S. and allied interests can be made. The hope it embodies for easing the Arab-Israeli standoff will, in the long run, provide the best antidote to the growth of fundamentalism. And a real transformation of the security context in the region will help, in the very long run, to eliminate the risk of war and thus relieve the United States of the burden of regional balancer.

Finally, in all three regions, a strategy of agility demands a clear and unambiguous set of criteria for U.S. military intervention in humanitarian or peacekeeping operations. This is less of an immediate question in Asia than in Europe or the Middle East, but the enunciation of a global standard for intervention is critical to U.S. foreign policy in all regions. If America is overcommitted to peacekeeping operations, it may not be able to respond quickly and decisively to regional provocations by such aggressors as Iraq and North Korea. Developing firm standards for peacekeeping operations will provide important indirect support for U.S. deterrent posture world-wide.

The Agile Strategy and International Economic Issues

Many elements of the agile strategy are equally applicable to U.S. global economic policy. They point to an economic strategy based on the interdependent policies of encouraging free trade abroad and investing in domestic renewal at home.

The highly fluid and mobile nature of the "new world disorder" is perhaps nowhere more apparent than in the international financial markets. In the absence of an agile strategy, the United States runs the risk of colliding with these new global markets rather than turning international financial integration to its advantage. Private markets were responsible for forcing Italy and the United Kingdom to withdraw from the European Exchange Rate Mechanism when these countries could not defend their currencies against enormous speculative pressures. The markets have frustrated almost all attempts by central banks to protect their currencies in recent years. And they reacted harshly—and instantly— to Mexico's peso crisis in December 1994 and to the Association of South East Asian Nations (ASEAN) market meltdown in late 1997.

Global capital flows have reached staggering proportions: More than a trillion dollars swirl around the planet each day, outside the control of central banks. On foreign-exchange markets alone, the volume of daily trading had increased from $20 billion to $30 billion in 1982 to more than $1 trillion in 1996. Daily global trading of bonds and securities is accelerating as rapidly.

The United States has eliminated its budget deficit, but it will rise sharply in the year 2001, at the very time there are major new requirements to finance defense modernization and acquisitions. During this same period, the United States will also have to finance the retirement of the baby boomers. Through the concurrent arrival of these two massive, yet inflexible, costs, the United States runs the risk of losing freedom of action—the basic feature of a carefully fashioned agile strategy. Miscalculation and aggression can result from this loss of freedom.

In the short term, the loss of freedom means higher costs to maintain U.S. economic activity. The United States will have to pay more to finance its deficits, especially when investors have a greater choice of high-return investment options across the world. It will mean driving capital formation offshore, and with it the possibilities for economic gain from innovation and commercial follow-through. In the longer term, the loss of freedom of action means the risk of forfeiting the leadership role that the United States has carved out for itself in the last several decades. If the United States insists on enfeebling itself by carrying large and growing external deficits, how can it expect to maintain its position of dominance in the age of markets?

If the United States is destined to lead in this new age of global finance, it must devise and enact an agile strategy that brings it economy into equilibrium; that recognizes the growing power of global market forces; that stresses international economic engagement as the key to domestic renewal; that adapts to the onset of the knowledge revolution in economic activity; and that positions the United States for continued prosperity and economic dynamism in the next century.

In the drive to promote free trade, an agile strategy would offer much the same counsel as it does on other issues of global significance and long-term scale: Keep in mind the ultimate goal—a world of unfettered trade—but recognize that it cannot be achieved all at once, and avoid pushing the issue too quickly in a manner that might promote a backlash. The symptoms are already apparent in Washington. Calls for mercantilism, economic nationalism, isolationism, and disengagement are resonating on both extremes of the political spectrum. As with political issues, this line between short- and long-term interests in economic issues is a tricky one to manage. Pushing hard for Japan and China to open their markets, for example, serves both goals even as it risks highlighting short-term concerns too much and sparking hostile reactions.

The agile strategy's emphasis on the need for U.S. domestic renewal also takes on special importance in an economic context. Addressing such issues as the U.S. budget deficit, the crises in Social Security and Medicare, the future of U.S. primary and secondary education, and related social issues such as the state of the American family will quite simply determine whether the United States can meet the economic challenges of the twenty-first century.

A Sound Defense Investment Strategy

If the United States is to have an agile strategy that continues to promote and defend U.S. national interests abroad, it needs the military tools to do the job. It needs, in other words, an agile military to go along with its agile foreign and economic policies. Current trends, however, are running in a dangerous direction—one of declining U.S. modernization, readiness and, ultimately, national security.

It is clear that the post–cold war era places onerous new burdens on the U.S. military. U.S. forces are involved in forward presence, peacekeeping, humanitarian rescues, and combat missions in dozens of countries across the globe. Increasingly, American armed forces are required not merely to man the ramparts of freedom, as they did during the cold war, but also to play important roles in a host of regional wars, ethnic conflicts, and natural disasters. As their numbers decline, U.S. forces must do more with less, responding to crises in distant corners of the globe on short notice. An agile strategy will help address the costs of such missions by enforcing stricter criteria for intervention, but it still demands a U.S. military capable of responding to sudden emergencies anywhere in the world—on short notice and, when necessary, with overwhelming force.

These requirements of U.S. strategy in the post–cold war era make it clear what sort of military establishment America needs. It must be professional and highly trained, composed of motivated and clever soldiers able to fight high-intensity wars as well as deliver food and medicine in a humanitarian operation. It must be modern, securing information dominance and using technology rather than numbers to achieve victory. Classical military strategy always advised holding the hill, and the strategic high ground is now space. To have true agility, the military must command this highest of grounds. It must be mobile, capable of racing to global trouble spots. It must have the weapons and training necessary to respond to the growing threat of proliferation, especially of ballistic missiles and weapons of mass destruction. And organizationally, such military agility demands continued reforms in the way the services operate—jointness—as well as an enriched professional military-education system, from the service academies and ROTC to the war colleges.

With modern telecommunications dissecting military operations, U.S. forces must be able as never before to win quickly. But above all, America needs the agile power and influence of a modern, technologically sophisticated military to shape the strategic environment in advance so as to deter conflict altogether.

Unfortunately, current trends in defense policy threaten to deprive the U.S. military of all these characteristics. The core problem is the aptly named "defense train wreck," an overall funding strategy that invests heavily in current force structure and readiness at the expense of future modernization. The military's basic fighting weapons are aging rapidly; after the turn of the century, most tanks, planes, and ships will be older than the troops who operate them. And given the U.S. budget situation, with Medicare and Social Security crises waiting ominously in the wings after 2000, there is little prospect of a substantial increase in procurement funds in future years.

The crushing overuse of the U.S. military in recent years magnifies the modernization crisis. Many units have shuttled from one conflict and peacekeeping operation to the next—from Desert Storm to northern Iraq to

Somalia to Haiti to Bosnia, not to mention dozens of smaller such operations. This high rate of commitment is beginning to take a toll. The military services have had to expend funds earmarked for training, spare parts, and other operational requirements to pay the costs of the missions. As a result, the readiness of some parts of the U.S. military—still believed on the whole to be reasonably high—may soon decline precipitously.

Morale will decline as troops find themselves overcommitted, underfunded, and operating older and older equipment. New thinking and military reforms have lagged as bureaucracies have dug in to fight turf wars. The revolution in military affairs—the array of new approaches to warfare and new technologies to support them—remains largely on the drawing board. Plans to improves U.S. capabilities against weapons of mass destruction and ballistic missiles are moving forward painfully slowly.

An agile strategy therefore demands an improved defense investment strategy, one designed to take advantage of the technological opportunities offered by a new era in warfare while upgrading missile defenses and preparedness for a nuclear, chemical, or biological battlefield. Information warfare—which will enable U.S. forces to see any battlefield in great detail—is the twenty-first-century military equivalent of a strategy of agility, applicable across the range of many possible futures they might encounter, from new geopolitical challenges to peacekeeping. In the long run, this strategy demands both agile means and agile minds—the dominant, flexible military capabilities of the revolution in military affairs, and farsighted leadership in the military services and the civilian offices of the Department of Defense to acquire those technologies and develop a military doctrine for them.

A Strategy for a New Era

The agile strategy is not a panacea. It is not a comprehensive geopolitical road map to guide the United States through the next century. It is not a coherent theory of international relations. But the fact that it is not all of these things is its strength. It deliberately avoids rigid doctrines that create mind-sets that destroy agility.

But an agile strategy does offer the best guidelines for a period of strategic uncertainty such as the one the United States (and all major powers) confronts today. It respects the realistic, power-based philosophies of world politics while recognizing the need for transnational actions to deal with transnational dangers. It attempts to lay the groundwork for an era of strong great-power harmony and cooperation in which the United States must be the catalyst. It reminds the foreign-policy community of the critical dependence of its field on U.S. domestic vitality. And most of all, it encourages and demands a focus on perhaps the preeminent task for a great power in a period of transition—distinguishing vital from merely important national interests, and not allowing initiatives aimed at the latter to undermine the required focus on the former.

In the process, an agile strategy will help the United States break out of two anachronistic mind-sets. One is cold-war security thinking—the paradigm of "deterrence," the use of the threat of nuclear holocaust to prevent war, and the abandonment of the most meaningful conventional options short of such an outcome. Such tactics represent the absence of classical strategy. The other mind-set is the historical U.S. reliance on attrition rather than maneuver, fighting by wearing the opponent down in direct combat rather than through agile means. Neither of those two mind-sets is appropriate for this fluid era. In an information age, warfare through attrition conducted in front of the cameras of world news organizations is simply not an option. In an age that is witnessing the proliferation of weapons of mass destruction, U.S. leaders cannot expect that an enemy will not be able to match an attrition strategy, bomb for bomb. Both these mind-sets will have to be abandoned if an agile strategy is to emerge.

In short, an agile strategy is an approach designed for an era of complexity and uncertainty, an era whose future is only dimly apparent, an era that holds powerful aspects of both promise and peril. As such it offers a promising approach for the global policy of the next administration. Yet it is not abstract, because it should discipline the military-force structure of the United States, and indeed its domestic economic policies as they relate to remedying the defects that make the nation vulnerable. It should also discipline U.S. diplomacy, which needs to understand the many dimensions of the use of power and influence to mold the world in a more orderly way.

NOTE

Chapter 25 is adapted from David M. Abshire, "U.S. Global Policy: Toward an Agile Strategy," *Washington Quraterly* 19, no. 2 (spring 1996): 41–61, copyright © 1996 by the Center for Strategic and International Studies (CSIS) and the Massachusetts Institute of Technology.

Chapter 26

Optimism and Advice about America and the World of the Twenty-first Century

George C. McGhee

The regional presentations on the current state of the world in previous chapters are excellent; the examinations of components of American foreign policy are insightful; and my distinguished fellow contributors' analysis and proposals for strategy are sage and sound. Based on them I will try to predict, insofar as possible, the major problems facing the world as a whole as we enter the twenty-first century, and comment briefly on how they affect our beloved country.

(1) **The U.S. world position.** The United States is and will in the twenty-first century continue to be by far the most influential country in the world in all key aspects—economic, political, military, and cultural. We face no important enemies or threats; however, I do not believe we fully understand the unique and awesome opportunities and responsibilities this entails. Rome at its peak of power and the United Kingdom during the colonial period dominated the world, but both faced powerful enemies that made it necessary to wage continuous war and rule by force. Our present position gives us freedom to choose how we share resources for the betterment of our own people; for aid to countries that have suffered catastrophes; to the less developed world; and toward preserving world peace. We must keep these claims in balance if we expect to make the most of our opportunities.

(2) **U.S. leadership.** The United States, with the failure of the Communist basis for the Soviet economy and aggression, became the leading world power, without our asking. Leadership is, however, not acquired by fiat, but must be granted by those willing to be led. Germany under Hitler became the strongest military power in a world that did not accept his leadership. We have occasionally faltered and lost face, by claiming leadership in the United Nations and failing to pay our dues; by assuming the lead without proper consultation, as I believe we did in the 1998 NATO expansion; and when we neglect to fill promptly key ambassadorial posts.

The United States demonstrated real leadership in putting together in NATO the coalition of democracies that won the cold war. One of our most important tasks now, I believe, is to assure that both Russia and China, the two states that give us most concern, are allowed to regain suitable roles among the world powers. Efforts to earn leadership must be undertaken tactfully. Our success will be greatly enhanced if we have the full support of our strongest world allies, which include at least Great Britain, Germany, Japan, and Turkey.

(3) **The organization of world security.** In considering U.S. obligations in world security, I believe we should accept the following assumptions. There is, I believe, no danger in the foreseeable future of any large-scale world wars of aggression of the type that occurred in this century. The nations that made such wars are now democracies, with even Russia making progress. Democracies do not start wars and do not have the incentive or resources to start wars of aggression.

Although we must continue to work hard at preventing proliferation of nuclear weapons, I believe there is no danger that any existing major state with a large nuclear arsenal will start a nuclear war. There is concern about states that have recently acquired nuclear weapons, or may do so soon. Nuclear weapons now existing were mainly created, I believe, for defense or prestige. We made our first nuclear weapon because we feared the Germans would make one. Russia made its because we had, China because Russia had, India because China had, Pakistan because India did, and Iran is trying because Israel did. In the event of a nuclear attack there could be retaliation by the Western powers with massive weapons. No country has or would risk such destruction.

The creation of the NATO Mutual Security Pact set an example for broadening such arrangements in other trouble zones. The expansion of NATO was well intended; however, the initial steps, I believe, created serious problems that will be difficult to overcome. As first steps, the NATO members should have sought an agreement on the enlargement and obtained approval by their respective governments for the scope and cost involved, and a clear agreement on Article 5 of the NATO treaty, guaranteeing assistance for any country attacked. They should then have negotiated with the Soviets before proceeding.

In the absence of any present or likely future aggressor, and with the present severe deficits of the NATO members as well as the new invitees, there appears to be no justification for the great expenses now being discussed for infrastructure and development of next-generation weapons. However, because we are committed to enlargement, it would seem to be best to delay taking more than the three new full members accepted and to substitute, for current planning, the more moderate NATO expansion plan, Partnership for Peace. NATO now helps twenty-three nonmember states, including Russia, to train, plan, and cooperate with NATO, providing a good, inexpensive start.

Local wars based on ancient rivalries, civil wars, and revolutions will, I am afraid, continue as far ahead as we can see. We should not shed our blood on wars such as the conflicts in Central Africa, Arabs vs. Israel, the Sudan civil war, the Sri Lanka civil war, or the Kashmir civil war, backed by India and Pakistan. We should use our moral influence and prestige in assisting peace negotiations and in furnishing humanitarian aid and, in some cases, weapons to the most worthy side. We should also help to prevent and minimize such conflicts by more control of conventional arms sales, in which we create much of the problem.

Ultimately, I believe, full NATO membership should be offered to all of the Partnership for Peace countries, fulfilling the goal of security from Vancouver to Vladivostok. To end all vestiges of the cold war, the new organization should come under the policy control of the European Organization for Peace and Cooperation. Its core staff should be drawn from the present NATO, with added appropriate representation of the new members. Its budget should be adjusted to face the maximum threat received at the time.

I believe the United States should also promote the creation of mutual security pacts in other troublesome parts of the world, starting with the Middle East, including most Arab states, Turkey, Iran, and Egypt, and another pact including the countries of Southeast Asia. Looking far into the future, it is hoped that the United States might someday expand its present Asian security base in Japan and South Korea by adding a united Korea and a China united with Taiwan. These security arrangements can be different from NATO in that they could include defense not only from outside hostile countries of the past, but also from hostile nations within the treaty.

(4) **War succeeded by peace.** The twenty-first century will, I believe, increasingly be a time of peace through the melding of an international spirit of community among independent states, increasingly bound together worldwide by strong and diverse ties. This will include not only intergovernmental treaties and relations and the United Nations and affiliated organizations, but also the great expansion of media connections and the exchange of people through tourism, sports, academics, and business. Wealth gained through fair-play competition in trade and investment, under the scrutiny of the World Trade Organization and national law, will be seen as being much more valuable than conquest by force. Governments must still protect and aid businesses and workers, but under conditions of optimum freedom for individual and national effort.

PART IX

Epilogue
and
Conclusions

Overview

Edward J. Perkins

This epilogue may at first appear unusual. We couple the summarized views and hard-nosed analyses of foreign-policy practitioners and scholars of the twentieth century—experts known for their pragmatic realism as well as their commitment to our nation's ideals—with the views and perspective of one of the world's better-known artists as a writer of fiction and romance. Moreover, the writer of fiction assumes her perspective and makes her critique in this instance not from the point of view of today or from the next millennium to which this book looks, but from the vantage of two millennia past, the period of the Roman Republic.

Colleen McCullough is a modern renaissance person with an eternal mind and an understanding of the way the world has been, is, and will be. She draws on her deep comprehension of human nature and her broad knowledge of the Roman Republic and the Roman Empire, taken from the study and writing of her *The Masters of Rome*[1] series of five novels—acclaimed for their authenticity in describing that period—to provide us with "lessons learned." She is a world citizen and a citizen of Norfolk Island in the South Pacific, an astute observer of Americans who knows us from having resided and worked for a few years in the United States. Dr. McCullough offers sound advice to the people of the United States as today's superpower confronting a new world. Rome teaches us, she advises, that America's leadership can best serve this new world by remaining true to our founders' ideals and convictions.

Following the epilogue, David Boren and I endeavor to summarize the incredible range of information and the wise counsel (sometimes conflicting) that the contributors to this book have provided us, and then to make observations and draw conclusions. In doing so, we will review historically contending themes in the formulation of American foreign policy; different models mankind has devised in the past in its search for lasting peace and progress; and some of the quickly evolving and waxing and waning ideas about the shape and nature of the rapidly changing world since the end of the cold war. As you will see, in the global situation we confront, we recommend that the United States, as the world's leader and lone superpower, draw heavily on the analysis and counsel of the inimitable Dr. Henry Kissinger and other sage contributors to this book.

NOTE

1. Colleen McCullough, *The Masters of Rome,* 5 vols. (New York: Morrow & Co, 1991–97).

Chapter 27

The Lessons of the Roman Experience for the United States as a Superpower in the Twenty-first Century

Colleen McCullough

Benjamin Disraeli said, "Read no history! Nothing but biography, for that is life without theory," a view shared by Ralph Waldo Emerson. Can these two eminent gentlemen of the nineteenth century possibly be right? Clearly, they object to history as a branch of philosophy, but are they also saying that in reading biography, the reader must under no circumstances form theories out of the verity of life? I would counter their argument by saying that even the most dispassionate of biographers theorizes about the subject, and that, further, concentrating on biography to the exclusion of general history is like admitting that although there are millions of trees, there is no such thing as a forest. All individuals are the product of their times, their places, their life's conditions, and the times, the places, the life's conditions are elemental components of history.

As an entity, the city-state of Rome existed for well over two millennia—from its first king, Romulus, in 753 B.C., to the Italian duchies of the Renaissance. And for the central thousand years of its existence it stood as a superpower, first in contention with other superpowers such as Carthage, then as the sole superpower in the basin of the Mediterranean Sea. Added to which, all truly Western nations are to some extent what Rome made them, for Rome left heirs to Roman thought and systems in commerce, politics and government, law and justice, and much more.

In the very beginning, perhaps not even the Gods could have predicted the fabulous future spread out before the feet of this determined, pragmatic, immensely industrious little group of Latins who inhabited the south bank of the Tiber River from the salt beds at Ostia, which they soon controlled, to a little village on the Palatine Mount, about fourteen miles upstream from the Tiber's mouth. They were farmers and businessmen, one of the humblest among many Italian peoples and states. More peculiarly, they cherished a sense of exclusivity which led them to cultivate the idea that the founder of their race was the Homeric hero Aeneas, son of a goddess, and that therefore a divine drop of ichor coursed through their veins. They also believed that the founders of the city-state of Rome, Romulus and Remus, were the twin sons of the god Mars.

Theirs was not a warrior society. They were prepared to go to war to defend their territory and their right to conduct trade beyond its borders. For the purposes of war, they marshaled an army composed only of those Roman citizens who owned solid property. They felt that a propertied man had more incentive to fight for his homeland than a citizen who owned nothing. They had a natural talent for soldiering. More importantly, they had a propensity to throw up capable generals, never more so than when the military situation looked hopeless. They revered bravery in battle as a criterion of a man's worth.

During the reigns of the kings of Rome, which spanned about 240 years, the Romans overcame their powerful neighbors. Rome's first treaty—with Gabii—was preserved and venerated. Many other treaties followed, simple documents guaranteeing the status quo of spheres of interest within the peninsula of Italy.

The last of Rome's seven kings was driven out in about 510 B.C. The Republic—Senatus Populusque Romanus—began. What emerged very soon was a complex and highly organized political system that reinforced collective Roman exclusivity but also denied the exclusivity of any one individual. From the electoral process to the legislature and the executive branch, the Republican democracy was democratic; the means test as administered by the censors ruled. So, too, did what almost amounted to ancestor worship, not surprising in a people that genuinely believed they had been founded by the sons of their gods. Some institutions were sacrosanct, in particular the family unit, the cornerstone of Roman society. Children owed their parents certain duties, all of which were geared to advancing the family clan in wealth and prestige. It is a mark of the Roman way of looking at things that, rather than abolish the aristocracy when the Plebeians overcame the Patricians, the Romans simply opened up the ranks of the aristocracy to a much broader consumer market. "You, too, can be a nobleman!"

As the Republic matured, political thought allied to the Roman propensity for legalism generated a sometimes fanatical devotion to the concept of equality, both of opportunity and of social eminence. By this I do not mean that Roman society was classless—indeed, the history of the ancient world is the history of its ruling class—but that Roman thought adapted Roman public systems to what might be called equal opportunity within that ruling class, and was even able to accept not only New Men into the ruling class but also their families as noble ever after.

The political system achieved a series of checks and balances designed to render it impossible for any one man to secure a degree of power deemed excessive. Thus the magistrates who formed the executive branch of government were elected on an annual basis, and the sole oligarchic body, the Senate, with its life membership of the best people, had no power to legislate. Legislation was confined to the People's Assemblies, of which there were three; all the Senate could do was to recommend laws to an assembly.

Republican Rome's dreams of empire were diffident. There were many among its ruling class who abhorred the very idea of empire and opposed expansionist tendencies strenuously.

The five original provinces—Sicily, Sardinia, Corsica, Spain, and Punic Africa (Tunisia)—fell to Rome as a result of three wars with the Punic (Phoenician) people of North African Carthage. The first of the wars occurred when the citizens of Sicilian Messana appealed to Rome after Punic forces occupied their city. By that time, 264 B.C., Rome had treaties with all of the Greek colonies around the toe of the Italian boot, and well understood the potential threat that the expanding Carthage posed to Italy. Even so, the Senate hesitated to commit Rome to war until the people in assembly directed it to honor Rome's treaties. Thus for well over a hundred years and three generations of propertied soldiers, Rome was locked into a periodic struggle that finally saw it triumphant and Carthage reduced to permanent impotence.

The moderate and conservative influences as embodied by the Senate were satisfied with the five provinces that Rome then possessed. Sicily, Sardinia, and Punic Africa provided bountiful supplies of wheat for Rome's rapidly growing urban populace, while Spain contributed huge amounts of iron, lead, zinc, and copper, not to mention silver and gold. Corsica just waited for Napoleon.

But how best to supervise the five provinces? The legislating assemblies could not conduct administration, nor could the special magistrates deputed to go out and govern do so, without there being an authoritative body back in Rome to assist and to restrain them. Rome had become a superpower, and it needed a department of foreign affairs. The onus of diplomacy was already shouldered by the Senate, because it had the traditional right to make Rome's treaties, receive ambassadors, declare and conduct war, and control the public purse. Therefore, the Senate took on the additional responsibilities arising out of empire.

By its very nature this body, it was agreed, could hope to make rational decisions because its members were disbarred from commercial enterprise not involving ownership of land, whereas by comparison, the three legislative bodies were controlled by Rome's businessmen, the knights, who were always in the vanguard of expanding Roman interests abroad. They constituted a powerful lobby, for wherever in the world there was a deal in the offing, a Roman knight was likely to be sniffing around. That made the Senate vulnerable to pressure from the knights, yet kept the decision making out of the knights' hands.

The Senate did have a foreign policy—namely, what was Rome's must remain Rome's, but there were more ways to skin a cat than by starting at its head and making war. War was a last resort. Part of senatorial reluctance to make war arose out of the Senate's shrewdness in realizing that, while victorious war might be profitable in the short term, in the long term it was an expensive hobby for the state to indulge in. Part of the Senate's reluctance was due to the composition of the Roman army, with its property-owning troops who expected to have sufficient time off from campaigning to attend to affairs back home. The Senate always preferred a treaty to a war.

One of its alternatives to actual Roman expansion was to bind the various kings and potentates on the periphery of the provinces with treaties assigning them the coveted status of Friend and Ally of the Roman People. These kings and potentates fought to have that title assigned to them by the Senate. In return for tribute and material assistance to Rome when requested, these client kings were entitled to appeal to the Senate for Roman intervention when threatened by an aggressor. Historical reportage sheds considerable light on what was expected of Rome and what was actually received. A client king was prone to petition the Senate if his own people rose up against him, but if the trouble was domestic the Senate confined itself mostly to serving up homilies about the prudence of being nicer to one's subjects. If the threat was external, the Senate usually stalled over its answer until after a fact-finding mission comprising one or more senators went out to investigate and report back in person. Only then would the senate debate the possibility of war. The eventual outcome was not always pacific, as in the case of King Eumenes of Pergamum's complaint about the conduct of King Perseus of Macedonia. But in most instances the client-king system did keep the peace without Rome's needing to mobilize the legions.

The style of senatorial reaction to a threatened client king is deliciously illustrated by the story of Gaius Popillius Laenas, whom the Senate sent in 168 B.C. to Egyptian Alexandria. Egypt's Ptolemaic rulers—a very complex trio at the time—had beseeched Rome to halt the invasion of Egypt by King Antiochus Epiphanes of Syria. Off went Popillius Laenas, accompanied by twelve lictors. He took no troops whatsoever. Because of either old age or bad bones, he supported himself on a staff as he walked out of Alexandria in the direction of the Canopic arm of the Nile. About where the Alexandrian hippodrome was located, he encountered Antiochus and his army, fresh from conquering Memphis and intent on subduing Alexandria.

"Go home, King," said Popillius Laenas placidly.

"No, I won't go home!" said Antiochus angrily.

Whereupon Popillius Laenas walked all the way around the person of the king, drawing a circle in the dust with the tip of his staff. Finished, he said, "When you step out of this circle, King, make sure your feet are heading in the direction of Syria."

Antiochus did not move for quite a long time, but when he did step out of the circle, his feet were heading in the direction of Syria. Nor did he stop until he got there. To prove his point, Popillius Laenas called in at Cyprus on his way home and evicted a Syrian army of occupation.

All of it had been done by one man in a purple-bordered toga, escorted by twelve men whose only weapons, the axes, were embedded inside their fasces among the thirty rods. Popillius Laenas was not unique, but his meaning is manifest. When that figure in the purple-bordered toga turned up in a trouble spot, his orders were obeyed. The nearest Roman legion might be hundreds of miles away, but behind Rome's solitary representative loomed the shadow of the superpower. A Roman senator deputed to emulate the mission of Popillius Laenas waltzed off convinced that no one would dare to harm a hair on his head. Thus Cato Uticensis restored the exiles to Byzantium and then turned up with three friends in the palace of the regent of Cyprus to annex that island into the empire. Although not unprotected, Ptolemy the Cyprian took what he saw as the only way out—he committed suicide. Cyprus was annexed peacefully.

A superpower is a superpower because it is perceived as having overwhelming military might backed by great resources. Yet Roman armies, especially under the Republic, were small in comparison to those of their foes. What distinguished the Roman military machine was its disciplined efficiency and its superior technology. It lost many a battle, but it did not lose the war.

That Rome the superpower would acquire more provinces was inevitable, but the intense conservatism at work within the Senate continued to resist expansion of the empire. A hardheaded lot, the senators were rarely consumed by the kind of passion which leads to indiscriminate war. On the other hand, Romans were tidy and liked tidy provinces. Once a region belonged to Rome, resistance to Roman rule was put down grimly. This was deemed in the national interest. It was not messianic; it was a part of Roman exclusivity. Roman ways were better.

When Macedonia and Epirus fell on the defeat of King Perseus at Pydna in 168 B.C., a senatorial commission was dispatched to inform the Macedonians that they would not be annexed, but would be given the gift of freedom. Their tribute to Rome was to be half what they had paid to their king, and they were deferred to in other respects as well. Four separate republics were created, each containing well-integrated peoples and having logical geophysical borders. The experiment did not work. The Macedonians preferred to live as a conglomerate under one king, so a series of pretenders to the throne resulted in Rome's annexing Macedonia and Epirus into the empire about thirty years later. Not all peoples want to enjoy even limited democratic government; some are just too used to autocracy.

Three more provinces were bequeathed to Rome in the last testaments of their kings: Asia Province, Cyrenaica, and Bithynia. Cilicia more or less ghosted into the empire, partly because the collapse of the Seleucid kings of Syria created a vacuum there, and partly because Rome could not afford to permit such a strategic area to drift into anarchy. Cyprus was a bequest, as was Egypt, though Rome under the Republic did not attempt to annex Egypt but merely used the threat of annexation to keep the Ptolemies and their unruly Alexandrian subjects in line.

Asia Province, which comprised a large slice of modern western Turkey, proved a specially difficult case. Rome's other provinces were not as fragmented, but Asia consisted of many little semi-independent city-states organized in the image of their Greek populace's forebears. In short, Asia Province was a government tax collector's nightmare, so Tiberius Gracchus legislated to contract out the collection of its revenues to companies of Roman tax farmers. This bright idea caused severe internal discontent and earned much hatred for Rome.

It was little wonder that when, in 88 B.C., King Mithridates VI of Pontus decided to expand westward, the suffering citizens of Asia Province hailed him as a savior—only to discover that the fire was far worse than the frying pan had been. In addition, about 80,000 Romans and Italians with a vested interest had settled in this very beautiful and pleasant part of the world. Mithridates rounded them up, massacred them, and filled a ravine with their corpses. Rome retaliated at once. Then internal power struggles at Rome itself caused a hiatus in serious hostilities, though the crimes of Mithridates were not forgotten. Finishing him took Rome thirty years, but finish him it did. Rome acquired two new provinces, Pontus and Syria, and doubled the contents of its treasury, a feat for which Pompey the Great took credit in 63 B.C.

Either through direct rule or through client kings, the empire now encircled the Mediterranean, and it was at about this time that the Mediterranean, hitherto known as Mare Internum, began to be called Mare Nostrum—Our Sea.

Until March of 58 B.C., Rome was able to congratulate itself that all of its foreign possessions had accrued by "legitimate" means. Carthage's foreign policy had been expansionist; Rome's was moralistic. There is also no doubt that the Senate got much better jollies from settling foreign crises with a few purple-bordered togas than it did from seeing the glittering Roman military snake wind itself out of sight among the Alban hills.

But when Gaius Julius Caesar invaded non-Roman Gaul, Roman foreign policy turned expansionist with a vengeance—*not* with the consent or collusion of the Senate, whose dominant conservative rump screamed in outrage and opposed Caesar literally unto death. Although a man of Caesar's vision and forethought knew exactly what he was doing and why, to many Romans of the ruling class his invasion of Gaul represented a betrayal of everything Rome stood for. They saw no honor or decency in conquest for the sake of conquest, and they vilified Caesar as a glory hunter. Yet among the classes lower than the very top, Caesar was a hero. He was seen as making Rome mightier year by year, and demonstrating to the non-Roman world that no other nation had ever generated anything like the Roman military machine, especially when it was generaled by a strategic and tactical genius who had the happy knack of inspiring his troops to love him.

Certainly a man of Caesar's phenomenal intellect, charisma, energy, and ambition would have been difficult to curb in any society, ancient or modern, but his conquest of Gaul was not undertaken for the sake of conquest alone. Caesar's strategic purpose was to install an integrated and Romanized buffer zone between Italy and the Rhine to keep the Germans inside Germania.

Fifty years earlier, Europe had been shaken by a mass migration of Germanic peoples originating in, according to Strabo, modern Denmark. Three-quarters of a million strong, they had wandered for twenty years from the Baltic to the Black Sea in search of a new homeland, until finally they entered Gaul. On several occasions during those twenty years they encountered a Roman army and trounced it, with massive loss of Roman life. In consequence Rome found itself unable to provide sufficient soldiers from among its propertied men and the propertied men of its Italian allies. Remembering the barbarian invasion of Italy and Rome in 390 B.C., Rome shivered in dread and repaired the city walls.

By a curious coincidence, it was Caesar's uncle by marriage, the great Gaius Marius, who solved both of Rome's dilemmas. He threw the Roman legions open to penniless recruits, then used his 38,000 penniless recruits to crush the Germans. Throwing the Roman army open to those recruits was to be the most significant among Marius' many innovations. The day of the career soldier had dawned, and with him he carried the seeds of the Republic's destruction. Why? Because the Senate refused to give these military paupers bonuses or pensions, leaving them to receive these perquisites from their generals, who were not slow to realize that their ambitions were greatly reinforced by owning legions more loyal to them than to Rome.

Julius Caesar was a child of the generation which had lived through the German threat; his uncle was the hero of that victory, and the men of his family had fought in the field to achieve it. We will never know from his detached, third-person commentaries on the Gallic wars just when Caesar's grand design crystallized. What we do know is that, having arrived at a policy, Caesar proceeded to implement it with characteristic ruthlessness. The buffer zone came into being at the cost of a million dead Gallic warriors, a million Gallic slaves, 400,000 dead Gallic women and children, and a quarter of a million Gallic families rendered homeless. After Caesar's grandnephew rose to autocratic power as Augustus, he made absolutely sure that the new provinces in Gaul were tended carefully and nudged into the Roman mold. When, more than 200 years later, German invaders began to overrun Gaul, it was strong enough in culture and tradition to recast its German settlers into the Latin mold. The name of France was taken from the Franks, but Caesar's grand design for Gaul as a bastion to contain the Germans still persists more than two millennia after his death. What began as a bloodbath became a national policy which may well make the unification of Europe a very painful, frustrating business.

So was the conquest of Gaul expansionist, or was it actually the practice of containment?

The Republic gave its last gasp at Actium in 31 B.C. After a disastrous half century of civil wars to see who would be the first emperor, Rome was politically, financially, and morally bankrupt. It fell to Augustus to put Rome on its feet again. Ever the prudent husbander of Rome's resources, Augustus was a most subtle and brilliant man whose foreign policy inclined far more to containment than to expansion. His two military forays—one in Illyricum (what was to become modern Yugoslavia) and one in Germany, towards the Elbe—were undertaken as long-term defensive measures. He saw his chief duty as reshaping Rome to deal with its empire and hold onto it. In the person of Augustus and his dozen or so immediate successors, Rome finally came to savor its superpower status and regard itself as the world's exemplar.

Rome then owned Spain, Gaul, Sicily, Sardinia, Corsica, Italy, Illyricum, Macedonia, Epirus, Greece, southern Thrace, Bithynia, Asia Province, Pontus and Little Armenia, Cilicia, Syria, Egypt, Cyrenaica, and an enlarged Africa Province. Its client kings ruled Mauretania (modern Morocco), Numidia (modern Algeria), Galatia, and Cappadocia in Anatolia, as well as a myriad of smaller realms. It had treaties with the Kingdom of the Parthians, which divided the east into spheres of influence separated by the Euphrates River.

Democracy in the form of an electoral process and the People's Assemblies had to go, although the Senate was permitted to stay as an obedient legislating body under the direct supervision of the emperor. The emperor himself was the entire executive branch, and he took over foreign policy, including the declaration and direction of war. He had sole authority over the armies and full control of the appointment and dismissal of their generals.

Things went along fairly well for almost 300 years as the Mediterranean basin enjoyed what came to be known as the Pax Romana. This was by no means as idyllic as the phrase implies, but it was sound propaganda that Augustus, the past master of propaganda, would have approved heartily. Foreign policy was usually based on maintaining the peace and prosperity of the empire, although there were some martial emperors, such as the relative upstarts Trajan and Hadrian. Thus, the empire continued to grow, but at a slower rate—Britannia, trans-Danubian Dacia (modern Hungary), all the lands south of the Danube, and a reshuffled Syria, which yielded the additional provinces of Judaea and Arabia. The client kingdoms of Galatia and Cappadocia were finally annexed.

Somehow the mighty empire and its rulers steadily became what the Republican Cicero would have termed less Roman, for Rome the city was ceasing to be what it had always been—the place that bred the ruling class and therefore kept its empire a personal thing. The armies were distributed mainly on the periphery of the provinces, leaving the Praetorian guard as the only military presence in Rome and Italy. From the time of the emperor Claudius, the Praetorian guard and then the army developed a tendency to choose the new emperor, which began to demoralize the people and weaken what influence the Senate had left. The massive financial demands of the military machine resulted in the imposition of unacceptable taxes on all classes of citizen, and from the time of Emperor Caracalla the emperors themselves—a vast parade—were mostly unsatisfactory. They became non-Roman in ancestry, which loosened their emotional ties to Rome the city-state, Rome the hub, Rome the idea.

By A.D. 258 things were not looking good. Grown old and rotten within, the Kingdom of the Parthians disintegrated and was replaced by Persia, reinvigorated by a new dynasty of Sassanian kings. Persia turned expansionist and began to nibble away at the eastern end of the empire. At that same time, two Germanic peoples, the Goths and Vandals, began to devour the Danube provinces before percolating remorselessly into Gaul, Spain, and even North Africa. Two more Germanic peoples, the Franks and the Alamanni, joined them. It is interesting to note, by the way, that during this third century A.D., history threw up two formidable women opponents of the empire, Victoria in Gaul and Zenobia in the East.

But Rome was not done. In A.D. 277, the new emperor, Probus, began to deliver Gaul from the Franks and Vandals, moving eastward to the Danube, sweeping all before him. He built a 200-mile-long stone wall from the Danube via the Neckar to the Rhine, but within one generation it lay in ruins. His most enduring legacy was not stone, however; it was a living one, stemming from his habit of exercising his troops by making them plant vineyards in northern Gaul and modern Austria. Outraged at being made to do the work of peasants, the soldiers rebelled and killed Probus. His murder marked the death of the Senate as a body having any authority at all; from then on it was not even asked to approve the installation of a new emperor. The army was the true ruler of the empire, for the army chose the emperors and the emperors did nothing to antagonize the army.

The child of Dalmatian slaves, Diocletian marked the beginning of Rome's superpower Indian summer, yet, simultaneously, he was the bitter winter of Rome's *mos maiorum*, which was the sum total of its customs and traditions. As much a statesman as a soldier, he reexamined the difficulties inherent in maintaining the empire at a time when all the peoples of northern Europe and the Russian steppes were on the move. He decided that the presence of an anointed emperor was necessary in several places at once, so he created first one co-ruler, then two more, making a total of four emperors, two senior and two junior. Each was allocated a segment of the empire to rule and fight in. The system worked quite well and enabled Diocletian personally to contend with the Persians without having to worry about what might be happening in Gaul or along the Danube. During the twenty years of his reign, Diocletian visited Rome, the city, only once—and loathed the place. His senior co-emperor, Maximian, custodian of Italy and Africa, preferred to rule from Milan.

Perhaps unwittingly, Diocletian destroyed the last remnants of the fiction that the Roman emperor was, at heart, the defender of Republican values. He wore the Hellenistic diadem of a king and clothed himself in eastern raiment. His court teemed with eunuchs, and people who were admitted to an audience were obliged to prostrate themselves. The whole idealistic fabric that once was Rome finally unraveled under Diocletian, who made the eventual permanent separation of East from West inevitable.

Constantine, the son of one of Diocletian's three assistant emperors, had nobler ancestors than any of the recent rulers. He also owned immense capability allied to consuming ambition. Gradually, he eliminated his set of co-emperors and gathered all the reins of government into his own hands.

But the best of what had been Rome was gone. The city of Rome did not matter, art could not summon up *one* good sculptor, and the practice of exposing unwanted children by families impoverished through taxation grew to such proportions that even Constantine himself became worried, although it never occurred to him to solve the problem by remitting a few taxes.

Instead, he did what no true Roman could ever have done; he transferred the center of the empire to ancient Byzantium on the Thracian Bosporus and officially made it the new capital under the name Constantinople. Born in Dacia, apprenticed to Diocletian in the Persian wars, then relegated to Britannia, Constantine neither knew Rome the city-state nor cared about its future.

Through the offices of his mother, Helena, this rather cold and formidably powerful man became a fervent Christian, thus assuring the Christian church of imperial patronage. The ideological struggle between Christianity and paganism had been going on ever since the basically Judaic religious sect had expanded out of Palestine 300 years before. Whereas the parent faith, Judaism, was exclusive by divine direction, Christianity had a voracious appetite for converts. Jew, barbarian German, Persian, Berber, Gaul, Greek, Egyptian—all were grist for the Christian mill, including Roman emperors.

At this point, I shall not carry the story any further. In Rome's decline I see less relevance for America's situation going into the twenty-first century than I see in Rome's rise and zenith. It took another 300 years for Rome to lose its superpower status, and a further 800 years before it ceased to be a political entity. Suffice it to say that Rome the city never perished as a vital center for Western thought. It became the principal see of the Christian, later the Catholic, church, which is in its own right a superpower, albeit of a different kind.

Many things contributed to Rome's downfall:

- loss of contact with the wellsprings of empire, its own beating heartlands
- inability to develop a system capable of properly assessing convulsions and trends on the periphery of the empire
- a progressive walling off of those who governed from those who were governed
- the elevation of the military machine to the summit of the power hierarchy
- the dwindling Romanness of the appearance and feel of government
- replacement of genuine Roman exclusivity with the sumptuous outward trappings of insecure, poorly self-identified men trying to be imperial
- blindness in perceiving the emergence of societies motivated by nationalism or new religious ideologies
- failure to understand that no people can keep up morale when taxed beyond endurance
- a general diminishing of the glory that was Rome.

What lessons then should the Roman experience teach the United States of America at the threshold of the third millennium? Whereabouts on the imperial evolutionary scale does America stand at this moment in time?

The greatest lesson of all is certainly that the systems, institutions, ethics, and ideals of democracy must be preserved internally at any cost, even if that means that they cannot always be propagated externally. America's finger on the pulse of the non-American world must be more sensitive than Rome's ever was, which means that its information/intelligence network must be attuned to the most subtle nuances of mood shifts and swings both outside and inside America. It must monitor the feelings of those who are governed as well as those who govern.

When a superpower loses its innate concept of itself, its decline is more devastating than if it suddenly loses all its material wealth. Let the United States of America remain true to the intentions and aims of its founding fathers, who were steeped in the classics and borrowed heavily from the legacy of Republican Rome; let America continue to survive as a beacon for the world until time immemorial.

Chapter 28

The Roman Experience:
Commentary and Discussion

J. Rufus Fears

Colleen McCullough is right to point out that parallels between America and Rome are as old as the republic itself. The Founders of our country crafted our Constitution to reflect the old free Roman Republic's constitution, with its balance of powers between a strong executive authority and a senate that controlled the purse strings. The Founders of the United States of America believed that the greatness of the Roman Republic resulted from the fact that its citizens were patriotic and possessed civic virtue—the willingness of the individual citizen to subordinate his own interests to the good of the community as a whole.

However, I think that the free Republic of Rome is no longer America's model. As the Founders themselves believed and feared would one day be the case, imperial Rome, the Rome of the Caesars, has become the model for Americans at the end of the twentieth century. It, too, is a model worthy of serious contemplation. In *The Decline and Fall of the Roman Empire,* Edward Gibbon wrote that the happiest period in human history was the Roman Empire of the Caesars.

The Roman Empire of the first and second centuries A.D. stretched from the moors of Scotland to the Tigris and Euphrates River valleys of modern Iraq, and from the forests of Germany and the North Sea to the sands of the Sahara. If today you were to take a tour of what was once the Roman Empire, you would start out in the United Kingdom and go through France, Belgium, western Germany, into Switzerland, Austria, and Hungary, and on to Rumania, Bulgaria, Greece, Turkey, Syria, Israel, Jordan, Egypt, Libya, Tunisia, Algeria, Morocco, and up to Spain. To take that trip today on your own, you would need a dozen languages and twice that many visas.

In the age of the Caesars, two languages—Greek and Latin—would take you anywhere in that empire. There was one law—Roman law—which guaranteed equal protection and individual rights to every citizen of that empire. Nowhere is this better illustrated than in the New Testament Book of Acts. The apostle Paul was arrested. Paul was a Roman citizen. The soldier who had arrested him did not know that and was preparing to beat him for causing a disturbance. "You may not beat me," answered Paul. "What is stopping me from flogging you?" asked the solder. "I am a Roman citizen," said Paul, "and as you well know, it is illegal to flog a Roman citizen who has not been convicted of a crime." Having ascertained that Paul was in fact a Roman citizen, the soldier was afraid that Paul would then bring him up on charges of violating the civil rights of a Roman citizen. Such was the equal protection afforded by Roman law even in a distant province such as Judaea.

Paul was, of course, a Jew as well as a Roman citizen. The Roman Empire and the great emperors who guided it recognized and even fostered cultural diversity. It was a multicultural, multinational empire in which local traditions, languages, and religions were tolerated and generally encouraged. At the same time, the emperors bound their vast empire together by giving it a common set of cultural, social, religious, and moral values, based on the great legacy of classical Greece. This rule of law, individual freedom, and diversity led to an age of intellectual creativity as productive in some ways as our own century has been. The spiritual, intellectual, scientific, and artistic foundations of Europe for the next thousand years were laid in the first and second centuries A.D.

The Roman Empire of the Caesars was peaceful and creative. It was also affluent. Under a free-market economy, the vast empire of Rome was bound together by a magnificent network of roads. Roman merchants sailed the seas in peace, traveling as far as India, Southeast Asia, and China to trade. Commerce flourished, and the trade goods of the world filled the markets and malls of Roman towns such as Pompeii in Italy, Leptis Magna in North Africa, and Londinium in Britain.

Making money was regarded as a social good. The empire rested on a large, prosperous, and public-spirited middle class that took pride in its philanthropic activities. The empire provided a safety net so that the children of the poor did not starve. But its welfare system did not dampen the entrepreneurial spirit. The free-market economy of the Roman Empire provided economic opportunity. A person could begin life as a slave and end up a wealthy and influential Roman citizen.

The Roman Empire of the first and second centuries A.D. was efficiently governed. It produced a series of great leaders such as Augustus, Vespasian, Trajan, Hadrian, and Marcus Aurelius, who kept the empire on such a steady course that not even the eccentricities of a Caligua or a Nero could seriously shake it. The Roman Empire was administered by a small, efficient bureaucracy that attracted dedicated public servants. It had the finest and most cost-efficient military force the world had ever seen. Only 360,000 soldiers were needed to guard the far-flung frontiers of the empire. This was the age of the Pax Romana. So peaceful did this army keep the Roman Empire that the great historian Tacitus, in the second century A.D., bemoaned the fact that there were not any great wars to write about in his own day, and hence he was denied the opportunity to describe the kind of martial grandeur that had marked the old, free Republic.

Above all, the Roman Empire of the Caesars had low taxes. The average inhabitant of the empire worked two days a year to pay his taxes. Compare that with our rate of taxation, even as you compare the excellent Roman roads with the pothole-strewed roads over which you drive home this evening.

Like too many of us, the ordinary Roman citizen did not think too much about foreign policy. That was the emperor's job. Yet despite all their great accomplishments, the Roman emperors never solved two great foreign-policy problems. To use today's language of geopolitics, these were the question of the Middle East and the question of central and eastern Europe. Rome thought of itself, as we have come to think of ourselves, as the only superpower. However, east of the Roman Empire, in today's lands of Iraq and Iran, lay the Persian Empire. To the north and east, stretching all the way from the Rhine River to the steppes of Russia, were the Germanic barbarians, divided into several tribes, fiercely warlike and proud of their independence.

With his characteristic brilliance and decisiveness, Julius Caesar believed the way to solve this foreign-policy problem was by conquest. When he was assassinated on March 15 of 44 B.C., he had been planning to leave almost immediately for a three-year campaign to conquer Iran and Germany. His successor, Augustus, forswore such foreign conquests. He made peaceful accommodations with the Persians and, after one military defeat in Germany, gave up any attempt to conquer the Germans. A century later, the emperor Hadrian literally sought to wall the Romans in and the barbarians out. The massive remains of Hadrian's Wall, still stretching across the north of Britain, stand as a monument to this desire of the Romans to isolate themselves from foreign-policy issues.

However, you cannot shut out foreign problems. In the third century A.D., foreign-policy issues of the Middle East and of central and eastern Europe would rise up and shatter the Roman peace. Persia would become united and revitalized by religious fundamentalism. Persian armies would sweep into Roman territory, capture a Roman emperor, flay him, and dye his skin purple. Germans would ravage the fairest parts of Gaul and penetrate into Italy. The Romans would respond to these challenges from foreign enemies, but their response destroyed what had made the empire so successful. The Romans created an enormous, inefficient bureaucracy and a massive and incompetent army. To pay for this, taxes were raised to exorbitant rates, with the middle class doing most of the paying. By their policy of taxation, the Roman emperors of the third and fourth centuries A.D. alienated and destroyed the middle class, and with it, the moral, political, and economic fiber of their empire.

Ultimately, the Roman Empire would fall. Under the banner of Islam, Arab invaders from the Middle East would sweep all the way to Morocco and into Spain. German conquerors would leave their homes in central and eastern Europe and begin the transformation of Roman Gaul and Britain into the new nations of France and England. In 410 and again in 455, German barbarians would sack the Eternal City of Rome.

If we could conjure up the ghost of Julius Caesar, that greatest of statesmen, he would warn us to be cautious about celebrating the end of the cold war too quickly. He would tell us that our failure to act with decisiveness and finality at the time of the Iranian hostage crisis and our unwillingness to remove Saddam Hussein in the Gulf War have left us with a bitter harvest in the Middle East, a harvest that we will one day reap. He would tell us that we are not the only superpower in the world today. There remains Russia, armed to the teeth with nuclear weapons and with a history and tradition that are chauvinistic, xenophobic, and expansionist. It is a Russia which feels a deep humiliation at the loss of an empire and a profound sense of betrayal at the hands of the United States. It does not take the statesmanship of a Caesar to understand the golden opportunity we lost with the collapse of Communism. We should have gone into Russia, as we did into Germany after World War II, with a new Marshall Plan. We should have materially assisted the Russians to create an economic structure that would make democracy finally viable in that unhappy land and would bind the Russians to us with unbreakable ties of economic mutual interest.

Julius Caesar exemplified what the Greeks and Romans believed to be the essential characteristic of a true statesman—foresight. The greatest of classical historians, Thucydides, defined foresight as the ability to see problems of the future and to solve those problems with solutions that are beneficial in both the short term and the long term. We Americans prefer not to think about foreign problems until it is almost too late. This book, based on a conference, is an example of true foresight, bringing together a stellar group of experts to discuss these deeply significant issues and to try to chart a course for the twenty-first century.

Alfred S. Bradford

One of the saddest things we historians learn from history is that if we do learn any lessons from history, we do not heed them. I think we do not heed lessons from history because they seem so simple and yet are so difficult. First, history has shown that even the victors in war are often worse off after the war. Second, it is better, as Colleen McCullough emphasized, to have consensus behind a mediocre idea than division behind a great idea. Third, we tend to find immediate solutions to immediate problems and seldom consider the more distant future or the collateral consequences of our solutions. Our failure to learn and heed these lessons has been a disaster for human beings.

Historians can look at the same facts and see them in a different way. I would like to take one period that McCullough has written about and tell you how I look at it—the struggle between the Senate and the generals.

McCullough put her finger on the moment the ideal of cooperation broke down—the Roman Senate lost control of the army when the senators tried to curb the power of the commanders by rejecting a bill to give benefits to veterans. Instead of cutting the commanders down to size, the unintended consequence was that the veterans turned to their commanders for help and supported them, even with arms. Roman generals had already discovered that the road to individual success, the road to wealth and power, was to get command of a Roman army to conquer something, because, in essence, they got to keep the fruits of their conquest. Once when a Roman general was called to account for all the booty he had taken, he brought his account books before the Senate and tore them in two.

I think Dr. McCullough is a little hard on Julius Caesar. I see him as the last in a long line of those men in the late Republic who used their armies for their own personal gain and turned on one another in their scramble to reach the top. The Senate never found the answer, but, as McCullough said, Augustus did. In one aspect, he had a good answer—he put an end to the competition among generals. The bad part of his answer was that he became an absolute ruler and he bequeathed absolute rule to his successors. The failure in the end was the failure of the senators and the Senate as a curb on absolutism. Thus, I wish to reinforce Dr. McCullough's conclusion: We must fight for our democratic institutions; we must strive for consensus and agreement; we must recognize that violence begets violence.

Some historians believe the Romans had a master plan for controlling the world during the centuries. The Romans were smart, but they were not that smart. They found solutions for the problems of their own day, and their solutions had unintended consequences. For example, Emperor Diocletian tried to control the horrible mess he had inherited—mutinous armies, usurpers, assassination—by sharing command and ruling through the army. Diocletian diminished the role of the Senate and replaced the traditional imperial bureaucracy with the army bureaucracy. He gained greater control over the empire, and so he solved the immediate problem, but he diminished the power of the Senate, which was the group most opposed to the spread of Christianity. Moreover, when a pagan priest told him that priests could not successfully carry out sacrifices because the Christians on his staff interfered, he ordered all Christians dismissed from offices they held in the Empire, and he began a great persecution. In the West, one of his co-emperors, the father of Constantine the Great, refused to allow such persecution. His son, who became the Roman emperor, also became a Christian, and thus changed the course of Roman history and culture.

To the end, the Senate was the repository of Roman ideals. When the Senate had no role left to play, the Roman Empire ceased to exist.

Q: I wonder if the lesson of the purple-robed senator has cognates in our time. Could the seeming loss of respect, increased terrorism, and other future problems be headed off by an assertion of power and authority?

Colleen McCullough

You have posed a very interesting question. I have friends in the Australian judiciary who are involved with the family court. The family court, particularly in the large cities, has been terrorized by a series of bombings of the judges. Some of my friends say that when the judge sat in remote estate on his podium, in his robes and wig, he was a god who dispensed the justice of apportioning the children or the property or whatever, and nobody thought to argue. Then they took the family court down to the conference table and dressed the judges and the officials of the court exactly the same as the people who came to that court to seek some kind of decision. I do not know, but I have a funny feeling that perhaps there is some truth implied in your question. I am not sure that complete egalitarianism is the right solution. Maybe the very sight of somebody in regal clothes tells you that this is a person of absolute authority, that there is a psychological element built into us that says, "OK, I believe you. Yes, I will do what you say."

The purple-bordered toga was a symbol of a Roman who had risen high enough to sit in the magistrate's chair, which was made of ivory. You could not wear a purple-bordered toga unless you had been a magistrate. The whole world knew this. When the purple-bordered toga appeared, nobody thought, "This is some minor official, some turkey, and I can pull the wool over his eyes." They were looking at somebody who would go back home to the old-boy network and create an awful lot of trouble unless orders were obeyed. I do think that authority can be conveyed.

Q: What is Rome's principal lesson for the United States at the beginning of the twenty-first century?

Colleen McCullough

I think the lesson is to hang onto democracy and not ever give up the values of a true democracy. I think democracy carries responsibilities that extend beyond the borders of the United States. To return to the isolationism between the two world wars would surely be a mistake, because the world is now too small to do that. Oceans are not infinite anymore. To me, the real lesson is that you have to stay true to your ideals, and that once you lose your ideals and your children are not taught them at school and at home, you will cease to be what you were.

I lived in the United States for many years and I have a great deal of love and respect for this country that I could not have learned had I not lived here. I cannot tell you how different democracy is in the United States from the concept of democracy in countries of the Westminster system of government. Children in those countries are not taught in schools to honor and cherish democracy the way American children are. Do not ever give it up. Democracy is too precious.

Chapter 29

Summary, Observations, and Conclusions on Preparing America's Foreign Policy for the Twenty-first Century

Edward J. Perkins and David L. Boren

The editors and contributors to this book are grappling with important and timely questions about America and its foreign policy as we begin the twenty-first century. In assembling and editing the thoughts offered at a foreign-policy conference at the University of Oklahoma in late 1997, the editors intend to contribute significantly to the dialogue that has been taking place among intellectuals, practitioners, and political leaders in their quest to develop a new paradigm for the United States' conduct of foreign policy. The policy of containment kept the peace in terms of preventing war among great powers for a longer period than any other during modern history except the reconstructed concert of Europe after the Congress of Vienna, from 1815 to 1914. A new paradigm is needed to replace and serve in a way similar to the policy of containment, which successfully guided the United States throughout the cold war during the last half of the twentieth century. This volume attempts to provide, if not a final answer, a timely and true definition of the challenges we face, and to suggest the course we should follow to fill the vacuum created by what Richard Haas has called "Paradigm Lost,"[1] until the outlines of the new world are clear.

Readers who have stayed with us to this point have encountered the views of America's most qualified and respected authorities on the state of regions of the world, the state of the major components that constitute foreign policy, and their ideas about a new paradigm for the conduct of American foreign policy as we enter the twenty-first century. By foreign policy we mean the policies and actions that a country takes to protect and advance its interests, especially its national security, the economic well-being of its citizens, and the advancement of its historical and cultural values and ideals. In this concluding chapter we will first summarize the rich and ample ideas put forth by the astute and experienced contributors. We will then discuss several contending themes in foreign policy that Americans have debated throughout most of United States history, and review evolving ideas that have been put forth since the end of the cold war about the nature of world politics. Finally, we will draw on the wisdom and direction of the contributors to reach some conclusions about a new paradigm for the conduct of American foreign policy in the coming decades.

In chapter 2 Professor Gaddis Smith succinctly reviewed the last 250 years of history to draw conclusions about five postwar eras and what they have in common. He found that they shared four things: an uncertainty about how winners treat losers and how losers behave; the appearance of powerful political ideologies; escalating technological change; and the fact that each era has been crucial to the United States' history and well-being. He stated that in today's post–cold war era we find the characteristics of the earlier five periods but, as yet, without agreed-upon goals among governments and societies. Smith finds that we are steering in a fog of uncertainty, which should make us more aware of our need for a map or new paradigm to find our way in conducting foreign policy.

An incomparable group of area experts advised us about the current state of the world. Pulitzer Prize–winning journalist Jim Hoagland suggested that with no single power or authority dominating Europe, constructive American leadership and an active cooperative role will be required for some time. The common traditions and interests of America and Europe, combined with the European Union's economic power and political influence, should make Europe and, it is hoped, a democratic Russia partners of America for a long time.

Former ambassador to Mexico James R. Jones said that for the past fifty years U.S. foreign policy has been the pursuit of freedom, and that policy has nowhere achieved greater success than in Latin America. The region has also adopted market economies, which has made Latin America the United States' most important emerging market in terms of trade. United States leadership is necessary to help Latin Americans continue to address problems of justice successfully and to close the opportunity gap between the rich and poor. For Jones, Mexico and China are the most important countries for future United States foreign policy.

There cannot be European stability without stability in Russia, former U.S. ambassador to the Soviet Union Jack Matlock said. Care must be taken not to threaten Russia by NATO expansion, which in his opinion is Europe's unfortunate substitute for the European Union's economic incorporation of eastern European countries (and Turkey). An overriding security interest of the United States is nonproliferation of weapons of mass destruction, and on this, cooperation with Russia is vital. Matlock argues that we should be careful that threatening NATO expansion does not derail the relationship. There are few conflicts in the United States and Russia's basic interests, and the two countries therefore should be able to cooperate constructively on most issues now and in the future.

Ambassador Edward Perkins argued that the United States ignores promoting economic expansion, sustainable development, and democratic institutions in Africa at the world's medium- and long-term peril. The United States needs a holistic vision and policy toward Africa that is proactive and that encourages African participation in regional and global trade régimes, market economies, and democracy.

Peter Rodman, a former deputy assistant to the president for national-security affairs, saw positive trends in the Middle East, such as the collapse of radical leftists without the support of the Soviet Union, and progress toward a Palestinian state. These positive developments are counterbalanced by a rising totalitarian, anti-Western Islamist fundamentalism (as distinguished from Islam as a religion) that sponsors state terrorism, and by rogue states that seek to acquire weapons of mass destruction. Because of unique historical social contracts, the traditional monarchies appear more resilient than was thought. The region is still problematical, but there are a few hopeful signs of moderation and some slight movement toward economic and political liberalization.

Because of its accelerated economic growth in the last two decades and its looming power and influence in the twenty-first century, Asia has been treated extensively in this book. China's former ambassador to the United States Li Daoyu emphasized in chapter 3 that the United States, as the world's largest developed nation, and China, as the world's largest less-developed nation, share great responsibility for the world's future peace, stability, economic prosperity, and environment. He said that because our common interests far outweigh our differences, we should be able to work together strategically. There is no reason for confrontation, although relations could be upset if the United States deviates from the "one country, two systems" formula for China's reunification with Taiwan. Chinese scholar Zhou Dunren reinforced Li Daoyu's position while arguing that China's economic strength is exaggerated and that Americans and Chinese must come to understand each other better.

Jan Berris, from the National Committee on U.S.-China Relations, and Professor Michel Oksenberg, a senior fellow at the Asia/Pacific Research Center at Stanford University, presented the United States' views of China in chapter 4. Berris pointed to tremendous changes in China that have improved citizen well-being and lessened state power over citizens, saying that Westerners who have followed China for a long time are inclined to see the glass as half full but newer comers are likely to see it as half empty. The Chinese likely will solve their major problems of corruption, transition to a market economy, and the environment one step at a time.

Oksenberg, too, cited China's sustained, highly accelerated economic growth and stated that China is coping with four enormous transitions: change from a rural to an urban society; change from a planned command economy to a market economy; a generational change in leadership from revolutionaries to bureaucrats; and the change from a monolithic society to one with a middle class. He stressed that American strategy toward China should be to develop a shared strategic perspective on the direction of world affairs; to help China into the world economy through the World Trade Organization (WTO); to accept any peaceful solution to the Taiwan issue that is acceptable to both sides; and to include a constructive human-rights plan. Because of Sino-Japanese animosity, the United States faces the dilemma of good relations with China and, hence, bad relations with Japan, or vice versa. However, for twenty-five years we have had simultaneously constructive relations with both these giants, and we must continue to do so.

A former American vice president and U.S. ambassador to Japan (1993-96), Walter F. Mondale described in chapter 5 the relationship between Japan and the United States as one of the greatest international success stories of the past half century, and as remaining the foundation of stability and our most strategic connection for the Asia-Pacific region. The United States and Japan are the two largest national economies. Japan needs to continue to open its economy. For the foreseeable future the U.S.-Japan Security Treaty, based on common interests, not common enemies, is perceived as essential to ensure peace and prosperity for the entire Asia-Pacific region. Japan's democracy belies assertions that democracy and human rights are alien to the "Asian way" or incompatible with economic growth. Finally, Mondale urges the need for greater intellectual and cultural understanding between Americans and Asians.

Ambassador and Japanese specialist Francis J. McNeil argued that Asia is more than just China, and that Japan, Southeast Asia, the Koreas, and other areas must be taken into account. A new structure of peace is needed that requires American engagement and a stable, peaceful balance of power. Japan is not seen as a military threat in Southeast Asia as long as Japan has security ties with the United States. The U.S. military presence in Asia is a must for Asian peace and stability, and China must come to regard it as such.

Dean of Asia scholars Robert Scalapino said in chapter 6 that U.S. policy toward Asia must deal simultaneously with three rising, conflictual forces: internationalism, nationalism, and communalism. In a sweeping review of Asian nations, he concluded that the United States should engage China, but with a "wait-and-see" attitude. Japan, he says, must make far-reaching economic reforms and move to true multiparty politics. Japan's relations with China and Russia are key. Although Russia will move more extensively into Asia, an alliance between Russia and Japan is unthinkable (although economic relations may be strong), and Russia's relationship with China is likely to be an accommodation, not an alliance. South Korean democracy will probably survive and accommodate with North Korea. He predicts that the future economic growth of Southeast Asia will be more moderate and the politics cloudy. Scalapino sees Taiwan as the most dangerous threat to peace in the early twenty-first century. He declares that the Asia-Pacific area is critical to the global economy and stability, and although violence and instability are likely, they will mostly be confined to the region.

In chapter 7 Professor Marlan Downey, former president and CEO of Shell Pecten and ARCO International, indirectly questions the statement that violence and instability can be wholly confined to the region. Picking up on a point in Mondale's piece, Downey pointed out that Asia's projected economic growth indicated an eventual $250 billion annual transfer from Asia to the Middle East for oil that will travel over an 8,500-mile sea lane. The control and protection of that route and the huge economic impact of such economic transfers will have great geopolitical consequences, not only around the Spratly Islands and in the South China Sea, but also along the entire sea lane and in the Middle East and the rest of the world. Professor Mikael S. Adolphson provided worrisome statistics that Americans must come to grips with if the United States is to gain sufficient understanding to deal successfully with Asia. Currently, 85,000 Chinese and Japanese study in the United States, most for degrees; only about 3,000 American students a year are in Japan and China, mostly for short stays.

Former ambassador and professor Edwin G. Corr stated that the experts' survey of the state of the world shows that America has small groups of persons who understand separate regions and countries of the world quite well, but the challenge is to take the concerns of each region and put them into an overall, prioritized, coherent, and viable strategy that the American people will support and finance. To gain American support for foreign policy, we must create a new paradigm for the conduct of foreign policy, while recognizing that no paradigm is a panacea that can relieve the United States and its top leaders from tough judgments and decisions about U.S. interests and about the certain consequences of engagement in ambiguous issues and conflicts.

Having completed a summary of the state of the world, the book turned to some of the more important components of foreign policy: defense, intelligence, trade and the economy, the environment, and the media and public opinion. Obviously lacking in treatment was diplomacy, although it is implicit throughout the book, especially in Part VIII's discussion of the overall architecture of our policy, and it is addressed briefly later in this chapter.

Senator Sam Nunn, former chairman of the Armed Services Committee, described in chapter 8 today's world as one with much lower risks to our national security but with greater instability. This contrasts with the higher security risks and greater stability that existed during the cold-war era. It is harder to define national-security threats and thus to develop an overarching policy. The spread of nuclear, chemical, and biological weapons of mass destruction is now the greatest security threat, and it will be for the next twenty to thirty years. Residual cold-war issues are a second important area of threat. As an example, Nunn outlined the intricacies and intractable attitude of the North Koreans that could ignite a war with global impact. Finally, Nunn introduced the reader to the reality that cyberspace warfare is not a phenomenon of the future but a growing current threat. The security posture he suggested is one of continuing and concerted vigilance to prevent proliferation and to control weapons of mass destruction, the management and cleaning up of residual cold-war conflicts, and meeting the challenge of cyberspace warfare, which is already upon us.

Ambassador Robert Oakley, who served as the president's representative in Somalia, suggested in chapter 9 that the direct defense of our territory, people, and armed forces is our only vital interest. "Very important U.S. interests" and criteria for the use of military forces are very difficult to describe. Citing U.S. government basic documents, he said America's leaders use military forces in less than war situations to "shape the international environment" in ways favorable to U.S. interests and global security; to respond to small-scale contingencies and major theater wars; and to prepare our forces against uncertain future threats. Oakley insists on the need for American leadership and on keeping our armed forces prepared.

Intelligence is the next component of foreign policy that our experts analyzed. In chapter 10 former CIA director Robert Gates evaluated the role of intelligence during the cold war, saying the CIA's failures had been trumpeted while its successes have been kept secret. Mistakes were made, but the intelligence community brilliantly monitored Soviet military strength and prevented any strategic surprises during the last half of the cold war, all the while in accord with presidential directives, law, and American values. George Tenet, current director of the Central Intelligence Agency, said in chapter 11 no responsible person would want our national security to be tended without the covert gathering of information. The intelligence community provides analysis, covert human and technological information gathering, counterintelligence, and covert action—the last being a small part of intelligence activity. He, too, stressed that people in the intelligence community reflect the values of the American people.

In the general discussion of Gates and Tenet's presentations, David Boren and Professor Stephen Sloan made important points in chapter 12, and a roundtable discussion in chapter 13 followed for C-Span, moderated by John Milewski of *Close-Up*. In the roundtable discussion were former CIA directors Richard Helms, Judge William H. Webster, James Woolsey, Professor Robert H. Cox, and Boren. Included among the many topics touched on were the need for the intelligence community to reach out to academia as a source of information and analysis; the successful and growing collaboration of the Federal Bureau of Investigation (FBI) and the CIA; and the statement that intelligence agencies should not gather information to give individual American firms a competitive advantage, although it should help to assure that they compete on a level playing field. The greatest innovation in the intelligence field in recent decades has been the evolution of a congressional oversight system, with which Senator Boren was deeply involved, and which other democratic countries are now trying to emulate.

During the roundtable, Helms stressed that intelligence's mission is "to save our skin." Webster amended this to say that the CIA does not save our skins, but gives essential, objective information to our nation's policy makers so they can do so. Woolsey believes the downsized intelligence structure of the cold war can be adapted to current needs and targets. Boren described the rapidly changing world and the necessity that we comprehend it. He stressed that early intelligence is now important because we have fewer military assets in "forward positions" around the world. He and Cox also stressed the rights of people in a democratic society to know the rule of law and accountability, and the moral behavior of intelligence officers.

The next component of foreign policy dealt with in the book was trade policy and preparing America's economy for the twenty-first century. In chapter 14 former secretary of agriculture and U.S. trade representative Clayton Yeutter put forth short-term priorities for the United States, such as persuading the American people of the benefits of free trade; the need for "fast-track" authorization for the president on trade legislation; advancing international trade reforms and rules for services, telecommunications, government procurement, standards, investments, and agriculture; and achievement of the Free Trade Agreement of the Americas and movement toward a United States–European Union Free Trade Area. For long-term priorities, he listed getting all the major players in the game (i.e., China and Taiwan into the World Trade Organization); transparency of nations' trade decisions; the WTO encompassing competition policies (i.e., antitrust laws); and a change in the psychology about trade negotiations among nations from the idea of "mutual concessions" to "benefits obtained."

Archie Dunham and Luke R. Corbett, presidents and CEOs of Conoco Inc. and Kerr-McGee Corporation, respectively, separately addressed in chapter 15 the question of unilateral sanctions as a tool of American foreign policy. Both argued that the use of unilateral trade sanctions has become excessive and counterproductive. They evoked case illustrations and studies to show that unilateral sanctions often result in undesirable leaders and policies targeted becoming more entrenched, while U.S. companies are denied markets or put at a competitive disadvantage. Corbett called for a review of policy toward each of the sixty-odd nations we sanction, blockade, or embargo. Dunham suggested alternative policies and actions, and contrasted the costs of such alternative actions with those of sanctions.

Ambassador John Wolf said in chapter 16 that the U.S. government focus is on opening markets and assuring equal treatment for American businesses—multilaterally, regionally, and bilaterally. He outlined, or mentioned, the World Trade Organization, the Organization for Economic Cooperation and Development (OECD), the Asia-Pacific Economic Council (APEC), and the Free Trade Agreement of the Americas (FTAA), describing APEC in greater detail. He emphasized the necessity of "fast-track" authority for the president, and said the private sector's role is key to a successful American foreign policy.

In chapter 17 enterpreneur Michael F. Price and distinguished Washington, D.C., attorneys W. DeVier Pierson and Max N. Berry examined aspects of strengthening the United States' economy for global competition. Price made it clear that American investors expect the U.S. government to enable them to do business freely and openly around the world. Pierson said the debate in the 1950s and 1960s over protectionism should have ended, because it is clear in the 1990s that we benefit from worldwide competition. However, the focus has shifted to a debate about attaching conditions about labor and the environment to trade negotiations. This is the essence of the fight over fast-track legislation, which is an important test for U.S. leadership. Berry, too, expressed great concern that the pendulum is swinging again toward protectionism, as seen by invalid criticisms of trade with Mexico under the North American Free Trade Agreement (NAFTA), and by the clumsy, too-late start by the executive branch in its efforts to obtain fast-track legislation and the congressional response. Berry pointed out American trade barriers that need to be eliminated, e.g., the long time required to process antidumping complaints filed by foreign firms under U.S. law. He also used the Jackson-Vanik Amendment to argue that trade policy should not be complicated by human-rights concerns and politics.

Treatment of environmental concerns as a component of American foreign policy centered on Richard L. Sandor's proposal in chapter 18. Sandor is the principal architect of interest-rate futures markets, and he outlined a limited-scale voluntary international greenhouse-gas emissions trading program. Philosopher Zev M. Trachtenberg of the University of Oklahoma pointed to deficiencies of direct regulation and taxation as a means to control industry, and to the attractiveness of Sandor's proposal to use market mechanisms to achieve environmental goals. In chapter 19 political economist Rajeev Gowda raised practical and ethical concerns that in schemes to limit and reduce pollution and environmental damage, the market unfairly distributes the benefits and burdens between wealthy, already modernized countries and poorer, less developed ones.

David Gergen, adviser to presidents and editor of *U.S. News and World Report*, posed the paradox in chapter 20 that although the United States is preeminent globally in terms of ideas, democratic and market values, military might, technology, and culture, American political culture and the media have turned inward. There is a lack of American public support and attention to international affairs. This causes the best and brightest people no longer to be attracted to the U.S. government foreign-affairs community. More important, the public's turn inward does not provide the president of the United States with the support necessary for the exercise of American global leadership that the world so vitally requires. The American news media and education system, especially universities, must provide the knowledge and information necessary for America's global competitiveness and leadership.

In chapter 21 Professor David Dary, director of the H.H. Herbert School of Journalism and Mass Communication at the University of Oklahoma, added the government to the media and universities as being responsible for informing and maintaining public interest in world affairs. Reporters Lee Cullum, of the *Dallas Morning News*, and Lois Romano, of the *Washington Post*, expressed concerns while pointing out that a few select newspapers are expanding their reporting of foreign news, although changing the topics covered.

With the experts' survey of the regions of the world and other authorities' examination of discrete components of American foreign policy, the foundation had been laid for noted geopolitical draftsmen to draw the framework of the architecture of an American foreign policy for the twenty-first century. Part VIII begins with former secretary of state and national security adviser Henry A. Kissinger's exposition in chapter 22 on America's strategy at this stage of the world's evolution. He pointed out that the United States—settled by immigrants, shielded by two oceans, and without powerful and hostile neighbors—had enjoyed the option of choosing to engage or not to engage in foreign policy until the mid-twentieth century, but we now live in a world environment of major powers and instantaneous global communications that no longer affords this luxury. Today we have no clear-cut enemy, nor do we confront serious military and ideological challenges. Yet we must reestablish some national consensus and determine our national interests, which include promoting our values. The historical American belief that the key to peace was to transform all countries into our image through the principle of self-determination has not been abandoned. No other country has undertaken so many great projects on an altruistic basis.

In creating a new architecture for foreign policy, Dr. Kissinger said we must root it in both the past and the present. We should build on our common history and shared values with Europe and Latin America. The establishment of the Free Trade Agreement of the Americas and of a North Atlantic Free Trade Agreement with Europe are of high priority. With respect to Russia, we must promote democracy and capitalism while persuading the Russians that they can develop and modernize without territorial expansion. Regarding the Middle East, the most important issue is between the fundamentalist and secular régimes of the Islamic world. The second critical issue is the stability of the Gulf area, i.e., Saudia Arabia and Turkey. Finally, there is the determination of final borders between Israelis and Palestinians.

Kissinger devoted most of his comments to our future relations with China, contrasting American and Chinese views of history and underlining that the United States will be far more powerful for some time to come, notwithstanding the astounding transformation of China since his visit as national security adviser in 1971. China is preoccupied with surrounding strong states and still has much to do internally. The importance to the world of China's stability and evolution toward constitutionalism should not be upset by the West demanding too much too soon on human rights, while still keeping them high on the agenda. In our dealings with Asia, the United States must not let any single nation dominate, nor should we anoint any single nation as our enemy. All this means it is essential for the United States to remain engaged and present in Asia.

Following Kissinger's analysis, Dr. Zbigniew Brzezinski, former national security adviser, proposed in chapter 23 a geostrategy for Eurasia which he clearly regards as essential for United States relations with Europe and Asia and for the control of the Middle East and Africa. (Brzezinski leaves Latin America and Africa—along with Antarctica—on the margins.) He distinguishes between short- and long-term strategy, and says the United States must balance matters so that no hostile coalition emerges in Eurasia that could challenge us. France, Germany, China, and Russia are seen as key players, but the United States is the "indispensable power," unmatched in the four key dimensions of power today—military, economic, technological, and cultural.

Brzezinski endorses NATO expansion, a transatlantic free-trade agreement, and incorporation of Turkey into the European Union. Russia must recognize that Europe and China are economically more powerful, while defining itself as nonimperial. India gets a mention in terms of its survival as a democracy being important. He says China and the United States have compatible interests and need each other. Japan should be our democratic and economic global partner but not an ally against China. A transcontinental Eurasian security system should emerge, consisting of Europe, Russia, China, Japan, and India, with the United States continuing to play the decisive role as Eurasia's arbitrator.

In chapter 24 Dr. Jeane Kirkpatrick, scholar, former U.S. ambassador to the United Nations, and former cabinet member, addressed the question of United States relations with nations emerging as leaders in the world arena. She stated that Russia, although now a fallen superpower, can also be categorized as a reemerging power, and it remains during the short and medium terms the country that most matters for the peace of Europe, the United States, the Middle East, and the world. Democratization of this historic European and reemerging power is very important. She draws on Jeffrey Garten's identification of Mexico, Brazil, Argentina, South Africa, Turkey, Poland, South Korea, China, Indonesia, and India as other emerging powers. Varying degrees of movement toward democracy and toward free markets in all of them are a good sign. This is the way in which they will be incorporated into a world system and structure for peace, and for increasing prosperity and justice. The current world is not devoid of serious problems—such as proliferation of weapons of mass destruction, Islamic extremism, and outlaw states—but America is well suited for the new era, and its future will be even more brilliant than its past.

The former president and chief executive officer of the Center for Strategic and International Studies (CSIS), Ambassador David M. Abshire, called in chapter 25 for an "agile strategy" while the United States develops a truly strategic framework for the post–cold war era. It will take five to fifteen years to move out of the current strategic interregnum in a now multipolar, interdependent world that is undergoing informational, business, and financial revolutions. The world is characterized by diffuse nuclear threats and expanded security issues, of which the proliferation of weapons of mass destruction is the greatest. In the meantime the United States, as the world's only superpower, must play a constructive balancing role grounded in U.S. vital national interests. After outlining the elements of an agile strategy, Abshire calls for the promotion of U.S. interests and ideals through short-term realism and long-term idealism.

In chapter 26 Ambassador George C. McGhee, who was a senior American official present with Secretary of State Dean Acheson at the creation of a new international system after World War II, concludes that the United States will continue to be the most influential nation in the world in all key aspects—political, economic, military, and cultural. There is no foreseeable danger of large-scale world wars of aggression or of nuclear war among major powers, although we will have to remain vigilant to keep internal and regional conflicts from expanding. America's leadership must be real and tactful. He urged that full NATO membership should be offered to Partnership for Peace countries, to create security from Vancouver to Vladivostok. The United States should promote the creation of regional security pacts that, distinct from NATO, should have provisions for defense against hostile nations within the treaty area as well as from outside. The twenty-first century, McGhee said, will be one of peace, with great expansion of nongovernmental relationships and optimum individual freedom, but with governments still playing a vital and powerful role in protecting and aiding their citizens in the global community.

Finally, the icing on the cake is noted novelist Colleen McCullough's essay in chapter 27 on "lessons learned" from the Roman experience for the United States as the world's lone superpower entering the twenty-first century. She suggests that the seeds of Rome's prolonged final destruction were sowed when Romans abandoned the principles and institutions from which the Roman Republic had evolved. In chapter 28 University of Oklahoma history professor Alfred S. Bradford pointed to the critical moment as when the Roman Senate lost control of the army by rejecting a bill to give benefits to veterans, who then turned to the generals who had learned that the road to individual power and wealth was by war and conquest.

J. Rufus Fears, classics professor at the University of Oklahoma, pointed out that America's Founders crafted our Constitution to reflect the Roman Republic, but that imperial Rome has increasingly become the model. He said the Roman Empire's failure to deal successfully with two foreign-policy problems led to its building a large bureaucracy and a massive, incompetent army, which necessitated exorbitant taxes that destroyed the prosperous, public-spirited middle class and the safety net for the poor. Dr. Bradford lamented that we do not heed the lessons of history.

Dr. McCullough stated that Rome's downfall was caused by losing contact with its wellsprings, by not being able to cope with convulsions on its periphery, a walling off of those governed from the governors, the elevation of the military to the summit of the power hierarchy, the dwindling of Romanness to imperialism, and the loss of morale caused by overtaxation—all resulting in the diminishing glory of Rome. What should Americans learn from this? The systems, ethics, and ideals of democracy must be preserved at home at any cost, and we should not become overextended in terms of trying to propagate them abroad too quickly, extensively, and thoroughly.

Having summarized the presentations of contributors to the book, let us address one essential component of foreign policy that was not given isolated attention and, until this point, has been treated only implicitly in the book—diplomacy. There is one sense in which diplomacy is the sum total of familiarity with countries and regions of the world, knowledge of the component parts of an overall policy (e.g., international trade policy), and the ability to design comprehensive policies and implement them—all of which are dealt with in this volume. In another sense, the conduct of diplomacy is knowing what our national interests are, how to formulate national goals and strategies, and how to achieve them through negotiations and dealing day to day with leaders and peoples of other countries. It is a tool and a profession to be mastered by our top political leaders and Foreign Service officers. And just as we did not give diplomacy a discrete section for special attention in this book, our leaders and the public unfortunately often give it low priority and insufficient attention and support.

Americans are uncomfortable with and reluctant to pay attention to or finance diplomacy adequately. The word *diplomat* evokes for many Americans nothing more than the image of a pinstriped, cookie-pushing, drink-in-the-hand, effete, and elitist sycophant floating from one cocktail reception or meaningless ceremony to another. During the twentieth century an attitude developed toward our armed forces that because they put themselves in harm's way, nothing was too good for our women and men in uniform, and certainly we the editors share that opinion. Ironically, for most of the last quarter of the twentieth century, the risks of being bombed, shot at, kidnapped, wounded, or killed have been higher on a per capita basis for the approximately 4,000 Foreign Service officers than for members of our much larger armed forces. In Vietnam, Foreign Service officers and U.S. military officers working as advisers in village development programs were often more exposed to the Vietcong than soldiers assigned to regular military units. American diplomats around the world, and their families, have been targets and victims of terrorists and insurgents. More ambassadors have been killed or kidnapped than general officers. There are marble slabs in the foyer of the State Department in Foggy Bottom with the names of 177 Foreign Service officers who were killed in the line of duty. Diplomats are our first line of defense, and our embassies and overseas missions are our forward trenches.

The threats to U.S. security are no longer largely military. Politics, economics, information culture, ecology, and technology are also important elements. Our national security rests on a triad of diplomacy, the military, and covert intelligence. In short, diplomacy—the traditional reporting and advocacy functions, public information, development assistance, and trade promotion—is our nation's most effective defense and tool for advancing American interests, when it is combined with the threat of strong and rapid military force. An ounce of prevention is worth a pound of cure, said diplomat Benjamin Franklin. You can be sure that any time our government resorts to deployment of units of our armed forces we are talking megadollars—many times the cost of what a crisis-preventive diplomatic solution would have cost.

Effective preventive diplomacy can keep political disputes that arise between or within states from escalating into armed, violent hostilities. There are myriad examples of such successes during our current era, although they are largely ignored. The range of diplomacy is far more than talking or war. There is a gamut of measures to influence and restrain or motivate parties in dispute. These include dialogues at the grassroots level; human rights and election observers; targeted economic and confidence-building exercises; membership in international organizations and working through them and through allies; peacekeeping missions; democracy building; use of good offices or mediation; multilateral sanctions; big-power pressures; show of military force; and mixes of such instruments. Moreover, preventive diplomacy can usually be effected at less political cost to a U.S. president than sending American soldiers into danger. American ambassadors are continually responding proactively to signs of potentially expanding crises, but unfortunately they are too often restricted in terms of the personnel and resources available to employ flexibly. As much as possible we should try to resolve problems before they reach the top levels of the State and Defense Departments and the National Security Council.

Although the number of countries with whom the United States maintains relations has doubled in the last forty years and the number of tasks and services for American citizens has multiplied many times, the United States has kept the number of Foreign Service officers at approximately the same level. A thousand officers could easily be added for the cost of one battalion or one piece of expensive military hardware. The payoff in terms of national security, the conduct of foreign policy, the promotion of our economic interests, and the provision of services to American citizens would be manifold. For the American public the costs of B-1 bombers, nuclear submarines, aircraft carriers, and Sherman tanks have never been too great. The annual defense budget reached $320 billion during the cold war, and it has declined to only about $260 billion. At the same time, from 1987 to 1997, the foreign-affairs budget dropped by 50 percent in real terms, to $19.15 billion in 1998, and it constitutes only about 1 percent of the federal budget.

Japan, with 130 million people, has surpassed the United States, with 260 million people, as the largest economic-aid provider in the world, using its aid in the form of Japanese products to help Japanese political influence and economic markets. Among the twenty-one richest countries in the world that belong to the Organization for Economic Cooperation and Development, the United States ranks last in terms of the percentage of gross domestic product it dedicates to foreign economic assistance. We are embarrassingly delinquent year after year in paying our dues to the United Nations and to international financial institutions. Something needs to change with respect to our foreign-affairs budget and staffing of the Department of State and foreign-affairs agencies if America is to remain, and fulfill its role as, a superpower.

Beyond giving attention to the Foreign Service and the State Department, there is an urgent need to examine our entire national-security structure to see if it is still appropriate for today's threats and the tasks that confront us. After World War II, the United States Congress passed the National Security Act of 1947 and led in creating the Bretton Woods international economic system, developed the policy of containment, and created new agencies and programs for dealing with the Third World. The National Security Act created an executive-branch management structure to implement the policy of containment, using both civilian and military assets. Because we again face a new and changed world and security environment, we sorely need to review our national-security establishment to see if it could be improved to serve the president better in meeting the challenges of the present. Perhaps we need a revamped or new National Security Act for the year 2000. The need to more closely integrate all of our intelligence assets, military and civilian, with academic analytical capability is also self-evident. There is also a need to strengthen the ability of the director of the CIA—who has much less than half the intelligence budget under his control—to set spending priorities for the entire intelligence community in the future.

We will now examine several themes that have historically been important in America's ongoing debates over United States foreign policy. Following this is a discussion of recently evolving ideas about the nature of world politics during the twenty-first century, and then some conclusions.

Each country and each generation is said to revise and rewrite its popular history and myths to reflect current needs. In stating this we are not negating the efforts of truth-seeking and trained historians to record and analyze events and trends objectively; we are merely saying that in each period each country popularly holds a particular view of its history. In the United States, dialogue and debate over foreign policy during the twentieth century have centered on at least four contending themes, and the discussion of each of these dialectics can be traced to some degree to the very beginnings of our republic. The contending themes are isolationism versus internationalism, realism versus idealism, balance of power versus collective security, and unilateralism versus multilateralism. These themes overlap greatly, but each has been the subject of debate and discussion.

Isolationism versus internationalism is particularly salient. School textbooks until the late 1970s most generally described the United States as isolationist from independence until about 1895, as internationalist (if not imperial) from 1895 to the period immediately after World War I, as isolationist from the end of World War I to Pearl Harbor, and as internationalist from World War II through the cold war. Today we are again examining the appropriate balance between our domestic concerns and foreign involvement.

Isolationists have long sought validation of their position by citing George Washington's advice in his farewell address, in which he warned America "to steer clear of permanent alliances with any part of the world." Secretary of State John Quincy Adams cautioned in his speech of July 4, 1824, that although America is the well-wisher of freedom and independence of all, "she goes not abroad in search of monsters to destroy." A critical examination of our early history suggests, however, that the United States was less isolationist in its early history and throughout the nineteenth century than is popularly depicted.

The geography and technology of the world at the beginning of the nineteenth century, the relative weakness of our recently independent country, and the dominance of western Europe in America's thought and international dealings were such that we wisely avoided embroilment in Europe's continental affairs. Not so for Europe's colonial holdings in the Western Hemisphere. The deliberate and aggressive quest of the United States to fulfill its "manifest destiny" of stretching across a huge continent from sea to shining sea was certainly regarded as "internationalist" by those whom we pressured or forced to cede and sell their claims over vast lands. Aside from the French, Spanish, and English giving up colonial territories against American insistence, the Mexicans—who had gained their independence in 1810 and from whom we took by conquest almost half of their claimed territory in 1848—certainly regarded the United States as imperialist, not isolationist, in outlook.

There is little historical dispute among Americans about our supposedly temporary and aberrant internationalism in our war with Spain at the turn of the century, colonial acquisition of the Philippines, and frequent interventions in Latin America, or about the period of deep isolationism into which our country sank—with disastrous consequences—between the two world wars. Many people blamed U.S. failure to accept leadership after

World War I for creating the conditions for World War II. After World War II we reluctantly stepped up to the plate and throughout the cold war exercised leadership, maintained the peace, and saw our values and ideals triumph. Now we Americans are again challenged by the question of whether, as we enter the new world of the twenty-first century, we will be willing to pay the price of world leadership, and what the consequences will be if we do not.

Let us turn now for a brief look at the debate on realism versus idealism. Realism in foreign policy has roots at least as far back as the wars of Athens and Sparta in the fifth century A.D., described in Thucydides' *The Peloponnesian Wars*. It is also evident in the ancient writings of China's Sun Tsu. Realism was manifest in Machiavelli's *The Prince,* about the conduct of relations among the medieval city-states of Italy. Otto von Bismarck was the master practitioner of realism. The twentieth century's Hans Morganthau described the system in *Politics Among Nations*;[2] and Henry Kissinger, as evidenced in his book *Diplomacy* (1994)[3] and other writings, is seen as the leading proponent of realism and balance-of-power politics today. Realism is based on a view of the state as the most important actor in an anarchic world arena in which states calculate their interests in terms of power.

Americans most identify idealism, the contending approach, with President Woodrow Wilson. Idealism has been associated with concern for international institutions, international law, disarmament and arms control, building a world community, and peace through collective security rather than through various iterations of balance of power as advocated by the realist school of thought.

On the debate between balance-of-power advocates and supporters of a collective-security approach, the balance-of-power argument is usually associated with realism and has been used in a variety of ways. In terms of preventing cataclysmic wars (not necessarily small wars or internal conflicts), *realism* refers to a system in which states follow a policy of preventing any one state from gaining a preponderance of power. The lesser states have effected this primarily through arms buildups and alliances with other threatened weaker states. Woodrow Wilson believed balance-of-power foreign policies caused World War I. The outbreaks of World Wars I and II as well as the bipolar cold war cast doubts on the efficacy of both realism and balance-of-power politics.

Collective security, as envisioned by Wilson and others, was to achieve peace by making aggression illegal, by outlawing offensive war, and by deterring aggression by a coalition of all nonaggressive states, with the coalition punishing aggressor states when deterrence has failed. The League of Nations embodied the doctrine of collective security. The United States rejected Woodrow Wilson and the League, and the League, without the United States, failed to prevent World War II. During World War II, at President Franklin Delano Roosevelt's instructions, the State Department drafted, by the end of 1943, what became with little change the United Nations Charter, and forty-nine nations signed it in San Francisco in 1945. The charter contained provisions meant to remedy the deficiencies of the League of Nations' approach to collective security. The founders again sought to maintain peace by outlawing the threat or use of force, except in self-defense or when used collectively for the world's security.

The UN Charter created the United Nations Security Council and gave it the power to pass universally binding resolutions for peace, while granting each of the five then "great powers" a veto, on the basis that it is better to make the lights go out temporarily in the house than to allow it to burn down in the form of a war against a great power. During the cold war the collective-security system did not function because of the hostility between the two superpowers, the United States and the Soviet Union, each of which freely exercised its right of veto. (There was one major exception: The Security Council voted for "police action" on the Korean Peninsula in the absence of the Soviets, who therefore were unable to veto.) As perceived by the United Nations' founders, the lights dimmed greatly from time to time without the house burning down, but it was not exactly a peaceful and progressive world, especially from the viewpoint of the Third World.

The cold war and the right of veto gave rise to preventive diplomacy in which the United Nations, instead of punishing aggressor nations, would identify them and interpose UN volunteer forces between warring parties. This was done during the Suez crisis, in the Sinai, and in Cyprus. Iraq's invasion of Kuwait saw the use of collective security in a major way for the first time in forty years. These types of operations foreshadowed the plethora of peace-building and peacekeeping operations that surged after the cold war's end. It is possible that we are entering an era in which a combination of some of the aspects of collective security with the realistic maintenance of our own power of deterrence may make more sense than viewing the two as competing solutions.

Unilateralism versus multilateralism, the final of the four contending themes in American foreign policy that we are examining, is related to the dialectic of balance of power versus collective security. It goes back to President Washington's enjoinder against entangling alliances. Multilateralism need not be globally comprehensive, as is demanded under pure concepts of collective security. Political scientists and historians tell us that unilateralism is a major trait of U.S. foreign policy—a strong tendency to go it alone and, when that is not possible, to be in charge or command of multilateral endeavors. It is akin to the concept of American exceptionalism to the normal conduct of nations. Although being the boss—that is, having our way—was not fully attainable in many cases during the cold war, it is even more difficult now. Even though we are the sole remaining superpower, other nations, because of greatly diminished threats, are less inclined to submit to American dominance. At the same time, the United States faces financial limits that make unilateral actions an impractical option in terms of domestic politics. Many people have concluded that we cannot afford to be the world's police force all by ourselves, taking all the risks and paying all the costs.

These four overlapping sets of themes, or dialectics, influence and shape the formulation of foreign policy in the United States. In Part VII, David Gergen's description of America's turning inward is reflective of the theme of isolationism versus internationalism. The realism-versus-idealism question is seen in the debate over human-rights issues in U.S.-China policy cited in Parts II and VIII. Realism versus idealism is also seen in the cautions put forth by Sam Nunn and Robert Oakley in Part III and by Admiral William J. Crowe Jr. in the foreword that we live still in a hostile world and must be prepared to deal with it. How do we strike the proper balance between protecting our vital interests of national security and economic well-being and the promotion of democracy and human rights? Dr. Kissinger and nearly all the contributors in Part VIII are proponents of realism in the short term and idealism in the long term. This prudent approach merits attention—providing we continuously bear in mind our short-, medium-, and long-term goals.

The argument over the United Nations that has been so acrid in the U.S. Senate since the end of the cold war reveals the contention between those who believe in, or incline to, collective security (and idealism) versus those who adhere to strict balance-of-power concepts. The example in chapter 1 of the debate over whether American soldiers should be placed under the command of officers of allied countries shows the unilaterialism proclivity of the United States versus multilateralism. Of course, there is no reason the United States cannot use both unilateral and multilateral approaches, and we do so.

In all these contending themes, no one of them is absolutely correct over the others, and they can be and are mixed. In each case an appropriate balance must be sought, both to design effective foreign policy and to garner the necessary public support to carry it out. Gaining the American public support necessary to carry out sustained and successful foreign policy requires a balance of contending themes, an explainable strategy, effective governmental decision-making bureaucratic mechanisms, and appropriate weapons and armed-forces structure, plus leadership. Ultimately, it comes down to the degree to which the American people are willing to give their treasure (taxes), time (service), and blood (allowing self or children to go into harm's way or to war) in support of a particular foreign policy. This, of course, depends on the merits of the foreign policy and the capability of America's leadership to present policy to the people persuasively.

It is important to examine the various systems which emerged historically to deal with the vital matter of preserving peace, or at least of preventing large-scale and nuclear wars. This examination is necessary to give ourselves a basis for evaluating the various suggested schemes that have been topical during the post–cold war period in the contemplation of world politics in the twenty-first century. The term *world politics* is employed, as opposed to *international relations,* because the nation-state system is a phenomenon of only the last 400 years. Because we are the world's only superpower at this juncture in history, knowledge of the ways in which the world has organized itself in the past might aid us to envision better where we may be heading. In brief, the various world systems that have existed have been characterized by some students of world politics as unilateral (empire or world-state), polylateral (diffusion of power, feudal), multilateral (balance of power), and bilateral (the cold-war period).

The establishment of empires, such as the one described by Colleen McCullough in the epilogue, was one way peace was assured in the past. Yet the ancient-empires model is not transferrable to the present because they were never global in scope. They could exist, in part, because the technological stage of communications and transportation was such that empires were affected little by other power centers simultaneously existent. Even if the United States wanted to, which it does not, the power of the United States relative to the remainder of the world's states is not sufficient to make it truly the hegemon of a world confederation. Much less is it sufficient to force all or most of the world into a unitary-style empire.

A second model for world politics is one similar to the situation that prevailed in Europe during the Middle Ages, after the fall of the Roman Empire and prior to the emergence of the nation-state system. During this interregnum there was a diffusion of power among various entities and power centers, such as the Vatican, principalities, city-states, leagues of city-states, and weak monarchs. None of them was sovereign or preponderant over nearly all aspects of life, as was the case in empires and in the fully developed countries of the nation-state system that evolved.

The emergence of the nation-state system out of the feudal order is usually dated by the signing of the Treaty of Westphalia, in 1648. Under this system of world politics, several peacekeeping models have been attempted. By the nineteenth century the prevailing thought in Europe about keeping the peace was embodied in the concept of balance of power among nations. The underlying thought was that sovereign states make shifting alliances with other states so that no single state can gain hegemony. The attractiveness of balance-of-power politics declined from the end of the nineteenth century while a new model was coming into vogue—the use of third-party dispute-settlement machinery. The outbreak of World War I interrupted the hopes for a peacekeeping model of international law, arbitration, and mediation. After this war "to make the world safe for democracy" came the idealism of Woodrow Wilson and the belief that international organizations—the League of Nations and the World Court—could manage and preserve peace. The appearance of totalitarianism and World War II dashed this model, while the United States lived briefly in splendid isolation with a false sense of security.

At the end of World War II, support for collective security again gained impetus by the United States' role in creating the United Nations, in an effort to pick up from when Americans had tried to exit the world in the 1920s and 1930s. Idealism and the global collective-security model were again set aside by the onset of a half century of cold war, and the inability of the Security Council to perform its peacekeeping role because of the veto. With the cold war's end, many people hoped that at long last the United Nations would be able to fulfill the peacekeeping role envisioned for it. The United Nations' track record in peace building and peacekeeping has disillusioned them. Increasingly, it is understood that an international organization can be no more than the major states allow it to be, and it is clear that the major powers are not yet ready to delegate peacekeeping entirely to the United Nations, although they resort to it in particular cases.

What is the thinking about future models of world politics since the end of the cold war? The fall of the Berlin Wall and the collapse of the USSR were greeted with euphoria in the United States and Europe (although not so enthusiastically in Latin America and Africa, from which the great powers transferred assistance and attention to eastern Europe). This euphoria, at least in terms of dreams of peace, was further heightened by the United Nations and United States' apparent triumph over Iraq's tyrant and aggressor, Saddam Hussein, in the Gulf War. However, the momentary "end-of-history" hype that the definitive victory of democracy and of the free market had been achieved, and predictions that the United Nations would guarantee lasting peace soon turned to cynicism. America's television and news media made Americans aware of growing conflict and strife in the Third World. Some pundits forecast "the end of the American century" and said Japan, China, or a political and economical European Union would "own the twenty-first century."

The United States, immediately after the cold war, was less and less confident as it contemplated its own economy and the seeming economic juggernauts of a uniting Europe and an expanding Japan. The picture depicted in some quarters was that the United States had sacrificed for a half century—by spending (in terms of percentage of its gross domestic product) for the world's recovery from World War II, free-world defense against Communism, and Third World development—twice what Europe had spent and six or seven times more than Japan. Supposedly, the struggle of the two dinosaurs locked in mortal combat had left the USSR slain, the United States debilitated and wounded, and Europe and Japan retooled and invigorated, along with Asian tigers and an emerging China, to vie with the United States in a world where economic competitiveness would be the most important factor. The utopian vision of a new world order was turning to one of disorder, and no model for peacekeeping in the world seemed satisfactory or attainable.

The nature of the global arena now is multipolar rather than bipolar. Russia remains a nuclear power with the capability of annihilating us. Its nuclear weapons could be retargeted against us in a matter of minutes if a nationalist leader decided to do so. A growing number of midlevel powers exist with chemical, biological, and nuclear weapons and delivery systems that, although still limited in number, constitute potential and real threats to world peace and United States interests. The end of the cold war and the bipolar world and lessened worry about a nuclear holocaust also took the lid off long ignored and suppressed struggles and rivalries in the Third World. Conflicts have boiled to the surface, sparked by religious-fundamentalist political movements, ethnic and nationality struggles, tribalism, terrorism, concerns about racism, the questioning of universal rights, and an enormous surge in crime and violence. United Nations and multinational peace-keeping efforts with dubious results (e.g., in Somalia) have frustrated Americans. Militarily, we were still the most influential world leader, but we were stricken temporarily by doubt and concerned about the eventual shape of the rapidly changing world arena.

Since the end of the cold war, what are the models of world order that peacekeeping experts and commentators have speculated on for the twenty-first-century world? One of the early, seriously discussed possibilities was the emergence of three large, powerful, and competitive economic blocs—East Asia, western Europe, and North America. There were, as stated, temporary concerns about how the United States would fare in such an economically centered and competitive world. Aside from the three blocs that would be the dominating players, Russia was a question mark that might sink further into disorder or recover to be a major power. There also was speculation about the possible creation of an Islamic confederation stretching from the Middle East across the Islamic former republics of the USSR, Afghanistan, Pakistan, and Bangladesh into Malaysia and Indonesia.

Another vision or model of the world of the twenty-first century picked up on the feudalism model described above. Conferences were held and political scientists discussed the possible decline in importance of the nation-state to such a degree that it would become only another player among other powerful entities. As in the Middle Ages, there would be no single sovereign over most aspects of most people's lives (as is the case in empires or of strong nation-states). Instead, there would be a diffusion of multicenters and layers of power, with no single entity dominating. The nation-states would be rivals of nongovernmental organizations, economic enterprises, and social institutions (such as the church and guilds) for people's loyalty and support.

Another model put forth came from dialogue originating with Samuel Huntington's "clash of civilizations" that would define the nature and be the source of conflicts in the world to come. Conflicts and hostilities would center on the geographic fault lines separating the states that make up these huge cultural groupings.

None of these models gained acceptance or validity. In this dynamic and rapidly moving period in world history, the idealistic view that world peace in the short term would be secured by the collective-security model through international organizations was quickly discarded, although it is recognized that international organizations will continue to play an important role. The idea of the emergence of three giant coherent economic blocs dropped by the wayside with the economic malaise of Europe and Japan, the looming market and economic power of China, and the resurgent vigor and steadiness of the American economy. The success of the European economic union and restored Japanese economic vitality could still lead to a situation in which the world could polarize along economic and not political lines.

Little by little, preoccupation with disorder and anarchy from ethnic and nationalist conflicts diminished, and the fear of wars from clashes of civilizations subsided with the realization that civilizations are not as monolithic and coherent as supposed. The interesting view that the nation-state is in decline and nongovernmental organizations and economic enterprises are eclipsing states also has lost ground, at least for the time being. This is because of the very obvious continuing strength of the wealthy states and of the newly emerging industrialized states, notwithstanding withering by several weak and poor "basket-case" countries.

The United States, as usual, rose to the post–cold war challenge and remade itself economically while Europe and Japan's seemingly powerful economies faltered. Through corporate downsizing, outsourcing, deregulation, innovativeness of mid- and small-sized firms, revolutions in science and technology, and our government's beginning at long last to put our fiscal house in order, the United States in the early 1990s entered a sustained period of economic growth. With this, we regained our confidence and recognition as the preeminent world power and leader for shaping the world of the early twenty-first century. Simultaneously we have increasingly returned toward the view of the world put forth by Henry Kissinger in his book *Diplomacy.*

What then are we to conclude about preparing America's foreign policy for the twenty-first century, from the information and ideas presented in this book by a very select group of analysts, practitioners, and scholars? In our deliberation we have the benefit of an accurate and insightful description of the geopolitical-economic current situation of each major region of the world; analyses of primary components that make up a comprehensive foreign policy; and proposals and strategies that singly or together could constitute a new paradigm for the conduct of foreign policy. The editors thus far, in this final chapter, have attempted to summarize and synthesize the experts' information, thoughts, and proposals. We then discussed some of the overlapping sets of contending themes that shape and influence the foreign policy of the United States; recounted the various political systems the world has employed historically in the quest for peace and the creation of an environment conducive for the progress of mankind; and reviewed provocative in-vogue views that quickly evolved after the end of the cold war about the nature of the future international system.

To analyze where the world is going, it is necessary also to discern where the world's most influential nation—the United States—wants it to go, what it requires to get there, and whether Americans have the leadership, will, and vision to pay the price required to take the nations of the world in that direction. In recent foreign-policy discourse there has been much emphasis on the need for vision, for analysts to picture the end state desired for strategies and operations. We know that in the large picture there really is no end state because life always moves on, but what is it that Americans want the nations and peoples of the world to attain over the next generation?

Generally, in the West, and particularly among Americans, it has been said that the ideal society is one that is prosperous and growing in wealth, socially and economically just, democratic, orderly, and in control of its own affairs (independent), even though it may be part of an interdependent world. Conversely, the undesired society for Americans generally is one that is poor, unjust, authoritarian or tyrannical, disorderly, and dependent. Please note that this view of the ideal society is not universal. There have been and are peoples who envision the utopian society to be one that is simple, austere, hierarchical, authoritarian, disciplined, and martial. And there are other utopias that can be conjured. Nevertheless, we believe it is valid to say that most Americans want the world to conform, to the extent possible, to something along the lines of the first ideal society depicted above, one similar to that sought by our founding fathers.

Now that we have suggested where we want this world to go, there is the question of how we will get there, or at least how we will move to approximate the next desired political order for the world. What will the road there resemble? Is it a paved superhighway, a rocky, devious road, or a new trail to be blazed? There are several views about how human affairs operate. Some people regard the flow of events in the world as basically harmonious or compatible—all things work together for good if we are of goodwill and if we try. This attitude is revealed in several past American foreign-policy initiatives and documents such as Woodrow Wilson's idealism, the Alliance for Progress, or the Jackson Commission Report on Central America. Perhaps in the long, long run this point of view has validity, but in the short run, experience tells us that in periods such as the present it is not pertinent and could be dangerous.

Certainly, with some exceptions, such as during the Roman Empire, most people and thinkers have seen the world as conflictive, if not anarchic and hostile. Out of this have grown conflict theories and the literature of conflict resolution. If then the nature of world politics is a mixture of the realists and idealists, we must seek balance and follow prevention and reconciliation policies in the present, while simultaneously and incrementally building our ideal society—one true to our founders' principles and dreams.

We hold the conviction that as Americans it is our privilege to meet the challenge and bear the burdens of leadership to assure peace and make the world an increasingly better and more just place to live, not only for Americans but for all peoples at this critical juncture in history. To do this we must understand the nature of the world system now and the direction of its evolution (which we have been discussing), and we must tactfully and decisively exercise realistic, bold, and consultative leadership, while recognizing the limits of United States power and outreach. To do this we need a conceptual framework or paradigm as a basis for our international leadership, decision making, and actions, although the paradigm will not be as simple as the policy of containment was.

Because a paradigm is a simplified reflection of society, its own degree of simplicity and clarity is probably correlated to the complexity of the society it is reflecting. Regardless of the degree of its complexity, a paradigm must be rooted in an accurate view of the current world scene; a vision of the kind of world we want to help build and live in; a sound perception of our national interests and idealistic goals; recognition of threats to the protection and advancement of these goals; and a realistic understanding of the limits of our own power and that of other major powers, both friendly and rival. Equally important, our leaders must be politically and morally effective at home in building and retaining sustained domestic support and a willingness to pay the costs of world leadership and an effective foreign policy. They also must have a governmental structure with the capabilities to provide essential information, make key decisions, and have the appropriate civilian and military organizations and tools to meet challenges and threats.

William Jefferson Clinton won the presidency at a time when many Americans were questioning the United States' future relative to economic strength. While global disorder surged in the wake of the euphoria of victory in the cold war and of President George Bush's masterful handling of the Gulf War, Bush's dreams of a new world order soon faded. The Clinton administration stated its intent to carry out America's leadership role by making the United States economically strong at home and assuming that global commerce is rooted in principles of openness, fairness, and reciprocity; by restructuring the U.S. armed forces to meet new and continuing threats to our security interests and international peace; by promoting the spread of democratic values and human rights; and by using more international institutions to address global problems such as the environment, narcotics trafficking, and refugees.

National security adviser Tony Lake issued in Clinton's first term what was posed as a successor to the doctrine of containment. He called for a strategy of engagement and enlargement of the world's free community of market democracies, but neither the words nor the concept captured the imagination of the American public or the American foreign-affairs community and scholars. This was despite the fact that with continuous fine-tuning, the goal of enlarging the number of market democracies has been a fundamental part of the Clinton foreign policy. His adherence to and fine-tuning of his theory of engagement is seen in his May 1997 *A National Security Strategy for a New Century.*

While the Clinton administration zigzagged to adjust the direction of our foreign policy in the fog of uncertainty about the nature of the new world—and after much conjecture about the possible features of a still hazy new world system whose outline on the horizon was becoming a little more perceptible—common sense, pragmatism, and wisdom have carried policy makers and most scholars back to an old but modified understanding of the world. Not surprisingly, it is very similar to the one described by Henry Kissinger in his book *Diplomacy*—at least for a couple of decades into the twenty-first century. The presentations of the contributors to this present book—be they scholars or practitioners, Republicans or Democrats—strongly reflect this view.

What is this view of the world? Kissinger and most of the other contributors to this book believe the international system of the twenty-first century will be similar to the European state system of the eighteenth and nineteenth centuries, but on a global scale. We believe that by the end of the first decade of the next millennium the world will have evolved to that situation. There is, in a sense, perhaps about a decade for U.S. leadership to better mold and shape this world in the directions we want it to go. After that our relative power will be less. The world will have at least six major powers (the United States, Europe, China, Japan, Russia, and probably India) plus several medium-sized powers (those addressed by Jeane Kirkpatrick in her excellent chapter). Among the medium-size nations will figure Brazil, Mexico, and Argentina from Latin America; South Africa and Nigeria from Africa; Iran, Egypt, and Turkey from the Middle East; and Korea, Indonesia, and Thailand from the ASEAN nations. They will provide a voice for those regions and can be lesser but important players in the balance of power. There will, of course, still be a large number of poorer developing states and, at the bottom of the heap, unfortunately, there still will be desperately poor basket-case states that require significant help to improve the lot of their citizens.

The successful functioning of this delicate system will require sensitive and decisive leadership among the leaders of the major powers, and Kissinger noted that none of the six major powers has previously engaged in balance-of-power international politics. Of course, those nations making up the European Union did so, and Russia, Japan, and the United States could be said to have played on the edges of the system.

The United States probably will continue to share a fairly common view of the kind of world we want to build with Europe and the long ignored and neglected Latin American nations, because of our common Judeo-Christian culture and traditions. The same should be true for much of Africa. Greater unity of actions and purpose may develop. Our relationship with

Japan should continue strong, even should the division of the Korean Peninsula be resolved. And in our relations with Asia, balance must be encouraged to avoid any single great power's becoming an enemy, or uniting of Asian states against the United States and/or the West (along Huntington's clash-of-civilizations lines). Presuming this perception of world politics for the next few decades to be correct, which we do, the responsibility of the United States as the strongest of the major powers and the primary arbiter of the balance-of-power system (as, for example, suggested in Brzezinski's piece) will be extremely important.

The prevalence of realism and balance-of-power politics in the next couple of decades, as we have tried to emphasize repeatedly, does not mean that in our leading, we Americans must set aside entirely our enthnocentric sense of "exceptionalism" and the promotion of democratic principles and ideals. Henry Kissinger, David Abshire, and many other authorities pointed out that although the United States should be (and has been) very pragmatic (the hallmark of our culture) in foreign policy, the universal-democracy dream has always been present in our diplomacy to the degree feasible—whether as a beacon on a hill or as an active effort to impose our democratic values on others. In this vein, it is worth making the distinction in politics that economists make routinely—the distinction among and sometimes the contradiction in our short-, medium-, and long-range goals. To achieve our democratic ideals in the long run it is at times counterproductive to push them too hard in the short term, which is exactly the argument made by several of the contributors with respect to human-rights objectives in China.

Edwin Corr pointed out in his comments on the experts' reviews of the various regions of the world that the challenge for American leaders is to take into account our proposed goals and actions for each region, to prioritize them, to analyze impediments to their achievement, and to match them against our capabilities. We must also be sure that we have the best national-security and foreign-relations structure to analyze the world, propose solutions, effect decisions, and implement those decisions. This is made more difficult because, distinct from the cold-war period, we have no major enemies threatening us directly and imminently at this time. It would be convenient and comforting if we could seize on a valid and simple concept such as that of containment to guide our actions, but at this stage and for the next couple of decades, we probably cannot do so. This means that as we practice realistic balance-of-power politics in the short term, we must simultaneously work for the kind of world we want in the future. We must find pragmatic ways to improve multilateral peacekeeping groups with common training and coordinated leadership. At the same time, we must not shrink from projecting our power alone when it is necessary.

At the same time, we must have well in mind our goals of a politically, economically, morally, and culturally strong America that relates to other states and cultures in a world characterized by peace, economic development, and prosperity through market economics, democratization, human rights, the rule of law, and justice. We must determine, for example, what we are willing to allow in terms of international inspections of our weapons systems to give us the moral standing and credibility to lead the world to a régime of international inspection and enforcement to stop the spread of dangerous weapons. We must also seriously consider the advisability of building expensive protection systems against random acts of terrorist nations or groups with the technical ability to strike targets in our country.

Understanding our goals, the nature of the world system, and other people's cultures and goals provides us with the foundation to lead in the creation of a better world. This comprehension is not a panacea. It does not alleviate our leaders from a myriad of tough decisions about the degree to which our national interests are at stake in ambiguous and difficult conflicts or in seemingly emerging positive world or regional developments.

In this book we have framed the issues for intelligent debate and have provided Americans with a framework for decision making in an uncertain but surely exciting, dangerous, and wonderful world. The genius of the American people is our pragmatic idealism, our willingness to analyze problems and opportunities, and then to work unstintingly and creatively to resolve matters and to take advantage of the moment. Historically, we have been more reactive and proactive than reflective, and we have been greatly troubled by ambiguity, but we must now assume the leadership that is ours and give our best to the current challenge, both intellectually and materially.

The editors hope that this book has been stimulating, and that it will contribute to our nation's historical call to better define the intellectual framework out of which Americans can formulate and implement a foreign policy to lead our citizens and those of all the world to more satisfying and fulfilling lives for themselves and their children.

NOTE

1. Richard N. Haas, "Paradigm Lost," *Foreign Affairs* 74, no. 1 (January – February 1995).

2. Hans Morganthau and Kenneth W. Thompson, *Politics Among Nations: The Struggle for Power and Peace* (New York: McGraw-Hill, 1993).

3. Henry A. Kissinger, *Diplomacy* (New York: Simon & Schuster, 1994).

Contributors

David M. Abshire

David M. Abshire is founder and president of the bipartisan Center for Strategic and International Studies (CSIS), in Washington, D.C. He graduated from West Point in 1951 and later received his doctorate in history from Georgetown University, where for many years he was an adjunct professor at its School of Foreign Service. He served as assistant secretary of state in the early 1970s and later as chairman of the U.S. Board for International Broadcasting. He has been a member of several government committees, including the transitional National Security Group for President-elect Ronald Reagan and the Council on Foreign Relations. More recently he was ambassador to NATO, where his efforts merited him the Distinguished Public Service Medal, and he served as special counselor to President Reagan, with cabinet rank. Abshire has written several books in his field of expertise. He is a member of the board of visitors of the International Programs Center at the University of Oklahoma.

Mikael Adolphson

Mikael Adolphson is an assistant professor in the Department of History at the University of Oklahoma who teaches surveys of Japan and East Asia and focuses his research on pre-1600 Japan. A native of Kalmar, Sweden, he graduated from Lund's University with a B.A. in history in 1984. He received a scholarship from the Japanese Education Ministry in 1986 and spent the next two-and-one-half years as a research student at Kyoto University. In 1989, Professor Adolphson entered Stanford's Ph.D. program in Japanese history, earning his doctorate in 1995 after several more visits to Japan.

Jan Carol Berris

Jan Carol Berris is vice president of the National Committee on United States–China Relations, a nonprofit organization which conducts policy discussions and exchanges among American and Chinese leaders in governance and civic affairs, international relations, economic management and development, education administration, communications, and global issues such as the environment. At the request of the United States State Department, she has played an active role in exchanges between the United States and China, such as the 1972 Chinese Ping-Pong Team and Premier Deng Xiaoping's 1979 visit to the United States. Prior to her current position, Berris was a Foreign Service Officer stationed in Hong Kong and Washington, D.C. She received her B.A. in Chinese studies in June 1966 and her M.A. in Japanese Studies in 1967 from the University of Michigan.

Max N. Berry

Max N. Berry is an attorney specializing in international trade law. A native of Tulsa, Oklahoma, he received his LL.B. in 1960 from the University of Oklahoma, and LL.M. in 1963 in international law from the Georgetown University Law Center in Washington, D.C. Prior to entering private practice, Berry served as an attorney with the International Affairs Division, among other federal offices, and received the U.S. Treasury Department's Certificate of Award for Meritorious Service for his work involving international trade. He has also received numerous awards from foreign governments for his work relating to the individual countries. Berry has written several articles on international trade that have been published in law journals. He is a member of the board of visitors of the International Programs Center at the University of Oklahoma.

David L. Boren

David L. Boren is the thirteenth president of the University of Oklahoma. Prior to coming to the University, he served in the U.S. Congress as a senator from Oklahoma and earlier as governor of Oklahoma, the first person in history to hold all three positions. President Boren is widely respected for his longtime support of education, his distinguished career as a reformer of the American political system, and his innovations as a university president. A graduate of Yale University in 1963, he majored in American history, graduated in the top 1 percent of his class, and was elected to Phi Beta Kappa. He was selected as a Rhodes scholar and earned a master's degree in politics, philosophy, and economics from Oxford University in 1965. In 1968, he received a law degree from the University of Oklahoma College of Law, where he was on the *Law Review,* elected to the Order of the Coif, and won the Bledsoe Prize as the outstanding graduate by a vote of the faculty. As a United States senator, Boren was the longest-serving chairman of the Senate Select Committee on Intelligence. Boren has served as a member of the Yale University board of trustees and as chairman of the Department of Political Science and chairman of the Division of Social Sciences at Oklahoma Baptist University.

Alfred S. Bradford

Alfred S. Bradford is the John Saxon Professor of Ancient History at the University of Oklahoma. Before coming to Oklahoma, he taught at the University of Wisconsin and was a research assistant and later a member at the Institute for Advanced Study, Princeton, New Jersey. He also taught at Rutgers-Newark and was a professor at the University of Missouri. Bradford was an honors graduate of the University of Wisconsin in 1964 with a B.A. in history. He attended the University of Chicago as a Woodrow Wilson Fellow in 1965 and received an M.A. in classical languages and literature in 1966. He returned to the University of Chicago and received his Ph.D. in classical languages and literature in 1973. He served in Vietnam on active duty in the United States Army and published a memoir about his service in Vietnam. In addition to his memoir, he has published *A Prosopography of Lacedaemonians* (C. H. Beck, Munich, 1977) and *Philip II of Macedon* (Praeger, 1994).

Zbigniew Brzezinski

Dr. Zbigniew Brzezinski is a Counselor at the Center for Strategic and International Studies and is professor of American foreign policy at the Paul Nitze School of Advanced International Studies at the Johns Hopkins University. Prior to his current position, he was national security adviser to the president of the United States during the Carter administration. Dr. Brzezinski has also served as a member of the Defense Department Commission on Integrated Long-Term Strategy and as a member of the President's Foreign Intelligence Advisory Board. In 1981, he received the Presidential Medal of Freedom for his role in the normalization of U.S.-Chinese relations and for his contributions to the human-rights and national-security policies of the United States. Dr. Brzezinski was born in Poland and received his Ph.D. from Harvard University in 1953. He has written many books in his field of expertise.

Luke R. Corbett

Luke R. Corbett is chairman and chief executive officer of Kerr-McGee Corporation. He received a B.S. in mathematics in 1969 from the University of Georgia. He began his career as a geophysicist and held positions involving domestic exploration of oil. He is a member of the American Association of Petroleum Geologists and several other professional organizations. He serves on numerous boards and is chairman of the advisory board of the Energy and Geoscience Institute at the University of Utah.

Edwin G. Corr

Edwin G. Corr is director of the Energy Institute of the Americas (EIA) and associate director of the International Programs Center (IPC) of the University of Oklahoma. Earlier, he was the Henry Bellmon Professor of Public Service and was professor of political science at the University of Oklahoma. Corr served as U.S. ambassador to Peru, Bolivia, and El Salvador. He was deputy assistant secretary of state for international narcotics matters and a career Foreign Service Officer with assignments in Mexico, Ecuador, and Thailand as well as in the Department of State. He was Peace Corps director in Cali, Colombia. Corr was a captain in the United States Marine Corps. He received his B.S. in education in 1957 and his M.S. in history in 1961 from the University of Oklahoma, and earned an M.S. in political science from the University of Texas in 1969. Corr has received awards from the governments of Ecuador, Bolivia, and El Salvador for helping to move countries to democracy and peace. He has published two books and several articles and chapters of books.

Richard A. Cosier

Richard A. Cosier is Dean and Fred E. Brown Chair of Business Administration in the Michael F. Price College of Business at the University of Oklahoma. He formerly served as associate dean for academics, professor of business administration, and chairperson of the Department of Management at Indiana University. In addition, he held a faculty appointment at the University of Notre Dame. His Ph.D. is from the University of Iowa. Prior to his academic career, he was a planning engineer with Western Electric Company. Dr. Cosier joined OU in 1993. He has concentrated on curricular improvement and private fund-raising. He has published more than sixty articles, has presented numerous papers at professional meetings, and has coauthored a management textbook. Dr. Cosier is the recipient of several Teaching Excellence Awards and a Richard D. Irwin Fellowship. He belongs to several professional organizations. He is on the board of directors at First Fidelity Bank, N.A., of Oklahoma City and chairs the Norman (Oklahoma) Economic Development Coalition. This unique partnership between the University, the city of Norman, and the Norman Chamber of Commerce generated the city's first economic-development plan.

Robert Henry Cox

Robert Henry Cox is associate professor and coordinator for European studies at the University of Oklahoma. He received his Ph.D. in political science in 1989 from Indiana University. A specialist in social policy and European politics, Cox has done extensive research on European welfare states. He is the author of *The Development of the Dutch Welfare State* (University of Pittsburgh Press, 1993). He has published numerous articles in such prominent academic journals as *Politics and Society, Comparative Political Studies, Journal of Social Policy, Governance, Publius,* and *West European Politics.* He has written essays on national sovereignty, and his recent research has concentrated on the politics of welfare reform in Denmark, the Netherlands, and Germany. In 1995 he was named a Fulbright Fellow to Denmark, and in 1998 he received a German Marshall Fund Fellowship. Cox also serves as book-review editor for *Governance: An International Journal of Policy and Administration.*

William J. Crowe Jr.

Admiral William J. Crowe Jr. is chairman of the International Programs Center board of visitors. He was the first holder of the chair in geopolitics established in his name at the University of Oklahoma. He is currently Shapiro Visiting Professor of International Affairs in the Elliott School of

International Affairs at George Washington University, in Washington, D.C., as well as chairman of the advisory board at Capitoline/MS&L, in Washington, D.C. Prior to his current position, he was U.S. ambassador to the United Kingdom, appointed by President Clinton. During the Reagan administration, Admiral Crowe was appointed the eleventh chairman of the Joint Chiefs of Staff, Department of Defense, in which position he served as the principal military adviser to the president, the secretary of defense, and the National Security Council. Crowe began his university studies at the University of Oklahoma and then moved to the United States Naval Academy, where he graduated in 1946. He received his M.A. in education from Stanford University and his Ph.D. in politics from Princeton. He is the author of several books and articles.

Lee Cullum

Lee Cullum is a syndicated columnist based at the *Dallas Morning News.* She is a regular commentator on the *News Hour with Jim Lehrer* and National Public Radio's *All Things Considered.* She has held positions as reporter, editor, executive producer, and on-air moderator of a nightly television program, and has produced programs for the Public Broadcasting Service. She has received numerous awards, including the J.B. Marryat Award from the Dallas Press Club. Cullum serves on the boards of the Council on Foreign Relations, the Pacific Council on International Policy, and many other organizations, including the board of visitors of the International Programs Center at the University of Oklahoma.

David Dary

David Dary is professor of journalism and since 1989 has been the director of the H.H. Herbert School of Journalism and Mass Communication at the University of Oklahoma in Norman. A native of Manhattan, Kansas, he was educated at Kansas State University and the University of Kansas. He worked as a journalist in Kansas and Texas before joining CBS News and later NBC News in Washington, D.C., in 1960. Dary covered the White House for CBS News during the Eisenhower and Kennedy administrations. At NBC News he was manager of local news. He returned to Kansas in the late 1960s and began to teach journalism in the William Allen White School of Journalism at the University of Kansas. He is the author of three books on journalism and nearly a dozen on the American West, including *The Buffalo Book, Cowboy Culture, Seeking Pleasure in the Old West,* and, in 1998, *Red Blood and Black Ink: Journalism in the Old West,* all published by Alfred A. Knopf, Inc., New York City.

Marlan W. Downey

Marlan W. Downey is chief scientist for the Sarkeys Energy Center and J. Denny Bartell Professor of Geosciences at the University of Oklahoma. He serves as an adviser for curriculum development and as a principal liaison with industry. He is the immediate past president of ARCO International Oil and Gas Company. In that position he directed oil and gas exploration and production for the company abroad. A native of Nebraska, Downey earned his bachelor's degree in chemistry from Peru State College, in Nebraska. He also earned bachelor's and master's degrees in geology from the University of Nebraska. He is active in several international scientific organizations and serves on numerous boards. In 1992, he served on President Jimmy Carter's team supervising the first free elections in Guyana. A fellow of the American Association for the Advancement of Science, Downey was a distinguished lecturer for the American Association of Petroleum Geologists. In 1986 the president of Cameroon knighted Downey for his services to that country, the first businessman to receive that honor.

Archie W. Dunham

Archie W. Dunham is president and chief executive officer of Conoco, Inc. A native of Ada, Oklahoma, Dunham holds a bachelor's degree in geological engineering and a master's degree in business administration from the University of Oklahoma. He is on the board of directors of the University's Energy Institute of the Americas and Sarkeys Energy Center, and the board of visitors of the College of Engineering. He has served on the boards of directors for Conoco and E.I. du Pont de Nemours & Co. and is a member of Du Pont's policy-making office of the chief executive. Dunham is a member of boards of several prominent institutions, including the Smithsonian Institution and the U.S.-Russia Business Council. He holds membership in several professional organizations.

J. Rufus Fears

J. Rufus Fears is professor of classics at the University of Oklahoma, where he holds the G.T. and Libby Blankenship Chair. Fears earned his Ph.D. at Harvard University. He has been a fellow of the American Academy in Rome, a Guggenheim fellow, and twice a fellow of the Alexander von Humboldt Foundation. He is the author of one book, three monographs, three volumes of edited works, and more than seventy articles and reviews on Greek and Roman history and the classical tradition. On ten occasions, he has won awards for undergraduate teaching. In 1996, Fears was named the University of Oklahoma Professor of the Year.

Robert M. Gates

Robert M. Gates is a member of the board of visitors of the International Programs Center at the University of Oklahoma. He served as director of the Central Intelligence Agency from 1991 to 1993. Dr. Gates was the only career officer in CIA's history to rise from entry-level employee to director, and the only intelligence analyst to become director. Prior to becoming CIA director, he served as assistant to the president and deputy national security adviser at the White House. He received his B.A. from the College of William and Mary, his M.A. in history from Indiana University, and his Ph.D. in Russian and Soviet history from Georgetown University. Dr. Gates is a member of several boards and is president of the national Eagle Scout Association, Boy Scouts of America. He published his memoirs in 1996.

David Richmond Gergen

David R. Gergen serves as editor-at-large at *U.S. News & World Report* and as a regular conversationalist on the PBS *News Hour with Jim Lehrer.* In addition, he is a visiting professor at Duke University and is writing a book on presidential leadership in the late twentieth century. A native of Durham, North Carolina, Gergen is an honors graduate of Yale University (A.B., 1963) and the Harvard Law School (LL.B., 1967). He is a member of the board of visitors of the International Programs Center at the University of Oklahoma and serves on several other boards, including the National Committee on U.S.-China Relations. He is a member of the Council on Foreign Relations, the World Economic Forum at Davos, Shamoda, and the International Institute of Strategic Studies. He has been an adviser to Presidents Nixon, Ford, Reagan, and Clinton.

M.V. Rajeev Gowda

M.V. Rajeev Gowda is a research fellow with the Science and Public Policy Program and assistant professor of political science at the University of Oklahoma. He obtained a B.A. from Bangalore University, India, an M.A. in economics from Fordham University, and a Ph.D. in public policy and management from the Wharton School, University of Pennsylvania. He has also served as a John M. Olin postdoctoral fellow at the Law School (Boalt Hall), University of California, Berkeley. His research interests focus on environmental policy, particularly on how people and societies make decisions under and about risks. He is a cofounder of the University of Oklahoma's Interdisciplinary Perspectives on the Environment Program. He has published several journal articles and is coeditor of two books: *Integrating Insurance and Risk Management for Hazardous Wastes* (Kluwer, 1990) and *Judgments, Decisions, and Public Policy* (Cambridge, forthcoming).

Richard Helms

Richard Helms was president of Safeer Company, an international business consulting firm in Washington, D.C., until his retirement in 1997. Prior to that he served as ambassador to Iran after several years as director of the Central Intelligence Agency under Presidents Johnson and Nixon. As CIA director, Helms was the senior intelligence officer of the United States government, served as chairman of the United States Intelligence Board, and was intelligence adviser to the president and to the National Security Council. He began his career by joining the U.S. Navy after the attack on Pearl Harbor. Having been assigned to the Office of Strategic Services (OSS) in Washington, D.C., Helms continued in the service of the OSS after leaving the navy and became a part of the successor organization to the OSS, the CIA.

Jim Hoagland

Jim Hoagland is the associate editor and chief foreign correspondent of the *Washington Post*. He has held the positions of reporter, copy editor, Africa correspondent, Middle East correspondent, and Paris correspondent. He became foreign editor and then assistant managing editor for foreign news at the *Washington Post*. He was a Ford Foundation Fellow at Columbia University in 1968–69. He received the Pulitzer Prize for international reporting in 1970, and the Overseas Press Club award for international reporting in 1977. Hoagland's book, *South Africa: Civilizations in Conflict*, was published in 1972. He was awarded his second Pulitzer Prize, for commentary, in 1991. Hoagland graduated with an A.B. in journalism from the University of South Carolina at Columbia.

James R. Jones

James R. Jones was U.S. ambassador to Mexico from 1993 to 1997, during one of the most important historical transitions ever. Among his accomplishments while ambassador were the passage and implementation of the North American Free Trade Agreement (NAFTA). Jones was chairman and chief executive officer of the American Stock Exchange in New York from 1989 to 1993. Before that, he was a partner in the Washington law firm of Dickstein, Shapiro and Morin from 1987 to 1989. Jones was a member of the U.S. Congress from 1973 to 1987, representing Oklahoma's first district. He distinguished himself as chairman of the House Budget Committee, the Social Security Subcommittee, and the U.S./Japan Trade Task Force; as deputy majority whip; and as a ranking Democrat on the Ways and Means Committee and its Subcommittee on International Trade. He began his career in national politics as personal assistant to President Lyndon Baines Johnson. Jones is a member of the board of visitors of the International Programs Center at the University of Oklahoma.

Jeane J. Kirkpatrick

Jeane J. Kirkpatrick is Leavey Professor of Government at Georgetown University and Senior Fellow at the American Enterprise Institute (AEI). Prior to that, she was the United States representative to the United Nations and a member of the cabinet of President Ronald Reagan, the first woman to serve in that capacity. She also was a member of the President's Foreign Intelligence Advisory Board (PFIAD). Dr. Kirkpatrick received her A.B. from Barnard College, M.A. and Ph.D. degrees from Columbia University, and studied at the Institute de Science Politique in Paris. She has written several well-regarded books, and she speaks widely on foreign policy and security affairs. Dr. Kirkpatrick was awarded the Medal of Freedom, the nation's highest civilian honor, and the Distinguished Public Service Medal, the highest civilian honor in the Department of Defense. She is a member of the board of visitors of the International Programs Center at the University of Oklahoma.

Henry A. Kissinger

Henry A. Kissinger is chairman of Kissinger Associates, Inc., an international consulting firm. He is also a Counselor to Chase Manhattan Bank and a member of its International Advisory Council; chairman of the International Advisory Board of American International Group, Inc.; a Counselor to and Trustee of the Center for Strategic and International Studies; and an Honorary Governor of the Foreign Policy Association. From 1986 to 1988 he was a member of the Commission on Integrated Long-Term Strategy of National Security and Defense Department. Dr. Kissinger was the national security adviser to President Nixon, and then was the fifty-sixth U.S. secretary of state, for Presidents Nixon and Ford. President Reagan appointed Kissinger to chair the National Bipartisan Commission on Central America, and he also served as a member of the President's Foreign Intelligence Advisory Board. Dr. Kissinger received the Nobel Peace Prize in 1973; the Presidential Medal of Freedom, the nation's highest civilian award, in 1977; and the Medal of Liberty in 1986. He graduated summa cum laude from Harvard College in 1950 and received his M.A. and Ph.D. degrees from Harvard University in 1952 and 1954. He was a member of the faculty at Harvard prior to entering government service. Dr. Kissinger is the author of several notable books, including *Diplomacy* (1994). He is a member of the board of visitors of the International Programs Center at the University of Oklahoma.

Li Daoyu

Ambassador Li Daoyu was the Ambassador Extraordinary and Plenipotentiary of the People's Republic of China to the United States of America until January 1998. In 1998 he was elected to the National People's Congress and is vice chairman of the Subcommittee on Overseas Chinese Affairs. He graduated from the University of Shanghai in 1952 and entered China's foreign service the same year. Prior to his current position he was deputy division chief, division chief, and deputy director of the Department of International Organizations and Conferences, Foreign Ministry of China. He then was deputy permanent representative of China to the United Nations office in Geneva. He is a member of the board of visitors of the International Programs Center at the University of Oklahoma.

Jack F. Matlock Jr.

Jack F. Matlock Jr. is the George F. Kennan Professor at the Institute for Advanced Study, Princeton University. Prior to his current position, he was Kathryn and Shelby Cullom Davis Professor in the Practice of International Diplomacy at Columbia University, New York City. During his thirty-five years in the American Foreign Service, he served as ambassador to the Soviet Union, special assistant to the president for national security affairs, senior director for European and Soviet affairs on the National Security Council staff, and ambassador to Czechoslovakia. Matlock has served as a visiting professor of political science at Vanderbilt University and has been an instructor in Russian language and literature at Dartmouth College. He received his A.B., summa cum laude, from Duke University and his M.A. from Columbia University. He has been awarded honorary doctorates by several colleges and has published several books, including his book on the Soviet collapse, *Autopsy on an Empire*.

Colleen McCullough

Colleen McCullough is a successful novelist whose work includes *The Thorn Birds*. Prior to her current success as a writer, she graduated in the Faculty of Science in Sydney, Australia, and obtained her master's degree from the Institute of Child Health at London University, U.K., in neurophysiology. For many years she was administrator of the research laboratories at Yale Medical School, where she taught neuroanatomy of the rhinencephalon and electronics, trained technicians, and supervised medical students. Her first book in a series about the fall of the Roman Republic, *The Masters of Rome*, earned her a doctorate of letters for excellence in history. She has now published the fifth book of this series. Dr. McCullough is a member of the board of visitors of the International Programs Center at the University of Oklahoma.

George C. McGhee

George C. McGhee joined the U.S. Department of State early in his career, became Coordinator for Aid to Greece and Turkey, and was assistant secretary of state for Near Eastern, South Asian, and African affairs. President Dwight Eisenhower appointed McGhee as ambassador and chief of the American aid mission to Turkey. During the John F. Kennedy administration, McGhee was undersecretary for political affairs and later ambassador to Germany. He has served as trustee or director of several organizations, including the School for Advanced International Studies of Johns Hopkins University. He received a B.S. degree in geology from the University of Oklahoma. McGhee was a Rhodes scholar and received a Ph.D. in physical sciences from Oxford University. He is a member of Phi Beta Kappa and Sigma Xi. He has authored several books on international interests. He is a member of the board of visitors of the International Programs Center at the University of Oklahoma.

Francis J. McNeil

Francis J. McNeil is Senior Adviser to the Pacific Task Force for the Chief of Naval Operations' Executive Panel, works part time for the Center for Naval Analysis, and serves as an unpaid member of the board of Founders of CRUSA, a binational foundation dedicated to the promotion of sustainable development in Costa Rica. Prior to his current position, he held three senior State Department posts relevant to East Asia—senior inspector, deputy assistant secretary for East Asian and Pacific affairs, and principal deputy assistant secretary for intelligence and research. McNeil was deputy assistant secretary for inter-American affairs during President Carter's administration. President Reagan appointed him as U.S. ambassador to Costa Rica and later as special emissary for the Grenada mission. McNeil served for nearly ten years in Japan, and the *New York Times* and the *Washington Post* considered him one of the best sources on Japan. He was a visiting professor at the Graduate School of International Relations of the International University of Japan. He has written several books and articles on foreign affairs.

John Milewski

John Milewski is a veteran broadcast journalist. He has reported on everything from space-shuttle launches and presidential elections to teen violence and the fall of the Berlin Wall. Milewski has interviewed leaders of nations and leaders of youth gangs. He is executive producer, managing editor, and host of one of the longest-running news and public-affairs discussion programs on television, *Close-Up* on C-Span. In addition, he serves as director of the Close-Up Foundation's Department of Television and Video. Milewski is a 1979 graduate of Pennsylvania State University.

Walter F. Mondale

Walter F. Mondale was vice president of the United States from 1977 to 1981 and the Democratic Party's nominee for president in 1984. Prior to that he was a U.S. senator from Minnesota. Mondale also served as ambassador to Japan from August 1993 to December 1996. During that period, he helped to negotiate several U.S.-Japan security agreements, including a resolution to the controversy about the American military presence in Okinawa. He also helped to negotiate numerous trade agreements with Japan, and he promoted the expansion of educational exchanges between the two nations. In addition, Mondale attended the annual Asia-Pacific Economic Cooperation (APEC) summit meetings in Seattle, Jakarta, Osaka, and Manila. In March 1998, Mondale served as President Clinton's special envoy to Indonesian President Suharto regarding economic reforms in response to the 1997–98 Asian financial crisis. Mondale is currently a partner with the Dorsey & Whitney law firm, with headquarters in Minneapolis.

Sam Nunn

Sam Nunn is a senior partner in the Atlanta law firm of King & Spalding, where he focuses his practice on international and corporate matters. Prior to his current position, he was elected to the United States Senate from Georgia for four terms. He graduated with honors from Emory Law School. In the Senate, Nunn served as chairman of the Armed Services Committee and was on other committees. He coauthored legislation creating the cooperative Threat Reduction Program, also known as the Nunn-Lugar Program, which provides incentives for the former Soviet republics to dismantle and safely handle their nuclear arsenals. He initiated many other projects while a senator, including cosponsoring legislation creating the nation's first national service programs, and he worked to combat waste, fraud, and abuse in government programs and agencies. He is a distinguished professor in the Sam Nunn School of International Affairs at Georgia Tech.

Robert B. Oakley

Robert B. Oakley is Distinguished Visiting Fellow with the Institute for National Strategic Studies at the National Defense University. Prior to his current position he was a U.S. Foreign Service Officer and served as Special Envoy for Somalia under Presidents Bush and Clinton. During his career as a Foreign Service Officer, Oakley was assigned to Abidjan, Ivory Coast; Saigon; Paris; Beirut; and the U.S. mission to the United Nations; and he was Senior Director for the Middle East and South Asia on the staff of the National Security Council. Oakley received the State Department Meritorious Honor Award and four Presidential Meritorious Service Awards, among other honors. He received his B.A. degree in philosophy and history in 1952 from Princeton University. He is a member of the board of visitors of the International Programs Center at the University of Oklahoma.

Michel Oksenberg

Michel Oksenberg is a senior fellow at the Asia/Pacific Research Center at Stanford University, where he is also professor of political science. He writes and lectures on contemporary China, Asia-Pacific affairs, and American foreign policy toward the region. His research specialties include Chinese domestic affairs, China's foreign policy, Sino-American relations, and East Asian political development. He received a B.A. from Swarthmore College and his M.A. and Ph.D. in political science from Columbia University. Dr. Oskenberg has authored several books in his area of expertise, and he lectures nationally and internationally. He is a member of the board of visitors of the International Programs Center at the University of Oklahoma.

Edward J. Perkins

Edward J. Perkins is William J. Crowe Jr. Chair Professor of Geopolitics and executive director of the International Programs Center at the University of Oklahoma. Prior to his current position, he was appointed as U.S. ambassador to the Commonwealth of Australia; U.S. representative to the United Nations, with the rank and status of ambassador extraordinary and plenipotentiary; U.S. representative in the UN Security Council; director general of the Foreign Service; U.S. ambassador to Liberia; and U.S. ambassador to South Africa. He received his B.A. from the University of Maryland and his M.P.A. and Ph.D. from the University of Southern California. Perkins has received numerous awards, including the Presidential Distinguished and Meritorious Service Awards and Kappa Alpha Psi Fraternity's highest honor, the Laurel Wreath Award for Achievement and Distinguished Diplomatic Service. As ambassador to South Africa, he worked to end apartheid. Perkins has published numerous articles in his areas of expertise.

W. DeVier Pierson

W. DeVier Pierson is a partner in the Washington, D.C., law firm of Pierson Semmes and Bemis. Prior to his current position, he practiced law in Oklahoma City. He received his A.B. degree and his LL.B degree from the University of Oklahoma. He is a member of the board of visitors of the International Programs Center at the University of Oklahoma, as well as several other boards. He is a member of the bars of the United States Supreme Court; U.S. Court of Appeals for the District of Columbia; Second, Fifth, Tenth, and Federal Circuits; Supreme Court of Oklahoma; and various federal and state district courts. He has held governmental positions as Special Counsel to the President of the United States; Associate Special Counsel to the President and Counselor of the White House; and Chief Counsel, Joint Committee on the Organization of Congress.

Michael F. Price

Michael F. Price is president and chief executive officer of Franklin Mutual Advisers, Inc. He is also chairman of the board and president of Franklin Mutual Series Fund, Inc. Price is a member of the board of visitors of the International Programs Center at the University of Oklahoma. After graduation from OU, he joined Heine Securities, where he began his career in managing mutual funds. He is a benefactor of the College of Business at the University of Oklahoma, and the college has been renamed for him.

Peter W. Rodman

Peter W. Rodman is Senior Director of National Security Programs at the Nixon Center for Peace and Freedom, and a senior editor of *National Review.* He is an author and has held the posts of Deputy Assistant to President Reagan for National Security Affairs, Special Assistant for National Security Affairs, and NSC Counselor for Presidents Reagan and Bush. Rodman also has served as Senior Adviser on foreign policy to the 1992 Republican platform committee, special assistant to Dr. Henry A. Kissinger, and a member of the National Security Council staff, among other posts. He received his A.B. degree, summa cum laude, from Harvard, B.A. and M.A. from Oxford University, and J.D. from Harvard Law School. He is a fellow of the Johns Hopkins Foreign Policy Institute and a senior associate at the Center for Strategic and International Studies. He is a member of the Council on Foreign Relations and the International Institute for Strategic Studies.

Lois Romano

Lois Romano is a journalist for the *Washington Post,* covering politics, campaigns, and cultural trends. Prior to her current position she worked for several other newspapers, and she has contributed to numerous periodicals. She has appeared as a commentator on various network and cable television news shows, as well as nationally syndicated radio programs. She received her B.A. from Emmanuel College in Boston and her M.A. in international affairs from George Washington University.

Richard L. Sandor

Richard L. Sandor is chairman and chief executive officer of Centre Financial Products Limited. Dr. Sandor has held senior executive positions in the financial-services industry and was vice president and chief economist at the Chicago Board of Trade, where he earned the reputation as the principal architect of interest-rate futures markets. He has been on the faculties of several universities, including Stanford, and was a visiting professor at other universities, including Columbia University Graduate School of Business. Sandor has served on numerous boards and is a member of the board of visitors of the International Programs Center at the University of Oklahoma. He earned his B.A. at City University of New York and his Ph.D. at the University of Minnesota. He has received numerous awards and scholarships from these institutions as well as from the National Science Foundation.

Robert A. Scalapino

Robert A. Scalapino is the Robson Research Professor of Government Studies Emeritus, Institute of East Asian Studies, University of California–Berkeley, and a member of the American Academy of Arts and Sciences. He also is a member of the board of visitors of the International Programs Center at the University of Oklahoma, and serves on the board of directors of Pacific Forum-CSIS. He was a founder and first chairman of the National Committee on U.S.-China Relations. Dr. Scalapino is a member of the board of trustees of the Asia Foundation and was recently named director emeritus of the Japan Society of Northern California and the Council on Foreign Relations. He is cochairman of the Asia Society's Asian Agenda Advisory Group. He is also a member of the board of the Atlantic Council and the National Bureau of Asian Research. He received his B.A. from Santa Barbara College and his M.A. and Ph.D. from Harvard.

Stephen Sloan

Stephen Sloan is professor of political science at the University of Oklahoma. Dr. Sloan pioneered the development of simulations of terrorist incidents. He has also conducted simulations for domestic and foreign law-enforcement departments, the corporate sector, and international airlines. He is involved in formulating counterterrorism doctrine for the military, as well as contributing to an evaluation of U.S. policies for the Vice President's Task Force on Combating Terrorism. Dr. Sloan also served as senior research fellow with the Center for Aerospace Doctrine, Research, and Education at the Air University at Maxwell Air Force Base in Montgomery, Alabama. He has lectured widely and has published several books in his area of expertise. He received his B.A. from Washington Square College of New York University, and his M.A. and Ph.D. degrees in comparative politics from the Graduate School of Arts and Sciences at New York University.

Gaddis Smith

Gaddis Smith is the Larned Professor of History at Yale University and chairman of the International Affairs Council at the Yale Center for International and Area Studies. He is also director of undergraduate international studies. Smith received his B.A. and Ph.D. from Yale. Prior to his current position, he taught at Duke University. He has written several books and was a senior consulting editor and major contributor to the four-volume *Encyclopedia of American Foreign Relations*. His articles have been published in newspapers and periodicals. Dr. Smith is a member of the board of visitors of the International Programs Center at the University of Oklahoma and a member of the Council on Foreign Relations, the Society of Historians of American Foreign Policy, and other historical organizations.

George J. Tenet

George J. Tenet is the director of the Central Intelligence Agency in Washington, D.C. Earlier, he served as the deputy director of Central Intelligence, Special Assistant to the President and Senior Director for Intelligence Programs at the National Security Council, and was a member of President Clinton's national-security transition team, among other posts. Tenet is a member of the board of visitors of the International Programs Center at the University of Oklahoma. He has served as staff director of the Senate Select Committee on Intelligence under the chairmanship of Senator David L. Boren. Tenet holds a B.S.F.S. from the Georgetown University School of Foreign Service and an M.I.A. from the School of International Affairs at Columbia University.

Zev M. Trachtenberg

Zev M.Trachtenberg is sssociate professor of philosophy at the University of Oklahoma, where he teaches introductory courses in philosophy as well as courses in social and political philosophy and environmental ethics. He is one of a group of OU faculty members from various departments who have developed a minor in Interdisciplinary Perspectives on the Environment. In his research Trachtenberg attempts to contribute a philosophical perspective to an interdisciplinary understanding of environmental issues, and he has published on the clash between property rights and environmental preservation. He is also the author of *Making Citizens: Rousseau's Political Theory of Culture* (Routledge, 1993), which explores the influence of culture on political life.

William H. Webster

William H. Webster is an associate of the law firm of Milbank, Tweed, Hadley & McCloy in its Washington, D.C., office. Prior to that, he was director of the Central Intelligence Agency under President Bush and director of the Federal Bureau of Investigation. Webster has practiced law in a private firm and as a United States attorney. He was appointed a judge of the United States District Court for the Eastern District of Missouri and was elevated to the United States Court of Appeals for the Eighth Circuit. Webster was chairman of the Judiciary Conference Advisory Committee on the Criminal Rules and a member of the Council of the American Law Institute. He received his B.A. from Amherst College and his J.D. from Washington University Law School in Saint Louis, Missouri.

John S. Wolf

John S. Wolf is the U.S. Coordinator for APEC, Bureau of East Asian and Pacific Affairs. Prior to his current assignment, Wolf served as Coordinator for the Secretary of State's Strategic Management Initiative. He has served as ambassador to Malaysia and as principal deputy assistant secretary of state for the Bureau of International Organization Affairs. He was a Department of State Foreign Service Officer. Wolf received his B.A. from Dartmouth College and was a Mid-Career Fellow at the Woodrow Wilson School, Princeton University. He has earned the President's Meritorious Service Award, as well as several other awards.

R. James Woolsey

R. James Woolsey is a partner in the law firm of Shea & Gardner of Washington, D.C. Prior to that, he was director of Central Intelligence. Before serving as DCI, he served as undersecretary of the U.S. Navy; general counsel to the U.S. Senate Committee on Armed Services; Adviser, U.S. Delegation to Strategic Arms Limitation; and in numerous other positions, including executive positions in corporate America. Woolsey was born in Tulsa, Oklahoma, and graduated from Tulsa Public Schools. He received his B.A. from Stanford (Phi Beta Kappa, with great distinction), his M.A. from Oxford University (Rhodes scholar), and his LL.B. from Yale Law School (managing editor, *Yale Law Journal*). He has served as chairman of the Executive Committee of the Board and as Regent of the Smithsonian Institution. Woolsey was a delegate at large for the U.S.-Soviet Strategic Arms Reduction Talks (START) and the Nuclear and Space Arms Talks (NST).

Clayton Yeutter

Clayton Yeutter is Of Counsel to Hogan & Hartson. He has served in cabinet and subcabinet posts under four U.S. presidents. In 1989 President Bush named Yeutter as secretary of agriculture, in which post he served as the administration's point man in steering the 1990 Farm Bill through Congress. In 1991 he was named Republican National Chairman, and in 1992 he returned to the Bush administration to coordinate domestic policy in the cabinet-level post of Counselor to the President. While serving as U.S. Trade Representative, Yeutter helped pass the 1988 Trade Bill and led the American team in negotiating the U.S.-Canada free-trade agreement. Yeutter received his law degree, cum laude, and the doctorate in agricultural economics from the University of Nebraska. He is a past president and chief executive officer of the Chicago Mercantile Exchange. Yeutter has received numerous public honors, including seven honorary doctorates. He is a director of several major corporations, and he regularly addresses groups throughout the world on trade and agricultural policy.

Zhou Dunren

Zhou Dunren is professor in the Center for American Studies, Fudan University at Shanghai, in the People's Republic of China. He is director and one of the founders of the center, and is also economic program director. He received his bachelor's degree at the Sichaun Institute of International Studies, his master's degree from Fudan University, and has done graduate work at the University of Leeds in England. He is the director of two academic societies and a member of the Shanghai International Relations Society. Zhou researches the U.S. economy in areas of corporation governance, mergers and acquisitions, and mutual funds. He has taught at major U.S. universities. He has translated several major works in his area of expertise and has published works of his own.

Board of Visitors and Staff of the University of Oklahoma's International Programs Center

Board of Visitors

David M. Abshire
Former President, Center for Strategic and International Studies; former Counselor to the President and Assistant Secretary of State for Congressional Affairs

James R. Adams
Former Chairman of the Board, Texas Instruments

Wayne Allen
Chairman of the Board and Chief Executive Officer, Phillips Petroleum Company

Michael H. Armacost
President, The Brookings Institution; Former Ambassador to Japan and the Philippines

Hannah D. Atkins
Former State Legislator; Secretary of State for Oklahoma; U.S. Delegate to the Thirty-Fifth General Assembly of the United Nations

Max N. Berry
Law offices, Max N. Berry

Ambassador John Burns
Former Ambassador to the Central African Republic; Ambassador to Tanzania; Director General of the Foreign Service of the United States

W. Hodding Carter III
President and Chief Executive Officer, The John S. and James I. Knight Foundation; former Assistant Secretary of State; Spokesperson for the Department of State

Jorge G. Casteñeda
Professor of Economics, Universidad Autonoma de Mexico

Admiral William J. Crowe Jr.
Chairman, Advisory Board, Capitoline/MS&L; former Ambassador to Great Britain; former Chairman of the Joint Chiefs of Staff

Lee Cullum
Columnist, *Dallas Morning News*

Secretary Lawrence S. Eagleburger
Senior Foreign Policy Adviser, Baker, Donelson Bearman, and Caldwell

James H. Everest
Business and civic leader, Oklahoma City, Oklahoma

Robert M. Gates
Former Director of the Central Intelligence Agency

David R. Gergen
Senior Editor, *U.S. News & World Report*

William R. Howell Jr.
Chairman Emeritus, J.C. Penney Company, Inc.; civic leader, Dallas, Texas

Stephen A. Janger
President, Close-Up Foundation

Ambassador James R. Jones
Former Ambassador to Mexico; Congressman; Chairman of the Board and Chief Executive Officer of the American Stock Exchange; Special Assistant to the President

Paul M. Kennedy
Dilworth Professor of History, Director, International Security Studies, Yale University

Lou C. Kerr
Vice President, The Kerr Foundation, Inc.

Ambassador Jeane J. Kirkpatrick
Leavy Professor, Georgetown University; Senior Fellow, American Enterprise Institute; former Ambassador to the United Nations; former cabinet member

Henry A. Kissinger
Chief Executive Officer of Kissinger Associates, Inc.; former Secretary of State and National Security Adviser

William W. Lewis
Director of the Global Institute, McKinsey & Company, Inc.; former Assistant Secretary of Energy and defense analyst

His Excellency Li Daoyu
Chairman, Foreign Affairs Committee in the National People's Congress; former Ambassador of the People's Republic of China to the United States

Ambassador Winston Lord
Former Assistant Secretary of State for East Asian Affairs; Ambassador to China; Director of Policy Planning Staff of the U.S. Department of State

Colleen McCullough
Author of *The Thorn Birds* and *The Masters of Rome* a series of novels on life in the Roman Empire, especially political and social activities

George C. McGhee
Former Ambassador to West Germany and Turkey; Assistant Secretary of

State for Near Eastern, South Asian, and African Affairs; Counselor and
Under Secretary for Political Affairs in the U.S. Department of State

Ambassador Robert M. McKinney
Editor and Publisher, *44   4*; Chairman of the Board, the New
Mexican, Inc.; former Ambassador to Switzerland

Harold J. Newman
Business leader in international finance, New York City

Ambassador Robert B. Oakley
Professor, National Defense University; former Ambassador to Zaire; UN
Special Representative to Somalia; other high-level assignments in The
U.S. Department of State

Michel Oksenberg
Professor and Senior Fellow, Asia/Pacific Research Center, Stanford
University

W. DeVier Pierson
Senior Partner, Pierson Semmes and Bemis

Michael F. Price
President and Chief Executive Officer, Franklin Mutual Advisers, Inc.

Ambassador Alain Rouquié
Ambassador of France to Ethiopia

Richard L. Sandor
Chairman and Chief Executive Officer of Centre Financial Products, Ltd.;
former Professor of Economics, University of California–Berkeley;
former Chief Economist, Chicago Board of Trade

Robert A. Scalapino
Robson Research Professor of Government Studies, Institute of East Asian
Studies, University of California–Berkeley

Stacy H. Schusterman
Executive Vice President, Samson Investment Co.; Founder and Chief
Executive Officer, Granite Properties, Inc.; civic and business leader,
Tulsa, Oklahoma

General Brent Scowcroft
Forum of International Policy; former National Security Adviser in the Ford
and Bush administrations

Secretary George P. Schultz
Distinguished Fellow, Hoover Institution; Lecturer in Economics, Stanford
University; former Secretary of State

Paul E. Sigmund
Professor of Politics and Director of Latin American Studies, Princeton
University

Commissioner Joseph J. Simmons III
President, The Simmons Co.; Vice Chairman, Surface and Transportation
  Board; former Commissioner, Interstate Commerce Commission

Gaddis Smith
Larned Professor of History and Chairman, International Affairs Council,
  Yale Center for International and Area Studies

William W. Talley II
Royal Danish Consul and Chairman of the Board, the RAM Companies

Ambassador Allan R. Taylor
Director-General, Australian Secret Intelligence Service (ASIS)

George J. Tenet
Director, Central Intelligence Agency

Cyril Wagner Jr.
Partner, Wagner & Brown, Ltd.; investor and civic leader, Midland, Texas

Helen Robson Walton
Entrepreneur and civic leader; founder of Walton Family Foundation

Staff

Ambassador Edward J. Perkins, Ph.D., Executive Director and William J.
  Crowe Jr. Chair and Professor of Geopolitics

Ambassador Edwin G. Corr, Associate Director

Millie C. Audas, Ph.D., Director, Office of International Relations

Gary B. Cohen, Ph.D., Director, International Academic Programs, and
  Professor of History

Sidney D. Brown, Ph.D., Professor Emeritus of History

Emily A. Gonzalez, Assistant Director, Office of International Relations

Julie R. Horn, Coordinator, Special Projects, International Programs Center

Barbara H. Lamb, Study-Abroad Adviser, Office of International Relations

Kathy J. Shahan, Administrative Secretary, International Programs Center

Diana D. Tiffany, Staff Assistant, Office of International Relations

Pat E. Wilson, Assistant Director, Office of International Relations

Claudia J. Braun, Secretary, International Programs Center

Mitchell F. Fuller, Graduate Research Assistant, International Programs
  Center

James Hochtritt, Graduate Research Assistant, International Programs
  Center

John Van Doorn, Graduate Research Assistant, International Programs
  Center

Index